lonely planet

Auckland

Christine Niven

LONELY PLANET PUBLICATIONS
Melbourne • Oakland • London • Paris

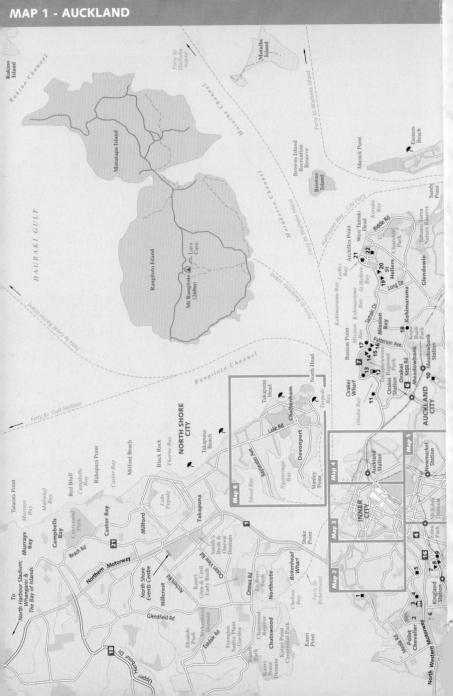

MAP 1 - AUCKLAND

Rakino
Island

Rakino Channel

Motutapu Island

Motuihe Island

Ferry to Waiheke Island

HAURAKI GULF

Ferry to Great Barrier Island

Ferry to Gulf Harbour

Rangitoto Channel

Rangitoto Island

Mt Rangitoto (260m)

Lava Cave

Motuihe Channel

Motukorea Channel

Ferry to Waiheke Island

Ferry to Rangitoto Island

Brown Island Recreation Reserve

Browns Island

Musick Point

Eastern Beach

Sandy Point

Karaka Bay

Tahuna Torea Nature Reserve

Glendowie

Halfmoon Bay - City Ferry

Achilles Point

West Tamaki Head

Riddle Rd

Churchill Park

Kohimarama Bay

Ladies Bay

Kohimarama

Kepa Bush Park

Kohimarama

St Heliers Bay

St Heliers

Long Dr

Tamaki Dr

Mission Bay

Mission Bay

21
22
19 20
18

Kepa Rd

Bastion Point

Mission Bay

Kohimarama

Patterson Ave

Thatcher

17
16 15
14
13

Meadowbank

Meadowbank Station

10

Orakei Wharf

Orakei Regional Park

Orakei Station

Orakei Kepa Rd

11

Okahu Bay

AUCKLAND CITY

NORTH SHORE CITY

North Head

Takapuna Head

Cheltenham

Torpedo Bay

Lake Rd

Devonport

Bayswater Ave

Takapuna Beach

Ngataringa Bay

Stanley Bay

Shoal Bay

Stokes Point

Map 6

Newmarket Station

Map 5

Auckland Station

Map 4

INNER CITY

Map 3

Mt Eden Park

Eden Park

Mt Eden

4
3
6
5
8 7
9
16

Kingsland Station

Point Chevalier

Nixon Rd

North Western Motorway

1
2
3
4
5

Takapuna

Lake Pupuke

Milford

Milford Beach

Castor Bay

Campbells Bay

Rahopara Point

Red Bluff Campbells Bay

Tatarata Point

Murrays Bay

Mairangi Bay

Castor Bay

Centennial Park

Beach Rd

2

Murrays Bay

Hillcrest

North Shore Events Centre

Archers Rd

Onewa Rd

Glenfield Rd

Wairau Rd

Smith's Bush & Onewa Domain

Northcote

1

Black Rock

Thorne Bay

Sulphur Beach

Birkenhead Wharf

Ferry to Birkenhead

Chelsea Bay

Te Roys Bush

Kauri Glen & Cecil Eady Bush

Kauri Point

Birkenhead Domain

Chatswood Reserve

Chatswood

Fernglen Native Plant Garden

Kauri Point Centennial Park

Kauri Point

Eskdale Park

Eskdale Rd

Kauri Point Domain

Glendfield Rd

To North Harbour Stadium; Whangarei & The Bay of Islands

Upper Harbour Dr

18

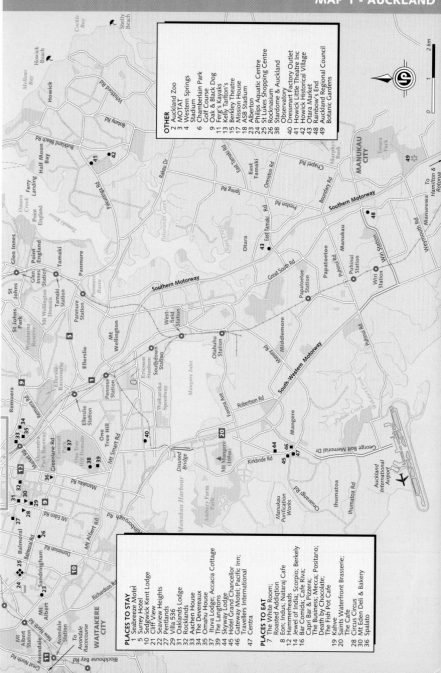

MAP 1 - AUCKLAND

OTHER
2 Auckland Zoo
3 MOTAT
4 Western Springs Stadium
6 Chamberlain Park Golf Course
9 Oak & Black Dog
11 Ferg's Kayaks
13 Kelly Tarlton's
15 Berkley Theatre
17 Mission House
18 ASB Stadium
23 Alberton
24 Philips Aquatic Centre
25 St Lukes Shopping Centre
26 Rockaround
38 Stardome & Auckland Observatory
40 Dressmart Factory Outlet
41 Howick Little Theatre Inc
42 Howick Historical Village
43 Otara Market
48 Rainbow's End
49 Auckland Regional Council Botanic Gardens

PLACES TO STAY
1 Seabreeze Motel
5 Surrey Hotel
10 Sedgwick Kent Lodge
21 Cliff View
22 Seaview Heights
27 Pentlands
31 Villa 536
32 Oaklands Lodge
33 Rocklands
34 Aachen House
35 The Devereaux
35 Omahu House
37 Ituva Lodge; Accacia Cottage
39 The Langtons
44 Skyway Lodge
45 Hotel Grand Chancellor
46 Gateway Motel; Pacific Inn; Travellers International
47 Centra

PLACES TO EAT
7 The White Room; Roasted Addiction
8 Eon; Indus; Nataraj Cafe
12 Hammerheads
14 Jewel of India; Scorpio; Berkely
16 Bar Comida; Cafe Riva; Capri Bar & Pizzera; The Business; Mecca; Positano; Death by Chocolate; The Fish Pot Cafe
19 Sahive
20 Sails Waterfront Brasserie; The Cafe
28 Circus Circus
30 Mt Eden Deli & Bakery
36 Spalato

Auckland
1st edition – January 2000

Published by
Lonely Planet Publications Pty Ltd A.C.N. 005 607 983
192 Burwood Rd, Hawthorn, Victoria 3122, Australia

Lonely Planet Offices
Australia PO Box 617, Hawthorn, Victoria 3122
USA 150 Linden St, Oakland, CA 94607
UK 10a Spring Place, London NW5 3BH
France 1 rue du Dahomey, 75011 Paris

Photographs
Many of the images in this guide are available for licensing from
Lonely Planet Images.
email: lpi@lonelyplanet.com.au

Front cover photograph
Auckland city over the waters of the Waitemata Harbour (David Wall)

ISBN 1 86450 092 1

text & maps © Lonely Planet 2000
photos © photographers as indicated 2000

Printed by The Bookmaker International Ltd
Printed in China

Contents – Text

Contents – Maps

EXCURSIONS

COLOUR MAPS   see back pages

The Author

Christine Niven

Christine joined Lonely Planet as an editor, but soon took to the road as an author. She has worked on *India*, *South India*, and *Sri Lanka* for Lonely Planet. She currently lives in Auckland and is co-authoring the forthcoming edition of *New Zealand*.

FROM THE AUTHOR

Many people went out of their way to assist with this project, which was done at lightspeed to a tight deadline. I would particularly like to thank Jan from Tourism Auckland, Vivian Naylor from the CCS, the Auckland Theatre Company, the very helpful and knowledgable staff at the Auckland Public Library's NZ research section, Lion Breweries, the ARC for kindly providing a map of Auckland's transport system, the Auckland Art Gallery staff for patiently showing me around their collections, and long-suffering Hilary who drew the short straw and got to edit this edition.

This Book

From the Publisher

Christine Niven worked tirelessly to author this first edition of *Auckland*. Brigid Shadbolt penned the Arts section, and Keith Stewart turned taste to text, writing the aside on Auckland wines.

The book was produced in Lonely Planet's Melbourne office. It was edited by Hilary Ericksen, with the expert help of Martine Lleonart and the advice of Mary Neighbour. Jane Thompson was responsible for proofing and Ann Jeffree did the indexing. Kusnandar put in many an hour on maps and layout; he was assisted by Jenny Jones and advised by Jane Hart. Helen Rowley did the colour wraps and Maria Vallianos the cover design. Matt King organised the illustrations and Fiona Croyden sourced the images. Ever indispensable, Tim Uden provided support throughout layout.

Foreword

ABOUT LONELY PLANET GUIDEBOOKS

The story begins with a classic travel adventure: Tony and Maureen Wheeler's 1972 journey across Europe and Asia to Australia. Useful information about the overland trail did not exist at that time, so Tony and Maureen published the first Lonely Planet guidebook to meet a growing need.

From a kitchen table, then from a tiny office in Melbourne (Australia), Lonely Planet has become the largest independent travel publisher in the world, an international company with offices in Melbourne, Oakland (USA), London (UK) and Paris (France).

Today Lonely Planet guidebooks cover the globe. There is an ever-growing list of books and there's information in a variety of forms and media. Some things haven't changed. The main aim is still to help make it possible for adventurous travellers to get out there – to explore and better understand the world.

At Lonely Planet we believe travellers can make a positive contribution to the countries they visit – if they respect their host communities and spend their money wisely. Since 1986 a percentage of the income from each book has been donated to aid projects and human rights campaigns.

Updates Lonely Planet thoroughly updates each guidebook as often as possible. This usually means there are around two years between editions, although for more unusual or more stable destinations the gap can be longer. Check the imprint page (following the colour map at the beginning of the book) for publication dates.

Between editions up-to-date information is available in two free newsletters – the paper *Planet Talk* and email *Comet* (to subscribe, contact any Lonely Planet office) – and on our Web site at www.lonelyplanet.com. The *Upgrades* section of the Web site covers a number of important and volatile destinations and is regularly updated by Lonely Planet authors. *Scoop* covers news and current affairs relevant to travellers. And, lastly, the *Thorn Tree* bulletin board and *Postcards* section of the site carry unverified, but fascinating, reports from travellers.

Correspondence The process of creating new editions begins with the letters, postcards and emails received from travellers. This correspondence often includes suggestions, criticisms and comments about the current editions. Interesting excerpts are immediately passed on via newsletters and the Web site, and everything goes to our authors to be verified when they're researching on the road. We're keen to get more feedback from organisations or individuals who represent communities visited by travellers.

Lonely Planet gathers information for everyone who's curious about the planet – and especially for those who explore it first-hand. Through guidebooks, phrasebooks, activity guides, maps, literature, newsletters, image library, TV series and Web site we act as an information exchange for a worldwide community of travellers.

Research Authors aim to gather sufficient practical information to enable travellers to make informed choices and to make the mechanics of a journey run smoothly. They also research historical and cultural background to help enrich the travel experience and allow travellers to understand and respond appropriately to cultural and environmental issues.

Authors don't stay in every hotel because that would mean spending a couple of months in each medium-sized city and, no, they don't eat at every restaurant because that would mean stretching belts beyond capacity. They do visit hotels and restaurants to check standards and prices, but feedback based on readers' direct experiences can be very helpful.

Many of our authors work undercover, others aren't so secretive. None of them accept freebies in exchange for positive write-ups. And none of our guidebooks contain any advertising.

Production Authors submit their raw manuscripts and maps to offices in Australia, USA, UK or France. Editors and cartographers – all experienced travellers themselves – then begin the process of assembling the pieces. When the book finally hits the shops, some things are already out of date, we start getting feedback from readers and the process begins again ...

WARNING & REQUEST

Things change – prices go up, schedules change, good places go bad and bad places go bankrupt – nothing stays the same. So, if you find things better or worse, recently opened or long since closed, please tell us and help make the next edition even more accurate and useful. We genuinely value all the feedback we receive. Julie Young coordinates a well travelled team that reads and acknowledges every letter, postcard and email and ensures that every morsel of information finds its way to the appropriate authors, editors and cartographers for verification.

Everyone who writes to us will find their name in the next edition of the appropriate guidebook. They will also receive the latest issue of *Planet Talk*, our quarterly printed newsletter, or *Comet*, our monthly email newsletter. Subscriptions to both newsletters are free. The very best contributions will be rewarded with a free guidebook.

Excerpts from your correspondence may appear in new editions of Lonely Planet guidebooks, the Lonely Planet Web site, *Planet Talk* or *Comet*, so please let us know if you *don't* want your letter published or your name acknowledged.

Send all correspondence to the Lonely Planet office closest to you:

Australia: PO Box 617, Hawthorn, Victoria 3122
USA: 150 Linden St, Oakland, CA 94607
UK: 10A Spring Place, London NW5 3BH
France: 1 rue du Dahomey, 75011 Paris

Or email us at: talk2us@lonelyplanet.com.au

For news, views and updates see our Web site: www.lonelyplanet.com

HOW TO USE A LONELY PLANET GUIDEBOOK

The best way to use a Lonely Planet guidebook is any way you choose. At Lonely Planet we believe the most memorable travel experiences are often those that are unexpected, and the finest discoveries are those you make yourself. Guidebooks are not intended to be used as if they provide a detailed set of infallible instructions!

Contents All Lonely Planet guidebooks follow roughly the same format. The Facts about the Destination chapters or sections give background information ranging from history to weather. Facts for the Visitor gives practical information on issues like visas and health. Getting There & Away gives a brief starting point for researching travel to and from the destination. Getting Around gives an overview of the transport options when you arrive.

The peculiar demands of each destination determine how subsequent chapters are broken up, but some things remain constant. We always start with background, then proceed to sights, places to stay, places to eat, entertainment, getting there and away, and getting around information – in that order.

Heading Hierarchy Lonely Planet headings are used in a strict hierarchical structure that can be visualised as a set of Russian dolls. Each heading (and its following text) is encompassed by any preceding heading that is higher on the hierarchical ladder.

Entry Points We do not assume guidebooks will be read from beginning to end, but that people will dip into them. The traditional entry points are the list of contents and the index. In addition, however, some books have a complete list of maps and an index map illustrating map coverage.

There may also be a colour map that shows highlights. These highlights are dealt with in greater detail in the Facts for the Visitor chapter, along with planning questions and suggested itineraries. Each chapter covering a geographical region usually begins with a locator map and another list of highlights. Once you find something of interest in a list of highlights, turn to the index.

Maps Maps play a crucial role in Lonely Planet guidebooks and include a huge amount of information. A legend is printed on the back page. We seek to have complete consistency between maps and text, and to have every important place in the text captured on a map. Map key numbers usually start in the top left corner.

Although inclusion in a guidebook usually implies a recommendation we cannot list every good place. Exclusion does not necessarily imply criticism. In fact there are a number of reasons why we might exclude a place – sometimes it is simply inappropriate to encourage an influx of travellers.

Introduction

The name Auckland refers both to a region, stretching from the towns of Wellsford and Warkworth in the north to roughly the Bombay Hills in the south, and a city, nestled between Waitemata and Manukau harbours.

Administratively, Auckland city consists of a number of cities, which form one vast urban sprawl. Auckland City proper lies between the Waitemata and Manukau harbours. North Shore City, centred on Takapuna, is just over the harbour bridge. Manukau City is to the south of Auckland proper, around the airport, and Waitakere City is to the west.

Auckland, with a population of over a million, is one of the world's most exciting waterside cities. A mere stroll down its main artery, Queen St, is not enough. You have to explore its heart – the magnificent harbour – reminiscent of Sydney, San Francisco, Hong Kong and Cape Town. Auckland has lots of enthusiastic yachties; it's very much the City of Sails, and is where the race for the 2000 America's Cup will be held.

Auckland is surrounded by water and punctured by volcanic cones, which bear evidence of former *pa* (fortified Maori villages) indicating a 1000-year occupation of the region. So many Islanders from Aotearoa New Zealand's Pacific neighbours have moved to Auckland that it now has the largest concentration of Polynesians in the world. More recently it has attracted immigrants from Asia. These foreign influences give Auckland a much more cosmopolitan feel than other NZ cities.

Facts about Auckland

HISTORY

In Maori mythology the demi-god Maui Tikitiki a Taranga hooks a great fish and hauls it to the ocean's surface. Settling there it becomes the North Island of Aotearoa New Zealand, Te Ika a Maui – the fish of Maui, with its head to the south. Maui's brothers, desiring part of the fish, beat and hack at it as it lies on the water. This, so the story goes, is why the isthmus is so lumpy, and so narrow at one point that the Maori used to be able to haul their canoes across it from one harbour to the other. The scales of the fish are said to have formed the Hauraki Gulf Islands.

According to local traditions, the first human inhabitants of the region were the Turehu, a fair-skinned people who were capable of extraordinary magical feats. Although the Turehu are regarded by the Maori as common ancestors, the identity of specific tribes is more closely linked with the individual *waka* (canoes) that arrived in the region. The great ancestor Kupe mai Tawhiti, for example, called first at Great Barrier Island, then portaged his canoe across the isthmus and sailed up the west coast. The rough seas of the west coast are said to have been created by Kupe who wanted to put a barrier between himself and his approaching enemies.

Of all the waka that visited the region, the Tainui has had the most lasting impact. This waka called in at many places before being hauled across the isthmus from the Waitemata to the Manukau Harbour. The descendants of this waka were known as Ngaoho, and although various tribal groups emerged and established their own identities, their common ancestry has formed an enduring bond. Until the 17th century, when tribes from the north and south challenged the isthmus dwellers, things were relatively peaceful.

Archaeological evidence of human settlement dates back some 800 years, with the earliest sites mainly located along coastlines and harbour mouths. The picture that emerges is one of a distinctly Polynesian society that depended on fishing, the gathering of shellfish and edible plants, and (increasingly as the centuries passed) agriculture. The natural environment back then was rather richer than it was when Europeans arrived. Repeated burn-offs for cultivation, the introduction of the Polynesian rat and the dog, hunting and forest clearance all took their toll on the environment over the course of the centuries.

The most accessible remains of pre-European Maori occupation are etched into the slopes of Auckland's volcanic cones. Here one can see the rectangular pits built to protect harvests of kumara (sweet potato) and other tropical crops from the damp and cold of winter, the terraces that were generally excavated for habitations and gardens, and the defensive earthworks. At one stage there were large stonefield gardens, but few remain. One Tree Hill (Maungakiekie) has the most extensive earthworks of any cone in the region and the information centre at Huia Lodge provides free pamphlets explaining the archaeology of this area. Evidence suggests that terracing began on the cones some time during the 14th century and that from this time the cones became important centres of habitation and cultivation, with gardens fanning across the slopes and beyond. It wasn't until the 17th century and the threat of invasion from outside tribes that some of the cones became heavily fortified.

In 1769 Captain James Cook, having paused at the Firth of Thames, sailed past the Waitemata Harbour during a storm, leaving behind several place names, such as Great Barrier and Little Barrier islands. In 1827 the French explorer Jules Dumont D'Urville entered the Waitemata in command of the *Astrolabe*. He climbed Mt Victoria (in Devonport) and reported no sign of any inhabitants. D'Urville also tried to scale

Mt Eden (Maungawhau), but was defeated by the heavy undergrowth. It seems that Tamaki Makaurau, 'Tamaki desired by many' (Auckland Isthmus), had been forsaken. The scrubby bracken-covered isthmus, which once supported quite a dense population, was virtually empty of people when Europeans arrived on the scene. This was largely the legacy of musket-bearing northern war parties of the 1820s. Many of the local inhabitants had fled to the Waikato, and only began returning in the 1830s.

Other pre-colonial visitors to the region included traders and whalers (from the 1810s) in search of business, and missionaries in search of souls. Various mission stations were established by Anglicans and Wesleyans from the Bay of Islands and Christianity appears to have been enthusiastically embraced by local Maori.

A pivotal date for Auckland is 1840. The year began with the signing of the Treaty of Waitangi, commonly seen as NZ's founding document. In Auckland, local chiefs gathered at Karaka Bay, Awhitu and Mangere to sign or put their mark to the document.

In this year too William Hobson, the Lieutenant-Governor of NZ, chose Auckland as the capital of the new colony. Sailing from New South Wales in Australia, he had made the Bay of Islands his headquarters, sending forth surveyor-general William Felton Mathew to investigate a suitable site. Felton Mathew favoured Tamaki, but Hobson preferred Waitemata (literally, 'sparkling waters'), and indeed Ngati Whatua chiefs residing at Okahu Bay also wanted Hobson to pick Waitemata. Hobson felt Waitemata was more central; he liked the fact it straddled two harbours and was impressed by the soil's fertility. So Waitemata it was, even though the decision was strenuously opposed by the New Zealand Company, the British agency of 'systematic colonisation', which, under the auspices EG Wakefield, sought to settle NZ from Wellington in the late 1830s. Wellington did, however, become capital in 1865.

The formal annexation ceremony took place on 16 September 1840 when officers from the ship *Anna Watson*, on which they had sailed from the Bay of Islands, landed at Official Bay and hoisted the British flag on Point Britomart (long since demolished). The flag received a 21-gun salute from the *Anna Watson* followed by 15 guns

**Looking south at the fledgling city from Queen Street Wharf, 1852
(lithograph from a drawing by PJ Hogan)**

from the accompanying ship *Platina*, which brought the framework from England for the new government house. Her Majesty's health was toasted at the foot of the flagstaff. The occasion was further marked by a regatta, a tradition which has been observed ever since on Auckland Anniversary Day. Auckland itself was named for Hobson's naval commander George Eden, Lord Auckland.

Auckland's foreshore was rather different then and probably more picturesque, with its little bays undisturbed. The sea came up to where Shortland St is today, and a stream ran down what is now Queen St. John Logan Campbell, one of Auckland's first settlers, wrote that the settlement really only consisted of a few boats and canoes on the beach, a few tents and huts, and a sea of fern.

By 1841 Auckland had just 1500 inhabitants, a number which was boosted in subsequent years by waves of immigrants from England, Ireland and Australia. Commercial Bay (near where Shortland St is today) was the main focus for the new township, with Official Bay the centre of administration. Mechanics Bay was where the township's industry (sawmills, shipyards and a brick kiln) took root.

It wasn't long before the settlers made a real impact on the landscape. By the mid-1840s farms producing meat and wheat covered the isthmus, and the Anglican Church was well established at Meadowbank and Parnell. But it was still a pioneering town. When the governor's wife held a ball at government house in the winter of 1843 the rain-soaked roads were so appalling that one man was reported to have transported his wife to the house in a wheelbarrow; other ladies put on boots to wade through the quagmire.

Lady Martin, wife of the chief justice Sir William Martin, lived at Judges Bay in Parnell from 1842. She described watching the canoes sailing across from the gulf islands into the little bay to trade, and how Maori who camped overnight in the bay cut fern for bedding and waded out to collect shellfish. During the township's early years relations with the Maori seemed quite cordial. Maori, in fact, supplied most of the fresh produce for the township; they traded widely and provided labour for public works and other projects. But there was an underlying uncertainty. Near-panic raced through the township in the mid-1840s when its inhabitants feared that clashes between British troops in the north and near Wellington

John Logan Campbell

John Logan Campbell – doctor, businessman, philanthropist – is a name that stands out among those who witnessed and took part in Auckland's establishment and early growth.

Trained in Edinburgh as a medical practitioner, Logan abandoned that profession to pursue a career in business. His ambition took him first to Australia and then to NZ, where at the age of 22 he landed at Coromandel and joined up with a like-minded young man, William Brown. While at Coromandel the pair heard that Governor Hobson was about to establish a capital at Auckland, so set off in that direction with the object of buying up land, subdividing it and selling to the settlers who would invariably follow. Things didn't go according to plan; the only land local Maori would agree to sell them was Browns Island (Motukorea). Using the island as a base, they started trading and before long moved across to Commercial Bay (near present day Shortland St) where they set up as merchants.

Brown eventually made enough money to retire to his home country, England. Campbell, whose first wooden dwelling is now on display in Cornwall Park, was also hugely successful. Eager to use his wealth for good works he gifted Cornwall Park to the people of NZ in 1901. He recorded his adventures in his book *Poenamo – Sketches of the Early Days of New Zealand*.

would put Auckland in danger of attack. The Albert Barracks were built and extra British troops called up, but the threat passed and Auckland continued to grow.

In the 1850s the creation of the Native Land Purchase Office and government attempts to individualise land title resulted in much land passing to the Crown, which in turn made it available on very attractive terms to settlers. This stimulated the growth of small settlements in places such as Waiuku and Warkworth, which, significantly, were situated on important waterways. Ten years later the government encouraged special settlements of certain groups of immigrants such as the Bohemians, who settled in Puhoi.

Meanwhile, in the Waikato, the King Movement (Kingitanga) was gaining momentum among Maori who wanted to stop further acquisition of their land. The government took the perceived threat seriously, building defensive blockhouses in south Auckland in response. In fact, only some of these were for defence; others were built to ensure the Great South Rd, which was to carry Imperial troops into the Waikato to fight the Maori, went ahead. The troops did indeed march down to the Waikato in 1863 and most of the fighting took place here; some, however, occurred on the southern borders of the Auckland region, around Pukekohe and Clevedon. This had a devastating effect on local Maori and many settlers also suffered heavy losses. Maori themselves refer to the land wars as Te Riri Pakeha, or white man's anger and claim, as did some European observers of the day, that they were only defending their land and their culture. The result was massive confiscations of land, the ramifications of which are still being addressed today.

The war may have destroyed lives and property, but the troops brought in to fight boosted the local economy. Similarly, their departure at the end of the hostilities, plus the transfer of the capital to Wellington, threw Auckland into the doldrums, something that was only arrested when gold was discovered on the Coromandel in 1867. Auckland gradually moved from a dependence on extractive activities (such as logging) to agriculture, and the introduction of refrigeration in the 1880s stimulated the growth of dairy farming.

Another invasion scare came in the mid-1880s when many Aucklanders believed they were in imminent danger of a Russian attack – these fears fuelled by an apparently increasing Russian naval presence in the Pacific. In response the government fortified North Head and Mt Victoria in Devonport and built a fort at Bastion Point. This was when the 'disappearing gun', state-of-the-art technology at the time, was installed at North Head. It was never actually needed, and has only ever been used for practise.

In 1891 Richard John Seddon (or King Dick, as he was also known) and the Liberals came to power, ushering in an era of social and economic reform: the old-age pension, the vote for women, the 40-hour working week. By the time the century drew to a close the economy was doing pretty well, buoyed by exports of butter, cheese and frozen meat to Britain.

As the Victorian era drew to a close and the Edwardian era began, NZ continued to prosper, gaining Dominion status in 1907. Auckland's prosperity was manifested in numerous public works: the ferry building, the chief post office, and the town hall. An electric tramline snaked through Auckland's southern and western suburbs. Then came WWI. NZ suffered heavy losses, with one in every three men aged between 20 and 40 killed or wounded fighting for Britain. The Auckland Museum was built as a war memorial to commemorate the nation's dead. With the returning soldiers came a deadly influenza, which hit Maori communities particularly hard.

The 1920s were economically stable but in the 1930s NZ, along with the rest of the world, was plunged into the Great Depression. In April 1932 Aucklanders, fed up with food shortages and the lack of jobs, rioted in Queen St and 2000 police and troops were called in. Thousands of men were put to work on relief jobs – Scenic Drive in the Waitakere Ranges being one of these projects.

In 1935 NZ's first Labour government, headed by Michael Joseph Savage, was elected by a landslide vote. Under Savage, NZ took its first steps to becoming a welfare state. Towards the end of the 1930s the hardship and suffering of the Depression years seemed to be over. But recovery was interrupted by the onset of WWII. Again, New Zealanders marched off to fight on Britain's side, although in 1941, when war was declared in the Pacific and NZ was directly threatened, a division was also established in the south-west Pacific. The Pacific War also brought many American servicemen to Auckland. Their camps, hospitals and warehouses endured for many years after the war ended, and some warehouses in south Auckland are still going strong.

The postwar years were good to NZ as the world was rebuilt. Prices for agricultural products were high. NZ had one of the highest per capita incomes in the world, and a social welfare system envied by many. By the close of 1956 a bridge spanned the harbour; people could now commute easily between the city and the North Shore. (In 1999 a second bridge was mooted.) Auckland hosted the Empire Games in 1950. European immigrants gave the city a more cosmopolitan feeling and rural New Zealanders migrated to the city, attracted by the prospect of jobs, money and excitement. By 1970 Auckland's population had grown to 650,000. In 1965 the Auckland Regional Authority was formed to coordinate planning and oversee the development of infrastructure for the sprawling city. Local body restructuring occurred in 1989 when the Auckland Regional Council was formed.

The good times stalled in the 1970s and 1980s. The closure of many of NZ's traditional European markets for agricultural products, combined with oil-crisis price hikes, caused a dramatic deterioration in the country's economy. In 1984 a Labour government was elected and, in a reversal of political roles, set about a radical restructuring of the economy; the finance minister, Roger Douglas, instituted his 'Rogernomics'. While the reforms produced some economic gains, they also resulted in rising unemployment.

This period also saw a resurgence of Maori culture, as leaders and activists pushed for social justice and highlighted Maori grievances. In 1975 the Treaty of Waitangi, which in 1877 was ruled a 'simple nullity', was reconsidered. The parliament passed the Treaty of Waitangi Act, establishing the Waitangi Tribunal to investigate Maori claims against the British Crown dating from 1975. In 1985 the act was amended to include claims dating back to the original signing of the treaty in 1840. Financial reparations were made to many Maori tribes whose lands were found to have been unjustly confiscated.

In 1983 NZ and Australia signed the Closer Economic Relations Trade Agreement, permitting free and unrestricted trade between the two countries. As NZ increasingly saw itself as a Pacific nation, rather than an 'efficient offshore farm' for the UK, its trade with the UK declined in proportion to its trade with Australia, the USA, Japan and the rest of Asia.

In 1984 NZ took a strong stand on nuclear energy issues by refusing entry to nuclear-equipped US warships. In response, the USA suspended its obligations to NZ within the ANZUS defence pact. Although this brave policy has caused many problems for NZ it has continued to stick by it.

NZ also became a leader in the Pacific in its opposition to French nuclear testing at Mururoa atoll in French Polynesia. In 1985 French secret service agents sank the Greenpeace ship, *Rainbow Warrior*, in Auckland Harbour (see the boxed text 'The Rainbow Warrior').

In the 1990s NZ continued to press on with free-market economics, with substantial cuts to welfare and deregulation of the labour market. Through a referendum in 1993 the people elected to adopt a Mixed Member Proportional (MMP) system based on the German model. But perhaps the most significant event of the 1990s – at least a great cause for national celebration – was NZ boat *Black Magic*'s historic win in the America's Cup yachting race in 1995.

The Rainbow Warrior

In 1985 the Greenpeace flagship *Rainbow Warrior* lay anchored in Auckland's harbour, preparing to sail north of Tahiti to protest against French nuclear testing. It never left Auckland. French saboteurs, with the backing of the French government, attached explosives to the side of the ship and sank her. Fernando Pereira, a green campaigner, was killed in the explosions.

It took some time to find out exactly what had happened, but in inquisitive, rural NZ the comings and goings of foreigners are not easily forgotten. Two of the saboteurs were captured, tried and found guilty, while the others have never been brought to justice.

The incident caused an uproar in France – not because the French government had conducted a wilful and lethal act of terrorism on the soil of a friendly nation, but because the French secret service had bungled the operation and been caught. The French used all their political and economic might to force NZ to release the two saboteurs, and in a farcical turn of events the agents were imprisoned on a French Pacific island as if they had just won a trip to Club Med. Within two years, and well before the end of their sentences, they returned to France to receive a hero's welcome.

Northland was the stage for the deadly mission involving several secret service agents. Explosives for the sabotage were delivered by a yacht (which had picked them up from a submarine) from Parengarenga Harbour in the far north. They were driven to Auckland in a Kombi van, by French agents posing as tourists. Bang! An innocent man dead, and international outrage – Auckland was in the news.

The skeletal remains of the *Rainbow Warrior* were taken to the waters of the beautiful Cavalli Islands. The masts of this oceanic crusader were sent to the Maritime Museum in Dargaville. The memory of the Portuguese photographer and campaigner who died endures in a peaceful bird sanctuary in Thames. A haunting memorial to the once-proud boat sits in peace atop a Maori pa site at Matauri Bay.

The world again focused on the *Rainbow Warrior* in 1995. Ten years after the sinking the French announced that they were resuming nuclear testing in the Pacific, and Greenpeace's new flagship, bearing the name of its ill-fated predecessor, set sail for the Mururoa test site. It entered the exclusion zone and was stormed by French marines.

The blasted hull of the *Rainbow Warrior*

GREENPEACE/MILLER

GEOGRAPHY & GEOLOGY

About 130 million years ago sediments deposited on the ocean floor near the great southern subcontinent Gondwanaland rose from the sea, forming a mountain range – the first outline of the land now known as NZ. The sediments (greywacke) were gradually eroded into a more subdued shape. Then, about 80 million years ago, the Tasman Sea opened in a process lasting about 20 million years, by the end of which NZ had moved into the Pacific.

The next important development occurred about 25 million years ago when the Pacific and Indian plates intersected the country. The tension between the two is largely responsible for NZ's present shape, the elevation of its mountains and its volcanic activity. Rock that makes up the Waitakere Ranges, for example, was thrown up by submarine volcanic activity that arced down Northland's west coast. Blocks of rock (the Waitakeres and the Hunua Ranges) were pushed up about 15 million years ago, and were modified by erosion over the next 10 million years; other areas, such as the Firth of Thames, Kaipara Harbour, were forced downward.

About 1.5 million years ago volcanic activity began in the Auckland region. It was also at about this time that the Ice Age closed in. During the peak of the Ice Age, some 15,000 to 20,000 years ago, the sea level dropped over 100m below its present level, draining the Waitemata, Manukau and Kaipara harbours as well as the Hauraki Gulf. Rivers that still exist extended their reach across the exposed land, but were themselves submerged when, about 10,000 years ago, the ice melted, creating the indented coastline one sees today.

Volcanoes are formed when magma deep below the earth's surface is forced upward. If magma encounters water when it bursts into the open, the result is superheated steam which, combined with dissolved gases, causes violent explosions that release clouds of ash and volleys of shattered rock. Eventually the volcano may expend its energy and its dead crater will fill with water (eg the Orakei and Panmure basins). But if, after the initial explosions, the lava rises again and meets no surface water, it fountains skyward. Glowing pieces of molten rock are flung into the air. The lava cools as it falls back to earth, and the porous, pocked pieces pile up on each other. This is how scoria cones, such as Mt Eden, were formed. Sometimes the lava flow is so great that it breaches the side of the cone, leaving a horseshoe shape in its stead, as is the case with One Tree Hill.

Auckland's oldest volcanoes (dating back at least 50,000 years) are thought to be

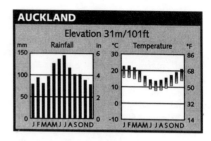

where Albert Park, Symonds St, the Auckland Domain and St Heliers are today. The youngest volcano, Rangitoto, erupted about 600 years ago and its creation was certainly witnessed by local Maori. Auckland apparently hasn't seen the last of its volcanic activity; the field is merely dormant.

CLIMATE

Auckland's maritime climate ensures that temperatures never go to the extremes they would were the city landlocked. Temperatures usually stay in the mid-20s (Celsius) in summer, and rarely fall near freezing in winter (June-August) – although the ground in some sheltered low-lying areas may at times receive a coating of frost. In summer the weather can become quite humid.

The gulf islands of Waiheke and Great Barrier are generally a few degrees warmer than the mainland. Rainfall is highest in the Waitakeres in the west, and the Hunuas in the south-east.

ECOLOGY & ENVIRONMENT

When Europeans first arrived on the Auckland isthmus they found a land covered in bracken and manuka, scrubby plants characteristic of regenerating bush – the legacy of repeated burn-offs mainly intended to clear land for cultivation. Kauri forest remained largely untouched in less accessible places like the Waitakeres and the gulf islands.

Not long after their arrival, colonists began logging kauri, especially in the Waitakeres. Great monsters of trees were felled and floated down rivers to be taken to the towns, or the docks for export. Gum diggers fossicked among the stumpy fields that were eventually burnt off and given over to pasture. Swamps were drained and mangroves eradicated. Introduced plants and animals quickly made an impact.

Auckland's scoria cones provided a ready-made and cheap material for roadworks and fill, and several have been quarried into oblivion. Those that remain are protected, but the gouge marks made by excavation machinery on some are clearly evident.

A network of regional parks and reserves (including three marine reserves) now protects important natural areas, although the majority of coastal habitats are not protected. There are, however, bans on harvesting shellfish at Karekare, Cheltenham and several other places.

The gulf islands, logged and farmed until relatively recently, are the focus of intensive and ongoing conservation efforts. Little Barrier Island, for example, is a sanctuary for endangered and threatened birds. Tiritiri Matangi, farmed until 1971, has been the focus of a major replanting program, aided over the years by thousands of volunteers. Threatened and endangered birds have been successfully released here. Currently Motutapu (next to Rangitoto) is the object of a Department of Conservation (DOC) program that aims to replant two-thirds of the island with indigenous species. Already rock wallabies and possums have been eradicated from both Rangitoto and Motutapu.

To understand more about the local environment and efforts to preserve it, visit the natural history floor at Auckland Museum and spend some time perusing the exhibit on human impact.

The Resource Management Act (1991) is NZ's most important piece of legislation concerning sustainable management, and regional and territorial authorities must defer to it. The Auckland Regional Council (ARC) is responsible for overall planning for the region, and has produced two important documents: the Auckland Regional Policy Statement (1999), which plans for 10 years out, and the Regional Growth Strategy (still in draft form), an environmental planning document with a 50-year outlook. At the end of 1999 the ARC for the first time released a document called the State of the Region Report, which details all issues and strategies as they relate to the environment of the entire region. Territorial authorities also have environment strategies, but they cannot conflict with those put forward for the entire region.

DOC controls about as much land as the ARC, but much of it centres on the gulf islands. DOC is a national body, whose responsibility is the protection of endangered species. Disputes involving sustainable management and apparent breaches of the Resource Management Act are heard before the Environment Court (formerly the Planning Tribunal).

Energy

Auckland draws most of its power from hydro-electric dams on the Waikato River to the south of the region. To a lesser degree it uses energy generated by natural gas plants at New Plymouth and Huntly. A cable that traverses Cook Strait brings power from the South to the North Island, but most of this is used in the lower half of the North Island. The national grid is operated by the government-owned Transpower. High-voltage lines are strung between pylons that cross the Waikato and the Bombay Hills, south of Auckland, to substations such as Otahuhu.

Auckland's CBD lost its power between February and April 1998 when all four cables, for various reasons, failed. Inner-city apartment dwellers became intimately acquainted with candles and staircases; restaurants threw out thousands of dollars in spoiled food from defrosting freezers. A sense of camaraderie developed among those affected. The construction of two new tunnels to carry cables into the CBD is under way: one from Mt Roskill and another from Penrose.

FLORA & FAUNA

Auckland has a surprising variety of habitats: rocky and sandy shores, tidal estuaries, forest and shrubland, wetlands and farmland, as well as urban areas.

On the coast is the tree most Aucklanders would associate with beaches and summer holidays: the pohutukawa, with its distinctive red flowers. Other coastal broadleaf trees include kowhai (yellow flowers in September), puriri and karaka (orange fruit). Also found in coastal areas are nikau, toii or cabbage trees (so-named by Captain Cook as its edible shoots reminded his crew of cabbage) and several species of fern including shield fern and maidenhair.

After the extensive logging in the 19th and early 20th centuries, little remains of the kauri forests that once covered large parts of the Auckland region. Among the best remaining stands are those at Kauri Grove and the Cascades in the Waitakeres. Associated with kauri in this area are rimu and northern rata. Rimu grows more than 50m high and has narrow, prickly leaves that drape down. Northern rata has red blossoms rather like a pohutukawa, but unlike pohutukawa it has leaves that are shiny and pointed at both ends. It starts life as an epi-

phyte (climber), usually attaching itself to rimu or puriri, which it eventually kills. Ponga, silver fern, and nikau (NZ's only native palm) can also be found in the region.

The Hunua Ranges, the largest forested area in the Auckland region, have been extensively logged for rimu and kauri. Tawa is now the main canopy tree; on the warmer northern slopes, it is taraire. Kohekohe and puriri are found on the lower slopes among the mixed coastal forest, and there are unusually (for Auckland) large stands of beech on the southern and eastern slopes of the ranges.

Manuka and kanuka (often collectively referred to as tea-tree) are scrubby plants characteristic of regenerating forest, and widely seen on land that's been logged or on abandoned farmland.

Auckland also has an impressive number of weeds (about 600 foreign urban types, one of the highest numbers recorded in any city), which flourish in its mild, moist climate. The appealing names that of some (eg old man's beard, cathedral bell and water poppy) belie their noxious status.

Auckland's diverse habitats harbour an equally varied array of birdlife. Introduced species found in urban areas include common house sparrows, starlings, song thrushes and blackbirds, black-and-white Australian magpies, pigeons, Indian mynahs, rock doves, silver-eyes, grey warblers, and the migrant shining cuckoos.

Native birds that inhabit city reserves include moreporks (native owls), fantails, tuis, wood pigeons, and in swampy areas, pukekos. In the countryside you may see harriers, native loners which patrol the skies above roads and fields seeking dead or alive small prey. Species found in the largest remnants of forest in Auckland (the Waitakeres and the Hunuas) include tuis, fantails, wood pigeons, moreporks, tomtits, and bellbirds (making a comeback after being regarded as extinct in the Auckland region). Kaka (a type of native parrot) is now only found on the gulf islands, and the North Island brown kiwi is found within Little Barrier Island's sanctuary.

MARTIN HARRIS

Toii, or cabbage tree

New Zealand native wood pigeon

Common coastal birds are gulls, both black-backed and red-billed, shags, terns, and the white-faced heron from Australia. Harbour flats attract curlews, oyster-catchers, banded dotterels, pied stilts and godwits.

Dolphins (common and bottle-nosed) are the most commonly sighted marine mammals around Auckland, sometimes coming into the harbour. Whales (black whale, white orca or killer whale, sperm whale, Bryde's whale) may sometimes be seen along the coast. In days gone by, there was a whaling station on Great Barrier Island. Fur seals are much less-frequent visitors to Auckland's waters.

For detailed information on NZ birds see BH & H Robertson's *Field Guide to the Birds of New Zealand*. For more detail on flora and fauna of Auckland get a copy of *A Field Guide to Auckland* by Ewen Cameron, Bruce Hayward & Graeme Murdoch, or *A Natural History of Auckland* edited by John Morton. Auckland Museum's natural history section is a great resource if you are interested in learning more about NZ's flora and fauna.

GOVERNMENT & POLITICS
National

The governmental structure of NZ is modelled on the British parliamentary system, with elections based on universal adult suffrage. The minimum voting age is 18 and candidates are elected by secret ballot. The maximum period between elections is three years. NZ is a constitutional monarchy. The traditional head of state, the reigning British monarch, is represented by a resident governor-general, who is appointed for a five-year term. An independent judiciary makes up another tier in government.

After a 1993 referendum on electoral reforms, New Zealanders voted overwhelmingly for proportional representation. The government introduced the MMP (Mixed Member Proportional) electoral system, a limited form of proportional voting based on the German electoral system.

Local

Auckland is made up of four cities (North Shore, Waitakere, Auckland and Manukau) and three districts (Rodney, Papakura and Franklin). Generally, districts can only become cities if they have a population of at least 50,000, are predominantly urban and can be identified as a distinct entity and a centre of activity for the region. The ARC has overall responsibility for planning for the region (roads, transport, environmental issues etc). The cities and districts also handle these issues, but must not be at odds with the overall regional planning. They are, however, more heavily involved in day to day service delivery: rubbish disposal, libraries and so forth. Local body elections are held once every three years. The inhabitants of the respective cities and districts elect their councillors and their mayors directly. The ARC consists of a council of 13 (the number of councillors representing a particular city or district is based on that city's or district's population) who elect a chairperson. Again, they all serve for a term of three years.

ECONOMY

Auckland's gross domestic output makes up about one-third of NZ's total. Auckland has a third of the country's businesses, and the same again of its workforce and retail sales. Auckland's seaports handle about a third of all goods arriving in the country by sea, and two-thirds of those leaving it. Seventy-four percent of all tourists to NZ arrive at Auckland's international airport.

The most important sectors of Auckland's economy are manufacturing, wholesale and retail, finance and business services and transport, as well as sectors related to agriculture. Within these categories are many dynamic and important areas of activity: viticulture and horticulture; software design; bloodstock; manufacture of building and construction materials; services such as packaging, refrigeration technology, transport and freight; and marine-related industries, eg electronics, software, and yacht design. (It's interesting to note that there are some 80,000 pleasure boats in Auckland, and it's claimed that the city's per capita boat-ownership is the world's highest.) Other areas in which Auckland has been innovative and successful include resource management law, whitegoods manufacture, filmmaking, telecommunications, education, aviation (including pilot training and engineering) and medical research.

POPULATION & PEOPLE

Some 1.2 million people live in the greater Auckland region – about 27% of NZ's population. Most are of European descent (61%) – mainly British. Pacific Islanders (from Samoa, Tonga, the Cook Islands, Nuie, Fiji and Tuvalu) make up the next largest ethnic group (13%), with people of Maori descent following at 12%. Those of Asian descent comprise 10% of the population. The remaining 4% is made up of people from various 'other' descents.

About 40% of Aucklanders were born elsewhere, either overseas (27%) or in some other part of the country. The majority of foreign-born Aucklanders are immigrants from the UK, with people from Asian and the Pacific Islands representing the next largest group.

EDUCATION

Auckland has two universities (Auckland, the longest established, and Massey), four polytechnics, a variety of research institutions and a teachers' training college.

As is the case in the rest of the country, there are both state and private (fee paying) schools and education is compulsory from age five to 15. There are also a great many pre-schools including kindergartens and playcentres. NZ has a good reputation as a place to learn English, with Auckland having the country's greatest concentration of English language schools.

There are 91 Kohanga Reo (Maori language-immersion schools for children aged up to six years) in the Auckland region. All teachers are Maori and all instruction is in Maori language. Kuru Kaupapa Maori language-immersion schools cater to kids up to Form 2 level (aged about 12 years). There are two Maori language-immersion schools in Auckland (at Glen Eden and Mangere) that cater for secondary-school children.

ARTS

Auckland offers the visitor a diverse range of arts to peruse. One of the positive aspects of its relatively small population is that different facets of the arts are closely interconnected. Auckland accommodates a small pool of artistic people who work in various guises. Many creative people often have dual reputations as artist/musicians or filmmaker/actors, dancer/designers and so on.

A lack of arts funding and the competitive nature of grants means that artisans living in Auckland adopt a kind of do-it-yourself attitude. Since the city has several tertiary institutions, students at universities and polytechnics initiate ventures that invigorate the broader arts community.

Literature

Literary life centres on book launches and poetry readings, which happen infrequently. The creative writing course at Auckland University produces a number of new authors who perform and print their work annually. Local pubs host poetry readings while more highbrow occasions such as the successful Alba readings are organised in cafe spaces from time to time.

In May 1999 Auckland held its first writers' week. This will most likely be an annual event, and bookings will be available through Ticketet. There is an unusual annual literary festival called 'Going West', which consists of readings on board a train travelling around the western suburbs.

Local writers' contributions can be read in a number of literary and fine-arts periodicals published in the city. In recent times two local magazines, *Quote UnQuote*, a mainsteam literary review publication, and *Monica*, a Creative NZ-funded arts periodical, have folded, leaving a considerable vacuum. However, this has created a space of opportunity that continues to be filled by various publications, such as *The Pander* or the internationally successful fashion/arts magazine *Pavement*. (See also the Books section in the Facts for the Visitor chapter.)

Visual Arts

A few artist-run spaces offer an alternative to the dealer galleries that dominate the art market. Although their gallery space is now closed, the Teststrip collective continues to produce the occasional micrograph, while Fiat Lux is due to reopen in new premises after an untimely demise. The two main exhibition spaces, the Auckland Art Gallery and its sister space the New Gallery, give an overview of historical and contemporary arts, while nearby the smaller George Fraser Gallery usually shows student work.

K Rd, renowned as a red light district, is now home to photographers, artists and performers, who live in converted warehouse spaces that double as studios. Recognising the need for improvisation in straitened circumstances, many artists have invented their own exhibition spaces around this area. You may happen across 'fixed cases' in the K Rd area, which hold temporary exhibits, or shops transformed into installation spaces.

A Pacific Island aesthetic is a distinct element in the craft and street fashion of Auckland – tapa cloth, woven baskets, shell jewellery, lava lavas and other ethnic elements are incorporated into many urban lifestyles. Especially in the last two decades, the Polynesian contribution to the arts scene has been considerable, with a number of visual artists and writers emerging into the mainstream. Because Polynesian cultural life tends to be communal, individuals often band together to organise dynamic fusions of dance, music and fashion.

Theatre & Dance

After a number of theatre closures and demolitions in the 1980s, Auckland has very few fixed outlets for dramatic productions. This means that drama tends to be produced sporadically, reliant on the enthusiasm of individuals rather than centering on a particular company. The most interesting work is done by impromptu theatre companies and at the flourishing university theatre.

The Auckland Theatre Company (ATC) is the city's only professional company, and despite the fact that it has no 'home' venue it has remained very active.

Dance performances are usually put on by NZ choreographers, such as Douglas Wright, and Maori drag-performer Mika, as part of a wider national or international circuit, rather than being confined to Auckland. (See also the Entertainment chapter.)

Film

Some of NZ's most renowned films have been shot in and around Auckland. Jane Campion's *The Piano* has immortalised the extraordinary beauty of Auckland's west coast beaches and Waitakere Ranges. Lee Tamahori's film of Alan Duff's novel *Once Were Warriors* has painted a bleak picture of a disenfranchised urban underclass in south Auckland. *What Becomes of the Brokenhearted?* (Duff's recent novel and film, and the sequel to *Once Were Warriors*) has also been set in the gritty urban environment of south Auckland.

Besides these and the production of *Xena*, there are a few ongoing film projects around town. The cinema studies school at Auckland University acts as a locus for discussion by film critics and practitioners alike. Short films are the preferred mode of experimentation because features are too expensive.

Speaking the Tongue

In many places Maori provide instruction in language and culture for young children, so they will grow up speaking Maori and English, and be familiar with Maori tradition. It is a matter of some pride to have fluency in the language. On some marae only Maori can be spoken, to encourage everyone to speak it and to emphasise the distinct Maori character of the marae.

Most consonants in Maori – h, k, m, n, p, t and w – are pronounced much the same as in English. The Maori 'r' is more like a flap of the tongue on the roof of the mouth behind the but not rolled. It's closer to the English 'd' in pronunciation. Two combinations of consonants are most challenging for visitors, and require special attention: 'ng', pronounced as in the English suffix '-ing' (singing, running etc), can be used at the beginning of words as well as at the end; and 'wh' also has a unique pronunciation in Maori – generally like a soft English 'f'. This pronunciation is used in many place names (particularly in the North Island), such as Whangarei, Whangaparoa and Whitianga (all pronounced as if they begin with a soft 'f').

The correct pronunciation of the vowels is all-important. To really get it right you need to hear them pronounced correctly. Every syllable ends in a vowel and there's never more than one vowel in a syllable. There are no silent letters in the Maori language.

There are many Maori phrasebooks, grammar books and Maori-English dictionaries if you want to study the language. Lonely Planet's *South Pacific Phrasebook* has a good section on Maori. The *Collins Maori Phrase Book* by Patricia Tauroa is excellent, with sections on everyday conversation and also on how the language is used in a cultural context, such as on marae. *Say it in Maori*, compiled by Alan Armstrong, is a pocket-sized book. *He Whakamarama: A New Course in Maori* by John Foster is an introductory language course and has an accompanying cassette. Other English-Maori dictionaries include the *English-Maori Maori-English Dictionary* by Bruce Biggs and the *Reed Dictionary of Modern Maori* by PM Ryan, one of the most authoritative.

It is increasingly common to be greeted on the phone or in the street with 'kia ora'. Depending on context there are a number of appropriate responses. You may want to learn a few basic greetings, especially if you plan to visit a marae, where you'll be greeted in Maori.

Haere mai!	Welcome!
Haere ra.	Goodbye; farewell. (from the person staying to the one going)
E noho ra.	Goodbye; farewell. (from the person going to the person staying)
Kia ora.	Hello; good luck; good health.
Tena koe.	Hello. (to one person)
Tena korua.	Hello. (to two people)
Tena koutou.	Hello. (to three or more people)
Kei te pehea koe?	How are you? (to one person)
Kei te pehea korua?	How are you? (to two people)
Kei te pehea koutou?	How are you? (to three or more people)
Kei te pai.	Very well, thank you; that is OK.

With the axing of the funding body *NZ On Air*, filmmakers will have to pursue closer relationships with the commercial sector.

SOCIETY & CONDUCT

Although NZ culture is essentially European, transplanted by the British to these far-off lands, Maori culture has always been an integral part of NZ and is a strong and growing influence. European New Zealanders once held so strong to their British traditions that they earned the tag of 'South Sea Poms'. However, a growing diversity of migrants and a wider global outlook has seen a real change in NZ society, and this particularly applies to Auckland. Resurgent Maori culture and the new corporate philosophy have also helped to shape a new worldview. NZ has always been proud of its traditions, but more than ever it is exploring its identity.

Though the majority of Auckland's population comes from British stock, there are other notable early influences. The Dalmatians came from Croatia to dig kauri gum and later established fine vineyards in West Auckland. Indians and Chinese are major immigrant groups; more recently, Koreans and a new wave of Chinese immigrants have arrived. Polynesians migrated to Auckland in large numbers in the 1960s and early 1970s when Auckland experienced severe labour shortages, bringing their cultures with them. Auckland is often described as the world's largest Polynesian city; you can go to a Samoan rugby match on Saturday afternoon, dance the *tamure* at a Cook Islands nightclub that night and go to a Tongan-language church service on Sunday.

Through a common history and culture based on British traditions, and a strong geographical link, Auckland shares many cultural attributes with, and has long been influenced by, neighbouring Australia. Many Aucklanders have emigrated to Australia, particularly Sydney, or at least travelled to and worked in Australia. However, many Kiwis are keen to distance themselves from their cousins across the Tasman (many of whom they see as brash and patronising).

LANGUAGE

NZ has two official languages: English and Maori. English is the most widely spoken, but Maori, long on the decline, has more recently made a comeback. Government departments now carry both Maori and English names, as do many other public institutions.

However, given Auckland's ethnic mix, a range of other languages can be added to the two official ones. They include several Pacific island languages (eg Samoan, Tongan and Cook Islands Maori), several Asian languages (Mandarin, Korean, Hindi, Tagalog and Japanese), and European languages such as Dutch, French, German, and Spanish.

Kiwi English

New Zealanders, like Australians and those from other former British colonies, have their own way with the English language. The elision of vowels is the most distinctive feature of Kiwi pronunciation. The New Zealand treatment of 'fish and chips' is an endless source of delight for Australians.

Maori

An oral language until recorded by the early missionaries, Maori is fluid and poetic. It's related to the Polynesian languages and has some similarity to dialects found in Indonesia. In recent years there has been a revival of interest in the language, an important part of the renaissance of Maoritanga. It is now taught in schools and there are also many language immersion schools for young people.

Facts for the Visitor

WHEN TO GO

The busiest tourist season is during the warmer months, from around November to April. The peak travel time in New Zealand is the summer school holidays from 20 December to late January. During these holidays, when both New Zealanders and international visitors are out on the road, transport and accommodation is likely to fill up, especially in the more economical places, so book as far ahead as possible. To a lesser extent the Easter weekend, Labour Day weekend (late October) and the mid-year school holidays are also busy. January and February are the best beach-weather months, but December and March are usually warm – even hot at times. November and April are slightly cooler and the beach weather has passed, but these months are noticeably quieter, and accommodation in areas with heavy tourist traffic is easier to find.

ORIENTATION

The commercial heart of the city (Map 3) is Queen St, which runs from Queen Elizabeth II Square (usually called QEII Square) near the waterfront and uphill to cosmopolitan Karangahape Rd (K Rd), passing Aotea Square en route.

Parnell (Map 4), just east of the city centre, is a fashionable area of renovated wooden villas. Parnell Rd continues on to fashionable Broadway in Newmarket and is lined with restaurants and boutiques. Tamaki Drive (sometimes called the waterfront drive) starts where Quay St (which skirts the harbour east of the downtown area) ends at Mechanics Bay, and continues all the way to St Heliers Bay, passing Okahu Bay and Mission Bay en route. Offshore lies Rangitoto and, to the east, flatter and smaller Browns Island. Also visible from Tamaki Drive is Devonport's North Head (Map 6), which juts into the ocean, and a little to the west of it, Mt Victoria.

Just west of the city centre is Ponsonby Rd (Map 2), packed with cafes and bars that spill over into neighbouring Jervois Rd, which runs through upmarket Herne Bay. Further west are the Waitakere Ranges, which can be seen from Ponsonby ridge. Visible from just about everywhere in Auckland is the Skytower, which soars above the city centre.

MAPS

Automobile Association (AA) members (or members of affiliate organisations) can present their cards at AA offices and get many free maps. These are among the best available. Wises' Streetmaster guides to Auckland and the Auckland region are also excellent. Land Information New Zealand (formerly the Department of Survey and Land Information – the name that still appears on the maps) publishes Topomaps, which are recommended if you intend bushwalking (or tramping, as it is known in NZ). Its Holidaymaker series, which covers the gulf islands, is also very useful. These are available at the Department of Conservation (DOC) shop in the ferry building or at Specialty Maps (☎ 307 2217), 58 Albert St.

Major bookshops, such as Whitcoulls, stock Wises and other maps, and Specialty Maps has an excellent range. Free maps are available at various tourist offices.

TOURIST OFFICES
Local Tourist Offices

Tourism Auckland offices (reservations @aucklandnz.com) are at:

Auckland Visitor Centre (☎ 979 2333, fax 970 2334), 287 Queen St. Open Monday to Friday from 8.30 am to 5.30 pm; weekends 9 am to 5 pm.
New Zealand Visitor Centre (no public phone number; the Queen St office handles all phone enquiries), Hobson Wharf. Open daily from 9.30 am to 5.30 pm.
Visitor Information Centre (☎ 275 6467, fax 256 8942), International Terminal, Auckland

Airport. Open daily from the first flight of the day (usually about 5 am) until the last flight of the day (usually midnight).

Visitor Information Centre (☎ 256 8480, fax 256 8225), Domestic Terminal, Auckland Airport. Open daily from 7 am to 7 pm.

Tourism Auckland's Web site is at www .aucklandnz.com.

Regional Tourist Offices

North Shore Information Centre
Devonport branch (☎ 446 0677/88), adjacent to the library, Victoria Rd. Open daily from 9 am to 5 pm in summer; 10 am to 4 pm in winter.
Takapuna branch (☎ 486 8670), 49 Hurstmere Rd. Open Monday to Friday from 9 am to 5 pm; weekends 10 am to 3 pm.

Hibiscus Coast Visitor Information Centre (☎ 09-426 0076, fax 426 0086), Hibiscus Coast Hwy. Open Monday to Friday from 9 am to 5 pm; weekends 10 am to 4 pm.

Warkworth Information Centre (☎ 425 9081, fax 425 7584), Rodney District Council Bldg, Baxter Street, Warkworth

Kumeu & District Visitor Centre (☎/fax 09-412 9886), Main Rd, Kumeu

Arataki Visitor Centre (☎ 817, fax 817 5656), Scenic Drive, Waitakere Ranges. Open daily from 9 am to 5 pm.

Franklin Information Centre (☎ 09-236 0670, fax 236 0580), State Hwy One, Mill Rd, Bombay. Open Monday to Friday from 8.30 am to 5 pm; weekends 9 am to 3 pm.

The Waiuku Information Centre (☎ 235 8924, fax 235 7278), 2 Queen St, Waiuku

Waiheke Visitor Information Office (☎ 372 9999, fax 372 9919,waiheke@iconz .co.nz), 2 Korora Rd, Artworks, Oneroa. Open daily from 9 am to 5 pm in summer; closes earlier in winter.

Great Barrier Visitor Information Centre (☎ 429 0033), Claris Airport, Great Barrier Island

Tourist Offices Abroad

The New Zealand Tourist Board (NZTB), whose role is to promote tourism to NZ, has representatives in various countries. Its head office (☎ 04-472 8860) is at PO Box 95, Wellington, NZ. Its overseas offices include:

Australia
(☎ 02-9247 5222, fax 9241 1136)
Level 8, 35 Pitt St, Sydney NSW 2000
Germany
(☎ 69-97 12 110, fax 97 12 11 13)
Rossmarkt 11, 60311, Frankfurt am Main
Hong Kong
(☎ 2526 0141)
Unit 1601 Vicwood Plaza, 199 Des Voeux Rd C
Japan
(☎ 6-268 8335)
Meiji Seimei Sakaisuji Honmachi Bldg, 2nd Floor, 1-7-15 Minami Honmachi, Chuo-ku, Osaka-shi 541
(☎ 3-5381 6331)
Shinjuku Monolith 21st Floor, 2-3-1 Nishi Shinjuku, Shunjuku-ku, Tokyo 163-09
Singapore
(☎ 738 5844, fax 235 2250)
Orchard Rd, Ngee Ann City, 15th Floor, Tower A, Singapore
UK
(☎ 020-7930 1662, fax 839 8929)
New Zealand House, Haymarket, London SW1Y 4TQ
USA
(☎ 310-395 7480, fax 395 5453)
501 Santa Monica Blvd, Suite 300, Santa Monica, CA 90401
(☎ 212-832 8482, fax 832 7602)
780 Third Ave, Suite 1904, New York, NY 10017-2024

DOCUMENTS
Passports

Everyone needs a passport to enter NZ. If you enter on an Australian or NZ passport, or a passport containing an Australian or NZ residence visa, your passport must be valid on arrival. All other passports must be valid for at least three months beyond the time you intend to stay in NZ, or one month beyond the intended stay if the issuing government has an embassy or consulate in NZ able to issue and renew passports.

Visas

Australian citizens and holders of current Australian Resident Return Visas do not need a visa or permit to enter NZ and can stay indefinitely if they do not have any criminal convictions. Australians do not require a work permit.

Citizens of the UK, and other British passport holders who can show they have permanent UK residency, do not need a visa; they are issued on arrival with a visitor permit valid for up to six months.

Citizens of the following countries do not need a visa and are given a three-month, extendable visitor permit upon arrival: Austria, Belgium, Brunei, Canada, Czech Republic, Finland, France, Germany, Greece, Iceland, Indonesia, Ireland, Italy, Japan, Kiribati, South Korea, Liechtenstein, Luxembourg, Malaysia, Malta, Monaco, Nauru, the Netherlands, Norway, Portugal, Singapore, South Africa, Spain, Sweden, Switzerland, Thailand, Tuvalu, USA.

Citizens of all other countries require a visa, available from any NZ embassy or consular agency. Visas are normally valid for three months.

To qualify for a visitor permit on arrival, or for a visa, you must be able to show your passport, valid for three months beyond the time of your intended stay; have an onward ticket to a country where you have right of entry, with firm bookings if travelling on special rate air fares; and have evidence of sufficient funds to support yourself for the duration of your intended stay. (This is calculated at NZ$1000 per month – NZ$400 per month if your accommodation has been prepaid. Funds can be cash, travellers cheques or bank drafts, or American Express, Bankcard, Diners Club, MasterCard or Visa credit cards.)

Work & Student Visas It is illegal to work on a visitor permit. If you have an offer of employment, before arriving in NZ you should apply for a work permit valid for up to three years. Permission to work is granted only if no NZ job seekers can do the job you have been offered. A work permit can be applied for in NZ after arrival but, if granted, it will be valid only for the remaining time you are entitled to stay as a visitor.

Citizens of Canada, Japan and the UK aged 18 to 30 can apply for a Working Holiday Visa, which is valid for a 12-month stay. It allows you to work while travelling around the country, but you must apply for it in your home country before entering New Zealand; it is only issued to those seeking a genuine working holiday, not permanent work.

You can study on a visitor permit if enrolling in a single course of not more than three months. For longer periods of study you must obtain a student permit.

Visa Extensions Visitor permits can be extended for stays of up to nine months, if you apply for an extension and meet the normal requirements. 'Genuine tourists' and a few other categories of visitors can be granted stays of up to 12 months.

Apply for extensions at any New Zealand Immigration Service office in Auckland, Manukau, Hamilton, Palmerston North, Wellington, Christchurch and Dunedin.

Be careful not to overstay; it will result in your being subject to deportation. Extensions are easy to get provided you meet the requirements.

Travel Insurance

A travel insurance policy to cover theft, loss and medical care is a good idea. Some policies offer varying medical-expense options; the higher options are chiefly for countries, such as the USA, which have extremely high medical costs. There are a wide variety of policies available, so check the small print.

Some policies specifically exclude 'dangerous activities', which can include scuba diving, motorcycling and even trekking. A locally acquired motorcycle licence is not valid under some policies.

You may prefer a policy that pays doctors or hospitals directly, rather than one that reimburses you later. If you have to claim your expenses later make sure you keep all documentation. Some policies ask you to phone (reverse charges) a medical centre in your home country for an immediate assessment of your problem.

Check that the policy you choose covers ambulance transportation and/or an emergency flight home.

Driving Licence & Permits

Take your driver's licence with you. A full, valid driver's licence from your home country is all you need to rent and drive a car in NZ. Members of automobile associations should take their membership cards, which can be useful if recognised by the AA.

Student & Hostel Cards

An International Student Identity Card (ISIC) entitles you to certain discounts, particularly on transport. Even better is an International Youth Hostel (YHA) card, which is well worth having even if you don't intend staying in hostels. This card provides a 50% discount on domestic air travel and a 30% discount on major bus lines, plus dozens of discounts on activities. A VIP Backpackers Card offers the same benefits and can be bought in NZ or Australia from VIP hostels.

Photocopies

All important documents (passport data page and visa page, credit cards, travel insurance policy, air/bus/train tickets, driver's licence etc) should be photocopied before you leave home. Leave one copy with someone at home and keep another with you, separate from the originals.

EMBASSIES & CONSULATES

As a tourist it's important to realise what your own embassy – the embassy of the country of which you are a citizen – can and can't do.

Generally speaking, it won't much help in emergencies if the trouble you're in is remotely your own fault. Remember that you're bound by the laws of the country you are in. Your embassy will not be sympathetic if you end up in jail after committing a crime, even if such actions are legal in your own country.

In genuine emergencies you might get some assistance, but only if other channels have been exhausted. For example, if you need to get home urgently, a free ticket home is exceedingly unlikely – the embassy would expect you to have insurance.

If you have all your money and documents stolen, it might assist with getting a new passport, but a loan for onward travel is out of the question.

Embassies used to keep letters for travellers or have a small reading room with home newspapers, but these days mail-holding services have been stopped and even newspapers tend to be out of date.

NZ Embassies & Consulates

Australia
    High Commission:
    (☎ 02-6270 4211, fax 6273 3194)
    Commonwealth Ave, Canberra, ACT 2600
    Consulate General:
    (☎ 02-9247 1999, fax 9247 1754)
    14th Floor, Gold Fields Bldg, 1 Alfred St, Circular Quay, Sydney, NSW 2000; GPO Box 365, Sydney, NSW 2000
Canada
    High Commission:
    (☎ 613-238 6097, fax 238 5707)
    Suite 727 Metropolitan House, 99 Bank St, Ottawa, Ontario K1P 6G3
    Consulate General:
    (☎ 604-684 7388, fax 684 7333)
    Suite 1200-888 Dunsmuir St, Vancouver BC V6C 3K4
France
    Embassy:
    (☎ 01-45 00 24 11, fax 45 01 26 39)
    7ter, rue Léonard de Vinci, 75116 Paris
Germany
    Embassy:
    (☎ 228-22 80 70, fax 22 16 87)
    Bundeskanzlerplatz 2-10, 53113 Bonn
    Consulate General:
    (☎ 40-4 42 55 50, fax 4 42 555 49)
    Heimhuderstrasse 56, 20148 Hamburg
Ireland
    Consulate General:
    (☎ 1-676 2464, fax 676 2489)
    46 Upper Mount St, Dublin 2
Netherlands
    Embassy:
    (☎ 70-346 9324, fax 363 2983)
    Carnegielaan 10, 2517 KH The Hague
UK
    High Commission:
    (☎ 020-7208 1130, fax 7973 0370)
    New Zealand House, Haymarket, London SW1Y 4TQ
USA
    Embassy:
    (☎ 202-328 4848, fax 667 5227)

37 Observatory Circle NW, Washington DC 2000
Consulate General:
(☎ 310-207 1605, fax 207 3605)
Suite 1150, 12400 Wiltshire Blvd, Los Angeles, CA 90025
Consulate:
(☎ 206-525 9881, fax 525 0271)
6810 51st Ave NE, Seattle, WA 98115

Embassies & Consulates in Auckland

Australian Consulate General
(☎ 303 2429), Union House, 32-38 Quay St
British Consulate General
(☎ 303 2973), Fay Richwhite Bldg, 151 Queen St
Cook Islands Consulate General
(☎ 366 1100), 1/127 Symonds St
Danish Consulate
(☎ 537 3099), Box 619, Auckland 1
French Consulate
(☎ 488 3453), 7a Barrys Point Rd, Takapuna
Italy
(☎ 486 1888), 102 Kitchener Rd, Milford, North Shore
Japan Consulate General
(☎ 303 4106), ASB Bank Centre, Level 12, 135 Albert St
Malaysian Consulate Office
(☎ 355 6016), 19 Morgan St, Newmarket
Netherlands Consulate
(☎ 379 5399), 1st Floor, 57 Symonds St
Philippine Consulate General
(☎ 303 2423), 1st Floor, 121 Beach Rd
Royal Norwegian Consulate
(☎ 355 1830), Level 38, Coopers & Lybrand Tower, 23-29 Albert St
Royal Thai Consulate
(☎ 373 2794), 44 Anzac Ave
Swedish Consulate General
(☎ 373 5332), Simpson Grierson Bldg, 13th Floor, 92-96 Albert St
Taipei Economic & Cultural Office
(☎ 303 3903), 11F Norwich Insurance Bldg, cnr Queen and Durham Sts
USA
(☎ 303 2724), General Bldg, cnr Shortland and O'Connell Sts

CUSTOMS

Customs allowances are 200 cigarettes (or 50 cigars or 250g of tobacco), 4.5L of wine or beer and one 1125ml bottle of spirits or liqueur.

Goods up to a combined value of NZ$700 are free of duty and GST. Personal effects are not normally counted. If you do not exceed your $700 passenger concession, and do not have any alcohol or tobacco in your possession, you can import two extra bottles of duty-free liquor.

As in most places, the customs people are fussy about drugs.

MONEY
Currency

NZ's currency is dollars and cents. There are $5, $10, $20, $50 and $100 notes, and 5c, 10c, 20c and 50c, $1 and $2 coins. Unless otherwise noted, all prices quoted in this book are in NZ dollars.

There are no limitations on the import or export of foreign currency. Unused NZ currency can be changed to foreign currency before you leave the country.

Exchange Rates

country	unit		dollar
Australia	A$1	=	NZ$1.26
Canada	C$1	=	NZ$1.29
European Union	€1	=	NZ$1.94
France	1FF	=	NZ$0.29
Germany	DM1	=	NZ$0.99
Hong Kong	HK$10	=	NZ$2.40
Japan	¥100	=	NZ$1.57
United Kingdom	UK£1	=	NZ$2.97
United States	US$1	=	NZ$1.91

Exchanging Money

The currencies of Australia, the UK, USA, Germany and Japan are all easily changed in NZ, and at consistently good rates. Most banks will exchange these and up to 30 other currencies, but exchange rates may be slightly lower for less frequently changed currencies.

Banks are open Monday to Friday from 9 am to 4.30 pm. Exchange rates may vary a few cents between banks. At most banks there's no service charge for changing travellers cheques.

Cash Major currencies can be readily exchanged at banks and moneychangers. Most moneychangers only accept cash.

Travellers Cheques All major brands of travellers cheques are accepted at most banks.

ATMs Following are location details of 24-hour ATMs in the downtown area. ATMs are widely available throughout Auckland's commercial hub and its suburbs.

ANZ Banking Group: cnr Queen and Victoria Sts; 126 Queen St; 230 Queen St; Sky Casino (two). ANZ machines accept any NZ-issued Diners Club International card, Visa, Master-Card, Bankcard and any card with the Cirrus logo.
ASB Bank: Downtown Shopping Mall (cnr Quay and Queen Sts); cnr Queen and Wellesley Sts; cnr Albert and Wellesley Sts; 138 Queen St. ASB machines accept Visa, MasterCard, American Express and any card with the Plus logo.
BNZ: Downtown Shopping Centre; 80 Queen St. BNZ machines accept Visa, MasterCard, Diners Club International and any card with the Cirrus or Plus logo.
National Bank: cnr Victoria and Queen Sts; 118 Queen St. National machines accept Visa and cards with the Plus logo.
WestpacTrust: 79 Queen St (two). WestpacTrust machines accept MasterCard, Visa, American Express and any card with the Cirrus logo.

Credit Cards Credit cards are a cheap and convenient way to carry money, provided you keep your account in the black and your bank does not charge exorbitant fees. Get a card with a PIN attached for ATM withdrawals.

For long stays, it may be worth opening a bank account; you can request a card for 24-hour ATM access.

International Transfers You can have money sent to you as a moneygram via Western Union (☎ 358 9173), at 32 Queen St, or Thomas Cook (☎ 379 3920), at Level 5, Telstra Business Centre, 191 Queen St.

Moneychangers Moneychangers have slightly longer weekday hours than banks and are usually open on Saturday and sometimes on Sunday. Rates may be competitive, but are usually lower than the banks'.

Thomas Cook offices have competitive rates and change a wider variety of currencies than most banks. Contact details for the various banks' branches and services are in the *Yellow Pages* telephone book.

American Express Foreign Exchange Bureau (☎ 379 8286), 105 Queen St. Open Monday to Friday 9 am to 5 pm (Wednesday from 9.30 am); Saturday 9.30 am to 12.30 pm. Most travellers cheques are accepted as well as cash, but no advances on credit cards.
Inforex Foreign Exchange (☎ 302 3066), the ferry building. Open daily from 8 am to 8 pm. Exchanges major currencies and travellers cheques.
Travelex (☎ 358 9173), 32 Queen St. Open Monday to Friday from 8 am to 8 pm and weekends 10 am to 8 pm.
Singapore Exchange & Finance (NZ) Ltd (☎ 302 0502), 11 Customs St East; (☎ 307 9333), cnr Albert and Quay Sts. Open Monday to Friday from 8.30 am to 7.30 pm; weekends 10 am to 6 pm.

Security
Travellers cheques are always the safest way to carry money, and their exchange rate is slightly better than for cash in NZ.

Costs
You can spend a lot or a little in Auckland, depending on where you stay and what you do. For example, backpacker accommodation costs around $20 for a hostel dorm bed, and if you add on food (eating at only inexpensive places, say $12 to $15 for a main meal), drink, transport and entertainment, you could do Auckland for about $50 a day with no frills. Middle-range travellers staying at B&Bs, eating out and going on occasional excursions would probably spend around $150 to$200 a day.

Tipping & Bargaining
Tipping isn't a way of life in NZ. At better restaurants and hotels a tip of up to 10% of the total bill may be given if the service etc is particularly outstanding. It's very much up to you.

Bargaining is virtually non-existent; all shops and most markets have fixed prices.

Bargaining would really only occur if you were buying something like a second-hand car at a car fair. Your ability to get the car for the price you want depends to a large extent on how well informed you are of current prices and market demand, something that generally comes with experience.

Taxes

A 12.5% GST (Goods & Services Tax) is applied to all goods and services including food and even fines, should you incur any. Generally, the prices given in this guide are inclusive of the tax unless otherwise stated. But it's always worth checking before you book or order to avoid an unpleasant shock.

POST & COMMUNICATIONS
Post

NZ post shops (they are not called post offices any more) are open weekdays from 9 am to 5 pm. Postal charges within NZ are 40c for a standard letter (80c for an extra large letter) and 80c for fastpost. Aerograms and postcards cost $1 to any destination. Letters to Australia and the South Pacific cost from $1 for medium size to $3 for extra large (maximum weight 200g/20mm thickness), to USA and Asia $1.50/6, and to Europe $1.80/6.80.

You can have mail addressed to you care of Post Restante. Your messages and mail will be held for up to three months, after which it will be returned to sender. Poste Restante (☎ 379 6714) is located at the Bledisloe Bldg, 24 Wellesley St.

Telephone

Local telephone calls from public booths using a coin or phonecard cost 50c, and you can talk as long as you like. Most booths have cardphones (green stripes) – booths with coin phones have a blue stripe, and credit card booths have a yellow stripe. You can make international telephone calls from some Internet cafes, including Net Central Cafe and Netcafe (see the Email & Internet Access entry later in this section). The national directory service number is ☎ 018 and the international service ☎ 0172.

Telephone numbers prefixed with 0800 are toll-free – though some companies will not allow this facility for calls made from the same area (ie you will have to use the local number). Numbers prefixed with 0900 attract a higher charge than local calls.

There's a wide range of local and international phonecards. Lonely Planet's eKno Communication Card (see the insert at the back of this book) is aimed specifically at independent travellers and provides budget international calls, a wide range of messaging services and free email. For local calls, you're usually better off with a local card.

You can join online at www.ekno.lonelyplanet.com, or by phone from anywhere in NZ by dialling ☎ 0800 11 44 84. Once you have joined, you can then access the cheap eKno local access rates from Auckland by dialling ☎ 912 8211. If you are elsewhere in NZ, you can use eKno by dialling ☎ 0800 11 44 78.

You can buy other prepaid/rechargeable cards from service stations, dairies and a few other places. Most will display a sign saying which cards they sell. New names seem to pop up all the time, although established ones include Smartel, Net Tel, CLEAR TalkPlus and Telecom Talkaway cards.

NZ Area Codes Within Auckland there are six different calling zones (all with the 09 prefix). They are Warkworth (telephone numbers beginning with 422, 423, 425, 4312, 4314, 4315), Helensville (420), Hibiscus Coast (424, 426), Great Barrier Island (429), Auckland and the gulf islands except for Great Barrier (3, 5, 6, 8, 25, 26, 27, 29, 41, 44, 47, 48) and Pukekohe (23). If you are dialling between these areas, say from Auckland to Warkworth or vice versa, you will need to insert the area code 09 before the telephone number.

NZ has the following area codes:

Northland/Auckland	☎ 09
Rotorua/Taupo	☎ 07
Hawkes Bay/Taranaki	☎ 06
Wanganui/Manawatu	☎ 06
Wellington	☎ 04
South Island	☎ 03

World Area Codes Use the following codes to dial outside NZ:

Country	Access Code
Australia	0061
Canada	001
France	0033
Germany	0049
Hong Kong	00852
Ireland	00353
Italy	0039
Japan	0081
Netherlands	0031
Singapore	0065
South Korea	0082
UK	0044
USA	001

Fax

Many hotels, motels and even hostels have fax machines. Many Internet cafes offer fax services, as do post shops. The charge to send a fax is about $5, plus the telephone charge. Receiving a fax costs about $1. You can also send and receive faxes at the Auckland Public Library, which charges $3.50 a page to Australia and $6 a page to other overseas destinations. It costs $5 to receive a fax.

Email & Internet Access

Net Central Cafe (☎ 373 5186), 4 Lorne St, is well organised and popular. Internet charges are $1.20 for five minutes and $12 per hour. Telephone calls to Australia, the UK, USA, Japan and Germany cost $1 per minute.

Netcafe (☎ 358 4877), at the Auckland Central Backpackers, 9 Fort St, is open 24 hours, seven days a week. It charges $2 for up to 10 minutes, $5 for 30 minutes and $10 per hour. International calls cost 80c a minute to Australia, $1 a minute to the UK and USA, and $1.85 to Germany and France.

Discount Dialling (☎ 355 7300), 7 Fort St, is open daily from 8 am to 11.30 pm. It charges in 10-minute blocks, but up to five minutes costs $1.50 and 40-60 minutes costs $10.

Live Wire (☎ 356 0999), Level 1 Mid City, 239 Queen St, is open Monday to Friday from 9 am to around 11 pm and weekends 10 am to 10 pm. It charges 16c a minute and $10 per hour.

Cyber City (☎ 303 3009), 29 Victoria St East (next to the Albert Park Backpackers), is open daily from 9 am to 11 pm. It charges $2.50 for 15 minutes and $10 per hour. Local and international calls can also be made from here.

Auckland Public Library (☎ 377 0209) has Internet-connected computers on the first floor, which are available on a first-come-first-served basis. You must buy a cash card ($1) on to which you load the amount you want to use; 15 minutes costs $3.

Cybercafe@MacJava (☎ 377 8082), 268 K Rd, Newton, is open Monday to Saturday from 10 am to 8 pm. It charges $10 per hour.

Click City (☎ 623 5001), 674 Dominion Rd, Balmoral, is open Monday to Saturday from 9 am to 11 pm and Sunday 10 am to 11 pm. It charges $3.45 for 15 minutes and $13.75 per hour.

Citinet Cybercafe (☎ 377 3674), Shop 4, 115 Queen St, is open daily from 10 am to 10 pm. It charges $1 for five minutes and $10 per hour. It has another branch just below Albert Park at 22-24 Kitchener St – same hours and rates.

USIT Beyond Travel Centre (☎ 379 3280), 18 Shortland St, offers ISIC and YHA card holders free Internet access for 15 minutes ($2.50 a minute thereafter).

Login I (☎ 522 9303), First Floor, Rialto Centre, 153 Broadway, Newmarket is open daily from 10 am to 10 pm. Internet costs $5 per half hour.

Gentronics (☎ 445 3740), 53a Victoria Rd, Devonport, is open Monday to Friday from 9 am to 5.30 pm and Saturday 10 am to 2 pm. It charges $5 for 15 minutes, $7.50 for 30 minutes and $10 per hour.

MBE Business Service Centre (☎ 623 0126), 453 Mt Eden Rd (near Oaklands Lodge and Villa 536), is open Monday to Friday from 8.30 am to 5.30 pm and Saturday 9.30 am to 1 pm. Email costs $5 for 15 minutes, and other services (eg fax, courier) are also available.

St Heliers Secretarial Service (☎ 575 9009), 26 St Heliers Bay Rd (upstairs in the main shopping centre), offers a range of services, including email at $5 for 15 minutes.

INTERNET RESOURCES

The World Wide Web is a rich resource for travellers. You can research your trip, hunt down bargain air fares, book hotels, check on weather conditions or chat with locals and other travellers about the best places to visit (or avoid).

There's no better place to start your Web explorations than the Lonely Planet Web site (www.lonelyplanet.com.au). Here you'll find succinct summaries on travelling to most places on earth, postcards from other travellers and the Thorn Tree bulletin board, where you can ask questions before you go or dispense advice when you get back. You can also find travel news and updates to many of our most popular guidebooks, and the subWWWay section links you to the most useful travel resources elsewhere on the Web. Other useful sites include:

www.aucklandnz.com
    Tourism Auckland's excellent site for anything to do with Auckland
www.outandabout.co.nz
    For restaurant listings, what to do and events
www.akcity.govt.nz/whatson/index.asp
    Auckland City Council guide to city events
www.manukau.govt.nz
    Manukau City site
www.nscc.govt.nz
    North Shore City site
www.govt.nz
    Waitakere City site
www.arc.govt.nz
    Auckland Regional Council site
www.itsoninnz.co.nz
    New Zealand Tourism Industry Association site for events nationwide
www.nztb.govt.nz
    New Zealand Tourism Board site
www.doc.govt.nz
    Department of Conservation site
www.devonport.co.nz
    Devonport Business Association's very useful site, listing places to stay and eat, galleries, events etc (updated regularly)
www.artguides.co.nz
    Updated every two months, a guide to goings-on at 30 Auckland galleries
www.rnzi.com/FRNZI.htm
    Radio New Zealand's site for news
http://nz.com/NZ/News/HardNews
    HardNews site for another slant on news
www.whitepages.co.nz
    Telecom's *White Pages* site with a link to the *Yellow Pages*

For sites relevant to the America's Cup, refer to the boxed text later in this chapter.

BOOKS

Most books are published in different editions by different publishers in different countries. As a result, a book might be a hardcover rarity in one country while it's readily available in paperback in another. Fortunately, bookshops and libraries search by title or author, so your local bookshop or library is best placed to advise you on the availability of the following recommendations.

Fiction

Old School Tie, by Paul Thomas, is a thriller centred on the City of Sails, in which occasional journalist Reggie Sparks is commissioned by a magazine to get to the bottom of a series of mysterious deaths.

The End of the Century at the End of the World, by CK Stead, focuses on former radical coffee-house owner Dan and one-time tennis champion Laura, who, 20 years after their youthful affair, meet again to find that things are not what they seemed.

Plumb, by Maurice Gee, is an award-winning first-person account of the life and fortunes of George Plumb (lawyer-turned-parson-turned-protestor) and his descendants. Also by Gee, *Going West* focuses on two friends, born in Auckland but on opposite sides of the tracks. When one friend drowns in the gulf, the other embarks on a quest to find out why.

In *Believers to the Bright Coast*, by Vincent O'Sullivan, Dr Crippen's mistress, a French nun and a slow-witted young man cross paths in Auckland and end up as hostages in a chase through the North Island.

Dove on the Waters, by Maurice Shadbolt, is in three linked parts. A middle-aged Auckland lawyer, a lonely spinster and a Boer veteran, each the subject of a story, seem unrelated but all share a special kind of love.

In *All the Nice Girls*, by Barbara Anderson, Devonport naval wife Sophie Flynn reconciles early 1960s social expectations with her personal loves and loyalties.

In *Provocation*, by Charlotte Grimshaw, a bright young law student and her successful criminal-lawyer lover become entangled in a case at the end of which everything has changed.

Waitemata Harbour and Auckland city from the air

Auckland Harbour Bridge

Westhaven Marina in the 'City of Sails'

The 328m Skytower dominates Auckland's skyline.

Cruising the Waitemata

Sunday morning on Auckland's waterfront

Leisure craft on Kohimarama Beach

The Warrior Queen, by Barbara Else, takes a black-humoured look at life inside a modern middle-class marriage in Auckland's mooned suburbs.

Paddy's Puzzle, by Fiona Kidman, is set in Auckland during WWII and examines a woman's struggle to assert her independence in the face of oppression and despair.

Feral City, by Rosie Scott, is set in a future Auckland, in whose crime-ridden, bleak centre two sisters set up a bookshop. In Scott's *Glory Days*, a budding artist and some-time nightclub singer finds that life starts to imitate art, with the violent themes in her paintings oddly reflected in events around her.

Then Again, by Sue McCauley, is a novel about various characters who come to live on subtropical Motawairua Island (based on Waiheke).

'A Game of Hide and Seek' is a short story by Frank Sargeson in the volume *A Man of England Now*. A man living in Auckland writes about his father and other people he has known.

Emily Perkins' *Leave Before You Go* is the story of a generation cast adrift, seen through the eyes of Daniel, who escapes London for the other side of the world, and Kate, an usherette at a local cinema.

Blowing My Top, by Kevin Ireland, is about the 1951 waterfront lockout, and evokes well the atmosphere of that time.

If the Tongue Fits, by Diane Brown, looks at the interconnected lives of three women and the relationship between them and men.

The Shark that Ate the Sun by John Puhiatau Pule is the first novel by a Niuean. It deals with the social disintegration a family experiences on migrating to a new land and culture.

Many of the 29 stories in *The Best of Albert Wendt's Short Stories* also explore the theme of cultural alienation, but from a Samoan point of view.

After Robert, by Sarah Quigley, follows the life of a young Irish woman who flees London to live in Auckland after the death of her boyfriend.

Non-Fiction

A Field Guide to Auckland: Exploring the Region's Natural and Historic Heritage, by Ewen Cameron, Bruce Hayward & Graeme Murdoch, is an excellent guide and virtually indispensable for anyone who wants to explore Auckland's natural and historic treasures.

Untamed Coast, by Bob Harvey, is another excellent book if you want to know about Auckland's wild west coast and its hinterland. In addition to interesting historical background, the book has maps, photos and plenty of information on walks in the area, as well as lots of anecdotes.

On the Road: K Rd, by Kevin Kearns, is a close up look at what is arguably Auckland's most colourful street. There is a good parade of characters – the stripper, the saint, the con, the gypsy and so on.

Pacific New Zealand, by Graeme Lay, is not purely about Auckland, but because Auckland has such a large Pacific Island population the city gets much coverage. This book provides an insight into Pacific Island customs, art and lifestyles.

Islands of the Gulf, by David Kerr & Kirsten Warner, is a coffee-table book with beautiful shots of the Hauraki Gulf's numerous islands. *Auckland: A Portrait*, by Ralph Talmont, is another coffee-table book that shows Auckland in various moods and poses.

A Natural History of Auckland, edited by John Morton, is a well-illustrated guide to the region's geology, fauna and flora.

The Natural World of New Zealand, by Gerard Hutching, is an encyclopedia covering the entire country's natural history. Although probably too broad if you just want something on Auckland alone, it's beautifully illustrated and a very tempting addition to one's bookshelf.

Auckland Architecture: A Personal View, by Sait Akkirman, has nearly 400 pages of colour photos of Auckland buildings. There's no explanatory text, but for those interested in architecture, it is a good record of buildings that have survived the vagaries of progress.

100 NZ Craft Artists, by Helen Schamroth, is a useful guide to NZ crafts people, and includes leading Auckland artists.

There are numerous books about NZ wine. *The Wines and Vineyards of New Zealand*, by Michael Cooper & John McDermott, is a beautifully illustrated book that has plenty of useful information. Although it covers vineyards countrywide, there is detail on Auckland vineyards. Michael Cooper's *Buyer's Guide to NZ Wine* is updated annually. Other guides include the *Good New Zealand Wine Guide* by Vic Williams, the *Penguin Good New Zealand Wine Guide*, Peter Saunders' *A Guide to New Zealand Wines*, and *The Wines of New Zealand* by Rosemary George. A handy book for the budget conscious is *Joëlle Thomson's Under $15 Wine Guide*. The most up-to-date survey of places to eat in Auckland (and nationwide) is Michael Guy's *Café: the Eating Out Guide*.

Many interesting books on Auckland's flora and fauna and history are out of print (or at least very hard to find in mainstream bookshops), but they can sometimes be tracked down through one of the city's good second-hand bookshops. See the Shopping chapter for details.

There are several helpful books that provide detail on places to stay. *Friar's Guide to New Zealand Accommodation for the Discerning Traveller* is a full-colour, annually published guide that provides details on guesthouses, boutique hotels and B&Bs throughout NZ. *The New Zealand Bed & Breakfast Book*, compiled by J & J Thomas, is also updated annually and covers the entire country in more than 700 pages. Its Auckland section is comprehensive. The *AA New Zealand Accommodation Guide* provides details on hotels, motels and B&Bs in Auckland and throughout the country. It's updated annually. Jason's *Corporate Traveller* is, as its name suggests, a handy reference for those visiting Auckland on business.

Lonely Planet guidebooks that are useful if you are travelling beyond Auckland include the *New Zealand* guide, *Tramping in New Zealand* and *Cycling in New Zealand* (March 2000).

For destinations even further afield, try Lonely Planet's new *South Pacific* guide (April 2000), which is accompanied by the *South Pacific Phrasebook*.

Finally, for a tongue-in-cheek peek at how the rest of NZ sees Auckland, get hold of the booklet *J.A.F.A Jokes (Just another F*@ing Aucklander)*, by anon. Fact or fiction?

NEWSPAPERS & MAGAZINES

The *New Zealand Herald* is Auckland's only daily newspaper (it comes out in the morning) and has comprehensive sections on sport and entertainment. The Saturday 'What's On' section and Thursday's '7 Days' are good for finding out what's happening in and around Auckland. The *NZ Herald* is published Monday to Saturday; on Sunday you can catch up with what's happening with the *Sunday Times* or the *Sunday News*.

Metro magazine contains features, reviews and gossip – an insight into Auckland's upwardly mobile set. *North & South* also runs features and columns, but covers the entire country. Both contain reviews of Auckland restaurants and cafes. *Pavement* is a magazine mainly aimed at the 20-something crowd. It has news, reviews, features and fashion.

Rip it Up is a monthly magazine dedicated mainly to NZ's contemporary music scene, with a gig guide at the back, and reviews and news. *The Listener* publishes television and radio programming for the week, plus features and reviews.

Two good places to get hold of both local and international magazines are Mega Mags, at 60 Queen St, and Magazzino, at 33 Victoria St East. Both places have branches in the suburbs.

RADIO & TV

Before deregulation made an impact over a decade ago, there were but a handful of radio stations, including National Radio, Radio Hauraki (which started out in the late 1960s as a pirate station broadcasting from a boat moored in the Tiri Channel), and bFM (which celebrated its 30th anniversary in 1999, having begun life as a student pirate venture called Radio Bosom).

Aucklanders now have around 27 stations from which to choose. National Radio can be heard on 756AM (music, some BBC, Pacific news, science etc), Concert FM on 92.6 (classical music and jazz) and BBC World Service can be picked up on 1476AM.

Local stations include Mai FM (88.6; Maori radio), Radio Pacific (702; talkback and music), Classic Hits (97FM; music from the 1960s to 1980s), Hauraki (99FM; mainstream popular music), bFM (95; a campus station – young, lively and distinctly Auckland), More FM (91.8) and George (88.2 FM).

For 24-hour tourist information tune in to 88.2FM (English), 100.4 (German) and 110.8 (Japanese).

There are six free-to-air TV channels (One, Two, 3, 4, Prime and Triangle) and one pay-TV channel (Sky Movies, Sky Sport, Sky 1, Discovery, CNN).

For details on programs and times (plus reviews and articles) for both television and radio get a copy of *The Listener* ($3.20), which is published weekly, or check the TV pages in the *NZ Herald*.

VIDEO SYSTEMS
Video recorders in NZ operate on the PAL system. Video supplies, equipment and maintenance are all readily available.

PHOTOGRAPHY
Film & Equipment
Fuji and Kodak are the most popular films, with Agfa also available. Film and processing prices can vary so it pays to shop around. There are numerous one-hour developing shops as well as professional laboratories; refer to the *Yellow Pages* under 'Photographic Developing' for location details.

Technical Tips
You should be familiar with your equipment and the type of film you are using before embarking on your trip. Some hints and tips for taking better photos are as follows.

- The quality of your photos depends on the quality of light you shoot under. Light is best when the sun is low in the sky – around sunrise and sunset.
- Don't buy cheap equipment, but don't load yourself down with expensive equipment you don't know how to use properly.
- A good SLR camera is advisable, but be aware that the quality of the lens is the most important thing. Zoom lenses are heavier than fixed focal length lenses and the quality isn't as good. An alternative to the zoom is a teleconverter that fits over your lens and doubles the focal length.
- Always carry a skylight or UV filter. A polarising filter can create dramatic effects and cut glare, but don't fit it over a UV filter.
- Take a tripod and fast film (at least 400ASA) or a film such as Fuji's MS100/1000, which can be set at any speed between 100ASA and 1000ASA. Flashes create hard shadows; a cable release is useful for shooting with a tripod.
- Settle on a brand of film and know how it works before you head off.
- Keep your film in a cool, dark place if possible, before and after exposure.
- Expose for the main component of a scene and fill the frame with what you are taking.
- Previsualise; it's one of the most important elements in photographic vision. You must 'see' your picture clearly before you take it.

Restrictions
There are very few restrictions on what you may photograph; places that have some sort of limitation will generally advertise the fact. If in doubt, ask.

Photographing People
When photographing people the only prerequisites are a reasonable degree of courtesy and commonsense. Most people won't object unless your efforts are intrusive and inappropriate – and it should be obvious to you if this is the case. If in doubt about whether it's OK, ask.

TIME
Being close to the International Date Line, NZ is one of the first places in the world to start the new day. It is 12 hours ahead of GMT (Greenwich Mean Time) and UTC

(Universal Time Coordinated), and two hours ahead of Australian Eastern Standard Time. When it is noon in NZ it is 10 am in Sydney, 9 am in Tokyo, 8 am in Singapore, midnight in London, 8 pm the previous day in New York and 5 pm the previous day in San Francisco.

In summer NZ observes daylight-saving time, when clocks are put forward by one hour in October; they are wound back the following March.

ELECTRICITY

Electricity is 230V, 50Hz, as in Europe and Australia. Australian-type flat three-prong plugs are used. Appliances designed for DC supply or different voltages need a transformer.

WEIGHTS & MEASURES

NZ uses the metric system, but you will still encounter vestiges of the imperial system that was in use until 1967. If you go skydiving you'll be taken up to 9000ft rather than to 2743m and if you ask someone how much they weigh, the answer may be in kilograms, pounds or stones (a stone is 14 pounds).

LAUNDRY

Most hostels and other places to stay have laundry facilities. However, a convenient laundrette in the city centre is the Clean Green Laundromat, at 18 Fort St. It is open Monday to Friday from 8.30 am to 7 pm and on Saturday from 9 am to 5 pm. A wash costs $3 and a dry $1. Washing powder is 50c a shot.

LEFT LUGGAGE

At the airport's international terminal you can store bags at Seal N Secure, on the ground floor, and at the Visitor Information Centre, in the Independent Travellers Hall. You can also store bags at the Collection Point (open daily from 6 am to 11 pm), which is near immigration.

There are storage lockers near pier 2, behind the ferry building on Quay St. You can also store luggage at the Visitor Information Centre at Oneroa, Waiheke Island.

HEALTH

There are no vaccination requirements for travel to NZ. Auckland is a clean, healthy city and a stay should present no health problems. Tap water is safe to drink.

Generally, it doesn't get too hot or too cold in Auckland, but the sun in summer can be strong, especially for travellers from a cooler climate, and you should wear a high-factor sunscreen – especially if you are at the beach. It's a good idea not to swim in inner-harbour beaches for at least a couple of days after heavy rain, as stormwater flushed into the sea may cause unacceptably high levels of pollution.

Medical care in NZ is excellent and a trip to the doctor is only moderately expensive. A typical visit to the doctor will cost $44. Medical practitioners are listed in the front of the *White Pages*, as are hospitals and 24-hour pharmacies. If you have an immediate health problem, go to the emergency section of one of the public hospitals, listed below, or call an ambulance on ☎ 111.

It's a good idea to always carry a basic medical kit with you, even though most of what you will need is available in Auckland. Bring any medications you are already taking. The contraceptive pill is available by prescription only, so a visit to the doctor will be necessary. Condoms are available from chemists, supermarkets and condom-vending machines in many hotel toilets.

Vaccinations for onward travel are available at the following places:

Traveller's Medical and Vaccination Centre (TMVC) (☎ 373 3531, fax 373 3732), Level 1, Canterbury Arcade. Open Monday to Friday from 9 am to 6 pm; Saturday 9 am to 2 pm.

Travelcare (☎ 373 4621), 5th Floor, Dingwall Bldg, 87 Queen St. Open Monday to Friday from 9 am to 4.30 pm

Traveller's Health and Vaccination Centre (☎ 520 5830), 21 Remuera Rd, Newmarket. Open Monday to Friday from 9 am to 6 pm (last appointment 5.30 pm); Saturday 9 am to 2 pm.

For information on HIV/AIDS call the AIDS Hotline on ☎ 358 0099.

Public hospitals such as Auckland (☎ 379 7440), at Park Rd, Grafton; Middlemore (☎ 270 4799), at Hospital Rd, Otahuhu; and North Shore Hospital (☎ 486 1491), at Shakespeare Rd, Takapuna, have accident and emergency clinics. There are also many private accident and emergency clinics. See the *White Pages* under 'Hospitals & Other Health Service Providers' for contact details.

WOMEN TRAVELLERS

Auckland is quite an easy city for women travellers, with few hassles. Women travellers should, however, exercise the same degree of caution as they would in any large city. We recommend that you observe all the commonsense safety measures, such as not walking through isolated areas alone after dark, not getting into private vehicles when you don't know the person/ people inside, and so on.

The NZ Police (☎ 379 4240), Auckland Central, cnr Cook and Vincent Sts, puts out free pamphlets called *Safety Guides for Women*, which contain plenty of good advice.

GAY & LESBIAN TRAVELLERS

Gay and lesbian culture in Auckland is fairly low key, and attitudes towards it are reasonably relaxed. Generally, the community mingles with the mainstream, and Ponsonby is one area where gay and lesbian identity is more obvious. The most public celebration of gay and lesbian identity is the Hero Festival, which is held over two weeks in February. The climax is a parade down Ponsonby Rd followed by a post-parade party.

See the Entertainment chapter for a list of nightlife venues.

Agencies specialising in information and bookings include:

Gaylink Reservations Centre
(☎ 302 0553, 0800 429 872, fax 358 1206, ak/travel@gaylink.co.nz), 7 St Kevins Arcade, K Rd
Harvey World Travel
(☎ 376 5011, fax 376 1288), 293 Ponsonby Rd
NZ Gay & Lesbian Tourism Association Inc
(☎ 04-384 1877, fax 384 5187, secretariat@ nzglt.org.nz), Box 11462 Wellington

Out! Travel Desk NZ
(☎ 377 9031, 100244.2734@compuserve.com), 45 Anzac Ave
Pride Centre
(☎ 302 0590, fax 303 2042), 33 Wyndham St (with drop-in centre – usually open Monday to Friday from 8 am to 5 pm – events noticeboard and plenty of helpful information)

You'll find there are some useful publications, including *Express* (☎ 361 0190) – a free fortnightly newspaper available from some cafes and bookshops – and *Out!* (☎ 377 9031) – a bi-monthly national gay magazine with useful listings at the back. *Out!* is available from most bookshops and at Magazzino outlets for $5, and its Web site is at www.nz.com/NZ/Queer/OUT/.

The campus radio bFM (95FM) has a program called 'In the Pink' on Sunday from 9 to 10 pm. Access Community radio (810AM) has the 'G&T Breakfast Show' (Thursday 7 am) and 'This Way Out' (TWOradio@ aol.com) gay and lesbian news on Saturday at 11.40 am.

TV2 periodically screens *Queer Nation*, a news and features program; you will need to check *The Listener* for program times or call the station for upcoming screenings if the show is temporarily off-air (at the time of writing it was screening Tuesday at 11 pm).

A bookshop dealing exclusively in gay and lesbian literature is Out! Bookshop (☎ 377 7770), at 45 Anzac Ave in the city. It is open Monday to Saturday from 11 am to 11 pm and on Sunday 1 to 11 pm. Another good bookshop for gay and lesbian literature is Hard to Find 2ndHand Bookshop (☎ 634 4340), at 171-75 The Mall, Onehunga. The Women's Bookshop in Ponsonby Rd, has an extensive collection of lesbian literature.

For religious services contact the Metropolitan Community Church (☎ 629 0927), the Methodist Church of NZ (☎ 358 0022) in Pitt St (Sunday 7.30 pm service), the Auckland Community Church (☎ 638 7796), or St Matthews-in-the-City (☎ 377 9798), cnr Hobson and Wellesley Sts (Sunday 7.30 pm service).

A useful contact for further information is gayline/lesbianline (☎ 303 3584). This is also point of contact for support and counselling. It operates Monday to Friday from 10 am to 10 pm and weekends 5 pm to 10 pm.

DISABLED TRAVELLERS

Big, sprawling Auckland is a place where, if you want to get out and about, you are better off with your own transport. Listed later in this section are companies with vehicles that have wheelchair hoists, and car-hire places where you can get cars with hand controls.

If you can't drive, or can't afford to hire taxis, there are a few other possibilities. Tuk-tuks are an inexpensive way to go, for example, and the Link bus service is extremely useful as it passes near many of Auckland city's major sights. Since July 1992 all new buildings have been required to provide access for people with disabilities, and buildings modified after this date must also do so as far as possible.

If you are a resident of NZ visiting Auckland you may get a 50% discount (to a maximum of $25 per trip) on taxi fares if you can prove you are unable to take public transport. Various regional councils throughout NZ use the voucher system (called the Total Mobility Scheme); if you already have vouchers valid for areas outside Auckland you can generally use them in the Auckland region as well. To find out more about the Total Mobility Scheme contact the Auckland Regional Council's Transport Division (☎ 366 2000 extn 8053). You can get a list from the council detailing all taxi companies whose drivers have had special training in serving disabled passengers.

Visitors from abroad are not eligible for these vouchers, but may purchase Mobility Parking Permits ($20) through NZ CCS (in Auckland contact the CCS at ☎ 373 5026, 9 Mount St – off Symonds St). You will need to show a medical certificate or a mobility card from your home country. This card allows you to use parking spaces with the wheelchair logo. You must display the card on the dashboard where it can be clearly seen by parking wardens.

Foreign visitors to Auckland can use the New Zealand CCS service, Dial-a-Ride (☎ 625 5599). Dial-a-Ride vehicles have hoists and can accommodate eight wheelchairs. As the service is subsidised, it's cheaper to use over long distances than ordinary taxis. However, it is in high demand in the mornings (until about 9.30 am) and again in the afternoons from about 3 pm, so you will have a better chance of getting a vehicle between these times. It's best to book well ahead.

Taxi companies that provide vehicles with hoists for wheelchairs follow. All operate throughout the Auckland region.

Auckland Co-Op Taxis (☎ 300 3000). This company has only one vehicle with a hoist, so you should book as far ahead as you can.
Cannons Total Mobility Transport (☎ 836 4386, 021 474 422). Bookings are generally heavy during the week. It operates one day per weekend, and you can book a taxi for the entire day if you wish.
Eastern Taxis (☎ 570 5055) has one car and one van with wheelchair hoists. It's best to book at least a day in advance. Contact Tina, the senior dispatcher.
Independence Mobility (☎ 836 6761, 025 540 487).
North Harbour Taxis (☎ 479 1300) has nine vehicles with wheelchair hoists, but is in heavy demand. Book a week in advance if you can.
R&R Passenger Transport Service (☎ 445 4369). Once again, the service is in high demand and booking at least two days in advance is advisable.

There are several car-hire companies catering to disabled drivers.

Avis New Zealand (☎ 526 2847, 0800 655 111, fax 526 3232, avis.res@xtra.co.nz), Box 53, 103 Auckland Airport, has portable hand controls that can be fitted on to any of their automatic vehicles at any of their branches in NZ; you need to give 24 hours notice.
Budget Rental Cars (☎ 375 2222, 0800 652 227, fax 375 2223), Private Bag 92, 144 Auckland, has a hand-controlled Ford Falcon. It's in heavy demand so you will need to book ahead.
Galaxy Motors (☎/fax 07-826 4020) Box 48, Te Kauwhata 2152, has a three-door Mazda hatchback with a roof wheelchair-hoist, and high-top automatic diesel vans which can carry

three wheelchairs and five passengers. Vehicles are available for trips anywhere in the country. Drivers can be provided if enough notice is given.

Maui (☎ 275 3529, fax 275 9690, mauiinf@maui .co.nz), Private Bag 92, 133 Auckland, has cars that can be fitted with hand controls, although it doesn't provide the controls. Contact the New Zealand Disabilities Resource Centre (details at the end of this section) for information on where to get hand controls and who is able to install them.

A handy and novel way of getting around is by tuk-tuk, an open-sided three-wheeler that can transport three or more passengers. On the city side of the harbour bridge, Auckland City Tuk Tuks (☎ 360 1988, fax 360 1954, tuk-tuk@titan.com) will take you on short trips in the city centre for $3, or for longer trips (eg along Tamaki Drive, to Auckland Museum etc). In Devonport contact Ultimate Tours (☎ 025 739 445, 482 0025). A trip up Mt Victoria and back costs $5 and a tour round the main sights costs around $12. Ultimate Tours also does trips with a motorcycle sidecar in Devonport and Auckland. Wheelchairs can be carried on board.

As for public transport, one reliable and extremely useful service is the Link bus (see the Getting Around chapter for details). This takes you past most of the inner-city sights. An electronic ramp allows you to board if you are in a wheelchair and there is room for two wheelchairs inside.

Fullers ferries go to Rangitoto, Devonport, Waiheke and Great Barrier (although you will have to make your own arrangements for transport and accommodation once you get there). Pacific Ferries runs a 'fast ferry service' to Waiheke as well as a slower service on the *Lady Wakefield*. The *Lady Wakefield* is the only ferry with an accessible toilet on board, although all ferries can be boarded by people in wheelchairs. Keep a note of the tides at Rangitoto; low tides may make it difficult to disembark as there are steps.

There is a Fullers trip to Rangitoto that involves touring the island on a 4WD tractor-towed passenger trailer (canopied). If you're using a wheelchair you will need someone to assist you into and out of the seat. A foldup wheelchair can be carried on board, but a non-collapsible chair will have to be left at the wharf at your own risk. You can fly to Waiheke and Great Barrier. See the Excursions chapter for details.

Tranz Metro trains are difficult to access alone if you are in a wheelchair. There is a 20-30cm step up to the train, realistically negotiable only with the assistance of an able-bodied person. A ramp is available if advance notice is given (call ☎ 270 5426 between 5 am and 9 pm weekdays). All stations have ramps leading to the platform, except for Tamaki. The only station with a wheelchair-accessible toilet is at Auckland station.

You can hire wheelchairs from Active Rehabilitation Equipment (☎ 0800 336 339, fax 622 4201), at 254 Church St, Onehunga, Auckland 6. Standard wheelchairs cost $30 per week plus GST, heavy-duty chairs $50, and lightweight chairs $60. Motorised wheelchairs cost $100 a week plus GST. There is a minimum rental period of one week for manual chairs and two weeks for motorised chairs. A bond of $50 is required for a manual chair and $100 for a motorised one; this is refunded when you return the item. The company also rents out various home-nursing aides. You can have chairs and other items delivered to your home, and possibly to your motel or hotel. However, the company does not deliver to the airport. Fisher & Paykel Healthcare (☎ 574 0100) sells scooters, walking aids and various other items through pharmacies in Auckland.

Silent pedestrian crossings are being installed throughout the city; tactile indicators are being installed underneath the control boxes.

Wheelchair-accessible attractions in Auckland include the Auckland Museum (there's a ramp to the right of the steps as you approach the museum, and access inside is via ramps and lifts); the Maritime Museum; Kelly Tarlton's (everything is accessible; there's a ramp at the entrance, a lift at the exit, and staff will remove seats in the snow cat to allow you to take the Antarctic tour to see the penguins); Auckland Zoo; MOTAT and Sky City (there is a lift up to the top for the view and the viewing area is accessible). For easy and mostly undercover access to Sky City from Queen St during office hours, go to Elliot St from Queen St via the Mid City Arcade and enter the Atrium; take the lift that goes up to the Centra Hotel foyer; take the pedestrian crossing over Albert St and enter the ASB building across the road; take the lift that's to the rear of the line of ATMs. This will bring you out opposite Sky City. All the places listed here have wheelchair-accessible toilets.

The Milford Beach walkway on the North Shore (Ocean View Rd) has a concrete path overlooking the beach, as does Cheltenham in Devonport. The footpath along Tamaki Drive takes you past Mission Bay, Okahu Bay, Kohimarama Beach and St Heliers Bay (where there is an accessible toilet at the community hall, behind the library), as well as to Kelly Tarlton's. Cornwall Park has sealed paths that are reasonably flat on the lower slopes (Twin Oak Drive). There are accessible toilets near Huia Lodge. The Parnell Rose Gardens are accessible and provide a good vantage point from which to view the harbour.

The Philips Aquatic Centre (☎ 815 7005), at Alberton Ave, Mt Albert, is fully accessible to wheelchair users. It's open from 6 am to 9 pm weekdays and 7 am to 8 pm weekends ($7 adults, $5 children). You can organise tours to the Royal Foundation for the Blind's Guide Dog Centre (☎ 266 4164), 30 McVilly Rd, Manurewa, any weekday between 11.30 am and 3.30 pm. You will need to book in advance. The tour is free, although a donation is appreciated, and lasts about an hour. Tours can also be arranged through the foundation's fully accessible headquarters (☎ 355 6900) at 4 Maunsell Rd, Parnell. The foundation is able to assist with queries you may have as a vision-impaired visitor to Auckland.

The Glenbrook Vintage Railway is also accessible (see South of Auckland in the Excursions chapter).

The Auckland Regional Council has a full list of facilities for disabled visitors for all its regional parks. If you call Parksline (☎ 303 1530), you can get a copy of this faxed to you immediately. One of the most convenient parks to visit from Auckland is the Botanic Gardens at Manurewa. These beautifully kept gardens are entirely wheelchair accessible (entry is free), but accessible toilets are only at the entrance. The Arataki Visitors Centre in the Waitakere Ranges has ramps leading to the centre and its viewing decks. It's possible for wheelchair users to go as far as the end of the first loop (it's a hard-packed earth surface) on the nature trail opposite the centre. The Long Bay Regional Park has a beach buggy (free) which can be used to get across the sand to the water. Contact Parksline on ☎ 303 1530.

A good point of contact for further information is the New Zealand Disabilities Resource Centre (☎ 06-952 0011, 0800 171 981, fax 952 0022, info@nzdc.govt.nz). The centre's Web site is at www.nzdrc.govt.nz.

SENIOR TRAVELLERS

If you are aged 60 or over you are entitled to discounts at most venues. You will need to produce some sort of document (driver's licence, passport, seniors' card) that verifies your age.

AUCKLAND FOR CHILDREN

Auckland is well catered-for when it comes to activities and parks. There's plenty to do (see the Things to See & Do chapter for ideas). Obvious choices include the Auckland Zoo (you can feed the black swans at the Western Springs Lake, just outside the zoo itself), MOTAT, the NZ National Maritime Museum, the Auckland Museum (the natural history section is excellent and kids really enjoy the fantastic activities centre), Skytower, and the Auckland Observatory and Stardome. There is also the new 3D-experience Imax Theatre, at the Force Entertainment Centre in Queen St, and Rainbow's End theme park in south Auckland.

Aucklanders are spoilt for choice when it comes to parks. A good one near the city centre is the Auckland Domain – bring some bread and feed the ducks at the pond near the Wintergarden, or if there's a breeze try flying a kite in the wide open spaces. (Kiteworks, ☎ 358 0991, at 111 Symonds St , has locally made kites of all shapes and sizes, and is nearby.) Cornwall Park has a working farm as well as plenty of space in which to run around. Auckland's volcanic cones offer unlimited scope to burn off surplus energy; Mt Eden (very steep crater) and One Tree Hill (in the middle of Cornwall Park – there is a very good information centre here) are exciting places to explore, and North Head in Devonport, with its WWII tunnels and 'disappearing gun', is also a good spot. On the North Shore there are numerous opportunities for walks through native bush; try Centennial Park and the Chatswood Reserve, Fernglen, and Le Roy's Bush, which has play equipment.

Take a ferry to Devonport (10 minutes) or further to Waiheke or one of the other Gulf islands.

Further out of the city centre there are working farms (eg Ambury in south Auckland), more beaches and parks, boat rides in historical vessels (at Kaipara Harbour, Waiuku), horse rides on beaches and farms, a bee farm in Warkworth (which also has a satellite station) and a chocolate factory at the Bombay Hills – about 45km south of Auckland – and more. See the Excursions chapter for details.

Not surprisingly for a city with water everywhere, Auckland offers umpteen opportunities for swimming and water sports. A good all-weather venue with lots of fun things to do is the Philips Aquatic Centre with its wave pool and slides (see Swimming in the Things to See & Do chapter). The Parnell Baths are only open during summer, but are perennially popular, with a small water slide and rafts in the shallow pool. The inner-harbour beaches are calm and safe, although swimming is best at high tide; at low tide exploring the rock pools at places like St Heliers Bay can be quite absorbing. Try fishing from the end of Orakei Wharf (on Tamaki Drive – near Kelly Tarlton's). On the North

Shore, beaches at Cheltenham and Takapuna are safe and popular. Both beaches can be reached by taking the ferry to Devonport. You can walk to Cheltenham, or take a bus from the Devonport wharf to Takapuna.

Kids 'n Action (☎ 273 3122, infoline 827 6600), at 219 Burswood Drive, Pakuranga, is an indoor playground for younger children. There are plenty of challenges and it's very safe. It is open daily from 9.30 am to 6 pm; entry for adults is free, children two to 12 years \$6 on weekdays, \$7.50 on weekends and school holidays. There is another Kids 'n Action (☎ 444 3366) at Croftfield Lane, Wairau Park, Glenfield, on the North Shore.

For pre-schoolers, there are storytelling sessions at public libraries. The Auckland public library has two sessions a week – Wednesday at 10 am and Thursday at 10.30 am (2nd floor, children's section). The sessions last half an hour and involve stories, dancing and singing (parents should accompany their children). No bookings are needed and there is no entry charge.

Most large bookshops have a children's section but one place that is dedicated to books for the young is Dorothy Butler Children's Bookshop (☎ 376 7283, fax 376 7243), at Fountain Court, Three Lamps, Ponsonby, which always has an excellent range.

A useful book to refer to is *Kids Go Auckland: A Fun Guide to Where to go and What to do* by Lynne Richardson, Nyla Breakspeare & Jennie Whyte. It contains lots of useful, practical information on parks and walkways, farms you can visit, libraries, museums, swimming pools and sport/leisure venues (plus a section on good venues for birthday parties, and a key indicating which venues are good on rainy days). It covers the entire Auckland region. The book is available at most bookstores (\$14.95). The visitor centre also has information on things to see and do with children.

Supermarkets and pharmacies will have just about everything you may need: disposable nappies (diapers), baby food, bottles and so on. Push chairs, backpacks and so forth are all readily available.

LIBRARIES

Auckland's main public library (☎ 377 0209) is at 44-46 Lorne St. It's open Monday to Thursday from 9.30 am to 8 pm, Friday 9.30 am to 9 pm and Saturday 10 am to 4 pm.

As a visitor there are two ways you may use it. The first is by paying $10 per day or $30 a week (Monday to Saturday), which allows you to peruse the library's shelves but not to borrow. The second way is to put down a deposit of $50, of which $40 will be refunded when you finish using the library. This second option gives you the right to borrow up to five items at a time.

UNIVERSITIES

The University of Auckland's main campus is at Princes St, across the road from Albert Park in the city centre. Most faculties are located here and along Symonds St. The university has more than 25,000 students. The Faculty of Medicine is in Park Rd, opposite Auckland Hospital, and there is another campus at Tamaki.

Massey University, based in New Plymouth, has a campus in Albany on the North Shore.

CULTURAL CENTRES

Alliance Francaise d'Auckland (☎ 376 0009, 0800 266 568) is at 9 Kirk St, Grey Lynn.

DANGERS & ANNOYANCES

As in any big city one should exercise a reasonable degree of caution and common sense. While Auckland is a relatively safe destination, it pays to follow a few simple guidelines. For example, avoid unlit, isolated places at night; this especially applies to women travelling on their own. If you feel threatened, it helps to act confidently and assertively. You should ask for help from the police if you are particularly concerned.

Don't tempt thieves. Valuables such as passports, cash, travellers cheques and so on should be carried as securely as possible, preferably in a money belt under your clothing. Similarly, don't leave valuables in hotel rooms or vehicles; use the hotel safe, or carry these things securely with you. Tourists have often lost money, passports, cameras and other things by leaving them in cars or campervans.

LEGAL MATTERS

If you are going to be driving in Auckland remember that heavy penalties await those who get behind the wheel under the influence of alcohol or drugs. If you are under 20 years of age, you are breaking the law if you have more than 30 milligrams of alcohol per 100 millilitres of blood or more than 150 micrograms of alcohol per litre of breath. For those aged 20 or more the limits are 80 and 400 respectively.

Exactly how many drinks it takes to reach this level varies from individual to individual. The advice in the *New Zealand Road Code* is unequivocal: if you drink at all, don't drive. The penalties for driving under the influence of drugs and/or alcohol range from the cancellation of your licence to time in prison. It's much better to take a taxi or bus, or have a non-drinker do the driving.

The legal drinking age was recently lowered from 20 to 18. You will need to show photo ID to prove you are indeed 18 or over. Under-age drinkers may be fined, and publicans serving them may also be fined and have their premises temporarily closed.

'New Zealand green' (or 'electric puha', if you're from Northland), the local sobriquet for marijuana, is widely indulged in but illegal. Don't get caught with it – fines can be stiff. Penalties for importing illegal drugs are severe.

Other rules to observe are that all occupants of a vehicle must wear safety belts, and cyclists and motorcyclists must wear a helmet.

BUSINESS HOURS & PUBLIC HOLIDAYS

Office hours are generally Monday to Friday from 9 am to 5 pm. These hours also apply to trading banks and shops. Late-night shopping on Friday (until 9 pm) is available on

Queen St and Newmarket. Shops in central Auckland, Parnell, Newmarket and larger suburban shopping malls are open Saturday from 9 am to 5 pm and Sunday from 10 am to 4 pm. Post shops are also open Monday to Friday from 9 am to 5 pm.

Auckland public holidays are as follows:

New Years Day	1 January
Auckland Anniversary	29 January
Waitangi Day	6 February
Good Friday	March/April
Easter Monday	March/April
ANZAC Day	25 April
Queen's Birthday	1st Monday in June
Labour Day	4th Monday in October
Christmas Day	25 December
Boxing Day	26 December

SPECIAL EVENTS

During summer the Auckland City Council always runs a People in the Parks program with various events; the visitor centre should have details, or contact the council on ☎ 379 2021.

To find out what's happening around the city for the new millennium, see the boxed text 'Millennium in Auckland' later in this chapter, and visit the Web site www.auck land2000.co.nz. For more general events in Auckland City visit www.akcity.govt.nz/whatson/index.asp.

The WOMAD (World of Music and Dance) festival is to be held around January/February in 2001 (it's a biannual event). Check with the visitor centre for further details.

The Whitbread Round the World Race also stops off at Auckland, and again, details available from the visitor centre.

January
ASB Bank Classic International Women's Tennis
  ASB Tennis Centre
Heineken Open Men's International Tennis
  ASB Tennis Centre
Auckland Anniversary & Regatta
  Waitemata Harbour
Offshore 2000 World Offshore Powerboat Championships
  Waitemata Harbour

February
Hero Parade
  Gay and lesbian festival, Ponsonby
Devonport Food & Wine Festival
  Devonport
Millennium Cup
  Super yacht race, Auckland to Kawau Island, 15-17 February 2000
Opera in the Park
  Family concert, Auckland Domain
National Dragonboat Festival
  Viaduct Harbour
Sky City Starlight Symphony
  Family concert, Auckland Domain

March/April
Round the Bays Run
  Fun-run along Tamaki Drive
Pasifika Festival
  Polynesian festival, usually held at Western Springs
Turangawaewae Regatta
  Dragon boats on the Waikato River, Ngaruawahia, closest Saturday to St Patrick's Day
Waiheke Jazz Festival
  Waiheke Island, Easter weekend
Easter Show
  Auckland Showgrounds, Ellerslie, Easter weekend

October
Annual Yacht Race
  Auckland to Russell in the Bay of Islands, Labour Day
Wine Waitakere
  Waitakere food and wine festival
BMW Marathon
  Half-marathon/wheelchair marathon, Tamaki Drive
Tall Ships Festival 2000
  Gisborne, Auckland, Wellington, Napier, Tauranga (arriving in Auckland 12 January 2000)

November
Ellerslie Flower Show
  Auckland Regional Council Botanic Gardens, Manurewa

December
Coca Cola Christmas in the Park
  Family concert in Auckland Domain
First to the Sun
  Auckland to Gisborne bicycle race
Auckland Cup Horse Racing
  Ellerslie Race Course

FACTS FOR THE VISITOR

The America's Cup

On 14 May 1995 a crew of NZ yachties on *Black Magic*, skippered by Russell Coutts, won the fifth straight race against *Young America*, skippered by US defence stalwart Dennis Conner. The 5-0 victory in this final challenge series off San Diego entitled the Kiwis to take the America's Cup (affectionately known as the Auld Mug) out of the USA for only the second time in 144 years. And it was only NZ's third cup challenge.

The cup has a long and illustrious history. In 1851 the *America* sailed to England, participated in and won the Round the Isle of Wight Race. A silver pitcher was presented to the skipper of *America*, taken back to the USA and, in 1857, entrusted to the New York Yacht Club (NYYC). It was first challenged (unsuccessfully) in 1870-71 by the British.

Challenge after challenge was mounted but the cup seemed to be cemented safely in its case at the NYYC. In 1983 *Australia II*, with its now legendary winged keel, beat the NYCC's *Liberty* 4-3, taking the cup out of the USA for the first time. Conner, skipper of the unsuccessful defender, vowed to get it back. He was true to his word and in 1987 wrested the cup from the Aussies off Fremantle, Western Australia. New Zealand's first real challenge was mounted in 1988 in San Diego. Amid legal wrangling, the defender's *Stars and Stripes* beat challenger *KZ1*. In 1992 the cup was again sucessfully defended by the San Diego Yacht Club.

After *Black Magic*'s 1995 win, the cup defence fell to Team New Zealand/Royal NZ Yacht Squadron. After some indecision, the Hauraki Gulf was chosen as the defence site. But perhaps the cup needs a defence of a different sort; in 1997 a protestor walked into the room where the cup was on display and smashed it with a sledgehammer; it has since been repaired.

The magnetism of the Auld Mug is immense. Obviously the Americans want it back: Team Dennis Conner, Young America Challenge, America True Challenge, America One Challenge and Aloha Racing (Hawaii) are all contenders. But the 13 teams who submitted their notice of entry by 1 August 1999 come from various nations. As well as the American teams noted above, the contenders include F.A.S.T. 2000 (Switzerland), Young Australia, Copa America Desafio Espanol (Spain), Nippon Challenge (Japan), Age of Russia Challenge, Le defi Bouygues Telecom Transiciel (France), Prada Challenge 2000 (Italy) and Le defi Sud (France).

Provided all 13 challengers pass the official boat measuring, they will go on to race for the Louis Vuitton Cup. This series will determine which one of the teams will compete against Team New Zealand (skippered by Russell Coutts) in the America's Cup Match.

Key Dates
Louis Vuitton Cup Series

Round Robin Series 1	18 October 1999	Semi-finals	2 January 2000
Round Robin Series 2	6 November 1999	Finals	25 January 2000
Round Robin Series 3	2 December 1999		

America's Cup Match

Race 1	19 February 2000	Race 6*	27 February 2000
Race 2	20 February 2000	Race 7*	29 February 2000
Race 3	22 February 2000	Race 8*	2 March 2000
Race 4	24 February 2000	Race 9*	4 March 2000
Race 5	26 February 2000		

*Race will take place only if necessary; the series is the best of nine. Dates are subject to change.

The America's Cup

Watching the Race

The race course is just off the East Coast Bays shore, between Rangitoto and the Whangaparaoa Peninsula. It's unlikely you'll see anything much from the shore, even with powerful binoculars. However, a viewing platform has been built on Mototapu Island, from which there are views from the gun emplacement. Facilities are to include a huge television screen and telescopes. Trips out to the island (half an hour each way) can be booked through Fullers Auckland (☎ 367 9111). Tickets (which include lunch) for the Motutapu Grandstand Experience start at $170 per person.

Viewing the race from the air is another possibility. Helilink (☎ 377 4406) and Heli Tranz (☎ 479 1991) are both available to take passengers. Helilink, which is based in Mechanics Bay, costs $220 per person for 20 minutes (the helicopters can seat up to six passengers) and Heli Tranz, which is at Rosedale Rd, Albany, on the North Shore, charges $1650 for a six-passenger helicopter (you only pay for the proportion of time you use). It's advisable to book as far ahead as possible.

There will also be numerous charter boats taking to the water. Be aware that even then you are unlikely to get close to the race itself, which is one reason why it's a good idea to choose a charter that has onboard TV. Before you decide on a charter vessel also make sure you are clear about what you are getting (eg does the price include lunch or snacks?), and that you know exactly when and where you will be picked up and dropped off. The visitor centre keeps a list of charter boat operators and can make bookings and sell tickets. Fullers (☎ 367 9111), Pacific Ferries (☎ 303 1741) and the tall ship *Soren Larsen* (☎ 411 8755) are all operating charter trips out to the course.

There will be plenty of organised entertainment at the America's Cup Village, not to mention the opportunity to gaze at some 80 multi-million dollar super yachts.

Useful Web Sites

To keep in touch with what's happening at the village and for the latest news on the syndicates, visit the following sites:

America's Cup: www.americascup2000.org.nz

Louis Vuitton Cup: www.louisvuittoncup.com

Team New Zealand: www.teamnz.org.nz

America's Cup Online: ac2000.co.nz

America's Cup Village: www.nzcupvillage.co.nz

Team Magic: www.team-magic.co.nz

Tourism Auckland: www.aucklandnz.com

Auckland 2000 Trust: www.auckland2000.co.nz

ANN JEFFREE

Millennium in Auckland

With the new millennium Auckland is really buzzing in the summer of 1999-2000. Listed below are the major events, but of course there will be many more.

Family Spectacular This will be held in the Auckland Domain, starting at 7 pm on 31 December, with music and video, choirs and cultural performances. The millennium show itself will begin at 9 pm and involve a non-stop three-hour epic of the history of the past two millennia, and visualise Auckland one thousand years on. At midnight there will be a fireworks display coordinated with other displays throughout the city.

First Night 2000 This party for young people will start at 1 pm in Aotea Square. There will be non-stop entertainment until the new millennium dawns at the stroke of midnight.

Fire in the Sky At midnight on New Year's Eve, the city and harbour will be lit up with a spectacular fireworks display.

Millennium Jump A group of Aucklanders intend to be the first people in the world to see the new century dawn. They will be skydiving 12,000ft (360m) over the International Date Line into the Pacific Ocean, 1280km from NZ at latitude 44. Their dawn is at 3.45 am NZ time, 15 minutes before the Chatham Islands, the nearest land, sees the light of day. A worldwide search for a non-jumper to go tandem has been launched. Check out details on the Web site at www.millenniumjump.co.nz.

Skytower Dawn Celebration A select group of guests will enjoy a dawn celebration on Skytower's outside observation deck. Video screens will show global celebrations. Tour packages, which include three nights luxury accommodation, breakfast, and a ticket to the millennium celebration, cost $2250 per person and can be arranged through most travel agents. For more information on the international party at Skytower visit the Web site www.nztb.co.nz/events/millennium.htm.

Dawn Ceremony This will begin at 4 am, 1 January, and entertainment will centre on the reserve at the eastern end of Okahu Bay, on Tamaki Drive. There will be illuminated pohutukawa trees and silk flags marking the gathering areas for church and social groups. Members of the local Ngati Whatua community will arrive at Okahu in a flotilla of *waka* (canoes). They will be greeted by a 2000-strong *haka* party, and various boats will bring people representing the past, present and future of Auckland.

DOING BUSINESS

Auckland boasts about 30% of the country's entire population, a third of its workforce, and a third of its manufacturing, food processing and service sector capacity. A good starting point for information on doing business in Auckland is the Auckland Regional Chamber of Commerce (☎ 309 6100, fax 309 0081, akl@chamber.co.nz), Box 47 Auckland. Auckland 2000 Trust has a useful Web site at www.auckland2000.org.nz. This has links to the following sites: Auckland City Council Economic Data, Enterprise North Shore, Manukau City Council Business Information, NZ Chambers of Commerce, NZ Tourism Board, NZ Trade Development Board's Investment Page, Tourism Auckland and the Waitakere City Business Development Unit. The Auckland 2000 Trust was set up to co-ordinate Apec, the America's Cup and other big events taking place in 1999-2000.

WORK

See the section on visas earlier in this chapter for information on visitors working in NZ. The Situations Vacant section in the *NZ Herald* provides the most comprehensive listings of jobs; the Wednesday and Saturday editions carry the most job advertisements.

DOC accepts volunteers for conservation projects. In Auckland these have in the past included various tasks on Little Barrier Island (track cutting, weed control and base maintenance), reserve management at Kawau Island, various tasks at Tiritiri Matangi Island and tree planting on Motutapu Island. Contact the Volunteer Coordinator, Auckland Conservancy, on ☎ 307 9279.

FACTS FOR THE VISITOR

Getting There & Away

AIR

New Zealand has six airports that handle international flights: Auckland, Wellington, Palmerston North and Hamilton in the North Island; Christchurch and Dunedin in the South Island. Most international flights go through Auckland. Wellington airport has limited runway capacity, and most of its international flights are to/from Australia. Flights from Christchurch are also mainly to/from Australia, although there are some connections to other countries.

Departure Tax

There's a $20 departure tax for all international flights from Auckland, Wellington and Dunedin airports, and a $25 tax from Christchurch, Hamilton and Palmerston North. This is payable at the airport.

Other Parts of New Zealand

Air New Zealand, Ansett New Zealand and Mt Cook Airlines connect Auckland with other major centres in NZ. For local operators based in Auckland, see Airline Offices later in this section.

Other Countries

USA & Canada Most flights between the USA and New Zealand are to/from the US west coast. Most travel through Los Angeles, but some through San Francisco. If you 're coming from another part of the USA, your travel agent can arrange a discounted add-on fare to get you to the city of departure.

Excursion (return) fares are available from various airlines but are more expensive than those from travel agents. Cheaper 'short life' fares are frequently offered for limited periods. The easiest way to get a cheap air fare from the USA is through a travel agency selling discounted fares; these fares are around US$650 return from Los Angeles or US$1050 return from New York. For as little as $100 extra you can fly from Los Angeles to Australia with a stopover in New Zealand.

The *New York Times*, *LA Times*, *Chicago Tribune* and *San Francisco Examiner* all produce weekly travel sections in which you'll find any number of travel agents' ads. Council Travel and STA Travel have offices in major cities nationwide. The magazine *Travel Unlimited* (PO Box 1058, Allston, MA 02134) publishes details of courier possibilities and the cheapest air fares from the USA to destinations all over the world.

If you want to visit other Pacific destinations on your way to or from NZ, compare carefully the stopover possibilities offered by each airline. Air New Zealand offers an excellent variety of stopover options on its route between Los Angeles and Auckland. You can tack on stopovers in Honolulu, Tahiti, Rarotonga, Western Samoa, Tonga and Fiji quite cheaply. Other airlines fly to NZ for the same price, or sometimes cheaper, but with more limited stopover options.

In Canada, the *Globe & Mail* and the *Vancouver Sun* carry travel agents' ads. Much of the advice about travel between the USA and NZ applies also to Canada, especially stopover options.

Australia NZ cities with flights to Australia are Auckland, Christchurch, Wellington, Dunedin, Palmerston North and Hamilton. Australian cities with flights to NZ are Brisbane, Cairns, Melbourne, Perth and Sydney. Air New Zealand, Qantas Airways and United Airlines (Sydney and Melbourne only) are the main carriers. Smaller carriers include Garuda Indonesia and EVA Airways (Taiwan) from Brisbane, and Aerolineas Argentinas, Thai Airways International, Royal Tongan Airlines and Polynesian Airlines from Sydney.

The fare depends on the day you fly out as well as where you fly to/from. The year is divided into peak and off-peak (low) times, which can vary between airlines. The main peak season is over the school summer holidays (10 December-15 January). Typical low-season, rock-bottom fares from an agent specialising in discount tickets from Sydney cost around A$515/550 one way/return to Auckland.

If you're travelling from Australia to the US west coast via NZ, the high season varies but is generally during the US summer (June to August). Low-season fares start at around A$1229/1749 one way/return; high-season fares are more like A$1429/2119.

Round-the-world (RTW) fares departing from Australia, which can include a stopover in NZ, vary with the season. The northern hemisphere summer (June to August) is usually the high season for RTW fares; tickets cost around A$2300 (with Philippine Airlines) to A$3000 (with Air New Zealand) in the high season, but can be around A$1800 in the low season.

STA Travel and Flight Centre are the major agents in Australia for cheap air fares and have branches in all major cities. Otherwise check the *Yellow Pages* and ring around.

The UK Trailfinders in west London produces a lavishly illustrated brochure which includes air fare details. STA Travel also has branches in the UK. Look in the Sunday papers and *Exchange & Mart* for ads. Also look out for the free magazines widely available in London – try outside the main railway stations.

Most British travel agents are registered with the Association of British Travel Agents (ABTA). If you've paid an ABTA-registered agent for your flight, and the agent then goes out of business, ABTA will guarantee a refund or an alternative. Unregistered bucket shops are riskier but sometimes cheaper.

The Globetrotters Club (BCM Roving, London WC1N 3XX) publishes a newsletter called *Globe*, which covers obscure destinations and can help in finding travel companions.

Economy return flights from London on major airlines such as Qantas, Air New Zealand, British Airways and Malaysia Airlines are approximately £550-600 (June), £700-750 (July to mid-August), £650 (mid-August to November), £700-plus (December). Depending on which airline you fly you'll cross Asia or the USA. If you come via Asia you can often make stopovers in places such as India, Bangkok, Singapore and Australia; via the USA stopover possibilities include New York, Los Angeles, Honolulu and a variety of Pacific Islands. Stopover options vary depending on the airline you use.

Since NZ is about as far from Europe as you can get, it's not much more to continue round the world rather than backtrack. Agents can organise a RTW route through the South Pacific for around £750.

Continental Europe Frankfurt is the key arrival and departure point for NZ flights, with connections to other European centres.

There are many bucket shops on mainland Europe where you can buy discounted tickets. The international student and discount travel agencies, STA and Council Travel, also have a number of offices in various European countries. Any of their offices can give details of which office is nearest you. In Amsterdam, make sure your travel agent has an SGR certificate or you may never see your money again.

Asia There are far more flights to NZ from Asia than there were only a few years ago. There are direct flights to Auckland from Tokyo, Hong Kong, Singapore, Denpasar (Bali) and Taipei, and connecting flights to most other places. Many of the connecting flights have stopovers in Australia.

Ticket discounting is widespread in Asia, particularly in Hong Kong, Singapore and Bangkok; Hong Kong is probably the discount air ticket capital of the region. There are a lot of fly-by-nights in the Asian ticketing scene so a little care is required. STA, which is reliable, has branches in Hong Kong, Tokyo, Singapore, Bangkok and Kuala Lumpur.

Air Travel Glossary

Baggage Allowance This will be written on your ticket and usually includes one 20kg item to go in the hold, plus one item of hand luggage.

Bucket Shops These are unbonded travel agencies specialising in discounted airline tickets.

Bumped Just because you have a confirmed seat doesn't mean you're going to get on the plane (see Overbooking).

Cancellation Penalties If you have to cancel or change a discounted ticket, there are often heavy penalties involved; insurance can sometimes be taken out against these penalties. Some airlines impose penalties on regular tickets as well, particularly against 'no-show' passengers.

Check-In Airlines ask you to check in a certain time ahead of the flight departure (usually one to two hours on international flights). If you fail to check in on time and the flight is overbooked, the airline can cancel your booking and give your seat to somebody else.

Confirmation Having a ticket written out with the flight and date you want doesn't mean you have a seat until the agent has checked with the airline that your status is 'OK' or confirmed. Meanwhile you could just be 'on request'.

Courier Fares Businesses often need to send urgent documents or freight securely and quickly. Courier companies hire people to accompany the package through customs and, in return, offer a discount ticket which is sometimes a phenomenal bargain. In effect, what the companies do is ship their freight as your luggage on regular commercial flights. This is a legitimate operation, but there are two shortcomings – the short turnaround time of the ticket (usually not longer than a month) and the limitation on your luggage allowance. You may have to surrender all your allowance and take only carry-on luggage.

Full Fares Airlines traditionally offer 1st class (coded F), business class (coded J) and economy class (coded Y) tickets. These days there are so many promotional and discounted fares available that few passengers pay full economy fare.

ITX An ITX, or 'independent inclusive tour excursion', is often available on tickets to popular holiday destinations. Officially it's a package deal combined with hotel accommodation, but many agents will sell you one of these for the flight only and give you phoney hotel vouchers in the unlikely event that you're challenged at the airport.

Lost Tickets If you lose your airline ticket an airline will usually treat it like a travellers cheque and, after inquiries, issue you with another one. Legally, however, an airline is entitled to treat it like cash and if you lose it then it's gone forever. Take good care of your tickets.

MCO An MCO, or 'miscellaneous charge order', is a voucher that looks like an airline ticket but carries no destination or date. It can be exchanged through any International Association of Travel Agents (IATA) airline for a ticket on a specific flight. It's a useful alternative to an onward ticket in those countries that demand one, and is more flexible than an ordinary ticket if you're unsure of your route.

No-Shows No-shows are passengers who fail to show up for their flight. Full-fare passengers who fail to turn up are sometimes entitled to travel on a later flight. The rest are penalised (see Cancellation Penalties).

Air Travel Glossary

On Request This is an unconfirmed booking for a flight.

Onward Tickets An entry requirement for many countries is that you have a ticket out of the country. If you're unsure of your next move, the easiest solution is to buy the cheapest onward ticket to a neighbouring country or a ticket from a reliable airline which can later be refunded if you do not use it.

Open Jaw Tickets These are return tickets where you fly out to one place but return from another. If available, this can save you backtracking to your arrival point.

Overbooking Airlines hate to fly empty seats and since every flight has some passengers who fail to show up, airlines often book more passengers than they have seats. Usually excess passengers make up for the no-shows, but occasionally somebody gets 'bumped' onto the next available flight. Guess who it is most likely to be? The passengers who check in late.

Point-to-Point Tickets These are discount tickets that can be bought on some routes in return for passengers waiving their rights to a stopover.

Promotional Fares These are officially discounted fares, available from travel agencies or direct from the airline.

Reconfirmation If you don't reconfirm your flight at least 72 hours prior to departure, the airline may delete your name from the passenger list. Ring to find out if your airline requires reconfirmation.

Restrictions Discounted tickets often have various restrictions on them – such as needing to be paid for in advance and incurring a penalty to be altered. Others are restrictions on the minimum and maximum period you must be away, such as a minimum of 14 days or a maximum of one year.

Round-the-World Tickets RTW tickets give you a limited period (usually a year) in which to circumnavigate the globe. You can go anywhere the carrying airlines go, as long as you don't backtrack. The number of stopovers or total number of separate flights is decided before you set off and they usually cost a bit more than a basic return flight.

Stand-by This is a discounted ticket where you only fly if there is a seat free at the last moment. Stand-by fares are usually available only on domestic routes.

Transferred Tickets Airline tickets cannot be transferred from one person to another. Travellers sometimes try to sell the return half of their ticket, but officials can ask you to prove that you are the person named on the ticket. This is less likely to happen on domestic flights, but on an international flight tickets are compared with passports.

Travel Agencies Travel agencies vary widely and you should choose one that suits your needs. Some simply handle tours, while full-service agencies handle everything from tours and tickets to car rental and hotel bookings. If all you want is a ticket at the lowest possible price, then go to an agency specialising in discounted fares.

Travel Periods Ticket prices vary with the time of year. There is a low (off-peak) season and a high (peak) season, and often a low-shoulder season and a high-shoulder season as well. Usually the fare depends on your outward flight – if you depart in the high season and return in the low season, you pay the high-season fare.

GETTING THERE & AWAY

Airline Offices

International airlines with offices in Auckland include:

Aerolineas Argentinas
(☎ 379 3675)
15th Floor, ASB Centre, 135 Albert St

Air Canada
(☎ 379 3371)
Dingwall Bldg, 87 Queen St
Air India
(☎ 303 1301)
Level 6, AMP Bldg, 214-18 Queen St
Air New Zealand
(☎ 336 2424, reservations 357 3000)

Buying Tickets

The plane ticket will probably be the single most expensive item in your budget, and buying it can be an intimidating business. There is likely to be a multitude of airlines and travel agents hoping to separate you from your money, and it is always worth putting aside a few hours to research the current state of the market. Start early: some of the cheapest tickets have to be bought months in advance, and some popular flights sell out early. Talk to other recent travellers – they may be able to stop you making some of the same old mistakes. Look at the ads in newspapers and magazines (not forgetting the press of the ethnic group whose country you plan to visit), consult reference books and watch for special offers. Then phone around travel agents for bargains. (Airlines can supply information on routes and timetables; however, except at times of inter-airline war, they do not supply the cheapest tickets.) Find out the fare, the route, the duration of the journey and any restrictions on the ticket. Then sit back and decide which is best for you.

You may discover that those impossibly cheap flights are 'fully booked, but we have another one that costs a bit more ...' Or the flight is on an airline notorious for its poor safety standards and leaves you in the world's least favourite airport in mid-journey for 14 hours. Or they may claim to have the last two seats available for that country for the whole of July, which they will hold for you for a maximum of two hours. Don't panic – keep ringing around.

Use the fares quoted in this book as a guide only. They are approximate and based on the rates advertised by travel agents at the time of going to press. Quoted air fares do not necessarily constitute a recommendation for the carrier. If you are travelling from the UK or the USA, you will probably find that the cheapest flights are being advertised by obscure bucket shops whose names haven't yet reached the telephone directory. Many such firms are honest and solvent, but there are a few rogues who will take your money and disappear, only to reopen elsewhere a month or two later under a new name. If you feel suspicious about a firm, don't give them all the money at once – leave a deposit of 20% or so and pay the balance when you get the ticket. If they insist on cash in advance, go somewhere else. And once you have the ticket, ring the airline to confirm that you are actually booked on the flight.

You may decide to pay more than the rock-bottom fare by opting for the safety of a better-known travel agent. Firms such as STA Travel, which has offices worldwide, Council Travel in the USA or Travel CUTS in Canada are not going to disappear overnight, leaving you clutching a receipt for a nonexistent ticket, but they do offer good prices to most destinations.

Once you have your ticket, write down its number, together with the flight number and other details, and keep the information somewhere separate. If the ticket is lost or stolen, this will help you get a replacement. It's sensible to buy travel insurance as early as possible. If you buy it the week before you fly, you may find, for example, that you're not covered for delays to your flight caused by industrial action.

Cnr of Customs and Queen Sts
(☎ 529 9000)
Broadway, Newmarket
(☎ 256 3999)
domestic terminal, airport
Air Pacific
(379 2404)
404 Queen St

Alitalia Airlines
(☎ 379 4457)
TrustBank Bldg, 229 Queen St
American Airlines
(☎ 309 9159, 0800 887 997)
15th Floor, Jetset Centre, 48 Emily Place
Canadian Airlines
(☎ 309 0735), Level 15, 48 Emily Place

Buying Tickets

Round-the-World Tickets & Circle Pacific Fares

Round-the-world (RTW) tickets are often real bargains. They are usually put together by a combination of two airlines and permit you to fly anywhere you want on their route systems so long as you do not backtrack. There may be restrictions on how many stops you are permitted and usually the tickets are valid for 90 days up to a year. An alternative type of RTW ticket is one put together by a travel agent using a combination of discounted tickets.

Circle Pacific tickets use a combination of airlines to circle the Pacific – combining Australia, New Zealand, North America and Asia. As with RTW tickets, there are advance purchase restrictions and limits to how many stopovers you can make. These fares are likely to be around 15% cheaper than Round-the-World tickets.

Travellers with Special Needs

If you have special needs of any sort – you've broken a leg or you're vegetarian, travelling in a wheelchair, taking the baby or are terrified of flying – you should let the airline know as soon as possible so that they can make arrangements accordingly. You should remind them when you reconfirm your booking (at least 72 hours before departure) and again when you check in at the airport. It may also be worth ringing round the airlines before you make your booking to find out how they can handle your particular needs.

Airports and airlines can be surprisingly helpful, but they do need advance warning. Most international airports will provide escorts from check-in desk to plane where needed, and there should be ramps, lifts, accessible toilets and reachable phones. Aircraft toilets, on the other hand, are likely to present a problem; travellers should discuss this with the airline at an early stage and, if necessary, with their doctor.

Guide dogs for the blind will often have to travel in a specially pressurised baggage compartment with other animals, away from their owner; smaller guide dogs may be admitted to the cabin. All guide dogs will be subject to the same quarantine laws (six months in isolation etc) as any other animal when entering or returning to countries currently free of rabies, such as Australia.

Deaf travellers can ask for airport and in-flight announcements to be written down for them.

Children under two travel for 10% of the standard fare (or free on some airlines), as long as they don't occupy a seat. They don't get a baggage allowance either. 'Skycots' should be provided by the airline if requested in advance; these will take a child weighing up to about 10kg. Children between two and 12 can usually occupy a seat for half to two-thirds of the full fare and do get a baggage allowance. Push chairs can often be taken as hand luggage.

Cathay-Pacific Airways
(☎ 379 0861)
11th Floor, Arthur Andersen Tower, 205 Queen St
Continental Airlines
(☎ 379 5680)
TrustBank Bldg, 229 Queen St
Delta Air Lines
(☎ 379 3370)
Dingwall Bldg, 87 Queen St
Emirates Airlines
(☎ 377 6004)
Level 5, 22 Fanshawe St
Freedom Air
(☎ 0800 600 500)
5 Short St
Garuda Indonesia
(☎ 366 1855)
120 Albert St
Japan Airlines
(☎ 379 3202)
120 Westpac Tower, 120 Albert St
Korean Air
(☎ 307 3687)
Finance Plaza, 92 Albert St
Malaysia Airlines
(☎ 373 2741)
12th Floor, Swanson Centre, 12-26 Swanson St

Warning

The information in this chapter is particularly vulnerable to change: prices for international travel are volatile, routes are introduced and cancelled, schedules change, special deals come and go, and rules and visa requirements are amended. Airlines and governments seem to take a perverse pleasure in making price structures and regulations as complicated as possible. You should check directly with the airline or a travel agent to make sure you understand how a fare (and ticket you may buy) works. In addition, the travel industry is highly competitive and there are many lurks and perks.

The upshot of this is that you should get opinions, quotes and advice from as many airlines and travel agents as possible before you part with your hard-earned cash. The details given in this chapter should be regarded as pointers and are not a substitute for your own careful, up-to-date research.

Polynesian Airlines
(☎ 309 5396)
Samoa House, Karangahape Rd
Qantas
(☎ 357 8900)
154 Queen St
Singapore Airlines
(☎ 303 2129)
West Plaza Bldg, cnr Albert and Fanshawe Sts
Swissair
(☎ 358 3216)
Dingwall Bldg, 87 Queen St
Thai Airways
(☎ 377 3886)
22 Fanshawe St
United Airlines
(☎ 379 3800)
Lumley House, 7 City Rd

Domestic airlines servicing Auckland include:

Air New Zealand
(☎ 357 3000)
Cnr Customs and Queen Sts.
Ansett New Zealand
(☎ 0800 267 388)
75 Queen St; 50 Grafton Rd
Great Barrier Airlines
(☎ 256 6500)
Auckland Domestic Air Terminal
Waiheke Air Services
(☎ 372 5001)
Ostend, Waiheke Island

BUS

The main bus company in Auckland, as in the rest of NZ, is InterCity. With a few exceptions, InterCity has buses to almost all bigger towns and main tourist areas; it operates from the Sky City Coach Terminal, at 102 Hobson St. For inquiries and reservations call ☎ 357 8400. The ticket office is open weekdays and Sundays from 7.30 am to 6.15 pm and on Saturdays from 7.30 am to 2.30 pm.

Newmans (☎ 309 9738) is the other main bus company, with a good North Island network and a more limited South Island service that runs along the east coast from Nelson to Invercargill. It operates from the Sky City Terminal. Northliner Express (☎ 307 5873) buses also operate from the

Sky City Terminal, with services heading north from Auckland to Whangarei, the Bay of Islands and Kaitaia.

Smaller services are the Geyserland Express (☎ 357 6616) to Rotorua, C Tours (☎ 758 1777) to New Plymouth, and the Little Kiwi Bus (☎ 0800 759 999) to Hamilton.

Backpacker buses operate in and from Auckland; both Kiwi Experience (☎ 336 9830, fax 366 1374) and Magic Bus (☎ 358 5600) offer door-to-door service, picking up and dropping off at any Auckland hostel.

Discount Fares

Although fares vary between companies, they are generally similar. Knowing the discounts available from various companies can cut travel costs by as much as 50% – you'll never have to pay full fare. All bus companies have free timetable booklets detailing discounts and schedules. Most of the following discounts apply only to trips that would otherwise cost $20 or more.

InterCity and Newmans offer a 30% discount to seniors (over 60) and anyone with a recognised backpacker card. These discounts are easy to get and have no special restrictions.

Saver and Supersaver fares, booked in advance (five days before the date of travel) and paid for two days before travelling, have a discount of 30% and 50% respectively, but limited seats are available at this rate. Discounts for return fares are 20%.

If you cancel up to two hours before the time of departure you will receive a 50% refund. There is no refund if you cancel within two hours of departure.

Travel Passes

The major bus lines offer discount travel passes valid for around 14 days to three months. InterCity, with the biggest network, has the most options. As with all unlimited travel passes, you have to do a lot of travelling to make them pay – they're best for people who want to see a lot in a short time. Book ahead to be sure of a seat.

InterCity, in conjunction with the Tranz Scenic rail network and the Interislander ferry, offers a '3 in 1 Travelpass' covering nationwide bus/train/ferry travel. Five days travel taken over 10 days costs $390 (children $261), eight days travel over three weeks $524 ($351), 15 days travel over five weeks $659 ($442) and 22 days travel over eight weeks $767 ($514). There is also a '4 in 1 Travelpass' that includes one domestic flight: for five days $655 ($437), eight days $789 ($527), 15 days $924 ($607), 22 days $1032 ($690). On this particular pass you can add an additional flight for $265 ($176).

There are other travel passes that are available at visitor information centres and bus depots. For example, InterCity has numerous North Island passes including Auckland-Wellington and points in between ($99, children $66), Auckland-Napier via Rotorua and the east coast ($149, $99).

Newmans' 'Stopover Pass' ($95) covers 14 days travel in all parts of the North Island except Northland; you can travel only in one direction (ie no backtracking).

Northliner Express offers several discount backpacker passes for Northland, with unlimited travel on various routes. The passes are valid from the date you start travelling. The 'Bay of Islands Pass' costs $49 and is valid for one month; the 'Northland Freedom Pass' costs $109 and is valid for one month (you can go as far north as Kaitaia and return via the west coast), and the 'Top Half Pass' costs $76 and is valid for two months.

TRAIN

Trains arrive at and depart from the train station (☎ 0800 802 802) on Beach Rd, about 1km east of the city centre. Several travellers have written to Lonely Planet saying that they felt intimidated at the station at night. You can check reservations and information daily from 7 am to 9 pm.

Two trains operate between Auckland and Wellington. The *Overlander* runs daily, departing Auckland/Wellington at 8.30/8.45 am, arriving Wellington/Auckland 7.30/ 7.35 pm. The *Northerner* is an overnight train that operates nightly, except Saturday, departing Auckland/Wellington 8.40/7.50 pm, arriving Wellington/Auckland 7.35/7 am.

GETTING THERE & AWAY

The *Geyserland* operates daily between Auckland and Rotorua, departing Auckland/Rotorua at 8.am/1.30 pm, arriving at Rotorua/Auckland 12.15/5.45 pm. The *Kaimai Express* operates daily between Auckland and Tauranga, departing Auckland/Tauranga at 6.05 pm/8.05 am, arriving Tauranga/Auckland 9.30 pm/11.40 am. Both services stop in Hamilton en route.

See the Getting Around chapter for details on Auckland suburban trains.

CAR & MOTORCYCLE

Driving around NZ is easy. Petrol (gasoline) costs 79c a litre, 91c for unleaded, and 84c a litre for premium unleaded. Petrol prices vary slightly from station to station and between the city and countryside, but only by a few cents. Diesel costs 45c a litre.

Driver courtesy is reasonably good in the towns, except perhaps for Auckland, but the highways are full of cowboys. Driving 20km/h over the speed limit and aggressive tailgating are common, despite the forever-twisting, narrow roads. Autobahns don't exist – apart from the occasional overtaking lane, highways are single-lane and pass through the towns. Traffic is generally light, but it is easy to get stuck behind a truck or campervan. Count on covering about 80km every hour on the highways.

Unsealed back-country roads are another hazard for the uninitiated. Many visitors lose control by moving onto the loose gravel verges and skidding into ditches.

Kiwis drive on the left, as in the UK, Australia, Japan and much of Asia. For those used to driving on the right – take care. Every year almost 100 serious or fatal accidents involve foreign drivers, many of them caused by driving on the wrong side of the road.

A 'give way to the right' rule applies. This is interpreted in a rather strange fashion when you're turning left and an oncoming vehicle is turning right into the same street. Since the oncoming vehicle is then on your right you give way to them.

Speed limits on the open road are generally 100km/h; in built-up areas the limit is usually 50km/h when conditions are unsafe due to bad weather; limited visibility; pedestrians, cyclists or animals on the road; excessive traffic; or poor road conditions.

The *New Zealand Road Code* is a wise investment; it will tell you all you need to know. It's available at NZ Automobile Association (AA) offices and bookshops. There is a similar book for motorcyclists.

A valid, unrestricted driver's licence from your home country is required to rent or drive a car in NZ. The AA staff can advise if you wish to obtain a NZ driver's licence. To drive a motorcycle you must have a motorcycle licence or a special endorsement on your home-country licence.

Excellent road maps are readily available in NZ, and are essential for exploring along highways where signposting is not always good. The best of the lot are AA's 1: 350,000 district maps (free to members).

Members of an equivalent overseas automobile association may qualify for reciprocal benefits from the AA; remember to bring your card. Otherwise AA membership (☎ 0800 500 222) is good insurance if you buy a car. Apart from free maps and publications, membership entitles you to free emergency breakdown service, free advice on traffic tickets and accidents, and various discounts on services and accommodation.

Theft from cars is a problem in NZ, particularly in isolated parking areas at scenic spots and walks. The North Island tends to be worse than the South Island, but no matter where you park do not leave valuables in the car. Hide your gear if you can't take it with you.

Rental

Car Usually you must be at least 21 years old to rent a car in NZ (sometimes 25). Under 25s often incur a larger insurance excess.

Car rental is competitive in the major cities, but Auckland is the cheapest place to rent a car. The surplus of operators means that you can often get special deals for longer rental, especially outside the peak summer months. Shop around by phone – quoting a competitor's rate may bring a reduction, even from the major companies. In peak season you may get a good, reasonably current model for $55 per day (all inclusive) for rentals of more than four days, while in off-peak periods the cost may drop to $45.

The major car-hire companies offer new cars, country-wide networks, more reliability, better insurance, and have high prices. The many smaller companies are much cheaper and have mostly older cars, but contracts and insurance policies should be looked at closely.

The big operators – Avis, Hertz and Budget – have extensive fleets, and offices in most towns. Unlimited-kilometre rental of a small car (a late-model Japanese car of 1600cc or less) starts at around $70 a day (more for rental of only a few days). For driving around town without an unlimited-kilometre option, expect to pay about 30c a kilometre. Medium-sized cars typically cost around $100 per day with unlimited kilometres. A drop-off fee applies if you're not returning the car to the city of hire. Overseas travel agents can often get better deals hiring new cars through major operators than you can yourself in NZ.

A huge number of smaller companies undercut the big operators, but there may be more restrictions on use, and one-way rentals may not always be possible. Some budget operators, such as Pegasus and Shoestring, have national networks.

Many small operators have older, second-hand cars, advertised for as little as $20 a day, but you get what you pay for. Advertised rates (and even quotes over the phone) are often misleading, and business practices can leave a lot to be desired. Always the check kilometre rate, whether the price includes GST, the minimum hire period, the age of the car, bond and the insurance coverage. Always read the rental agreement before you sign.

Rock-bottom rates usually apply to minimum one-month hire in the off season for a beat-up car over 10 years old with limited (or even no) insurance. Full payment in advance and a credit-card bond is usually required. Because rental-car accidents (usually minor) are so common in NZ, insurance premiums are very high. Bigger companies will remove the excess for around $10 a day extra, but insurance from the cheaper rental agencies is usually subject to a $700 excess for any accident or damage to the car (some even include tyre replacement and puncture repairs), even if it is not your fault. Most of these companies, however, will cash your bond and refund it later if the other driver's blame can be proved and they have insurance (don't count on it). Insurance coverage for all hire cars is invalid on certain roads, typically beaches and unsealed roads in major tourist areas.

If you are prepared to risk the insurance excess, second-hand car hire can be good value. By shopping around, you can hire a 1990 model Japanese import for a month in the off season for as little as $30 a day, or a more recent model for $40 a day (sometimes less). Prices are up to 50% higher in the peak season and are also higher outside Auckland.

Campervan Campervans (also known as mobile homes, motor homes or, in US parlance, Winnebagos or RVs) are an enormously popular way of getting around NZ. In tourist areas in the South Island, it seems that almost every other vehicle is a campervan. Campervans combine transport and accommodation in one neat package, and you'll have your own kitchen on wheels.

The cost of renting a campervan varies with the type of vehicle and the time of year. A small van, suitable for two people, typically has a sink, hot and cold water, a gas cooker, 12V fridge and 240V heater. The dining table and seats fold into a double bed. Usually of minivan size with a 2L unleaded petrol engine, campervans are easy to drive, manoeuvrable round town and have enough pep for the hills. Slightly larger varieties may have toilets and showers. Others may be kitted-out Kombi vans or 4WDs, or even station wagons with pop-up tents fitted on top.

Four to six-berth campervans are light-truck size and usually contain the works. They are very comfortable, with an extra double sleeping-cabin at the front, a microwave, toilet, shower etc. Fuel consumption is similar to smaller vans, but larger ones may run on much cheaper diesel fuel. The only drawback is their size – they're not much fun to drive in cities and are sluggish on hills. They are tall (around 3.3m), so the top is easily scraped, especially on signs or verandahs when parking on the camber of a road.

Campervans usually have 240V power systems (just plug them in at a motor camp) with backup 12V systems, so you can still camp in luxury out in the wild or at basic campsites. Dispose of waste water properly; toilets must be emptied at designated dumping stations, found at camping grounds or provided by some councils.

Maui and Britz New Zealand are two of the biggest operators and the main car hire companies also rent campervans. For details on companies renting campervans in Auckland see the Car & Motorcycle section in the Getting Around chapter.

Motorcycle Most of the motorcycle-hire shops are in Auckland, but Christchurch has a few too (see the Getting Around chapter for the Auckland dealers). You can hire anything from a little 50cc moped (nifty-fifty) for zipping around town, to a big 750cc touring motorcycle.

Remember you will need a motorcycle licence to hire a regular motorcycle (rental bikes are usually from 250cc to 750cc in size); a car driver's licence will get you by if you want to tootle around on a moped.

Purchase

Car For a longer stay and/or for groups, buying a car and then selling it at the end of your travels can be one of the cheapest and best ways of seeing NZ. You're not tied to the bus schedules, nor do you find yourself waiting by the roadside with your thumb out looking for a ride.

Auckland is the easiest place in NZ to buy a car. Christchurch is the next-best place for overseas visitors, but a distant second. One of the easiest ways to buy a cheap car is to scour the hostel notice boards, where other travellers sell their cars before

moving on. You can pick up an old car for only a few hundred dollars. The really cheap backpacker specials, beat-up 15 to 20-year-old cars that somehow are still running after many circuits of New Zealand, are so cheap that it many be worth taking the risk.

Otherwise, cars are advertised in newspapers just like anywhere else in the world. Cars are advertised in the *NZ Herald* on Wednesday, the *Trade & Exchange* on Monday and Thursday, and in the weekly *AutoTrader* magazine. Buy-backs, where the dealer agrees to buy back your car for an agreed price, are not usually a great deal but are an easy option. Auckland dealers who work on this system include:

Budget Car Sales	☎ 379 4120
Downtown Rentals	☎ 303 1847
Geraghty McGregor Motors	☎ 307 6700
Rex Swinburne Motors	☎ 620 6587
Rock Bottom Rentals	☎ 622 1592

Auckland also has a number of popular auctions and car fairs, where people bring their cars to sell. Manukau is the biggest and best, but the Ellerslie Racecourse car fair is also good. In the city centre, there is a car fair next to the old Oriental Markets (near the train station building), but it is relatively small. Arrive early, between 8.30 am and 9.30 am, for the best choice – the fairs are over by about midday. For a credit check phone ☎ 0800 658 934; quote chassis and licence plate numbers. Mechanical inspection services, credit agencies and Auto Check details are all on hand at the car fairs, which are:

Ellerslie Racecourse (☎ 529 2233), near the Greenlane round-about, Sunday 9 am to noon
Manukau City, South Auckland (☎ 358 5000), in the car park of the giant shopping mall near the Manukau off-ramp of the Southern Motorway, Sunday 8.30 am to 1 pm
Old Oriental Markets (☎ 636 9775), Beach Rd in the city centre, Saturday 9 am to noon

Alternatively, you could try the car auctions. Two of the best-known are:

Hammer Auctions (☎ 579 2344) is at 830 Great South Rd, Penrose. Auctions are held several times a week with Monday, Wednesday and Friday at 6 pm set aside for budget vehicles.

Turner's Car Auction (☎ 525 1920) is on the corner of Cain Rd and McNab St, Penrose. Auctions are held several times a week, with Wednesday at 11.30 am set aside for budget vehicles.

BICYCLE

Cycling is a cheap, convenient, healthy, environmentally sound and – above all – fun way of travelling. One note of caution: before you leave home, go over your bike with a fine-toothed comb and fill your repair kit with every imaginable spare part. You won't necessarily be able to buy that crucial gismo for your machine when it breaks down somewhere in the back of beyond as the sun sets.

Bicycles can travel by air. You can take them to pieces and put them in a bike bag or box, but it's much easier simply to wheel your bike to the check-in desk, where it should be treated as a piece of baggage. You may need to remove the pedals and turn the handlebars sideways – check all this with the airline well in advance, preferably before you pay for your ticket.

Currently, bicycles may be carried free on trains when accompanied by a fare-paying adult.

Lonely Planet's *Cycling in New Zealand* (March 2000) is a comprehensive guide, so if a two-wheeler is your mode of transport, get hold of it.

HITCHING

Hitching is never entirely safe in any country in the world and we don't recommend it. The well-publicised murder of two Swedish hitchhikers a few years ago highlights the fact that even in relatively safe NZ hitchhik-ing can be a risky undertaking. If you are determined to hitch, then bear in mind that getting out of Auckland is hard work. The only legal way to hitch out of town is to stand by the motorway on-ramps, or to take a bus to Mercer or Albany and start from there.

BOAT

Cruise ships aside, there are no longer any regular passenger-ship services to NZ. Even arranging to work your way across the Pacific as crew on a yacht is much more difficult than it used to be. There are many yachts sailing around the Pacific but nowadays they're usually only willing to take on experienced yachties as crew.

To try your luck finding a yacht, go to the appropriate port at the appropriate time. There are lots of favourite islands, ports and harbours where you're likely to find yachts, such as Sydney and Cairns in Australia, Bali in Indonesia, various ports in Fiji and Tahiti, and Hawai'i, San Diego and San Francisco in the USA. In NZ, popular yachting harbours include the Bay of Islands and Whangarei (both in Northland), Auckland and Wellington.

There are certain times when you're more likely to find yachts. From Fiji, October to November is a peak departure season as cyclones are on their way. March-April is the main departure season for yachts heading to/from Australia; be prepared for rough seas and storms when crossing the Tasman Sea.

ORGANISED TOURS

As well as the host of tours you can arrange in Auckland, many can be arranged from outside the country. The New Zealand Tourism Board (NZTB) can provide the details of tour companies; its offices around the world are listed in the Tourist Offices section of the Facts for the Visitor chapter.

GETTING THERE & AWAY

Getting Around

THE AIRPORT

Auckland airport (☎ 256 8899) is 21km south-west of the city centre. It has an international terminal and two domestic terminals (Ansett and Air New Zealand), each with a tourist information centre. A free shuttle service operates between the terminals, and there's also a signposted footpath. The airport Web site is at www.aucklandairport .co.nz.

At the international terminal there's a freephone for accommodation bookings, and many places to stay provide a free shuttle to/from the airport. A bank is open for passengers of all arriving and departing flights to change money, but it charges a $3 transaction fee. Both terminals have left-luggage facilities and car-rental desks, though you get better rates from companies in town.

TO/FROM THE AIRPORT

The AirBus shuttle (☎ 272 9396) runs every 20 minutes between the airport and the Downtown Airline Terminal ($10/16 one way/return, 50 minutes). (Reservations are not required; buy a ticket from the driver.) The first bus leaves from outside the Sheraton Hotel in the city at 4.40 am, the last bus at 8.25 pm, calling in at the Sky City bus terminal, the Downtown Airline Terminal and several major hotels before heading through Parnell and Newmarket to the airport. The first bus leaves the international airport at 6.20 am and the last bus at 10 pm. During rush hour allow at least an hour for the trip.

Door-to-door shuttles run to/from the airport, and competition is cut-throat. The two main operators are Super Shuttle (☎ 307 5210) and Johnston's Shuttle Link (☎ 275 1234). The cost between the airport and the city centre is around $15 for one person and $20 for two; all sorts of deals are available.

A taxi to the airport from the city will cost around $38.

BUS

The Downtown Bus Centre is on Commerce St, between Quay St and Customs St East, but not all buses leave from here. Local bus route timetables are available from the bus terminal, newsagents and visitor centres (see the Facts for the Visitor chapter for tourist office locations), or you can phone Rideline (☎ 366 6400) for information and schedules. The bus information kiosk at the Downtown Bus Centre is open from 7 am to 6.30 pm Monday to Friday and from 9 am to 5 pm Saturday and Sunday. The *Auckland Busabout Guide*, available at information centres and the bus information kiosk, shows routes and departure points for the city's major attractions. There is also a useful colour pamphlet called *Auckland's Top Stops*, showing which buses go to Auckland's main attractions. This is also available at the places mentioned. See also the bus and ferry map at the back of this book for bus routes in and from the city centre.

Where an *x* appears in the bus numbers given in this guide, it indicates that any bus with the digits preceding the *x* will get you to the given destination. For example, 'bus Nos 25*x* will get you to Timbucktoo' means any buses whose first two digits are 25 will get you there.

Inner city fares cost 50c for an adult and 30c for a child or senior citizen (you pay the driver when you board). Trips farther out cost from $1.10 per adult (70c child/senior citizen). Auckland*pass* day concessions cost $7 (adult/child/senior citizen) and this allows you to travel on any Stagecoach bus in Auckland (including Whenuapai Bus Travel buses). There is also a Family*pass* for $14, available after 9 am Monday to Friday, all day on weekends and public holidays. Monthly passes are also available. Passes may be bought on the bus or at the Link ferry ticket office.

The Link is an excellent bus service which travels clockwise and anti-clockwise around a loop that includes Queen St, the casino, Ponsonby Rd, K Rd, the university, Newmarket, Parnell, the train station and QEII Square. The service operates every 10 minutes from 6 am to 7 pm on weekdays (every 20 minutes on weekends), then every 20 minutes until 11 pm. The all-white buses are easy to spot and the fare to most places is only $1 ($2.20 for the entire loop). For exact times telephone Rideline (☎ 366 6400), or pick up a timetable at the visitor centre.

Plans to have trains and buses leave from a single terminus (Britomart), roughly where the present Downtown Bus Centre is, are in the offing. Work on the new transport hub is expected to get under way in the final months of 1999.

TRAIN

There's a limited Tranz Metro (Rideline ☎ 366 6400) train service, with just two main lines running west to Waitakere ($4.30/ $2.80 adult/child) from the city and south to Papakura (prices as for Waitakere). The first stop out from the main train station is Newmarket ($1/60c). Auckland station is on Beach Rd, behind the imposing but now disused former Auckland Central Railway Station. Bicycles can be carried on board free as long as they're accompanied by an adult fare-paying passenger.

CAR & MOTORCYCLE

Auckland is crawling with car-hire operators and is the best city in which to hire a vehicle for touring NZ. Some good deals can be had for long-term hire, but be warned that the cheapest is not necessarily the best.

The major companies – Avis, Budget, Hertz and Thrifty – are the most reliable, offering full insurance and offices at the airport and all over the country. They are expensive, but rates are often negotiable for longer rentals.

If you are prepared to take limited insurance and risk losing an excess of around

$700, then the cheaper operators offer some pretty good deals. Prices vary with the season, the age of the car and length of rental. In the off-season, for rental of a month or more, a good 1990 model car costs as little as $30 a day. For shorter rentals in the high season, expect to pay $50 or more a day. A campervan or kitted-out minibus starts at around $70 per day. Ignore prices quoted on brochures and shop around by phone. Always read the rental agreement thoroughly before you sign.

Auckland has more than 60 rental operators, including:

A2B	☎ 377 0825, 0800 222 929
Ace*	☎ 0800 502 277
Alternative Rental Cars	☎ 373 3822
Avis	☎ 526 2800
Britz NZ*	☎ 0800 831 900
Budget*	☎ 375 2270, 0800 652 227
Hertz	☎ 309 0989, 0800 654 321
Maui*	☎ 275 3013, 0800 651 080
Thrifty	☎ 309 0111, 0800 737 070

* Rents out sleepervans and/or campervans as well as cars

You can rent a small scooter for $24 for 24 hours; only a car licence is needed. New Zealand Motorcycle Rentals (☎ 377 2005, fax 377 2006, info@nzbike.com), 31 Beach Rd, has one-day hire from $90 (Yamaha SR250cc) to $215 (BMW K750cc); the daily rate progressively decreases the longer you hire the bike. Its Web site is at www.nzbike.com.

For further information on driving and rentals, see Car & Motorcycle in the Getting There & Away chapter.

TAXI

There are many taxis in Auckland that usually work from ranks but also cruise popular areas. You often have to phone for a taxi; Auckland Taxi Co-Op (☎ 300 3000) is one of the biggest companies, and others are listed in the *Yellow Pages*. Taxis charge a flagfall of $2, and around $1.59 per kilometre.

TUK-TUK

Three-wheelers or tuk-tuks are a novel alternative to the more usual forms of transport, and are handy for getting around Auckland's pubs and nightspots. On the city side of the harbour bridge, Auckland City Tuk Tuks (☎ 360 1988, fax 360 1954, tuk-tuk@titan.com) will take you on short trips in the city centre ($3) or for longer trips (eg along Tamaki Drive, to Auckland Museum etc). Auckland City Tuk Tuks can generally be found outside the ferry building. In Devonport contact Ultimate Tours (☎ 025 739 445, 482 0025). A trip up Mt Victoria and back costs $5 and a tour round the main sights costs around $12. Ultimate Tours tuk-tuks can be found outside Devonport Wharf, where there is a special tuk-tuk stand. Ultimate Tours also does trips using a motorcycle sidecar in Devonport and Auckland.

BOAT

Fullers Auckland (☎ 367 9111, enquiries@ fullersakl.co.nz) operates ferries between the city and Devonport, Stanley Bay, Birkenhead and Bayswater on the North Shore, the gulf islands and, most recently, Half Moon Bay in Howick. Ferries to Devonport ($7/3.50/14 adult/child/family return, 12 minutes one way) run every half hour; the last ferry from the city is 11 pm on weekdays and 1 am on weekends. Fullers also has several tours (see Sailing & Cruising in the Things to See & Do chapter). The Excursions chapter gives details on the gulf island ferries. Fullers' ticket office is at the ferry building and its Web site is at www .fullers.co.nz.

Pacific Ferries (☎ 303 1741) has a 'fast ferry' service to Waiheke and another, slower, service on the *Lady Wakefield*, a former Manly (Sydney, Australia) ferry (see the Waiheke section in the Excursions chapter for details). Pacific Ferries' ticket office is at Princess Wharf, not far from the ferry building, and its Web site is at www.pacificferries.co.nz.

There are ferry services to Kawau (Kawau Kat and Matata Cruises). Fullers also runs services out here. See the Excursions chapter (North of Auckland) for details.

Getting to gulf islands that are not serviced by the commercial ferry companies means chartering a boat (easy to do in Auckland). See the Things to See & Do chapter for details.

BICYCLE

Several companies around Auckland hire out bicycles, usually mountain bikes, by the day, week, month or longer. They also hire gear. A handy place in the city centre is Adventure Cycles (☎ 309 5566), 1 Fort Lane (just off Fort St). A mountain bike for use in the city (ie not to be ridden on sand or other areas that will require special bike cleaning) costs about $18 a day, otherwise they start at around $25 a day. Helmets, pumps, locks and so on are included.

The Penny Farthing Cycle Shop (☎ 379 2524), on the corner of Symonds St and Khyber Pass Rd, hires out mountain bikes for $25 per day, helmets etc included.

Pleasant places to cycle include Tamaki Drive (but avoid the afternoon traffic; early on weekend mornings is recommended), Cornwall Park (which has numerous trails) and around Devonport (you can't ride over the harbour bridge, but you can take your bike across the harbour on the ferry). There is a signposted 50km cycling route along the waterfront, looping back to the city centre; a free pamphlet with a map of the route is available from the visitor centre. Bicycle hire places will also advise on cycling routes, or take a look at Lonely Planet's *Cycling in New Zealand* (March 2000), which has a good section on Auckland and the surrounding region.

WALKING

In Auckland the car is king. But having said that, there are all sorts of possibilities for walks in and around Auckland city: bush, beach, arts and crafts trails, historic buildings – there's plenty of choice, and plenty of information from the various visitor centres (see the Things to See & Do chapter for details).

ORGANISED TOURS

You can tour the major Auckland attractions in the United Airlines Explorer Bus (☎ 571 3119, info@explorer-bus.co.nz) for $20 – all day. It departs daily from the ferry building on the hour every hour from 10 am to 4 pm in winter and every half hour from 9 am to 4 pm from October to April. It goes to Mission Bay, Kelly Tarlton's Antarctic Encounter & Underwater World, Parnell Rose Gardens, Auckland Museum, Parnell Village, Victoria Park Market and back to the ferry building. At the museum you can pick up its Satellite Link (summer only) to Mt Eden, St Lukes Shopping Mall, Auckland Zoo, Motat, Auckland Art Gallery, the America's Cup Village and Sky Casino. Its Web site is at www.explorer-bus.co.nz.

Auckland has many tour operators. Three-hour tours (about $38/19 adult/child) will typically cover the city centre, harbour bridge and Tamaki Drive, including stops at Mt Eden, the Auckland Museum and Parnell. Other tours (eg Sea City Tours ☎ 0800 732 2489) do the same, and include a harbour cruise for $98. ABC Tours (☎ 0800 222 868), Scenic Tours (☎ 634 2266) and Great Sights (☎ 0800 744 487) are all reputable companies. Hotel pick-up and drop-off is usually included in the price. The Devonport Tour Company (☎ 357 6366, 0800 868 774) runs daily trips in a mini-bus that meets the ferry from the city. For $22 ($11 children) you get a one-hour tour of Devonport's volcanic cones plus a bit of history (the fee includes the return ferry fare).

Auckland Adventures (☎ 379 4545, fax 379 4543, auckland-adventures@acb.co.nz) has a tour that includes a Maori cultural show at Auckland Museum, a trip up Mt Eden, a visit to a winery, orchards and farms, as well as to the gannet colony at Muriwai ($55). It's Wilderness Adventure ($75) provides a more extensive trip in the West Coast region.

Other possibilities include a tour of Auckland's volcanic cones and other geological features as well as flora and fauna. Geotours (☎ 525 3991, murray@geotours.co.nz) charges about $99 for a day trip or $59 a half day. You can visit its Web site at www .kiwipages.co.nz/geotour.html. Mike's Garden Tours (☎ 846 5350) start at $49 for a half day or $95 for a full day.

For trips to West Auckland, see the Excursions chapter. Many companies, such as Bush & Beach Nature Tours, will pick up/drop off in the city centre. (You can see where the movie *The Piano* and episodes of the cult TV classics *Xena: Warrior Princess* and *Hercules* were filmed.)

GETTING AROUND

Things to See & Do

MUSEUMS & GALLERIES
Auckland Museum Te Papa Whakahiku (Map 5)

The museum is a must-visit attraction. Expansive, green lawns sweep up to the entrance, before which stands a cenotaph and a couple of cannons, reminders that this museum is also a war memorial.

The museum has a fine collection of art and artefacts from the Pacific Islands, including a sacred canoe from Tikopia. One room is dedicated to significant Maori *taonga* (treasure). There is also a **Maori cultural performance** on the first floor of the museum at 11 am and 1.30 pm daily. It costs $8 per adult and $5 for children, seniors and students (a family pass is $15 – two adults, three children).

The museum houses reminders of various wars past, and includes the exhibition 'Scars on the Heart', which features Auckland's Jewish community.

An entire floor is dedicated to NZ's natural history. This excellent display has interactive consoles that allow you to discover what NZ's birds both look and sound like. But there's lots more, including a whole bank of computers (for looking up all sorts of information), books, a video room and an impressive collection of dinosaur skeletons. Also on this floor is the children's activity centre, a wonderful place with all manner of attractions.

The museum is open daily from 10 am to 5 pm; a donation of $5 per adult is encouraged. The Explorer Bus passes the museum's front door every 30 minutes. The Link bus stops nearby at Parnell Rd, from where it's a short walk to the museum, every 10 minutes on weekdays until 6 pm and every 20 minutes after 6 pm and on weekends.

NZ National Maritime Museum (Map 3)

Located on the downtown waterfront, this museum (☎ 373 0800, 0800 SALTYSAM,

fax 377 6000, mmuseum@wave.co.nz) is dedicated to one of NZ's national obsessions – sailing. The extensive museum explores 1000 years of NZ's seafaring history. Dozens of sailing craft and displays are exhibited, including the huge 25m (76ft) outrigger canoe *Taratai*, which modern navigator Jim Siers constructed using 1000-year-old methods and sailed across the Pacific. Outside is **KZ1**, the Bruce Farr designed 1988 America's Cup challenger.

Other exhibits illuminate the Maori and European discovery of and migration to NZ. There are exhibits on navigation, fishing and oral history. The inside of a 19th century sailing ship, of the sort immigrants would have travelled in, has been recreated, complete with creaking timbers. Another display – one that will strike a chord with most New Zealanders who grew up in the 1950s and 1960s – includes a typical seaside bach (complete with the formica and vinyl, and the popular 1950s soap *Dr Paul* playing on a valve radio) and a seaside dairy with the ubiquitous Tip Top ice cream sign.

The newest exhibit centres on the history of NZ yachting and the America's Cup.

It's open daily from 9 am to 5 pm (6 pm in summer). Entry is $10 for adults, $5 for

Victoria Park Market, under the shadow of the historic brick chimney

Parnell Village on the city's eastern flank

CHRISTINE NIVEN

Expansive views from Bastion Point, site of a significant land-rights struggle during the late 1970s

CHRISTINE NIVEN

Urban meets rural at North Head, Devonport

CHRISTINE NIVEN

Cornwall Park, a beautiful city oasis from dawn to dusk

children, students and seniors, and $25 for families – two adults, three children. Guided tours are conducted – usually at 11 am or 2 pm – as are sailing trips (season and weather permitting). The sailing scow *Ted Ashby* departs for a trip around the harbour at noon, although in the summer of 1999-2000 there will probably be more frequent departures (adults $7, children, students and seniors $5, families $15). The journey takes about 45 minutes. Salty Sam's luncheon heritage cruise departs at noon (summer only) and includes lunch. Bookings are recommended (last sales on the day at 11 am).

Bruce Wilkinson Collection (Map 3)

Located in the original gatekeeper's house at Albert Park (see Parks & Gardens below), this museum displays items collected by Auckland philanthropist Bruce Wilkinson who, in 1974, gifted his home in plush Paratai Drive and its contents to the city of Auckland. The collection features ceramics, crystal and an extraordinary assortment of clocks. It is open daily from 10 am to 4 pm (free).

Museum of Transport & Technology (Map 1)

This museum has two sections. MOTAT I has exhibits on transport, communications and energy, including a display on pioneer aviator Richard Pearse. This eccentric South Island farmer may have flown before the Wright brothers. During his life he produced a steady stream of inventions and devices, but he was a lousy farmer. Also at MOTAT I is the infotainment Science Centre with hands-on exhibits.

MOTAT II, at nearby Sir Keith Park Memorial Airfield, features rare and historic aircraft. Exhibits include a V1 flying bomb and Lancaster bomber from WWII, but pride of place goes to the huge Solent flying boat that ran a Pacific islands loop in the luxury days of flying. The ticket you buy at the main entrance covers both sections (the tram goes most of the way between the two), but you must show it when you enter MOTAT II and have it stamped.

MARTIN HARRIS

'Those magnificent men in their flying machines...'

MOTAT is open daily from 10 am to 5 pm. Entry is $10 for adults, $5 for children five to 16 years (under fives free) and $5 for senior citizens and students.

Rugby Hall of Fame (Map 1)

This was being re-established at Eden Park in Sandringham at the time of writing. It will open daily, but times and entry fee details were unavailable. The Rugby Hall of Fame (☎ 849 5555) will provide a comprehensive display of the game and its star players. Bus Nos 23 and 24 will take you from Victoria St West (opposite Elliot St) in the city to Eden Park on Sandringham Rd.

Howick Historical Village (Map 3)

This fascinating 'living' museum with costumed staff evokes the atmosphere of the Fencible settlement as it was from the 1840s to the 1880s. There are 33 buildings, many re-located here from other parts of the region. The streets, the pond with ducks and geese and the village gardens are faithful reconstructions of Victorian fashion. There is a cafe with homemade goodies as well. There is a theme day on the 3rd Sunday of each month during which you will be treated to something special, for example the black-smith working at the forge, the 65th Regiment firing their muskets or maybe the school in session. Check with the village for details (☎ 576 9506, fax 576 9708, fencible @ihug.co.nz). It is on Bells Rd, Lloyd Elsmore Park, Pakuranga, and its Web site is at www.fencible.org.nz. It's open daily from 10 am to 5 pm and entry is $9 for adults, $7 for seniors and students and $5 for children.

Royal NZ Navy Museum (Map 6)

This museum, in Spring St, Devonport, provides an insight into New Zealand's naval history. Most of the exhibits have been donated by ex-servicemen and servicewomen and their families. Entry is free, although donations are appreciated. The museum is open daily from 10 am to 4.30 pm.

Devonport Museum (Map 6)

Situated on the Mt Cambria Reserve, just east of Devonport's Mt Victoria, this small museum chronicles the area's history. It is open on weekends from 2 to 4 pm; entry is free, but donations are appreciated. It also sells few books on Devonport's history.

Auckland Art Gallery Toi o Tamaki (Map 3)

The Auckland Art Gallery (☎ 309 7693) has New Zealand's largest collection (more than 10,000 pieces) of local and international art. There are two parts to the gallery: the original gallery (opened in 1888), at the foot of Albert Park, and the New Gallery (opened 1995), across the road, on the corner of Wellesley and Lorne Sts.

Colonial landscape paintings and early images of Maori are particularly well represented in the NZ collection at the main (original) gallery. Early colonial artists, such as Reverend John Kinder (1819-1903) and William Fox (1812-93), were often amateurs or draftsmen who depicted an orderly and prosperous landscape with newly built roads and fences. In contrast to the pre-colonial works of Augustus Earle (1793-1838), in these paintings Maori culture was very often ignored as was any hint that suc-

cessful colonisation might be threatened by hostilities. By the 1880s this sort of painting had given way to grand landscapes that reflected European conventions of the day, idealising nature in subdued, muted colours redolent of the northern hemisphere. It was at least 50 years before sharper more realistic images became the norm.

A large part of the collection focuses on two of NZ's most well-known colonial artists, Gottfried Lindauer (1839-1926) and Charles Goldie (1870-1947). Both artists specialised in producing portraits of Maori for European audiences, and both were highly successful. Lindauer, born in Bohemia and trained as a portraitist in Vienna, did numerous paintings of well-known Maori chiefs (sometimes using photographs) as well as of customs such as tattooing. Goldie, New Zealand's self-styled 'old master', was born in Auckland and attended art school there as well as in France. His portraits of elderly Maori with facial tattoos (*moko*) reflect a commonly held, albeit erroneous, belief at the time that the Maori was a dying race.

Auckland Art Gallery Toi o Tamaki

The first two decades of the 20th century saw an exodus of NZ artists to the art schools of Europe. Frances Hodgkins (1869-1947), one of New Zealand's most well-known painters, was among them. She regularly sent work back to New Zealand for exhibition, and many of her sketches and paintings are in the gallery's collection. In the 1930s and 1940s artists searched for a sense of place and local identity. Rita Angus' (1908-70) *Portrait of Betty Curnow* (1942), which is rich in symbolism, is one of the most important works in the history of NZ painting.

The collection also includes works by Colin McCahon (1919-87), considered to be NZ's most important painter, as well as works by contemporary Maori artists, such as Robyn Kahukiwa and Kura Te Rewiri.

Works from the gallery's Mackelvie, Grey and Chartwell collections are also on display. One room, decorated salon-style, contains works from leading European masters Breughel, Millais, Joshua Reynolds and Thomas Gainsborough; another focuses on contemporary painting and sculpture, and includes important works by NZ artists. There is also a good collection of *ukiyo-e* (Japanese woodblock prints) and a small display of European religious art, from medieval to baroque.

The gallery is open daily from 10 am to 5 pm. General admission is free and to special exhibitions it is waived on Mondays. There is a 45 minute guided tour daily at 2 pm (free), and a regular program of talks and lectures – check with the gallery or its Web site (www.akcity.govt.nz/around/places/artgallery) for details.

The New Gallery (☎ 307 4540) is a place for exhibitions and installations of contemporary media and new ideas. At the time of writing there were six different shows. Keep an eye out for the current exhibition in the McCahon Room, a space dedicated to one of New Zealand's most influential artists. The New Gallery is open daily from 10 am to 5 pm; entry is $4 for adults, $2 for children, seniors and students (children under 12 are free). The entry fee is waived on Mondays. There are good cafes in both galleries.

HISTORIC BUILDINGS

Although Auckland has lost a number of its older buildings (many were demolished during the 1980s), there is a growing pressure to preserve those that remain. The gentrification of inner-city suburbs such as Ponsonby, Herne Bay and Parnell has helped save many dwellings now a century old.

In the city centre (Map 3) there is the **ferry building** (1912) on Quay St; the **Bank of New Zealand facade** (1865) in Queen St, made of Tasmanian sandstone and designed by a Melbourne architect in Greek Revival style; and the English baroque-style former **chief post office building** in QEII Square.

The **Old Custom House,** on the corner of Albert and Fanshawe Sts, is a French Renaissance-style building that was spared demolition in the 1970s and is now restored and filled with upmarket shops. The **Civic Theatre** has a wonderful Eastern-fantasy interior with stars in the ceiling, minarets, gilded elephants, and red-eyed lions crouched in alcoves. It recently opened after extensive restoration. The **Auckland Art Gallery** on the corner of Wellesley and Kitchener Sts (1888) is styled in early French Renaissance design.

Former guests of the creeper-covered **Northern Club**, on the corner of Kitchener and Princes Sts, include the Duke and Duchess of Cornwall and York and Anthony Trollope. The nearby **Old Government House** was built in 1856 and, although Auckland lost out to Wellington as the national capital, the building has played host to various visiting royals, including Queen Elizabeth II.

Other significant buildings in the city centre include the wealthy **merchants' houses** in Princes St; the **old synagogue** (1884) on the corner of Princes St and Bowen Ave, now restored and occupied by a bank; the University of Auckland's **old arts faculty** building with its distinctive **clock tower** and the remains of the **Albert Barracks wall** behind it; and the red-bricked, gargoyled **High Court** building on Waterloo Quadrant.

The Auckland City Council (ACC) has a booklet with a map with history on and pictures of these buildings. You can pick up a copy from the visitor centre or from the council's Heritage Division, 10th Floor, 1 Greys Ave, during office hours.

Parnell (Map 4) has a number of historic buildings, many associated with the Church. These include **St Mary's**, now tucked beside the Cathedral of the Holy Trinity (having been moved from across the road in 1982) and **Hulme Court** (1843) on Parnell Rise, a Regency-style building and the oldest Auckland building on its original site. **Selwyn Bishopscourt**, on St Stephens Ave in Parnell, was designed by Frederick Thatcher, who also created beautiful wooden churches for Bishop Selwyn (see the boxed text, 'Selwyn Churches'). Also from this era is the old **Deanery**, on the corner of Brighton Rd and St Stephens Ave, which has recently been restored; it is not open to the public. (The new Auckland Cathedral of Holy Trinity has

free guided tours daily at 11.30 am and 2.30 pm.)

A pamphlet with a walking tour map and background on the various buildings is available from the Department of Conservation (DOC) and from the city council's Heritage Division, details above.

The oldest surviving wooden house in Auckland is **Acacia Cottage** (Map 1) which has been re-located to Cornwall Park at the foot of One Tree Hill. Built in 1841, the cottage was originally where Shortland St is today. The NZ Historic Places Trust has opened the following buildings to the public.

Highwic (Map 5) at 40 Gillies Ave, Epsom, is a fine example of a timber Gothic Revival structure. Built in 1862 by the Bucklands, wealthy colonial landowners, it was named for the Devonshire village of Highweek. It remained in the Buckland family until its acquisition by the Auckland

Selwyn Churches

George Augustus Selwyn was Anglican Bishop of New Zealand from 1842 to 1868. He was a man of action rather than a theologian, whose interest in architecture has given rise to a genre, a Selwyn style. Frederick Thatcher is the architect he appointed to design the churches, beautiful creations in wood characterised by vertical boarding, a steep roof pitch, lancet windows, rose windows over the doorways and a belfry where the four arms of the cross-shaped church meet.

St John's College Chapel at Meadowbank was Thatcher's first architectural undertaking for Selwyn, who in fact considered wood second-best to stone. But stone proved too expensive

and problematic. So wood it was. St John's College served as a sort of workshop for Thatcher's churches; eight were prefabricated here, worked on by European and Maori craftsmen. All Saint's Church in Howick, built in 1847, is one of these. Another beautiful little church, again designed by Thatcher, is St Stephen's Church in Parnell, near Judges Bay (Map 4). Based on the shape of a Greek cross, it vies with All Saints as one of the loveliest in the country. The headstones in its graveyard read like a who's who of prominent Aucklanders of that era.

St Stephen's Church, Parnell

CHRISTINE NIVEN

City Council and the NZ Historic Places Trust in 1978. Bus No 297 or 298 from Wellesely St West near the Civic Centre in the city will get you there.

Alberton (Map 1), at 100 Mt Albert Rd, Mt Albert, started life as an upmarket farmhouse to later become an 18-room mansion. Built in the mid-19th century, it once formed the centrepiece of a large estate and was well-known for balls, musical evenings and hunts. The property stayed in the family until 1972 when it passed into the hands of the NZ Historic Places Trust. The layout of the house illustrates the Victorian class system at work, with basic servant accommodation in the attic, and grand rooms for entertaining in the main part of the house. There's no direct bus here from the city centre, but if you don't mind walking for 10 to 15 minutes along Mt Albert Rd, a No 233 or 243 bus from Victoria St West will get you to Mt Albert Rd.

Ewelme Cottage, at 14 Ayr St, Parnell, was built from kauri in the 1860s for V Lush, the first vicar of Howick. Little altered since its construction, Ewelme House remained in possession of the Lush family until 1968 when it was bought by the Auckland City Council. It's now administered by the NZ Historic Places Trust.

Kinder House (1857) was designed by Bishop Selwyn's favourite architect, Frederick Thatcher, who designed two other buildings in Parnell. It was built from Rangitoto basalt as a dwelling for John Kinder, Anglican minister and first headmaster of Auckland Grammar School. Kinder was a photographer and artist and some of his works are displayed within, along with various other memorabilia relating to his era. The Link bus will bring you close to both Ewelme Cottage and Kinder House.

Highwic, Alberton and Ewelme are open Wednesday to Sunday from 10.30 am to noon and from 1 to 4.30 pm. Entry to Highwic and Alberton is $5 (accompanied children free) and to Ewelme it is $3 (accompanied children free). Kinder House is open Monday to Saturday from 11 am to 3 pm, entry $2.

PARKS & GARDENS

Below are listed the major parks and reserves reasonably close to the city centre. There are of course many, many more, some of which are listed under Activities below as places with walking tracks through native forest.

Albert Park (Map 3)

Albert Park, opposite the University of Auckland, was once the site of a Maori

MARTIN HARRIS

Once a place of high society, Alberton is now under the care of the Historic Places Trust.

kainga (village). In the 19th century it was given over for the Albert Barracks, which catered to the needs of some 900 Imperial troops until their withdrawal in 1870. In the 1880s the Auckland City Council developed it as a park laid out along formal Victorian lines. During WWII air-raid shelters and tunnels were burrowed beneath it – although these are not accessible to the public. Many of the fine, old trees in this park were donated by Governor Grey. The large **floral clock** was created to mark Queen Elizabeth II's 1953 visit. Other reminders of days gone by include the muzzle-loading guns commissioned during the 1897 Russian scare and a meteorological station dating from 1909. The **gatekeeper's cottage** (1882) is now a museum (open daily from 10 am to 5 pm).

Myers Park (Map 3)
Right in the heart of the commercial district, this park is wedged in between Queen St and Greys Ave and extends all the way up to K Rd (stairs take you up to St Kevins Arcade). It's a popular place for lunching office workers.

Symonds St Cemetery (Map 3)
This is one of Auckland's first cemeteries, established in 1842 in what was then a rural outskirt of the township. Today it's at the busy junction of K Rd and Symonds St.

Auckland Regional Parks

The Auckland Regional Council has an extensive network of parks covering some 37,280 hectares. There are farm parks, parks with archaeological sites and historic homesteads, marine reserves and botanic gardens. You may camp at many of these places. For information on the parks, or for campsite bookings, contact Parksline on ☎ 303 1530. The council publishes a free pamphlet called *Natural Masterpieces*, detailing park locations (available from the council and many visitor centres).

Originally there were sections for five denominations: Jewish, Presbyterian, Wesleyan, Anglican and Roman Catholic. The remains of more than 4000 people were exhumed, mainly from the Anglican and Roman Catholic sections, when the Southern Motorway was put through Grafton Gully in the 1960s. They are now marked by two memorials. Much of the native forest was also destroyed when the motorway was cut through. The cemetery is the final resting place of many prominent Aucklanders, including New Zealand's first governor, William Hobson.

Grafton Bridge dominates the eastern end of the cemetery; it was built in 1910 of reinforced concrete and at the time was believed to be the world's longest, concrete single-span bridge.

North Head (Map 6)
One of Auckland's oldest volcanic cones (believed to have erupted more than 50,000 years ago), North Head is a historic reserve and included in the Hauraki Gulf Maritime Park.

Once it served as a Maori pa, known then as Takapuna after the springs that flowed into Torpedo Bay. Because of its sweeping views over the harbour, a pilot station was established here in 1836. In the late 1800s it was fortified when (hard to credit now) there was a real fear of a Russian invasion (a minefield stretched from North Head to Bastion Point). The *pièce de résistance* was the eight-inch **disappearing gun**, state of the art technology at the time – disappearing because, after firing, it recoiled underground for reloading. The Russians never came and the gun was only ever used for practise.

During both world wars North Head was ready for action, and in the 1950s it served as the base for military training. Today its historic sites are looked after by DOC. Pick up DOC's pamphlet *North Head Historic Reserve: Self Guided Walk* ($1) from the DOC outlet at the ferry building. This will help you navigate your way round the site and give you a bit of history on the way.

There is a road up to a car park just before the main magazine. Vehicle gates open daily from 6 am to 6 pm.

Mt Victoria (Map 6)

Mt Victoria is higher than North Head. It provides a great 360° view and has a map pointing out all the landmarks and names of the many islands you can see. You can walk or drive to the summit of Mt Victoria. Vehicle gates are open from 6 am to 6 pm daily.

Western Springs (Map 1)

Located next to zoo, this park is so named because until 1907 its springs supplied all of Auckland's fresh water. There are plenty of waterbirds, attracted by the lake and the surrounding wetlands; children can feed the black swans that live on the lake. There is a good playground, and toilets and a refreshment stand are near the playground.

Auckland Domain (Maps 3 & 5)

This popular 81 hectare park sprawls across one of Auckland's oldest volcanoes. Auckland Museum is perched on top of what's called a tuff ring – the now-consolidated debris that was spewed out during the volcanic eruption. This spot was known to the Maori as Pukekawa, or hill of bitter memories, a reference to bloody tribal battles fought in ancient times.

The playing fields near the Wintergarden occupy the crater, which was a swamp until drained by early European settlers. In the middle of this area is a small scoria cone known to Maori as Pukekaroro, or hill of the black-backed gull. It was once a pa, but is now partly covered in oak trees and topped with a totara tree, planted by Princess Te Puea Herangi in 1940. The tree is surrounded with traditional **Maori carvings** which are enclosed by a palisade. In summer months outdoor concerts (eg Opera under the Stars) are held in the crater, a natural amphitheatre.

The domain is Auckland's oldest park (established in 1845) and one of its most attractive. Pathways meander through the grounds and around the formal gardens, which boast various items of statuary. Near

CHRISTINE NIVEN

The disappearing gun, trained to the south-east

the tea kiosk (built along with the band rotunda for the 1913-14 Auckland Exhibition) is a duck pond fed by freshwater springs which, in 1866, supplied Auckland with its first piped water. The springs were used to raise NZ's first rainbow trout in 1884, and by the Acclimatisation Society to propagate European plants.

The **Wintergarden** consists of a cool house and a tropical house (both established in the 1920s) containing a selection of carefully tended specimens. From November 1 and March 31 it is open Monday to Saturday from 9 am to 5.30 pm, Sunday 9 am to 7.30 pm; from April 1 to October 31 it is open daily from 9 am to 4.30 pm (entry free).

The nearby **Fernz Fernery**, which occupies a disused scoria quarry, has more than a 100 types of fern. It is open daily from 10 am to 4 pm, and on Sundays until 7 pm from December to March (entry free).

Dove-Myer Robinson Park & Parnell Rose Gardens (Map 4)

Named for a former mayor of Auckland, this park is perhaps better known for its rose gardens (entry free). Here you will find some 5000 rose bushes that are at their best between October and April. The park sweeps down to Judges Bay and it's a short walk from here to the **Parnell Baths** and the historic **St Stephen's Chapel**.

The *Gardenview Restaurant* (☎ 377 3619), situated in a fine old building overlooking the harbour and gardens, is open daily for breakfast, lunch and dinner. Bus No 703 from the Downtown Bus Centre ($1.10) will get you to the gardens.

Tamaki Drive & Bastion Point (Map 1)

Tamaki Drive starts at Mechanics Bay and runs parallel to the shore as far east as St Heliers. Along the way are several beaches, Kelly Tarlton's Antarctic Encounter & Underwater World and numerous places to eat and drink.

Bastion Point (accessed from Tamaki Drive between Okahu Bay and Mission Bay) has a commanding position with great views. In 1978 Maori gathered here to stop the proposed development of luxury housing. Helicopters, army vehicles and police encircled the protestors' encampment and there were numerous arrests. The land was never built upon. From the point the land sweeps up to the Maori settlement (you can just make out the carved gables of the meeting house).

Michael Joseph Savage, popular Labour prime minister in the 1930s under whom NZ was transformed into a welfare state, is buried in the vault of the old fort here.

Eden Gardens (Map 5)

This 2.5 hectare garden, nestled at the foot of Mt Eden (Maungawhau), is a tribute to the energy and foresight of a small group of citizens who, in the 1960s, transformed an abandoned scoria quarry into what is now a peaceful retreat. Work began in 1964 when Jack Clark and 15 other garden enthusiasts began clearing truckloads of broken bottles and other refuse from the site, which they then landscaped and planted. They were assisted by many volunteers over the years, and volunteers still keep the gardens going.

Pathways meander through extensive plantings; a **waterfall** and **watergarden** have been established; and a cafeteria has been built. Eden Gardens has something of interest year round, but during July and August the camellias, for which the gardens are renowned, come into full bloom.

The gardens are open daily from 10 am to 4 pm – enter the from Omana Ave, Epsom. Admission costs $4 for adults and $2 for senior citizens (it is free for children accompanied by an adult).

Mt Eden (Map 5)

Named by Governor Hobson for his naval commander George Eden, this 196m scoria cone (the highest in Auckland) affords excellent views. From the trig station near the car park you can view the Waitemata Harbour on one side and the Manukau Harbour on the other. Familiar Auckland landmarks (Skytower, One Tree Hill etc) are also visible.

Known to Maori as Maungawhau, it was once heavily defended and is still pitted with the remains of the ancient defensive earthworks. Bus Nos 274 to 277 from the Downtown Bus Centre will get you here.

Cornwall Park & One Tree Hill Domain (Map 1)

The beautiful Cornwall Park spreads over the lower slopes of One Tree Hill, or to give it its Maori name, Maungakiekie (literally, 'mountain of kiekie', a flax-like plant with edible bracts – *Freycinetia banksii*). There is another, lesser known name for the summit: te Totara i Ahua, a reference to the sacred totara tree that grew there until it was cut down in the mid-19th century. The **solitary pine** that now grows on the summit (planted by John Logan Campbell) is a distinctive landmark – and a survivor. A 1994 attack by a chainsaw-wielding activist to avenge the felling of the original totara failed to kill it off. It's now firmly braced with cables.

Maungakiekie (183m) erupted some 20,000 years ago, and is one of the largest volcanoes in Auckland. It is the most extensively **terraced volcanic cone** in Auckland – more than 170 of these terraces still exist – and was the site of one of NZ's largest pa (it was the stronghold of chief Kiwi Tamaki in the early 18th century, and the head pa of Te Wai o Hua tribes). Its proximity to fertile volcanic soils (the cone still bears the signs of gardens and kumara storage pits), abundant seafood from the Waitemata and Manukau harbours (with convenient portage between the two) made it very attractive and able to support a population of thousands. However, by the late 18th century it had been abandoned.

Maungakiekie was bought from the Maori in 1845 by an Irish merchant, Thomas Henry. One Tree Hill Domain was set aside as a reserve in 1848 by Governor George Grey and the area around it was bought by the company Brown & Campbell in 1853. From 1873 it was owned exclusively by Sir John Logan Campbell, city mayor and a partner in Brown & Campbell, who gifted the park to the people of Auckland in 1901. It was named for the Duke and Duchess of Cornwall, who visited Auckland that year. An **obelisk** was built on the upper summit (*tihi* – to the Maori, the most sacred area) in 1948, damaging some of the ancient earthworks. Campbell's grave is nearby.

The park contains a **working farm** with Perendale sheep, Simmental cattle and chickens, and extensive plantings of native trees (a wonderful sight during summer are the red-blossomed pohutukawa). There are paths for cyclists and joggers, BBQ sites (no bookings), and various sportsgrounds (it's home to the Auckland Archery Club).

There is an information centre at the restored **Huia Lodge** (☎ 630 8485, huialodge@xtra.co.nz), originally built by Campbell as a caretaker's dwelling. It is open daily from 10 am to 4 pm and you can pick up free brochures including *Cornwall Park New Zealand Native Tree Arboretum*, *Maungakiekie Archaeological Trail*, *Cornwall Park Tree Trail*, *Cornwall Park Bird Species*, and *Maungakiekie Volcanic Trail*. Throughout the year there is a program of guided walks; the visitor centre has details. There is also a 15-minute video available to anyone interested.

Across the road is **Acacia Cottage** (opening hours as above; entry free) which was built by Campbell in 1841 near Shortland St, in the city centre, and which was moved to its present site in 1920. Sir John himself

CHRISTINE NIVEN

The lone pine on One Tree Hill (Maungakiekie)

referred to the place as 'comfortless and dreary' and in its restored state it gives some indication of how basic life was for settlers in mid-19th century Auckland.

The pleasant Cornwall Park Garden Cafe (open Monday to Friday from 9.30 am to 4 pm and weekends 9 am to 4 pm) serves snacks and meals and is also licensed. You can buy ice creams and snacks around the corner from the cafe.

Star-gazers should head to the **Stardome Planetarium** (Map 1) on Manukau Rd, on the south side of One Tree Hill (see Other Attractions below).

The main gates to Cornwall Park off Greenlane Rd close at dusk. But the summit and the observatory can be reached from the southern entrance via Manukau Rd.

Auckland Regional Council Botanic Gardens (Map 1)

More than 10,000 different plants can be found in this 64 hectare expanse of garden, which was established in 1974 and officially opened in 1982. Since 1997 the Ellerslie Flower Show, the country's most important horticultural fair, has been held here annually in mid-November. There is a visitor centre (☎ 267 1457, fax 266 3698, rprice@arc .govt .nz), which is open weekdays from 9 am to 5 pm and weekends 10 am to 4 pm, and a cafe, open from 8.30 am to 4.30 pm. The gardens themselves are open daily from 8 am till dusk. Guides are available for groups Monday to Friday. The gardens are well signposted and the plants labelled, so there is really no problem navigating your way around alone.

If you are coming by car from Auckland take the Southern Motorway and turn off at Manurewa. Turn left at Hill Rd; the entrance to the gardens is on your left. Buses leave from the Downtown Bus Centre every half hour (catch a Papakura, Pukekohe or Drury bus). Get off at Great South Rd, Manurewa, just before Hill Rd, and walk east along Hill Rd (20 minutes approximately) to the entrance on your left.

Ambury Park (Map 1)

This is one of the Auckland regional parks and is a **working farm** right on the city's doorstep. The park is about 15km south of Auckland city, near the airport, on the shores of the Manukau Harbour. Take the South-Western Motorway from the city towards the airport and turn off at Mangere Bridge; the farm is signposted from there. The main entrance is at the end of Kiwi Esplanade. There are sheep, cows, horses, goats, chickens, peacocks, turkeys and kune kune pigs. Some 86 species of birds live on the foreshore including pied stilts, welcome swallows, and oyster-catchers. It's also a favourite wintering ground for migrant birds. You can wander freely around the farm (remember to close the gates) and there's no entry charge.

A detour across Wallace Rd takes you to **Mangere Mountain**, a volcanic cone created some 18,000 years ago and the site of one of Auckland's largest Maori pa (the remains of kumara pits can still be seen). You can take a horseback tour through the park ($25 for one hour, $45 for two hours; contact Ride the Parks ☎ 0800 743 384). Auckland Regional Council puts out a guide to Ambury

Park which is available from visitor centres. There is an unstaffed information centre at the entrance to the park itself.

OTHER ATTRACTIONS
Auckland Zoo (Map 1)

The beautifully landscaped Auckland Zoo is close to MOTAT, with travel between the two made easy by an electric tram running every 20 minutes on weekdays and 10 to 20 minutes on weekends and holidays (adults $1 one way, $2 return; children half that).

An ongoing renovation program has seen the animals' concrete cages replaced by naturalistic surroundings, and the viewing possibilities have been made much more interes- ting for visitors. There is a nocturnal compound for the tuataras and kiwis and an enclosure (**Pridelands**) for the African animals: lions, hippos (eye-to-eye viewing as they wallow in the pond), zebras, giraffes and gazelles. (For something a little different, try out the **talking termite** when you reach its mound.)

The McDonald's **rainforest** section is very popular (you can get surprisingly close to the primates – or is it the other way around?), and it has an impressive array of tarantulas (safely glassed off). The rainforest Web site is at www.zoorainforest.co.nz. A favourite with children is the meerkat enclosure. Tunnels beneath the enclosure give access to plastic domes from which you get a ground-level, eye-to-eye view of these very busy and very cute little desert dwellers.

There is also a good cafe, and near to this is a children's playground with lots of interesting things to explore.

The animals are fed at various times during the day; on entry you receive a pamphlet with a map of the zoo and the feeding times. The zoo is open daily from 9.30 am to 5.30 pm (last admission 4.15 pm). Entry is $12 adults, $7 children aged five to 15 (under five free), $8 senior citizens and $9 students (there are various concessions for families). At the visitor centre, just inside the entrance, you can arrange a guided minicart tour ($10 for an hour; tours run between 10 am and 2 pm daily).

Kelly Tarlton's Antarctic Encounter & Underwater World (Map 1)

If you want to see real penguins waddling about on real snow, then Kelly Tarlton's – right on the waterfront (23 Tamaki Drive) – is the place to come. Your trip to Antarctica begins with **Scott's hut** at Cape Evans, which has been faithfully recreated – you even get a whiff of seal blubber-fuelled lanterns. The spirit of the era has been captured wonderfully with various displays (including a working pianola and a film of **Shackleton's expedition**). A drawcard is the ride in special carriages past the penguins. You can wander through an excellent interactive display and learn about scientific research in the Antarctica and about the animals and plants that live here. This section opens into an area with a souvenir shop and several tanks with various interesting specimens, including giant eels. A moving walkway (which you can step off if you want) will take you through perspex tunnels through which you can get a diver's view of **marine life**; this will probably be as close as you're ever likely to get (or want to get) to stingrays and sharks. The sharks and stingrays as well as the penguins are hand-fed periodically during the day; check the times by phoning ☎ 528 0603.

The cafeteria attached to Kelly Tarlton's is across the road, on the water's edge; you can enter via an underground tunnel leading from the souvenir shop area. Free parking is available until 9.30 pm from November through March, and until 7 pm from April through October. Entry is $20 for adults, $10 for children aged five to 12, $6 for four year olds (under fours free) and $16 for seniors and students (13 years and over). There are also family concessions. Kelly Tarlton's is open daily from 9 am to 9 pm from November through March and from 9 am to 6 pm from April through October (from 10 am to 5 pm Christmas Day). The last entry is one hour before closing time.

Kelly Tarlton, the person behind the eponymous attraction, was himself a local diver and salvage expert. His vision was to create an environment in which non-divers could experience the underwater world he found so fascinating. He pioneered the use of the clear plastic tunnels to allow for this. Kelly Tarlton's opened in 1985, but sadly Tarlton himself died of a heart attack at the age of 47 only weeks after.

Victoria Park Market (Map 3)

Victoria Park Market (information hotline ☎ 309 6911) is at the western end of Victoria St West, opposite a park and playing fields. The market is overshadowed by a 38m-high **brick chimney**, which was once part of a giant incinerator used to dispose of Auckland's refuse. The depot was closed in 1972 and the buildings restored. Victoria Park Market is a good place to come for handicrafts, inexpensive clothes, ceramics, woollen items and food. On weekends extra stalls spill out into the adjacent car park.

The market is open daily from 9 am to 6 pm, and you'll find its Web site at www .victoria-park-market.co.nz. The Link bus goes past the market.

Skytower (Map 3)

The imposing Skytower on the corner of Federal and Victoria Sts is part of the Sky City complex (with a 24-hour casino, revolving restaurant, cafes and bars). It is NZ's tallest structure at 328m, and higher than the Eiffel Tower. A lift takes you from the ground up to the **observation decks** in 40 seconds and in a 200km/h wind the top of the building sways up to 1m.

From the preliminary observation levels you can see ant-like humans scurrying around the inner-city. For techno-junkies, there are all sorts of interactive displays, audio guides, powerful binoculars and weather monitors. You can catch the Skyway lift to the top, which costs $15 for adults, $7.50 for children five to 14 years (it's $3 extra to go to the ultimate viewing level; the spectacular views over the city and harbour are well worth the extra cost). The cost of the ticket is waived if you spend a minimum of $25.50 at the Orbit restaurant ($15-plus for kids).

Lion Breweries (Map 5)

Lion Breweries (☎ 377 8840) is NZ's largest multinational brewery and gives free tours of the plant at 368 Khyber Pass Rd in Newmarket. See the process, guzzle a 'Steinie' and try other popular commercial beers. Tours of about 1½ hours are held on request at 10.30 am and 2 pm on Tuesdays, Wednesdays and Thursdays. Bookings are essential.

Rainbow's End (Map 1)

The country's largest theme park, Rainbow's End, is on the Great South Rd (corner of Wiri Station Rd) at Manukau. There is a log flume and rollercoaster, as well as go karts, flight simulators and so on. It's open daily from 10 am to 5 pm. Super-passes offer unlimited rides all day (adults $30, children four to 13 $20); otherwise a $15 entry buys three rides. For details call the 24-hour information line on ☎ 262 2044 or visit the Web site at www.rainbowsend .co.nz. Bus Nos 454-57 and 487-497 from the Downtown Bus Centre will get you there (adults $4.50, children $2.70).

Stardome & the Auckland Observatory

This is the place to learn more about the southern sky. There is a changing program that includes a **laser light display**, occasional music performances under the stars and a special show for pre-schoolers. Weather permitting, there are large-telescope (50cm) viewing sessions on Wednesday, Thursday and Saturday (1½ hours) after the 7.30 and 8.30 pm Stardome shows (adults $3 with a Stardome ticket, $5 without; children under 15 $2/3). Bookings are advisable for Stardome shows (☎ 624 1246).

Admission for adults is $10, for children three to 15 years $5, seniors and students $8, and family concessions are also available. Some shows have translations in Japanese, German and Mandarin (headsets $2). To find out sessions times phone ☎ 625 6945. The Web site is at www.stardome.org.au. The Stardome is situated on the lower slopes of One Tree Hill. Bus Nos 302, 305 and 312

will take you from downtown via Newmarket to the gate of the park.

Maori Cultural Tours

Maori Heritage Tours (☎/fax 278 0932) offers a view of Auckland through indigenous eyes. Among other things, tours include a marae visit, art viewing, a cultural performance and a hangi. Bookings are essential as minimum numbers apply.

ACTIVITIES
Swimming

Auckland has many beaches within easy reach of the downtown area. They include Okahu Bay, Mission Bay, Kohimarama Beach and St Heliers Bay, which are along Tamaki Drive (Map 1; bus No 725 or 769 from the Downtown Bus Centre); Northshore's Cheltenham Beach (Map 6; walking distance from Devonport) and Takapuna Beach (Map 1; bus Nos 80x and 90x from Victoria St); and the East Coast Bays beaches (Map 1; bus No 839 or 858 from Victoria St for Long Bay). These beaches tend to be best at high tide. Further afield are the good surf beaches of the west coast (Map 8) – Karekare, Piha, Te Henga, Anawhata. Entry to all is unrestricted.

There are also numerous public swimming pools in Auckland. Some are only open in summer only.

The Tepid Baths The Tepid Baths (Map 3; ☎ 379 4794, 100 Customs St), in downtown Auckland, were built in 1914, and until 1974 were filled with salt water from the Viaduct Basin. In the mid-1980s they were modernised, a gym added and the sauna and steam baths renovated. There are two pools: a 25m pool, which is used for lap swimming, and an 18m pool. The baths are open weekdays from 6 am to 9 pm and on weekends and public holidays from 7 am to 7 pm. Entry is $4.50 for adults, $3.50 for students and $2 for seniors and children. Concessions are available for 10 swims.

Olympic Pool & Fitness Centre The Olympic Pool (Map 5; ☎ 522 4414, Broadway), in Newmarket, was built in 1940 for the 1950 Empire Games. Once an open-air pool, it has been converted into an indoor complex with a fitness centre. The main pool (50m) is primarily used for lap swimming; a smaller 15m pool is used for instruction and recreation. There is also a spa as well as a sauna and steam rooms. The complex is open Monday to Friday from 6 am to 10 pm and weekends and public holidays 7 am to 8 pm. A swim, spa and sauna costs $4.50 for adults, $2 for children and seniors, and $3.50 for a students. Adult entry to the fitness centre is $12 and an aerobics session costs $10. Concessions are available for 10 visits or more. Goggles, towels, kickboards and aquajoggers can be rented ($2).

Parnell Baths The Parnell Baths (Map 4; ☎ 373 3561), next to Judges Bay in Parnell, comprise a 60m saltwater, open-air pool and smaller one beside it. There is a water slide at the main pool, and rafts in the shallower pool. The baths are open in summer months – Monday to Friday from 6 am to 8 pm and weekends and public holidays 8 am to 8 pm.

Point Erin Pool This open-air pool (Map 2; ☎ 376 6863), on the corner of Shelley Beach Rd and Sarsfield St, Herne Bay, has great views of the Waitemata Harbour. Additional facilities include a BBQ area and basketball and volleyball courts. It's open during the summer months – Monday to Friday from 6.30 am to 8 pm and weekends and public holidays 10 am to 8 pm.

Philips Aquatic Centre This popular indoor complex (Map 1; ☎ 815 7005), on Alberton Ave, Mt Albert, has a 25m competition pool as well as a wave pool, a rapid-river ride and a hydro slide. It's open weekdays from 6 am to 9 pm and weekends 7 am to 8 pm. Entry is $7 for adults and $5 for children.

Cruising & Sailing
One of the best ways to appreciate the City of Sails is to take to the water.

Fullers Auckland (Map 3; ☎ 367 9111) has the largest selection of cruises and op-

erates almost all the ferries. The cheapest option is the 12-minute ferry ride to picturesque Devonport. Ferries also go to many of the nearby islands in the gulf. Rangitoto and Waiheke islands are easy to reach and make good full or half-day trips from Auckland. Pacific Ferries (☎ 303 1741) also has trips to Waiheke (see the Excursions chapter for details).

Fullers also has popular tours around the inner-harbour, including a two hour coffee cruise stopping at Devonport, Rangitoto and Kelly Tarlton's (adults/children $20/10; departs Auckland daily at 9.30 am, 11.45 am, 2 pm and, in summer, 4 pm). Fullers' Devonport Explorer tour takes two hours and includes a coach tour of Devonport ($22/11; departs daily at 10 am, noon and 1, 2 and 3 pm). The Devonport Explorer Lunch & Tour is the same as the Explorer Tour but with lunch at McHughs in Devonport ($40/30; departs daily at noon and 1 pm). The Devonport Explorer Harbour Lights Dinner & Tour takes three hours and includes a coach tour of Devonport and a three-course dinner at the Watermark Restaurant in Devonport ($55/35; departs daily at 6 pm).

Pride of Auckland (Map 3; ☎ 373 4557, fax 377 0459, pride.of.akl@xtra.co.nz), which is based at the NZ National Maritime Museum (Map 3), operates a fleet of four monohulls and a catamaran, all with distinctive blue and white sails. Cruises include Experience Sailing, about 50 minutes on the inner-harbour (adults/children $40/25; departs 11 am); the Coffee Cruise, about 90 minutes sailing ($50/28; departs 1 pm); Sailing the New Zealand Way, 1½ hours and includes lunch ($60/30; departs 1 pm); and Dining Afloat, 2½ hours and includes dinner ($85/50; departs 7 pm). Charters can also be arranged.

The NZ National Maritime Museum (Map 3; ☎ 373 0800) has a sailing scow the *Ted Ashby*, which departs daily at noon for luncheon and harbour cruises (see Museums & Galleries above for details).

For one of the best experiences on the water take a trip on the tall ship *Soren Larsen*, a square-rigged, 19th-century brigantine beauty with 12 sails. The *Soren Larsen* was built from oak in Nykøbing Mors in Denmark and achieved fame as the star of the TV series *The Onedin Line*. It returned to NZ and the Pacific in October 1994 after a circumnavigation of the globe. Over summer there are three-hour coffee cruises departing most Saturdays at 1 pm, and six-hour harbour daysails most Sundays departing at 10 am. For details contact ☎ 411 8755 (sorenlarsen@ voyager.co.nz); the Web site is at www .squaresail.q.co.nz.

Plenty of other companies offer cruises and sailing ships. Caprice Yacht Charters (☎ 0800 804 835), charters a catamaran for day cruises at $75 per person (English, Dutch and German spoken). Charterlink (☎ 445 7114, charter@charterlink.co.nz) has a fleet of vessels including catamarans; the Web site is at www.charterlink.co.nz. Most charter companies offer skippered, crewed and skippered, or bareboat (you skipper yourself) charters, as well as instruction. Fishing charters are also available. Penny Whiting Sailing (☎ 376 1322) has well-run courses for those who want to learn to sail.

Sea Kayaking

Fergs Kayaks (Map 1, ☎/fax 529 2230, 12 Tamaki Drive), at Okahu Bay, hire out a variety of kayaks from $7 to $15 an hour ($30 to $60 a half day and longer hires possible). Lessons are available, but complete novices can paddle along near the shore. You can also undertake more ambitious (guided) trips with Fergs Kayaks to Rangitoto ($50 per night trip or $55 per day trip), Browns Island ($55) or Devonport/North Head ($42 overnight). Combinations of these are also possible. There is a family trip out to Puhoi and Wenderholm as well.

Auckland Wilderness Kayaking (☎ 630 7782, fax 630 7768) has half and full-day tours out to the gulf islands, an overnight trip to Mahurangi Regional Park (Map 7) north of Auckland – where there are **sea caves**, a **shipwreck**, **phosphorescence** – and night kayaking excursions. Prices start at about $50 for half-day tours. The Web site is at www.nzkayak.co.nz.

There are numerous kayaking opportunities from Waiheke and Great Barrier, as well as from Puhoi north of Auckland. See the Excursions chapter for details.

Windsurfing

In summer windsurfing boards can be hired near the car park at Mission Bay, and at other spots along Tamaki Drive.

Surfing

For good surf less than 50km from the city, try Te Henga (Bethells Beach) on the west coast where the water is often very rough. You should also check out Piha, Karekare, Muriwai and Whatipu. Most of the surfing beaches have surf clubs and lifeguards. Farther afield, but possible as day trips, Raglan on the west coast and Tawharanui and Pakiri on the east coast near Warkworth, have some of NZ's best waves.

The *Yellow Pages* ('Surfboards & Accessories') lists places to buy and trade gear. You can find out the conditions on 'Auckland's Surf Report' (☎ 0900 47873), the 'West Coast Surf Report' (☎ 0900 95951) or 'Wave Track Surf Report' (☎ 0900 99777) – these information lines cost about $1.20 a minute. Radio bFB has a surf report at 9.30 am on Saturday.

Jet Skiing

Jet Ski Tours (☎/fax 486 0880, ernsthansen@ hotmail.com) offers two-hour, guided spins around the harbour. You'll go under the harbour bridge, past the **America's Cup Village** (Map 3), Rangitoto Island and the North Shore beaches ($100 per person).

Diving

Most dives start at Leigh (Map 7), near Warkworth, north of Auckland – eg for dives at the Hen & Chicken Islands or Mokohinau Islands – and Tairua on the east coast of Coromandel Peninsula. If you are doing a day trip from Auckland allow for the travelling time to and from these places. The starting point for dives at the Poor Knights Islands (one of the world's top diving experiences) is Tutukaka, which is about 20 minutes north of Whangarei. Trips closer to Auckland include Goat Island and Little Barrier Island. The visitor centre has a list of dive operators, although they are also listed in the *Yellow Pages*.

Walking

Heritage Walks In suburbs such as Ponsonby, Grafton and Parnell you can still view the vestiges of the city's Victorian and Edwardian past. There are also some notable 19th century structures in the downtown area.

The Auckland City Council has recently put out two heritage trail booklets for the downtown/waterfront area and the CBD (Map 3). The **CBD trail** starts at the ferry building and goes down Queen St via Vulcan Lane and Shortland St to the university and back. The booklets are available from the visitor centre and from the ACC's Heritage Division (☎ 379 2020, 10th Floor, 1 Greys Ave).

Parnell Heritage Historic Places Map covers 50 sites that includes historic buildings and local parks. Allow about two to 2½ hours for this walk. Another inner-city walk is the **Historic Ponsonby Heritage Walk**, which starts at Victoria Park (Map 3) and wends its way round Ponsonby (Map 2), taking in 28 sites. The pamphlet which details the walk has a map and a snippets of local history on each place. Both pamphlets are available from the visitor centre and the ACC.

Grafton (Map 5) is another old inner-city suburb where the remnants of its Victorian and Edwardian past remain. The walk starts at the Auckland Domain grandstand, passes the Parkside Backpackers Inn (which dates from 1910) and loops around Grafton Rd, then back down Khyber Pass Rd to the starting point. It's detailed in the pamphlet *Grafton Heritage Walk*, available from the visitor centre or the ACC.

Devonport (Map 6) has its share of historic places with the added attraction of North Head and Mt Victoria. Pick up a copy of *The Old Devonport Walk* from the Devonport Information Centre. The walk takes about an hour and covers 21 sites. It starts

Auckland's historic ferry building

DAVID WALL

at the wharf, goes along King Edward Parade on the waterfront, and loops around Albert Rd back to Victoria Rd and the wharf. DOC puts out the pamphlet *North Head Historic Reserve Self Guided Walk*, which details 16 places of interest and much about the mountain's military and strategic value ($1 from DOC's ferry building shop).

See also the Historic Buildings section earlier in this chapter.

Bush & Beach Walks (Map 1) The ACC (☎ 379 2020) publishes a pamphlet entitled *A Walker's Guide to Tahuna-Torea Nature Reserve, Kepa Bush Reserve, Point to Point Walk*.

The **point-to-point trail** starts at Cliff Rd, at the eastern end of St Heliers Bay and continues to Point England, 8.7km away (about three hours one way). En route you will pass Ladies Bay (named for the wife of Governor George Grey), Achilles Point (named for the

NZ navy ship that fought the German cruiser *Graf Spee* in the 1939 Battle of River Plate), parks and reserves, and Karaka Bay (the place where local Maori signed the Treaty of Waitangi).

The **Kepa Bush Reserve** starts between Nos 251 and 253 Kepa Rd, Kohimaramara, and continues to Purewa Creek. The walk takes about 45 minutes to complete.

The **Tahuna-Torea Nature Reserve** is a 25 hectare wilderness on the Tamaki Estuary. Its mangroves and swamps provide a haven for many birds, including the migrant godwits.

The **Waiatarua Reserve**, behind the Remuera Golf Course (enter from Grand Drive, St Johns, near the intersection with Abbots Way), is a wetland area where farm stock wander freely, and which you can explore along boardwalks and paths. There is some parking at the reserve's entrance, as well as public toilets and a playground (entry free). Bus No 635 from the Downtown Bus Centre will take you to Grand Drive.

South of Auckland there are two good places for a stroll. **Awaroa Walkway** in the south-east takes you from Shelly Park to Musick Point, passing Cockle Bay, Howick Beach, Mellons Bay and Eastern Beach on the way. Pamphlets on the walk are available from the Manukau City Council (☎ 263 7100) and the Howick Historical Village (see Museums & Galleries above).

Murphys Bush (4km from the Southern Motorway turn-off to Manukau city; enter from Murphys Rd) is a good, flat bushwalk through regenerating kahikatea forest. There are various paths; the one from the car park on Murphys Rd is suitable for wheelchairs. There are picnic tables and toilets – and an ostrich farm and a worm farm across the road from the main entrance.

The **Coast to Coast Walkway** follows a trail between the Waitemata and Manukau harbours. The four hour walk encompasses Albert Park, the university, Auckland Domain, Mt Eden, One Tree Hill and other sites, keeping as much as possible to reserves rather than city streets.

North Shore City's Parks Department (☎ 486 8400) has put out a series of informative pamphlets on the area's reserves, all of which have walking tracks through native bush. (They are available from the Devonport Information Centre). Some tracks, such as Le Roys Bush and Kauri Glen & Cecil Eady Bush, can be reached by taking the Birkenhead ferry from the city to Birkenhead wharf; from there it is a short walk. Rideline (☎ 366 6400) can advise on buses that pass near the following walks.

Entry to **Awaruku Bush** is via Awaruku Rd, Torbay. The track takes you past a variety of native flora (there are 90 numbered stakes), including orchids, ferns, flax, pohutukawa, nikau, gold totara, rimu and more.

You get to **Centennial Park** from Beach Rd or Rae Rd, Campbells Bay. Kauri forest once covered this area, although the extent can only be judged by the remnants of kauri gum found in the remains of gum diggers' huts. It's been extensively planted with native flora; the pohutukawa along the park's southern border were planted in WWII by servicemen shortly before they departed for war.

Eskdale Park is a regenerating forest, with matai and mature rimu. You enter the park from Lauderdale Rd, Glenfield.

There is a short bushwalk at **Fernglen Native Plant Gardens** that will take you from the fern collection to a steam-side bank where you may see glow worms. You can continue on to Kauri Park from here. Enter from Kauri Rd, Birkenhead; it's open from 9 am to 4 pm daily.

Access to **Kauri Park** is from Rangatira Rd, Birkenhead. There is a walking track that takes about 1½ hours to complete and that will take you past stands of kauri, puriri and kahikatea. The park's rich plant life attracts many native birds.

You can reach **Kauri Glen & Cecil Eady Bush** from Kauri Glen Rd, Northcote. The Cecil Eady Bush walk takes about an hour to complete and the Kauri Glen walk about 1½ hours. Although this area was once logged, a few kauri, possibly as old as 300 years, remain.

The shingled tracks at **Kauri Point Centennial Park** will take you down to Kendall Bay; other tracks will allow you to loop

Public art in Albert Park

Double vision: St Mary's in timber and in glass

The stunning Wintergarden in the Auckland Domain

Detail of One Tree Hill obelisk honouring the Maori

Magnificent Kauri north of Auckland

back to **Chatswood Reserve**. Here you'll see what's left of the beech and kauri forest that once covered the area– the oldest remaining kauri are around 400 years old. Access to the park is via Onetaunga Rd, Birkenhead.

To reach **Le Roy's Bush** you enter from Onewa Rd, Birkenhead. Here you'll find plenty of native flora including kauri, totara, puriri, nikau and many other kinds of fern. The walking track takes about one hour return and will take you to Little Shoal Bay. Nearby, there is a BBQ area and a swimming beach.

Smith's Bush can be accessed from **Onewa Domain**, which is on Northcote Rd. Unusually, this area has no kauri but plenty of puriri. There is a short nature trail which loops around a stand of these trees.

The North Shore also has three coastal walks for which there are pamphlets: *Long Bay – Coastal Walk*, the *Two Foot Tour – East Coast Bays* and the *Devonport Coastal Walks*. The **Long Bay walk** starts at Milford Beach and finishes at Takapuna Beach; allow 1½ hours at an easy pace. The **two-foot walk** goes from Campbells Bay to Tororoa Point and can be done in a couple of hours.

The pamphlet *Auckland Walkways* details 14 walkways that are part of the NZ Walkways System, a network that covers the entire country. Some of these are on the gulf islands, others are in the greater Auckland region. You can get this pamphlet from the DOC outlet at the ferry building.

There are endless possibilities for walks in the Waitakere Ranges and along the west coast beaches. Tracks range from dead easy to very demanding (see the Excursions chapter for more information).

Free pamphlets on all the above walks are generally available from visitor centres, but you can also get them from the relevant city councils and from DOC.

Art & Craft Trails The art trails really need to be done by car, and there are possibilities for detours to nearby parkland. Pick up the *Harbourside Art Trail* map from the Devonport Information Centre. It marks eight

Listen for the extraordinary song of the Tui

studios and workshops that can be visited in Birkenhead and Northcote, and gives their contact details and opening times. The map also incorporates many of the parks mentioned above, so you could bring a picnic and make a day of this.

Art Out West is a glossy map that shows you how to get around the workshops and studios of Titirangi and the Waitakeres (see West of the City Centre in the Excursions chapter for details). The map is available from the DOC outlet at the ferry building and from the visitor centre.

Jogging
The ACC (☎ 379 2020) puts out a pamphlet called *Inner City Jogging* which details jogs ranging from 5km to 30km. You can get a copy of this from the council or the visitor centre. An easy and popular route from the city is along Quay St to Tamaki Drive and from there to St Heliers Bay (about 7km one way).

Inline Skating
This is very popular along Tamaki Drive; there is a cyclists path which skaters may use. Inline skates can be hired from Fergs Kayaks (☎/fax 529 2230, 12 Tamaki Drive). Prices start at $10 for an hour ($5 for each hour thereafter; pads $1 per item). There is usually a mobile van hiring out inline skates at Mission Bay during summer.

Rock Climbing

The Rocknasium (☎ 630 5522, 610 Dominion Rd, Balmoral) is an indoor rock climbing venue open daily from 10 am to 10 pm (unitl midnight on Wednesday). It has 600sq metres of rock climbing surface, more than 15m of vertical height and over 35 separate lines of roped routes. Gear (carabiners, shoes, chalk bags, harnesses etc) is available for hire, and instruction is on offer. Daily rates (no time limits) are $14 for adults and $10 for children (under 16). Bus Nos 25x and 26x, departing from near the Civic Centre in Queen St, will take you along Dominion Rd.

There is another indoor climbing wall at the Birkenhead Leisure Centre (☎ 418 4109, Mahara Rd) on the North Shore. It's open daily from 10 am to 10 pm. There's a good lead climb and a variety of challenges for experienced climbers, as well as instruction. Entry is $10, a harness is $3 and other gear (chalk bags etc) is also available for hire. Bus Nos 973 and 974 from Victoria St West (between Federal and Albert Sts) in the city centre will take you to the Highbury Shops in Birkenhead, within walking distance of the centre.

Urban Rap Jumping

For the most exhilarating view of Auckland's skyline, rap jump (face down abseil) from the top of the Novotel Hotel on QEII Square. The crowd below samples your fear, especially when you're dropped six storeys in a spread-eagled free fall – you can actually hear their gasps. You can even see your folly reflected in nearby skyscrapers.

The cost is $50 for a single jump. It's best to do three jumps for $75 – this will give you an initial heart starter, a second spinning jump, and a third where you free fall, spin and go 'hog wild'. Phone Absolute Adrenalin Adventures (☎ 483 8553) to book. (At the time of writing Adrenalin Adventures were not operating but there were plans to resume in November or December 1999).

Bungy Jumping

The 'extreme air bungy' (Sky Screamer) on Quay St, near the former Oriental Markets, is a carriage that's suspended on a bungy line; the ride can reach 200km/h in two seconds. It costs $30 (there's a minimum height requirement of 1.1m). The ride's open from 11 am to 10 pm daily (later on weekends).

Abseiling

Cliffhanger Tours (☎ 021 661 851 mobile) takes abseiling trips to several locations in and around Auckland. A half-day abseil at Mt Eden quarry costs $65 per person; at the world's highest tourist abseil (110m), located in the Waitakere Ranges, it costs $145 for one abseil and $162 for two. The company will pick-up in the inner city and all gear is provided.

Canyoning

Canyonz (☎/fax 534 1468, canyonz@xtra .co.nz) takes trips into the Waitakeres (Map 8) where, suitably wetsuited, helmeted and harnessed, you get to slide, leap and abseil down a gorge, negotiating waterfalls, streams and pools. It's an adrenalin rush and a lot of fun. Trips last a full day, with everything (including food and city pick-up/drop-off) included in the price of $125 (one to three people), $115 (four to six people) or $109 (seven or more). French, German and Spanish are spoken. The season runs from the beginning of October to the end of May.

Awol Adventures (☎ 630 7100, awoladv@ talk.co.nz) also takes canyoning trips out at the west coast. Trips start at the top of the canyon, near a kauri logging dam built in 1911. It costs $125 per person; lunch and drinks included.

Horse Riding

The closest place to the inner-city area is at Ambury Park (Map 1) in south Auckland (contact Ride the Parks ☎ 0800 743 384; see under Parks & Gardens above).

There is also riding on Waiheke and at Waiwera (see the Excursions chapter for details).

Cycling

You can hire a mountain bike and explore the city yourself (see the Getting Around and the Excursions chapters). Auckland Adventures (☎ 379 4545) has a full day mountain bike adventure trip that takes you across farmland and Muriwai Beach on the west coast (Map 8). It costs $75 or $55 if you bring your own bike.

The Little Adventure Company (☎ 445 1451) organises bicycle tours of Devonport that combine scenic stops with a bit of history. They cost $20 per person and last one to two hours.

Beyond the Road (☎ 0800 245 386) takes bike tours to Woodhill Forest and Riverhead north of Auckland (free pick-up in the city) for $55 with bike hire included.

Go Karting

Indoor Karting Parnell (☎ 358 1232) has a Go Kart course on the corner of The Strand and Ronayne St, not far from the Auckland Station. It's open Sunday to Thursday from noon to 9 pm and Friday and Saturday noon to 10 or 11 pm. Ten minutes costs $15 and half an hour $30. There is a $5 discount for students with ID.

There is another place called Extreme Indoor Superkarts and Dirt Bugs (☎ 273 5552) at 82 Kerwyn Ave East Tamaki. It's open Monday to Friday from noon to 10 pm and weekends 10 am to 10 pm. Ten minutes on either the dirt or regular track costs $15.

Tennis

There are courts open to the public at the ASB Tennis Centre (☎ 373 3623, 72 Stanley St). Outdoor courts cost $8 per person per hour (singles) or $6 per person per hour (doubles). Indoor courts cost $10 per person per hour. The courts are available daily until about 11 pm. You must have your own racquet; there is a pro shop at the centre.

Golf

Auckland has more than 30 golf courses. For a full listing, refer to Tourism Auckland's Web site at www.aucklandnz.com/go. You should book ahead if you wish to play. If you are not affiliated to a NZ club, you will pay rather more. Golf Plus Tours (☎ 0800 487 225) arranges trips to courses

in and around Auckland, and organises clubs, green fees and so on.

In addition to the courses listed below, there are several mini-golf courses. The nearest to the city centre is Lilliput Mini Golf (☎ 524 4096, 3 Tamaki Drive) on the waterfront. It's open from 10 am to 9.30 pm daily; adults $7, children $4. Nevada Bob's Golf (☎ 526 0056) is a popular nine-hole course at 69-71 Ballarat St, Ellerslie. It's open daily and costs $10 to play on weekends and $8 during the week. Half-sets of clubs can be hired for $5.

Formosa This world-class course, designed by Bob Charles, is at Beachlands, south-east of the city (☎ 536 5895, 110 Jack Lachlan Drive). It costs $100 to play if you are not affiliated to a club in NZ, although on Mondays and Tuesdays there is a special rate of $35. Affiliated players pay $55 Wednesday to Sunday. The fee includes a cart; a set of clubs can be hired for $35. Facilities include a bar, restaurant, accommodation and a full sporting complex, complete with swimming pool and tennis and squash courts.

Whitford Park Country Club This club is on Whitford Park Rd, Whitford, in south Auckland (☎ 530 8823). It costs $30 to play a round of 18 holes, $20 to hire a set of clubs and $25 to hire a cart.

Manukau Golf Club This course is south of Auckland, at 333 Great South Rd, Manurewa (☎ 266 8297). It costs $60 to play 18 holes if you're not affiliated to a NZ club. A set of golf clubs costs $25 and a cart $20.

Gulf Harbour Country Club This north of Auckland course was the site of the World Cup Golf championships in 1998. You can play 18 holes for $65 (Monday to Friday) or $75 (weekends and public holidays), with a cart included in the price. You can hire a standard set of golf clubs for $25 and an executive set for $45, and there is a pro shop.

Gulf Harbour is on the Whangaparaoa Peninsula, some 50km north of Auckland city. You can either drive or take the ferry (contact Gulf Harbour Ferries ☎ 0800 424 5561). It's a little too far to walk from the ferry landing, but you can arrange in advance to be picked up.

Chamberlain Park Public Golf Course

It costs $18 to play a round of 18 holes on this popular public course at 46a Linwood Ave, Western Springs (☎ 846 6758). Carts can be hired for $30 for a full round, and clubs for $15 a half set or $35 a full set.

Waitemata Golf Club

This course at 15 Derby St is very handy if you are staying in Devonport. You can play 18 holes for $30 or nine for $15 as a casual player – $25/12.50 if you are affiliated with another NZ golf club. Equipment can be hired from the pro shop: $15 for a half set of clubs or $25 for a full set (half these prices for nine holes). Carts cost $13 to rent. The best times to play (ie, non-club days) are Monday, Thursday and Friday, or Saturday and Sunday afternoons. Book at least two days in advance on ☎ 445 8716.

Hot Air Ballooning

Balloon Safaris (☎ 415 8289) and the Balloon Expedition Company of NZ (☎ 416 8590) do trips for about $200 per person – about an hour in the air, with breakfast and bubbly afterwards. The meeting point for Balloon Safaris is Albany, on the North Shore, and for the Balloon Expedition Company at the Westgate Shopping Centre at the end of the North-Western Motorway.

Scenic Flights

Flight 2000 (☎ 422 6334), based at Ardmore Airport in south Auckland, has bi-plane trips ($99 per person with two passengers per craft for 20 minutes), Cesna 172 flights ($200 for the craft, which seats up to three, for one hour) and trips with the Warbird Dakota DC3 ($45 per adult, $30 per child, $120 family concession – two adults, two children). The Warbird flights last about half an hour and leave at 1 pm on Sunday. You can get to Ardmore by taking the Southern Motorway and turning off at Takanini. It's on Hamlin Rd.

For helicopter flights try Helilink (☎ 377 4406), which has flights, from $130 per person for 12 minutes, over the city centre, One Tree Hill, the Harbour Bridge and Rangitoto. The flights leave from Mechanics Bay in the city.

Paragliding & Skydiving

Sky Wings (☎ 570 5757, 025 982 345 mobile) will take you paragliding, weather permitting, any day of the week. The site varies depending on conditions at the time. It costs $110 for a full day of paragliding and instruction. Pick-up from the city centre can usually be arranged if you give advance notice.

For tandem skydiving, try Action Adventures (☎ 0800 865 867), the Parakai Parachute Centre (☎ 0800 753 000; see the Helensville section in the Excursions chapter), Auckland Parachute School (☎ 0800 586 777) and Auckland Skydivers (☎ 373 5323).

COURSES

People from around the world, especially Asia and the Pacific, come to NZ to study English. Auckland has the highest concentration of language schools in New Zealand, and the visitor centre keeps a complete, up-to-date list of these (check in *Auckland A-Z*).

You can do short courses in various sports including kayaking and diving; the details of some courses are given under Activities in this chapter.

Places to Stay

New Zealand has a Goods & Services Tax of 12.5%. Unless otherwise stated, the prices given here for accommodation include this tax. It is, however, always worth checking that it's included in the price quoted when making your booking.

PLACES TO STAY – BUDGET
Camping & Cabins
Four kilometres north of the Harbour Bridge is the four-star *Auckland North Shore Caravan Park, Cabins & Motel* (☎ 418 2578, 52 Northcote Rd, Takapuna). Take the Northcote Rd exit from the Northern Motorway and it's 700m west, beside Pizza Hut. Tent and powered sites cost $22 for one person, $30 for two, cabins start at $44/55, tourist flats cost $77/88, leisure lodges cost $116 for up to four people, and motel units start at $96 for a double.

The *Takapuna Beach Caravan Park* (☎ 489 7909, 22 The Promenade, Takapuna) is 8km north of the city centre, right on the beach, and has a view of Rangitoto. It's an easy walk to the shops and central Takapuna, and a 10 minute drive into downtown Auckland. Tent sites are $24 for two, powered sites start at $26, cabins $38 and on-site vans $48.

The *Tui Glen Motor Camp (Map 8; ☎ 838 8978)* is beside the swimming pool complex at Henderson, 13km west of Auckland. Tent and powered sites cost $15/20 for one/two, cabins cost $38 for two, and tourist flats $48 for two.

The closest camping ground to the city is the quiet and secure *Remuera Motor Lodge & Inner City Camping Ground (Map 4; ☎ 524 5126, 524 5639, rml@xtra.co.nz, 16 Minto Rd)*, 8km south of the city centre. Take bus No 64 or 65 from the Downtown Bus Centre. It has a large swimming pool and is just 100m from the shops and bus stop. Tent/powered sites cost $13/15 per person, a self-contained bunkroom costs $50 for one or two, and tourist flats start at $75 for two.

The *Avondale Motor Park (☎ 828 7228, 46 Bollard Ave)*, off New North Rd, is 9km south-west of the city centre and close to MOTAT and the zoo. Tent/powered sites cost $9/10, on-site vans $40 for two people, cabins with ensuites $55 for two, and tourist flats $60.

South Auckland has many caravan parks, such as the *Manukau Central Caravan Park (☎ 266 8016, 902 Great South Rd)* and *Meadowcourt Motor Camp (☎ 278 5612, 630 Great South Rd)*, that are close to Manukau and the airport. Tent/powered sites are around $9/22 for two people.

The Auckland Regional Council has camping grounds in the regional parks around Auckland, many in coastal areas. Some are accessible by vehicle, others by tramping only. Contact Parksline (☎ 303 1530) for information and bookings.

City Centre (Map 3)
Hostels *Auckland Central Backpackers (☎ 358 4877, fax 358 4872, backpackers@ acb.co.nz, 9 Fort St)* is NZ's largest hostel, with room for 300 people. ACB's amenities include two cafes, a lively rooftop bar (Rat's), a dairy, a video theatre and an excellent backpacker travel agency. Netcafe is handy for sending and receiving email, and is open 7 am to midnight (30 minutes $5). Singles/ doubles with linen cost $33/45, a bed in a three or four-bed dorm costs $19, a twin bunk costs $18 per person (supply your own linen) and a bunk in a room with up to 10 beds costs $16 per person if you supply your own linen.

Downtown Queen St Backpackers (☎ 373 3471, fax 358 2412, 4 Fort St) is opposite ACB and has beds in small dorms for $15 a person, twin rooms for $37, and singles/doubles for $26/37.

The *City Backpackers Hotel (☎ 0800 220 198, fax 307 0182, reservations@ citybackpacker-hotel.co.nz, 38 Fort St)* provides apartment-style accommodation in the heart of the red-light district. A bed in a dorm costs $17 to $20, a double room $40 to $65, and a two-bedroom serviced apartment $120 to $150.

De Brett's International Backpackers *(☎ 377 2389, fax 377 2391, cnr High and Shortland Sts)* was renovated in mid-1999 and has a bar, fax and Internet services and a self-catering kitchen. Dorm beds start at $16, single rooms cost $40, double and twin $65 to $75 (all with ensuites), and a two-room family apartment $90.

Central City Backpackers *(☎ 358 5685, fax 358 4716, cccbnz@xtra.co.nz, 26 Lorne St)* has 160 beds, a kitchen, dining room, rooftop garden, bar, and travel counter. A dorm bed in a room of 10 costs $18, in a room of four $20. Rooms cost $46 for a double and $23 per person for a twin. All bathrooms are shared.

Albert Park Backpackers *(☎ 309 0336, fax 309 9474, 27-31 Victoria St East)* is only 50m from Queen St and the eateries of High St. It has all the necessary facilities, and will store luggage and make bookings for activities. Dorm beds cost $10 (10-12 beds per room) or $18 (six beds per room). Double rooms cost $45. Quilts are supplied if needed.

Auckland City YHA Hostel *(☎ 309 2802, fax 373 5083, yhaauck@yha.org.nz, cnr Liverpool St and City Rd)* is one of Auckland's biggest hostels. Comfortable, multi-share rooms cost $19 per person, and double and twin rooms $22 ($4 extra if you are not a member).

At the time of writing a new YHA hostel, ***Auckland International YHA*** *(☎ 302 8200, 5 Turner St)*, was about to open. This is a 160 bed hostel. Dorm beds and twin/double rooms cost the same as the Auckland City YHA, and it also has ensuites ($66). This hostel has fully accessible accommodation.

Bay City Backpackers *(☎ 303 4768, 6 Constitution Hill)*, near the University of Auckland, has dorm beds (four to eight per dorm) for $15, double rooms with ensuites for $40 and double rooms with shared bathrooms for $35.

The ***YMCA*** *(☎ 303 2068, 0800 367 962, fax 377 6770, hostel@auck.ymca.org.nz,*

cnr Pitt St and Greys Ave) accommodates both sexes in single/twin rooms for $35/55 (linen included).

Kiwi Hilton Backpackers *(☎/fax 358 3999, 430 Queen St)* is rather worn but is cheap enough at $10 for a bed in a 14-bed dorm (maximum three nights), $12 in a dorm with up to 12 beds, and $38 for a double room. (There's one women-only dorm.)

Guesthouses, Apartments & Hotels

Albion *(☎ 379 4900, cnr Hobson and Wellesley Sts)* has 20 rooms in an old, restored building. Double rooms with ensuites cost $65.

City Central Hotel *(☎ 307 3388, 0800 323 6000, fax 307 0685, cnr Wellesley and Albert Sts)* has standard rooms with ensuites for $79 and studio rooms for $99 (both options sleep up to two).

Choice Plaza *(☎ 302 0888, fax 366 6689, choiceplaza@xtra.co.nz, 10 Wellesley St)* is a distinctive, red, pagoda-like building with partly furnished single and double rooms ranging from $130 to $180 a week. There is a communal kitchen with stove and microwave (bring your own pots and crockery) and a laundry. The minimum stay is one week and linen is provided.

The ***Aspen Lodge B&B*** *(☎ 376 5046, 62 Emily Place)* looks out on a delightful little park. It's about a five minute walk from Queen St, and has a convivial dining and common area. Single/double rooms cost $54 /78 and bathrooms are shared.

The ***Harbourview Station Hotel*** *(☎ 303 2463, fax 358 2489, 131 Beach Rd)* is rather better inside than its exterior would suggest, and its location near the railway station is handy. Standard rooms with ensuites cost $50/70 for a single/double, and superior rooms (ie those recently renovated) cost $70/80.

West of the City Centre (Map 2)

The ***Brown Kiwi*** *(☎/fax 378 0191, guest phone ☎ 778 0192, bookings@brownkiwi .co.nz, 7 Prosford St, Ponsonby)* is a friendly, well-run place handy to restaurants and cafes on both Jervois and Ponsonby Rds. There are two eight-bed dorms (one for women and one for men) and two four-bed dorms (mixed), plus three double rooms. A bed in an eight-bed dorm costs $18 and in a four-bed dorm $20 (sheets and pillowcases are supplied; duvets can be hired for a one-off charge of $3). All linen is laundered weekly. The double rooms cost $45. The shared bathrooms are all clean and tidy. Other facilities include a sunny outdoor area at the back of the house, and a sitting room with a library and television. At the time of writing, the owners were planning to open another, larger hostel at the other end of Ponsonby Rd.

Ponsonby Backpackers (☎ *360 1311, 2 Franklin St, Ponsonby*) is in a rambling Victorian-era house, close to Ponsonby Rd. Dorm accommodation costs $15 (four beds to a dorm; mixed and single sex available), single rooms cost $25 to $30, and double and twin rooms $40. The rooms vary in quality.

East of the City Centre (Map 4)
Upmarket Parnell is within walking distance of the city centre and is well serviced by restaurants, cafes and shops. It's also handy to Auckland Museum and the Auckland Domain. The Link bus, which goes along Parnell Rise, will take you into the city centre and back.

Leadbetter Lodge (☎ *358 0665, 17 St Georges Bay Rd, Parnell*) is cosy, if a little threadbare. Dorm beds cost $13 and double rooms $30 to $35.

City Garden Lodge (☎ *302 0880, 25 St Georges Bay Rd, Parnell*) is one of the best accommodation options in this area. It's a large, impressive place, originally built for the queen of Tonga. Dorm beds cost $18 to $19, and twin/double rooms $42/44.

Lantana Lodge (☎ *373 4546, 60 St Georges Bay Rd, Parnell*) is friendly and well run, with good views of the city from the rear of the lodge. Dorm beds cost $17 and twin/double rooms $42 (duvets provided).

South of the City Centre
Georgia Parkside Backpackers (Map 5; ☎ *0508 436 744 toll free, 189 Park Rd, Grafton*) is on the corner of Carlton Gore Rd, overlooking the domain. This rambling old place boasts a variety of comfortable rooms. A bed in a 12-bed dorm is $17 (all dorms are mixed). There are three double rooms for $44, one slightly smaller double for $42; single rooms cost $30. Linen is included in the price and all bathrooms are shared. Tent sites are also available.

The *YWCA* (Map 5; ☎ *379 4912, fax 358 1628, ywca.auckland@clear.net.nz, 10 Carlton Gore Rd*) is a women-only hostel. It's an older, well-kept, secure building. Facilities include kitchens, TV, and laundry (coin operated). Linen is included in the price of $35 for a single room and $25 per person for a twin.

International Backpackers (Alan's Place) (Map 5; ☎ *358 4584, 8 Maunsell Rd, Newmarket*) is in a quiet residential location near the museum. This large brick building has plenty of individual rooms, as well as a commercial-style kitchen, a lounge, TV room, dining area and reading room, plus off-street parking. Dorm beds cost $16, though most are in double and twin rooms ($19 per person; singles $25).

Grafton Hall of Residence (Map 5; ☎ *373 3994, fax 377 9134, graftonhall@ auckland.ac.nz, 40 Seafield View Rd*) caters mainly to students during term time, but from the last week of June to the second week of July, and again from 20 November to 20 February, it takes budget travellers. There are 107 single rooms and 30 twins. Each floor has a fully equipped laundry (free to guests) and a telephone booth for local calls, which are free (coin and card phones for toll calls are on the ground floor). In the main living areas downstairs there are three TV lounges, a cafeteria, a microwave and 24-hour (free) tea and coffee-making facilities. There is also a tennis court (racquets are hired out for $2 per hour). Bed and breakfast costs $32 per person; dinner, bed and breakfast costs $39. Children under the age of five are free; older children are half price. There is off-street parking.

Mt Eden, a pleasant residential area 4km south of the city centre, has hostels that tend to be the last to fill up in summer. Buses run from the Downtown Bus Centre, on Quay St, to Mt Eden Rd.

Eden Lodge (Map 5; ☎ 623 4267, fax 623 2101, 22 View Rd) is fairly upmarket, set in a huge colonial-era home and surrounded by gardens. The rooms are comfortable and there are large, pleasant communal areas. A bed in an eight-bed dorm costs $15, and twin and double rooms cost $40. Bus Nos 255, 256, 258, 265 and 267 stop on the corner of Mt Eden and View Rds.

Oaklands Lodge (Map 1; ☎ 0800 222 725, fax 638 6545, bookings@oaklands .co.nz, 5a Oaklands Rd, Mt Eden) is in a quiet tree-lined street at the foot of Mt Eden. Bus Nos 274, 275 and 277 from the city stop at the Mt Eden shops, 100m away. It charges $15 to $17 for dorms, $20 per person for twin and double rooms, and $30 for a single. Linen and duvets are included in the price. There is a kitchen, dining room, TV lounge and laundry, and free baggage storage.

Rocklands (Map 5; ☎ 630 0836, fax 630 9721, ywca.auckland@clear.net.nz, 187 Gillies Ave, Epsom) is a YWCA-run hostel that accepts men and women (it also has a women-only wing). Once a grand home, its glory is now rather faded. It's popular with students from the nearby Teachers' Training College. There are 160 beds, a TV lounge, kitchen, and coin-operated laundry. It costs $25/75 per person for singles/doubles (linen included and some rooms with ensuites). The easiest way to get there is on Link bus; get off at Manukau Rd and walk down Bracken Ave.

PLACES TO STAY – MID-RANGE
City Centre (Map 3)

Prices here are merely a guide. Discounts and specials are often available.

New President Hotel (☎ 303 1333, fax 303 1332, reservations@newpresidenthotel .co.nz, 27-35 Victoria St West) has double rooms/suites for around $118/165.

Novotel (☎ 377 8920, 0800 668 683, fax 302 0993, 8 Customs St) has twin/double rooms starting at $178.

Park Towers Hotel (☎ 309 2800, 0800 809 377, fax 302 1964, parktowr@ihug .co.nz, 3 Scotia Place) is a 79-room hotel with single rooms for $120, doubles/twins for $146, and triples for $162.

The Heritage Auckland (☎ 379 8553, 0800 368 888, fax 379 8554, res.heritageakl@ dynasty.co.nz, 35 Hobson St) is located on the site of one-time Auckland shopping icon, Farmers department store. A superior room (king, queen or twin) costs $169, a one-bed-room deluxe/executive suite costs $196/211, and a two-bedroom executive/director's suite costs $332/480 (prices exclude GST). The executive and director's suites have a separate lounge and dining area with a full kitchen.

Citylife Auckland (☎ 379 9222, fax 379 9223, 0800 141 780, res.citylifeal@dynasty .co.nz, 171 Queen St) has hotel rooms and suites, plus a fully equipped kitchen. Double rooms cost $290 (plus GST) and suites start at $340 (plus GST).

Hyatt Regency (☎ 366 1234, 0800 441 234, fax 303 2932, auckland@hyatt.co.nz, cnr Waterloo Quadrant and Princes St) has 274 rooms starting at $235 plus GST.

Sky City Hotel (☎ 912 6000, 0800 759 2489, fax 912 6032), is part of Sky City. Rooms cost $150 to $290, and suites start at $210 (plus GST).

Rydges Auckland (☎ 359 9100, fax 379 8051, aklsales@rydges.co.nz, cnr Kingston and Federal Sts) has 188 rooms at $170 to $180 (plus GST) for a double.

Kiwi International Hotel (☎ 379 6487, 0800 100 411, fax 379 6496, Kiwihotel@ xtra.co.nz, 411 Queen St) has economy rooms ranging from $20 (bunks) to $49 (double or twin). Suites cost $130 and family rooms (without a kitchenette) cost $100.

Best Western Whitaker Lodge (☎ 377 3623, fax 377 3621, 21 Whitaker Place) is handy to the university and museum. Singles/doubles cost $113/123.

Apartments *First Imperial Hotel & Apartments* (☎ 357 6770, 0800 687 968, fax 0800 682 828, 131-39 Hobson St) has 60 hotel rooms and 44 executive apartments. Hotel rooms (single or double) cost $185, a studio apartment suite costs $225, and a two-bedroom apartment suite costs $337 ($22 for each extra person – maximum of six per apartment).

Cintra (☎ *379 6288, 0880 246 872, fax 379 6277, reception@cintra.co.nz, 3 Whitaker Place*) has 64 furnished apartments: studios cost $128 and one/two bedrooms $150/195. All have kitchens, and a continental breakfast is included in the price.

Darlinghurst Quest Inn (☎ *366 3260/ 3269, arc@questapartments.com.au, 2 Eden Crescent*) has studio apartments with kitchenettes for $144 and two-bedroom apartments with kitchens for $210.

Quay Regency (☎ *377 4848, 0800 500 148, fax 377 6688, 148 Quay St*) has one-bedroom apartments with city views for $225, and with harbour views $253. All units have kitchens and bathrooms.

Quest Auckland (☎ *366 5190, 0800 944 401, fax 366 5199, questauck@xtra.co.nz, 363 Queen St*) is a four-star apartment hotel with 96 apartments, each with fully equipped kitchens/kitchenettes and laundries. Most apartments have separate fax/modem lines. A studio apartment with a city view costs $184, and with a park view $200. A one bedroom apartment with a city view costs $220, and with a park view $235. A two bedroom executive apartment costs $259.

Nautilus Apartments (☎ *356 1024, fax 356 1028, 16-18 Hobson St*) has fully furnished, self-contained apartments for $180/220 a single/double.

Anzac Avenue Apartments (☎ *379 6288, 0800 246 872, fax 379 6277, reception@ cintra.co.nz, 97 Anzac Ave*) has 13 self-contained apartments. A studio apartment costs $128, a one/two bedroom is $150/195.

West of the City Centre

Guesthouses & B&Bs *The Great Ponsonby Bed & Breakfast* (*Map 2; ☎ 376 5989, fax 376 5527, great.ponsonby@xtra .co.nz, 30 Ponsonby Tce, Ponsonby*) is a restored 19th century house with spacious rooms (all with ensuites) and a very pleasant sitting and dining area. There are five rooms (one king and four queen) and six studios (one executive). The studios, which accommodate two people, have their own kitchens. Standard rooms for two people cost $135 and studios range from $165 to $170.

The *Ponsonby Potager* (*Map 2; ☎ 378 7237, fax 378 7267, raywarby@compuserve .com, 43 Douglas St, Ponsonby*) has a self-contained cottage with two double bedrooms, a bathroom (with bath and shower) and a fully equipped kitchen. There is a very pleasant garden room, a library and Sky television. One bedroom has its own deck and private garden. Everything you need to make breakfast is supplied and is included in the price of $90/120 for a single/double occupancy. If two couples book the entire cottage it costs just $140.

Colonial Cottage (*Map 2; ☎ 360 2820, fax 360 3436, 35 Clarence St, Ponsonby*), a restored kauri villa from the turn of the 19th century, is a friendly, relaxed place close to the cafes and restaurants of Ponsonby and Jervois Rds. Comfortable single/double rooms cost $80/100 (shared bathroom).

The French Cottage (*Map 2; ☎ 376 6046, 025 909 012 mobile, 7 Georgina St, Freemans Bay*) is, as its name suggests, built in the French provincial style. This self-contained cottage has a courtyard, and costs $150 a night or $500 for a week; all breakfast ingredients provided.

Hotels & Motels *Surrey Hotel & Conference Centre* (*Map 1; ☎ 378 9059, fax 378 1464, shotel@ihug.co.nz, 465 Great North Rd, Grey Lynn*) has 60 rooms and an indoor heated pool. Prices start at $95 for a bedsitter unit, $105 for a two room unit (both have kitchen facilities); and $150 for a superior hotel room or family hotel room (sleeps five).

Acapulco Motel (*Map 2; ☎ 376 5246, 0800 222 785, fax 378 1528, 20 Shelly Beach Rd, Herne Bay*) has superior/executive/two-bedroom units for $118/126/128 (the rates apply to one or two persons; each extra is $18).

Best Western Unicorn Hotel (*Map 2; ☎ 376 2067, fax 376 0685, 31 Shelly Beach Rd*) has 16 self-contained units. The rates are the same as for the Acapulco Motel.

Abaco Spa Motel Apartments (*Map 2; ☎ 376 0119, fax 378 7937, abacospa@xtra .co.nz, 59 Jervois Rd, Herne Bay*) has studio

PLACES TO STAY

rooms for $99 to $104, apartment suites for $115 to $125, and apartments with spas for $135 (each additional person is $18).

Motel Westhaven (Map 2; ☎ 376 0071, fax 378 4293, motel.westhaven@xtra.co.nz, 26 Hamilton Rd, Herne Bay) has 14 self-contained units. It's a pleasant place set back from the road. A standard/superior one bedroom apartment costs $160/170 (one or two persons; each additional adult is $15).

The Harbour Bridge Motel (Map 2; ☎ 376 3489, fax 378 6592, 6 Tweed St, Herne Bay) is a building dating to 1886. At the time of writing it had just changed hands and there was talk of renovation. It has 16 units, all with bathrooms and kitchens. Rates are $70/80/110 for a double/queen/family. Family units sleep up to seven people.

The *Seabreeze Motel* (Map; ☎ 376 2139, fax 376 3177, 213 Jervois Rd, Herne Bay) has 10 units – some with balconies and sea views. All are equipped with kitchens and bathrooms. Prices range from $99 for a studio deluxe unit, to $120 for a two bedroom unit. Each extra adult costs $16 and there is no charge for children under three years.

East of the City Centre
Parnell (Map 4) Guesthouses & B&Bs
The *Ascot Parnell* (☎ 309 9012, fax 309 3729, AscotParnell@compuserve.com, 36 St Stephens Ave) is a long-standing favourite, with 11 guestrooms costing $95 for singles and $145 to $185 for queen-size rooms. All have ensuites and telephone facilities; the service includes breakfast to order.

Birdwood House (☎ 306 5900, 025 777 722 mobile, fax 306 5909, info@birdwood .co.nz, 41 Birdwood Crescent) is a delightful, restored 1914 bungalow overlooking the Auckland Museum. It has two pleasant balconies, leadlight windows, a kauri staircase and an Inglenook fireplace. There are five rooms: four have ensuites and one has a bathroom across the hall. Prices are $155 to $175 for two people, and $130 to $150 for one.

St Georges Bay Lodge (☎ 303 1050, fax 303 2055, enquiry@stgeorge,co.nz, 43 St Georges Bay Rd) is a peaceful, tastefully restored Victorian villa with four centrally heated bedrooms (ensuites available), a lovely conservatory, balcony and verandah. Rooms cost $130 to $145 for a single and $145 to $165 for a double.

Chalet Chevron (☎ 309 0290, fax 373 5754, 14 Brighton Rd) is a Tudor-style hotel with beautiful harbour views. Single rooms cost $68, doubles with a sea view cost $110 ($98 without). All rooms have ensuites, and the price includes a cooked breakfast.

Amersham House (☎ 303 0321, fax 303 0621, stirling@xtra.co.nz, 1 Canterbury Place) is a luxurious home with four huge guest rooms (all with ensuites), plus a heated pool and spa. There are extra telephone lines for those wishing to use the Internet. The topmost room has 360° views, a balcony, double spa, and sitting room. Prices start at $200 (single) and range up to $380.

34 Awatea St (☎ 379 4100) is a spacious Parnell home with wonderful sea views. It has three bedrooms (two queen-size, one double), which cost $120, and two guest bathrooms.

Redwood (☎/fax 373 4903, 11 Judges Bay Rd) is a modern house with two double rooms and a single. The double rooms have ensuites; the single has share facilities. Over December 1999-January 2000 the prices are $100/145 for a single/double.

Hotels & Motels *Parnell Inn* (☎ 358 0642, reservations 0800 472 763, fax 367 1032, parnelin@ihug.co.nz, 320 Parnell Rd) is tucked away behind The Other Side restaurant. Singles/doubles start at $75/110.

Parnell's Village Motor Lodge (☎ 377 1463, fax 373 4192, 2 St Stephens Ave) has Victorian-style rooms and modern one-bedroom apartments. All have kitchens. The studio rooms have kitchenettes.

Barrycourt Motor Inn (☎ 303 3789, reservations 0800 504 466, fax 377 3309, 10-20 Gladstone Rd), opposite the Parnell Primary School, has a selection of accommodation options (double and twin rooms, studio apartments, and suites). Prices start at $86 and range up to $300.

Quality Hotel Rose Park (☎ 377 3619, 0800 808 228, fax 303 3716, quality

.rosepark@cdlhms.co.nz) is opposite the Parnell Rose Gardens. It has 107 guest rooms, five suites and five villas (with kitchen, lounge and laundry). Prices start at $140 for a double or twin room.

Remuera *Aachen House Boutique Hotel (Map 1; ☎ 520 2329, 0800 222 436, fax 524 2989, info@aachenhouse.co.nz, 39 Market Rd)* is a renovated Edwardian-era home at the foot of Mt Hobson. There are nine guest rooms (including three suites), each with ensuites and furnished in period style. The suites each have a fax point, two direct phone lines and a writing desk. Breakfast is served in the beautiful, marble-floored conservatory, which looks out onto a pretty garden. Prices range from $150 to $275 (the Victoria Suite), plus GST.

Omahu House (Map 1; ☎/fax 524 9697, 524 9697, fax 524 9697, 35 Omahu Rd) is another beautiful Remuera guesthouse. Built in 1928, it was completely renovated in 1997. There are four bedrooms (ranging in price from $140 to $160); the two upstairs rooms have views of Mt Hobson and Mt Eden and Cornwall Park. A spacious verandah opens onto a peaceful garden with a swimming pool.

The Devereux (Map 1; ☎ 524 5044, fax 524 5080, the.devereux.hotel@xtra.com.nz, 267 Remuera Rd) is a spacious 1890s villa, with a conference room. There are 13 guest rooms: four double rooms, six master suites, two single rooms with a shared bathroom, and one double with a shared bathroom. Each room is imaginatively furnished to theme (Provence, Cairo, Bodrum, Tuscany etc). Prices start at $120 for singles and range up to $250 for two people in a master suite.

Sedgwick Kent Lodge (Map 1; ☎ 524 5219, fax 520 4825, accommodation@ sedgwick.co.nz, 65 Lucerne Rd) is a two-storey restored 1910 farmstead, furnished with antiques, Persian rugs and original artwork. A double room costs $160, which includes a cooked breakfast.

Longwood (Map 5; ☎/fax 523 3746, longwood@ihug.co.nz, 54 Seaview Rd) was built in the 1880s, when this part of Auck-

land was farmland. The original homestead in this area, it once presided over some 300 acres. There are two guest rooms: upstairs is a twin-bed room and downstairs a room with both a queen-size and a single bed. Each room has its own bathroom. Prices range from $90 to $130. There is a pleasant, sunny deck that overlooks a large back garden with a swimming pool.

St Heliers (Map 1) *Cliff View (☎ 575 4052, fax 75 4051, 51 Cliff Rd)* is a contemporary, self-contained apartment with one of the best harbour views in Auckland. From the large, curved windows in the sitting room (which opens up onto a balcony) you can gaze towards Rangitoto and take in the expanse of the Waitemata Harbour; at night the city lights to the west glitter and sparkle. The secluded Ladies Bay beach is at the foot of the cliff across the road (there is a track leading down). The apartment has a kitchen, an office (with its own telephone line), a bathroom and a queen-size bedroom, and costs $195 a night.

Seaview Heights (☎ 575 8159, fax 575 8155, seaview@bitz.co.nz, 23a Glover Rd) is a 1960s home with great views of both the Waitemata Harbour and Glover Park from its hilltop location. There are two suites (one queen-size, 'Parkview'; one super-king/twin, 'Bayview'), a twin-bed room ('Crows Nest Snug') and a queen-size room ('Charlotte'). Bayview has a twin spa. German, French, Italian and Spanish are spoken fluently at Seaview. Crows Nest Snug and Charlotte cost $180, Parkview $220 and Bayview $260.

South of the City Centre

Mt Eden (Map 1) *Pentlands (☎ 638 7031, fax 638 7031, hoppy.pentland@xtra.co.nz, 22 Pentland Ave)* is a large place (suitable for groups) in a quiet cul-de-sac. It has a tennis court, picnic tables and a kitchen for guests. There are 15 bedrooms (five single, five double, three twin, two family) with shared bathrooms. Singles/doubles cost $59/89.

Villa 536 (☎/fax 630 5258, annasvilla@ hotmail.com, 536 Mt Eden Rd) has three rooms in a restored kauri villa. There is one en suite room downstairs with a queen-size and a single bed ($120/130 for a single/double), and two rooms upstairs – one with an en suite and a queen-size bed (plus great views to One Tree Hill), which costs $140 (double), and another, smaller room with twin beds (the bathroom is downstairs) for $85/95. All rooms have a TV. There is a very pleasant lounge with television, and a sunny room that opens out onto a large deck with good views (guests may use the kitchen to make tea and coffee any time). There is a sizeable back garden. If you are coming from the city centre, take one of the Three Kings/Mt Eden buses (Nos 274, 275, 277). If you are coming by airport bus, ask to be dropped off at Fairview Rd (which is opposite the B&B).

One Tree Hill (Map 1) *The Langtons* (☎ 625 7520, fax 625 7520, thelangtons@ xtra .co.nz, 29 Haydn Ave)* is a beautiful, spacious home opposite one of Auckland's finest parks, One Tree Hill Domain. It has a swimming pool, a lovely garden, a music room (with a piano) and a guest lounge with a sundeck. There is a separate building by the pool that's currently available for business meetings. There are four bedrooms (each with super king-sized beds that can be separated into twin beds), which cost between $185 and $225. All rooms are airy and tastefully furnished, with views towards either the park or the Manukau Harbour. Guests have access to fax and email facilities, and gourmet meals are also available. The owners will pick you up from, or drop you off at the airport or train station. There are regular buses from the city centre (Nos 302, 304, 305 and 312).

Airport (Map 1) There is a cluster of motels on Kirkbride Rd, Mangere, about five minutes by shuttle from the airport. Nearest to the motorway are *Pacific Inn* (☎ 275 1129, 0800 504 800, fax 275 1128, 210 Kirkbride Rd)*, *Gateway Hotel* (☎ 275 4079, fax 275 3232, Gateway@xtra.co.nz, 206 Kirkbride Rd)*, *Travellers International* (☎ 275 5082, 0800 800 564, fax 256 0106, 190 Kirk-

bride Rd)*, *Hotel Grand Chancellor* (☎ 275 7029, 0800 803 322, fax 275 3322, reservations@granda.co.nz, cnr Kirkbride and Ascot Rds)*, and *Centra* (☎ 275 1059, fax 275 7884, cnr Kirkbride and Ascot Rds)*. The first three charge around $89 for a double room; Grand Chancellor and Centra are more expensive. However, there are usually specials on offer, especially when things aren't busy.

A couple of minutes drive farther along Kirkbride Rd is another cluster of motels. *Skyway Lodge* (☎ 275 4443, fax 275 5012, 30 Kirkbride Rd)* has budget accommodation: bunks/singles/doubles cost $18/45/55, and units cost $75 for two people. There is a BBQ, swimming pool and guest kitchen.

All motels will arrange shuttle buses to the airport.

North of the City Centre
Devonport (Map 6) Devonport is well supplied with B&Bs, many in beautifully renovated Victorian or Edwardian villas. If you are coming from the airport, the most convenient way to get to Devonport is by the airport shuttle, which will drop you off at the place of your choice. The trip costs about $20 (one person) to $35 (two people) and takes approximately half an hour. If you are coming from downtown Auckland, the most pleasant way to travel to Devonport is by ferry (10 minutes). Of course, if you have a car, you can drive over the harbour bridge.

Hyland House Fine Accommodation (☎ 445 9917, mobile 021 986 221, fax 445 9927, hyland@voyager.co.nz, 4 Flagstaff Tce)* is a large, elegant house with two rooms costing $225 and $275. The latter is especially large, with a four-poster bed and a Victorian day-bed. The other room is furnished in traditional French style. It has a swimming pool and a lovely garden.

Peace & Plenty Inn (☎ 445 2925, fax 445 2901, peace&plenty@xtra.co.nz, 6 Flagstaff Tce)* is one of the country's most outstanding B&Bs. Beautifully restored and elegantly furnished (fine art, oriental carpets, antiques), it has five queen-size bedrooms with ensuites. Breakfasts include goodies such as

Belgian waffles, scrambled eggs with smoked salmon, and eggs benedict, served on fine china on tables dressed with white linen cloths and silver cutlery. Singles/doubles cost $200/230.

Parituhu Beachstay (☎ 445 6559, *parithuhu@iprolink.co.nz, 3 King Edward Pde)* is a quite little place with one single room with a shared bathroom for $60, and a double with en suite for $80.

Jeong-K Place by the Sea (☎ 445 1358, *fax 446 1358, jeong-k@ihug.co.nz, 4 King Edward Pde)* is a refurbished 1910 villa with period furniture. There are four rooms (three queen-size and one twin), each with an en suite and access to the garden. Rooms cost $190 to $210 for a single and $200 to $230 for a double.

Top of the Drive (☎ 445 3362, 15c King Edward Pde) is a relatively new house built in traditional style. There are three rooms (a single, a queen-size, and a king). The larger two have ensuites and the single room has its own toilet and vanity, but guests use the shower in the main bathroom. Rooms for one person range from $70 to $100, for two from $110 to $140.

Albertine (☎ 445 6443, 45 Church St) is a colonial-style house with sea views from the verandah and a pretty garden. Singles/doubles cost $110/130.

Auntie Janet's Homestay (☎/fax 445 8589, puff@ihug.co.nz, 7 Albert Rd) is a tidy cottage with a lovely back garden and comfortable rooms (the bathroom is shared). The sunny kitchen-dining area overlooks the garden and deck. Singles/doubles cost $70/105.

Devonport Village Inn (☎ 445 8668, fax 445 2668, 9 Albert Rd) is nearby and has four double rooms upstairs, which share two bathrooms. Rooms cost $90/130 for a single/double.

The Garden Room (☎ 445 2472, 23 Cheltenham Rd) is on a quiet street that leads directly to the beach. Two rooms are available: one in the garden, with an ensuite, and the other inside the villa itself, which shares a bathroom. Each room costs $150.

The Secret Garden (☎ 445 3605, zenia@nadara.co.nz, 18 Eton Ave) is tucked away near the playing field at the end of Eton Ave. It's a quiet, pleasant spot with one double room for $70.

Villa Cambria (☎ 445 7899, fax 446 0508, villacambria@xtra.co.nz, 71 Vauxhall Rd) is a truly lovely Victorian villa (built in 1904 of kauri) with attentive hosts and great breakfasts. There are three queen-size rooms, one double room and one with twin beds. Prices range from $180 to $200 (the $200 room is a loft with its own balcony).

Karin's Garden Villa (☎/fax 445 8689, 14 Sinclair St) is a very pleasant restored villa with a huge back garden (great for children). Single rooms cost $85 to $105, doubles $125 to $155, and the cottage (with a double bed and balcony) costs $155. The cottage and one double room have couches that can be folded out to make an extra bed.

Devonport Villa Inn (☎ 445 8397, fax 445 9766, dvilla@ihug.co.nz, 46 Tainui Rd) is an elegant Edwardian villa made of solid kauri. It's been beautifully renovated and is set in a very lovely garden. There are five rooms and two suites. A cottage in the garden contains two rooms furnished in period style. From November 1999 to March 2000 rooms cost $210 and suites $245, dropping after this to $190 and $225 respectively.

Cheltenham-by-the-Sea (☎ 445 9437, 2 Grove St) is a modern, friendly home with singles/doubles for $65/90, a twin for $45 per person and a queen-size room for $120. The queen-size room has an ensuite.

Ivanhoe (☎ 445 1900, fax 446 0039, 82 Wairoa Rd) is a modern home, seconds from Cheltenham Beach and close to the golf course. The self-contained unit, with good views, costs $100/150 for a single/double.

Rainbow Villa (☎/fax 445 3597, 17 Rattray St) is an 1880s restored villa that's much larger than its street appearance would suggest. There is a spa pool in the sunny back garden. The spacious rooms (two doubles and one twin) all have ensuites and cost $120/150 for a single/double.

Khorasan Bed & Breakfast (☎ 446 1111, 5 Kerr St) is an older place with a sunny guest room (with ensuite) upstairs. The breakfast room is downstairs and opens onto the garden; the hens may even supply your breakfast eggs. Bed and breakfast costs $150 a night.

Badger's of Devonport (☎ 445 2099, fax 445 0231, badgers@clear.net.nz, 30 Summer St) is a friendly place, five minutes walk from the Stanley Bay ferry which runs at peak hours during the week. There are three double rooms (although twin beds are available on request). Rooms with en suite cost $89 for one person and $125 for two; the room with a separate bathroom costs $119 for two. There is also a two-bedroom, self-contained unit behind the main house that costs $135 a double ($20 for each additional person). The rear verandah leads onto a pleasant garden. The owners will pick you up or drop you off at the Devonport ferry terminal or elsewhere in Devonport.

Aniwaniwa Cottage (☎ 445 4454, pgoldsbury@stratex.co.nz, 20 Hastings Pde) has a self-contained unit at the back of the main house with two bedrooms and shared bathroom (you can use the kitchen in the main house). It costs $40 per person.

Bakers' Place (☎/fax 445 4036, baker@ ihug.co.nz, 30 Hastings Parade) is a modern, self-contained cottage, nestled in bush behind the main house ($120 a night). It's private, quiet and sunny; there's a choice of one double or twin beds. Facilities include a kitchen, washing machine, dryer and ironing board. There is an outdoor spa on the deck.

Amberley Bed & Breakfast (☎/fax 446 0506, amberley@xtra.co.nz, 3 Ewen Allison Ave) is a quiet home with three queen-size rooms and one twin. There are two bathrooms for guests (bathrobes are supplied). Rooms cost $72 to $100 for one person and $100 to $130 for two.

Wharemoana Bed & Breakfast (☎ 445 7549, 4a North Ave) is a modern and unpretentious place with two rooms – one single and one double – which share a bathroom. A lounge with TV is available to guests. The single room costs $40 a night and the double $70; it's possible to hire both rooms and have this end of the house to yourself if desired. In summer you can use the spa pool, and there's a deck with a garden to sit out in.

Ducks Crossing Bed & Breakfast (☎ 445 8102, 58 Seabreeze Rd, Narrow Neck) is a contemporary home with a lovely garden. Ducks do in fact live nearby, and you can easily see them waddling by the stream that runs parallel to Seabreeze Rd. They also appreciate being fed, if you have a few spare moments. The queen-size room, with its own balcony and ensuite, costs $100; the garden room costs $95 (French doors lead outside); and there is a small room which goes for $65/85 for a single/double.

Bayswater Point Lodge (☎ 445 7163, fax 445 7166, titchener@xtra.co.nz, 27 Norwood Rd, Bayswater) is a simply stunning two-storey home with brilliant views across the harbour. There are four spacious rooms, all with ensuites (two with baths as well as showers). Two of the rooms have balconies with fantastic views. There is a guest lounge with coffee and tea-making facilities and a deck. Guests may also use the modern laundry downstairs.

The lodge (a 90-year-old mansion) has been beautifully furnished and the guest rooms are tastefully and thoughtfully finished. The lovely garden extends right to the cliff and the lodge has its own jetty. You can easily get to/from downtown Auckland on the Bayswater ferry, which is a four-minute walk away; the owners will also drop you off or pick you up from Devonport. Email, fax and telephone facilities are all available to guests at any time. Rooms range in price from $165 to $195 (including a great breakfast).

Esplanade Hotel (☎ 4445 1291, fax 445 1999, reservations@esplanadehotel.co.nz, 1 Victoria Rd) is one of the oldest hotels in Auckland. This lovely old place is modelled on fashionable Brighton (UK) homes from the turn of the 19th century. Prices start at $106 for doubles and go up to $264 for a suite.

PLACES TO STAY – TOP END
City Centre (Map 3)
Various rates are available for the following upmarket city hotels, depending on whether

your booking is for a weekend or week day, how far in advance you book and so on. Prices range upwards of $200 a night for a double room.

Carlton Hotel *(☎ 366 3000, 0800 227 5866, fax 366 0121, reservations@carlton-hotel.co.nz, cnr Mayoral Drive and Vincent St).*

Centra *(☎ 302 111, fax 302 3111, centrabusiness@ xtra.co.nz, 128 Albert St).*
Copthorne Harbour City *(☎ 377 0349, fax 307 8159, copthorne.harbourcity@cdlhms, 196-200 Quay St).*
Sheraton *(☎ 379 5132, 0800 443 535, fax 377 9367, 83 Symonds St).*
Stamford Plaza *(☎ 309 8888, 0800 442 519, fax 379 6445, Albert St).*

PLACES TO STAY

Places to Eat

FOOD

Once upon a time eating out in Auckland invariably meant Chinese – or perhaps steak and chips. It wasn't that many years ago that drinking wine with one's meals was considered a little eccentric – a strange foreign custom. All that's changed. Dining out in Auckland is exciting, and the quality and variety just keep getting better. The emphasis is on fresh, innovative food imaginatively served.

Flavours reflect Asia and the Pacific, with Mediterranean cuisine also featuring strongly. Seafood figures large: try New Zealand's own unique sweet and juicy greenlipped mussels, whitebait fritters, the fat, succulent Bluff oysters, or perhaps tuatuas (a shellfish), paua (abalone), scallops, smoked salmon or crayfish. Try it raw (oysters in their shells with a little pepper and lemon juice, sashimi or Polynesian raw fish in spicy coconut milk), grilled, panfried, deepfried, steamed, seared, baked, sauteed or casseroled. For meat eaters, there is the traditional NZ favourite, roast lamb with mint sauce, as well as venison and other game, steak of course, and poultry in numerous guises. Pasta is also pretty popular.

Where to eat it? The inner-city suburbs of Ponsonby, Herne Bay and Parnell are bursting at the seams with great dining options. But in big, sprawling Auckland this isn't the end of the story. Further out, in areas not covered by our survey in this chapter, are more excellent places to eat. They include Hurstmere Rd in Takapuna, Dominion Rd in Mt Eden, the eastern beaches area north of Takapuna (Torbay, Browns Bay etc), Remuera and more.

To go with the food, why not try a NZ wine, perhaps one produced by one of Auckland's own vineyards. Most restaurants these days are licensed (ie licensed to sell liquor), although many also allow you to bring your own (BYO). A few places are BYO only. Finish your meal with a platter of excellent NZ cheeses (Puhoi, near Auckland, produces a range of gourmet cheese).

PLACES TO EAT

For the Pleasure of the Palate

If you drink Auckland wine, expect high quality, and be prepared to pay for it. Although its resident wine companies account for 95% of national production, Auckland is not a major growing area. Its vineyards are an historic remnant of the small holding industry that sold wine, along with peaches, cabbages and apple juice, at roadside stalls. This has changed with New Zealand's wine revolution, and what remains of Auckland's vineyards produces highly sophisticated, cosmopolitan wines.

The two leading Auckland producers are Collards and Kumeu River, both of whom make chardonnay from their West Auckland vineyards that is as good as any in the country. All Kumeu River's suave wines and Collard's pristine Rothesay labels are grown north-west of the city. Both also make good local sauvignon blanc, and Kumeu River has rare merlot and pinot noir reds of note.

Another range of superb Auckland wines is grown on Waiheke Island, usually on cute lifestyle vineyards that demand high returns. Goldwater Estate and Stonyridge make impressive, expensive cabernet/merlot reds known in London and New York for their class. Te Motu and Peninsula Estate are not far behind in price and quality.

Keith Stewart

More informal dining is catered for by Auckland's burgeoning cafe culture: espresso any way you like it, panini, bruschetta, foccacia, bagels, cakes of various descriptions, and so on. On weekends, inner-city cafes, their tables spilling out onto the sidewalk, are full of people happily brunching on cholesterol-and-calories-be-damned feasts of bacon, eggs, sausages, fried tomatoes, pancakes with bacon and syrup, hot buttered toast, croissants and bagels with cream cheese and conserves. Buy a copy of the weekend newspaper, head down to your favourite all-day breakfast place and hunker down for a couple of hours, or more – at least until lunchtime or dinner, when you can saunter off to sample the fare somewhere else.

If you want to know more about NZ cuisine and Auckland restaurants, get hold of a copy of *Cuisine* magazine, which has the latest news, reviews and features on wine and food. The magazine *Café* covers the country's cafe scene.

CITY CENTRE
Budget (Map 3)
Downtown Auckland has a large number of Asian food places, many of which are very inexpensive. Sushi bars are everywhere. Middle Eastern food is also popular and there are numerous inexpensive kebab places.

Lorne St, between Wellesley and Victoria Sts, has several inexpensive eateries, mainly Asian. They include the *Moghul Indian Restaurant*, with mains from $12, and *Chef 2 Asian Cafe* and *Bokcholee Korean Restaurant* where you can fill up for $10 or less. Choice Plaza (cnr Wellesley and Lorne Sts) has a couple of Asian food places including the inexpensive *Noodle Fast Food*, which has filling dishes under $10, and *Sushi & Sake* (udon from $7.50 and sushi from $5.50).

Tony's Restaurant & Bar (☎ 373 2138, 32 Lorne St; ☎ 373 4196, 27 Wellesley St West) must be doing something right because it's continued unchanged while other places have come and gone. It has a basic steak-house menu which also features lamb dishes and pasta (steak from $12 and pasta from $12.50). It's open weekdays from 11.30 am to 2.30 pm and 5 to 10 pm, Sunday 5 to 9 pm.

At the southern end of Lorne St (No 57), opposite Auckland Public Library, is *Pizza Pizza*, a popular place with students from nearby Auckland Institute of Technology. Regular and large pizzas go for $8.50 and $12.50 respectively and there is an interesting selection of beer on offer: DB, Lion (Lion Red $2.80), Mac's Gold (from Nelson), Black Mac, and imported beers, including Fosters and Carlton Cold from Australia.

Victoria Yeeros (15 Victoria St) is a good spot for felafel, shawarma, doner kebab and salads. The surroundings aren't flash but prices are low. It's open daily from 11 am to 10 pm and Friday until late.

At *Foodoo*, on the corner of Victoria West and High Sts, you can get a range of hot meals, such as pasta, soup, curry or stew, for less than $10.

Khymer, in Vulcan Lane, serves large bowls of steaming noodle soup (chicken, beef, seafood) for $5, satay for $5 and fried noodles from $6. *Raw Power Cafe* is above Khymer and serves a range of healthy food, from free-range eggs for breakfasts, to tofu burgers, soups, salads ($7 for a bowl) and pasta. There is also a good selection of juices and smoothies (about $5). It's open weekdays from 7.30 am to 4 pm, Saturday from 10 am to 3 pm. Opposite, tucked away next to Vulcan Cafe, is *Sushi Factory* where you can eat all you possibly can within an hour for $15.

Kebab Valley (239a Queen St) is busy at lunch time. Doner kebabs start at $6.50 and shish kebab at $7. Vegetarian options, such as felafel, hummus rolls and dolma, are $5.

Middle East Restaurant (23a Wellesley St West) is tiny and often crowded. The food is excellent and reasonably priced. For great Turkish food try the similarly priced *Cafe Midnight Express* (59 Victoria St West), near the Mexican Cafe. Another good Turkish place is *Sultan's Table* (68 Victoria St West). *Okonami-yaki*

(23 Wellesley St West) offers 'Japanese alternative cuisine'. There are lunch-box specials for around $12 and other mains (eg soba, udon, tempura) for around $16.

Mohammed's Curry Den, in the Customs St end of Queens Arcade, serves halal takeaways for under $10. It's open Monday to Saturday from 9 am to 5 pm, Friday to 9 pm.

Tucked away in Tyler Lane, just of QEII Square, is **Daikoko Ramen**, with sushi and steaming ramen for less than $10.

On Upper Queen St **Hare Krishna Food for Life** serves filling, wholesome vegetarian food at rock-bottom prices. For $3 you'll get a plate heaped with rice, dhal, subzi (curried veges) and a pappadam; $6 buys you all you can eat. It's open weekdays from noon to 3 pm.

On the eastern side of Upper Queen St is a row of eateries. Closest to the K Rd end is **Peter's Pies** where, for $5, you can choose between steak, lamb, curry, vegetarian and so forth. Beyond Peter's is a string of Asian restaurants – plus one Middle Eastern place – all very reasonably priced.

Caravanserai, next to the Kiwi Hilton Backpackers hostel, is a long-running place with inexpensive Middle Eastern food (mains about $12). Opposite is the **Merchant Mezze Bar**, which is popular with the young office-crowd at lunch time.

Wun Loy (156 Hobson St) doesn't look all that promising from the outside but the food – standard Chinese (chop suey, fried rice, noodles, sweet and sour) – is inexpensive (from $7 for a main) and filling. Steak and chips is also on the menu. It's open daily from 11 am to 8.50 pm.

Food halls in central Auckland are mostly open during shopping hours only. The Downtown Shopping Centre on QEII Square, on the corner of Queen St and Customs St West, has the **Downtown Food Court**. Other food halls are on the lower ground floor of the BNZ Tower on the corner of Queen and Swanson Sts, and on the 4th floor of the Finance Plaza on the corner of Queen and Durham Sts. On the 4th floor of the Countrywide Bank Centre at 280 Queen St, there's an international food hall

with kebabs, fish and chips, Chinese, Japanese (**Fujiyama** for Sushi) and traditional cafes. The Atrium on Elliot St has seven international outlets in its food hall. For Asian fare you can't beat **Food Alley**, in Albert St, opposite the Stamford Plaza Hotel. Thai, Chinese, Malay, Korean and Japanese meals mostly cost under $10. It's open daily from 10.30 am to 10 pm.

The Victoria Park Market has several restaurants, cafes and a food hall.

Pub food is usually good value. Try **Shakespeare Tavern & Grill** on the corner of Wyndham and Albert Sts, the bistro of the **London Bar** on the 1st floor at Wellesley St West. **Bird Cage** on the corner of Victoria St West and Franklin Rd, opposite Victoria Park Market, is a fancier pub that serves meals but is noted for its good value breakfast.

If **McDonald's** is a favourite – especially the tasty Kiwiburger – you'll find it on Queen St and in the Downtown Food Court on K Rd. There's a **Wendy's** upstairs on Queen St, just north of Wellesley St. In the same block but a bit farther down the hill, opposite McDonald's, there's a **Pizza Hut** downstairs in Strand Arcade. Nearby, on the opposite side, is a **Burger King**.

The cheap eats and late night quandary can be solved with the **White Lady** mobile hamburger stand, an Auckland institution. It's on Shortland St, just off Queen St, and is open in the evenings until around 3 am during the week, 24 hours on weekends and holidays. It's a good place for burgers, toasted sandwiches or a steak.

Supermarkets There is a **New World** supermarket at 2 College Rd, near Victoria Park Market. It's open daily from 8 am to 10 pm. Mini supermarkets can be found in the basement of Deka (48 Queen St; open Monday to Thursday from 7.30 am to 7 pm, Friday until 9 pm, Saturday 9 am to 5.30 pm and Sunday 10 am to 5 pm), and the **Mid Town Mini Supermarket** (ground floor of the Landmark Building, on the corner of Durham St West and Queen St; open Monday to Thursday 6.30 am to 7 pm, Friday until 9 pm, Saturday 8.30 am to 6 pm and Sunday 10 am to 5 pm).

Wah Lee *(214-20 Hobson St)* is a good Asian foodstore, which offers lots of opportunity to browse through all manner of interesting things. Apart from fresh and dried food, there's crockery, chopsticks, bamboo steamers, brushes and colours for ink painting, paper kites and more.

Mid-Range to Top End

Most of the places listed here have mains between $18 and $25.

Cin Cin on Quay Brasserie & Bar *(Map 3; ☎ 307 6966)* and **Harbourside Seafood Bar & Grill** *(Map 3; ☎ 307 0556)*, both in the ferry building at 99 Quay St, are innovative and stylish restaurants. They are not cheap, but neither are they outrageously expensive for the quality. In a similar vein, **Kermadec** *(Map 3; ☎ 309 0412)* at Viaduct Quay, on the corner of Quay and Lower Hobson Sts, serves top quality seafood. Another good place nearby is **Viaduct Central** *(Map 3; ☎ 377 1200, 204 Quay St)*.

Seamart *(Map 3; ☎ 379 4928)*, on the corner of Fanshawe St and Market Place, has no problem getting really fresh fish as the market and restaurant are in the same location. There are daily specials.

Sails *(Map 2; ☎ 378 9890, Westhaven Marina, Westhaven Drive)* has a ringside view of the marina, and is generally busy at lunch time with local business people. Seafood is its specialty. It's open for lunch and dinner weekdays, and for dinner weekends (from 6.30 pm).

The Yacht Club *(Map 3; ☎ 373 5776, 11 Westhaven Drive)* is another popular place; the fish 'n' chips is recommended. It's open for lunch weekdays (noon to 3 pm) and for dinner Monday to Saturday from 6 pm until late. The bar menu is available from 11.30 am until late.

Paramount Restaurant & Bar *(Map 3; ☎ 377 9973)*, on the corner of Lorne and Wellesley Sts, is tucked away near the New Art Gallery. Dinner is served Monday to Saturday, and lunch weekdays. Fresh flavours from the Pacific and Asia are a specialty, but

the menu varies to include North African and other interesting cuisines. A vegetarian main course is available.

Orbit Restaurant *(Map 3; ☎ 912 6000)*, Sky Tower, on the corner of Victoria and Federal Sts, is a revolving restaurant in Auckland's tallest building. It's open daily for breakfast (from 10 am), lunch and dinner, and there is also a kids' menu. The cost of your ticket up the Skytower is deducted from the cost of your meal. Sky City has four other eateries, including the fine-dining **Tamarind** (Pacific Rim cuisine; mains about $30), and the **Fortuna Buffet Restaurant**, which has all-you-can-eat breakfast ($15), lunch ($20.95) and dinner ($25.50) buffets.

O'Connell St Bistro *(Map 3; ☎ 377 1884, 30 O'Connell St)* is a bar and restaurant that's open weekdays from 11.30 am to 2.30 pm for lunch and from 6 pm daily for dinner. The food is simple and fresh, and the dining area cosy and intimate.

Toto *(Map 3; ☎ 302 2665, 53 Nelson St)* is an Italian place with a welcoming atmosphere, and live opera on Thursday. The food is good and so is the service. It's open weekdays from 11 am until late.

Five City Restaurant *(Map 3; ☎ 309 9273, 5 City Rd)* is a fine-dining place with excellent food and service ($75 for a three-course menu, $90 for a four-course set menu). There are, in addition to the upstairs dining room, two private dining rooms.

Mikano *(Map 4; ☎ 309 9514, 1 Solent St)* is in a great spot at Mechanics Bay, right on the water's edge. Besides the excellent and innovative food, helicopters (including the Westpac Rescue helicopter) buzz in and out from the helipad nearby. It's open daily for lunch except Saturday, and for dinner every night. There is a bar area behind the main dining space.

The French Café *(Map 5; ☎ 377 1911, 210 Symonds St)* is not a cafe but a restaurant, and is a long-time favourite for French cuisine. Entrees include ravioli of snails with wild mushroom sauce and rocket leaves ($14.50) and roasted goat's cheese with parma ham, tamarillos and red wine ($15.50). Mains include aged beef, salmon, snapper, chicken and veal ($21 to $26). It's open for lunch Tuesday to Friday and for dinner Monday to Saturday.

Cafes (Map 3)

In the city centre there is a concentration of cafes on Lorne St, High St, and Vulcan Lane.

Alba (303 Lorne St) is a classy place with Mediterranean-style food (mains $18 to $22). It's open Monday to Saturday until 10.30 pm.

Also in Lorne St, a couple of doors from Central City Backpackers, is *City*, an understated place with a row of white-clothed tables. The food is fresh and good, but what makes this place special is that all meats served are organic or free range (mains $18 to $22).

The New Gallery's cafe also has a good selection of delights and is reasonably priced.

Paneton (60 High St), near the corner of Victoria St East, is ever reliable, with all manner of bakery products to go with your espresso. Nextdoor are *Cima* (with a double-level dining area) and *Wofem Bros Bagelry*, and further along are *Ginger*, at No 48, and *Rosinis*, at No 20. On the other side of the road is *Jolt*, a hip little place, and *Colombus*, which is seriously dedicated to coffee (it has another outlet in Newmarket).

In Vulcan Lane, in the section bordered by High and O'Connell Sts, are two very popular places: *Mecca* and *Cafe Melba*, both with good food and both busy on weekends. On the corner of Freyberg Place and High St is the stylish *D72*, which stays open until late (24 hours Friday to Saturday). *Vulcan Cafe*, in the section of Vulcan Lane that runs down to Queen St, is a popular lunch-time cafe. *Firellos Cafe (10 Durham St East)*, with its slow-turning overhead fans, is another long-time favourite with cafe-goers.

K ROAD (MAP 3)

Karangahape Rd (K Rd) has a range of interesting dining options, from Maori fare to Indian thali. There are also some good cafes, mostly towards the eastern end of the street, and prices are very reasonable.

Te Ao Kohatu (☎ 309 1841, 553 K Rd) serves Maori cuisine. A sign in the window announces that it's alcohol, smoke and eftpos-free. This is the place to try things like *kina* (sea egg), muttonbird and paua, although lamb, duck, chicken and emu are also on the menu, with watercress and kumara appearing as accompaniments. Boil-ups (wao koorau koohua – vegetarian; komi koohua – pork bones, greens, kumara, doughboys) cost $10.50. Hangi-in-a-pie is $6.50. Desserts include roroi (caramelised kumara) and kanga pirau (fermented corn). A full cooked breakfast is $6.50. Te Ao Kohatu means 'things from the past are things for the future'. It's open daily from 10.30 am until late.

Armadillo (☎ 303 3515), on the corner of Hereford St and K Rd, is one of the newest places in this part. A stylish lounge and bar (with an open fire), it's a good place either for a meal (mains are around $18 to $22) or a drink (there's an extensive wine list).

The Monkey Bar, towards the Queen St junction, is another stylish cafe that's popular for lunch (noon to 3 pm), but which also draws a lively crowd in the evenings (Monday to Saturday from 6 pm).

Caluzzi Bar & Cafe, next door, is usually busy at lunch time with local office-workers calling in for focaccia ($9.50) or soup, as well as for more substantial fare (eg red curry chicken at $17). It's open Monday and Tuesday from 9 am to 4 pm, Wednesday to Saturday 9 am until late.

Habanero (65 Pitt St), just off K Rd, is popular and has good food inspired by Asian and Pacific flavours. Mains cost about $18. It's open Monday to Wednesday from 7 am to 7 pm, Thursday and Friday until late, Saturday from 8 am until late, and Sunday from 9 am to 3 pm.

Back on the main road is *Brazil*, a barrel-roofed, very bohemian cafe in a former fruit store – the signs are still there from the old days.

Little Turkish Cafe (217 K Rd) is a brisk, bright place with kebabs from $5 and moussaka from $7.50. It's open daily until late.

Rasoi Vegetarian Restaurant is the place to go for Indian thali. You can order a serving of plain rice and two curries for $5.50 or go the whole way and splurge on all-you-can-eat maharaja thali for $13.50. There are also dosa, lassi and a range of delicious Indian sweets.

Right at the back of St Kevins Arcade is *Alleluya Bar & Cafe*, in a great spot overlooking Myers Park. It has a selection of brunch dishes for under $10 as well as more substantial fare. If you aren't worrying about cholesterol try the K Rd fry-up (bacon, eggs and toast) for $11.50. Alleluya's good for a drink in the evening as well, and periodically there are music performances and poetry readings. In the same arcade is *Mumbai*, which serves inexpensive Indian vegetarian food, and *Ambush*, which has panini, soups, burritos and waffles.

Past St Kevins Arcade, heading towards Queen St, are *Wagamana*, which serves tasty Italian food (music from 11 pm on Friday and Saturday), and *Verona*, which has good, reasonably priced soups, spaghetti, pizza and organic chicken. Verona's bar is a pleasant, low-key place for a drink.

Near the intersection with Liverpool St, at the eastern end of K Rd, is *Ken Yakitori Bar* (☎ 303 3366, 89 K Rd), which has a variety of chargrilled goodies on skewers (from $2.50 for two) as well as Japanese beer.

KXQ Cafe, right on the corner of Queen St and K Rd, is a spacious and quite stylish place, and has a pleasant upstairs area with comfy, soft lounge chairs. Panini, nachos, lasagne, salads and soups go for under $10, and there's a good selection of cakes and coffees.

PONSONBY & HERNE BAY (MAP 2)

Auckland's busiest restaurant district is strung out over many blocks on Ponsonby Rd. You can walk along here in the daytime or evening and see what captures your fancy. On Saturday night get there early or book.

Cafe Cezanne (296 Ponsonby Rd) is a small, casual place with a great atmosphere and good food at good prices. Breakfasts, light meals, gourmet burgers and unusual pies are served all day – all for around $7.50 – and there's a good dinner menu.

Tuatara, at No 198, and *SPQR*, at No 150, are two of the trendiest eating spots. Tuatara has straight-forward, well-prepared food, and good coffee. The tables outside are popular during the day, but this place also packs them in until late at night. The smaller SPQR is similar, with stylish decor, hearty breakfasts and a good range of moderately priced snacks and light meals. The food is a prelude or complement to the wine quaffing, which goes on into the early hours.

Opposite SPQR, *Atomic Cafe*, at No 121, is a breakfast and day-time hang-out with arguably the best coffee in town (its roasters supply many other cafes). *Atlas Power Cafe*, at No 285, is a gay-friendly cafe. Other popular cafes are *Dizengoff*, at No 256, where Jewish food is a speciality, and *Expresso Bambina*, at No 266, a busy little place with all-day breakfasts, soup ($7.50), bruschetta ($6.50), salads and so on. The newer *Bambina Bistro* next door is equally busy.

For fabulous food to take home try *Rocket Kitchen* at No 234a. Here you can get all manner of gourmet entrees and meals (eg goat fetta and roasted tomatoes on baked polenta, cured salmon with mustard and dill, Mexican port and caper empanadillas). Prices are reasonable considering the quality.

Another irresistible place is *The City Cake Company*, at No 186, which has yummy cakes, tarts and desserts-to-die-for. Eat in or take away (there's another outlet at 426 Mt Eden Rd).

Prego (☎ 376 3095, 226 Ponsonby Rd) is a popular place for good Italian cuisine. Pizzas start at $17, pasta at $16.90. It's licensed and open daily from noon until 12.30 am.

Estasi (☎ 378 7888, 222 Ponsonby Rd) specialises in Pacific Rim cuisine.

GPK (☎ 360 1113, 260 Ponsonby Rd) is a classy place serving gourmet pizzas cooked in a wood-fired stove ($18.80). There is also a selection of curries and salads. It's open weekdays from 11 am until late, from 9 am on weekends.

Musical Knives (☎ 376 7354, 272 Ponsonby Rd) is a stylish, but not cheap, vegetarian restaurant which has a selection of organic fare. Mains (eg special organic

PLACES TO EAT

soba, organic vegetables with tofu) start at around $24.

Masala (☎ *278 4500, 169 Ponsonby Rd*) is open weekdays from noon until late, weekends from 5 pm until late. Mains start at $13.50 and include Punjabi-style lamb curry, a tasty butter chicken ($15.50) as well as a selection of vegetarian dishes (thali $13.50, vegetable korma $12.80).

Freiya's (☎ *376 3738*), on the corner of Ponsonby Rd and Pompallier Tce, is a Parsee place (the Parsees – or Zoroastrians – were Persians who migrated to India). It has atmosphere, music and good food and is open daily from 5 pm until late. Mains start at $13 (eg butter chicken and chicken Madras).

For Thai try ***Thai Palace*** (☎ *378 4469, 244 Ponsonby Rd*) where you'll find a wide choice (from seafood to vegetarian) of moderately priced dishes.

The Noodle Box (☎ *376 6875, 113 Ponsonby Rd*) does takeaways in neat boxes, although there is also a sit-down area if you want to eat in. Prices range from $8.50 for stirfried vegetables and noodles, to $12.50 for wok-seared kingfish.

Yum Yum Noodle Bar & Restaurant (☎ *376 6373, 43 Ponsonby Rd*) is open Monday to Saturday from 6 pm until late and offers a range of Asian dishes: Thai, Malay, Vietnamese, Chinese, and so on. Mains start around $13.

At ***XTC***, on the corner of Picton St and Ponsonby Rd, you can sample one or more of 50 exotic teas or try a range of blended coffees. It's open Monday to Saturday from 9 am to 6 pm, Sunday until 5 pm.

Ponsonby Pies, at No 134, has everything from traditional mince or steak to smoked fish, Thai beef curry and other innovative fillings. Next door is the ***Open Late Cafe***, an option during the wee small hours.

Santos, at No 114, is open daily from about 6 am to 5 pm and is a popular cafe with the media and entertainment crowd. At the nearby ***Burger Fuel*** you can choose from a range of innovative burgers for less than $10. It's open Sunday to Thursday from noon to 10 pm, Friday and Saturday until midnight.

The ***Ponsonby Fire Station*** (☎ *378 6499, 1 Williamson Ave*) features modern NZ and continental cuisine. It's open Tuesday to Friday for lunch, and daily for dinner from 6 pm. Mains are around $22.

Provence (☎ *376 8147, 44 Ponsonby Rd*) specialises in southern French cuisine. It's open Monday to Saturday for dinner.

Jervois Rd has several good restaurants and cafes. The ***Sierra Cafe***, at No 50, and ***Fusion***, nearby, have good coffee, breakfasts and lunches, and are open daily. ***Gannet Rock***, a cafe and deli at No 38, has an all-day breakfast menu and also serves salads, seafood (whitebait fritters, Tahitian raw fish), burgers (Cajun chicken bagel burger) and other interesting items – many for under $10. It's open weekdays and Saturday from 7 am until 5 pm, Sunday from 8 am.

Essence (☎ *378 0740, 70-72 Jervois Rd*) is a stylish, award-winning restaurant. It has an innovative menu (mains around $25) and a good wine list.

Vinnies (☎ *376 5596, 166 Jervois Rd*) is another award-winning place with European-influenced cuisine. It's open daily from 6.30 pm until late. Mains are around $25.

Andiamo (☎ *378 7811, 194 Jervois Rd*) is popular and busy. There is a blackboard menu with plenty of variety (pasta, Asian dishes, salads and so on) and a good wine list. As Andiamo opens daily at 7 am, it's a favourite for breakfast (the 'big breakfast' – scrambled eggs, bacon, two hash browns, sausage and toast – costs $14.50). It closes around 1 am.

The Cooker (☎ *378 8566, 190 Jervois Rd*), next door, is also popular, with a menu ranging from bangers & mash ($16) to red lentil & onion pakora ($14.50). It's open daily 8 am until late.

Further west, ***Toss-it*** (☎ *376 0722, 236a Jervois Rd*) specialises in 'body friendly' gourmet salads: vegan, organic, wild food, game, seafood – in fact, just about anything you can think of. Prices range from $8.50 to $20. You can eat in (there's an upstairs dining area) or take out.

The Gables (☎ *376 4994*), on the corner of Kelmarna Ave and Jervois Rd, is a traditional

PLACES TO EAT

tavern and grill restaurant with steaks, seafood and, at lunch time, open sandwiches and light meals. It is moderately priced, and open Monday to Saturday from 11.30 am, Sunday from noon.

KINGSLAND (MAP 1)
Kingsland (bus Nos 210, 211, 212 and 223) has a happening strip of trendy restaurants, galleries and designer homeware, and is well worth visiting.

For starters, there's a good pub, the *Oak & Black Dog* (427 New North Rd), which has live music on Thursday and Friday nights and cheap counter meals ($10). Further west is a string of trendy places to eat. *The White Room* (☎ 815 0913, 487 New North Rd) is colour-coded, 'conceptual dining', with imaginative dishes such as 'hot goats envy' and 'blue fish green fish'. *Roasted Addiqtion* (287 New North Rd) is The White Room's alter ego. It has great coffee (the eponymous Roasted Addiqtion) and an imaginative daytime menu (it's not open for dinner), with dishes such as 'the lamb that got away' – naturally a vegetarian dish. *Eon*, just off New North Rd, near the railway station, combines espresso with art; *Indus* serves good Indian cuisine (beef vindaloo, dhal makana etc); and *Nataraj Cafe* (463 New North Rd) specialises in South Indian food (masala dosa, iddli etc).

PARNELL (MAP 4)
Strawberry Alarm Clock (☎ 377 6959,119 Parnell Rd) is a popular cafe with plenty of atmosphere.

Oh Calcutta (☎ 377 9090, 131 Parnell Rd) is a good place to come for tandoori; prices are very reasonable with mains under $15. It's open daily from 5.30 pm until 11 pm, Wednesday to Sunday from noon until 2 pm.

Gibraltar (☎ 307 3224, 215 Parnell Rd) specialises in woodfired pizza ($18). *Maruhachi* (☎ 357 3535) has consistently good Japanese food. It's open Monday to Saturday from 11.30 am to 2.30 pm, 6 to 10.30 pm.

Alligator Pear (☎ 377 2223, 211 Parnell Rd) is a popular place with excellent food, including pasta, salads, chicken and fish. Mains are between $13.50 and $21.00. It's open Tuesday to Sunday from 5.30 pm until late.

La Bocca (☎ 375 0083, 251 Parnell Rd) is a small place that serves great Italian food. Mains are in the $18-22 range. It's open weekdays from 11.30 am until late, weekends from 9 am.

Non Solo Pizza (☎ 379 5358, 259 Parnell Rd) has some 20 pizza toppings to choose from. Prices start at $18.50 for classic pizzas, with others in the $20-24 range. It is open daily from noon until late. Tucked away next to it is *Toto*, a small, licensed place, that's a pleasant spot to enjoy panini, bagels and bruschetta.

Iguaçu (☎ 358 4804, 269 Parnell Rd) is a perennially popular restaurant, which also has consistently good live jazz (see the Entertainment chapter).

The Other Side (☎ 366 4426, 320 Parnell Rd) has a selection of German food, as well as steaks, fish and venison dishes (mains start at $32).

For fine dining *Antoines* (☎ 379 8756, 333 Parnell Rd) is one of Auckland's best. In a renovated house, it's one of those silver-service, gold-credit-card emporiums where the best local produce is tantalisingly presented in French style. Bookings are essential.

The Parnell Village has some good mid-priced restaurants hidden away, several with tables in open courtyards. They include *Thai Friends* (☎ 373 5247) for good Thai food, with mains from $15.80; *Asahi* (☎ 358 1227), which has tempura from $15 and rice meals from $10; *Java Room* (☎ 366 1606), which has good Indonesian and Thai food (mains from $16.50); and the *Chocolate Cafe*, which has a wide selection of coffees, snacks and desserts (eg chocolate cake infused with whisky syrup).

Verve (☎ 379 2860, 311 Parnell Rd) has an imaginative and appealing approach to food, with an evening menu that includes roasted venison and herb-crusted lamb rack. It has a pleasant outdoor eating area and is open for dinner from Tuesday to Saturday, daily for brunch and lunch.

PLACES TO EAT

Cibo (☎ *309 2255, 91 St Georges Bay Rd)* has great food, and you can enjoy courtyard dining in summer.

Kebab Kid (363 Parnell Rd) does great doner kebabs and shwarmas (including vegetarian) from $6.50. It's open Tuesday to Saturday from noon to 11 pm (Friday to 2 am), Sunday and Monday noon to 10 pm. There's another Kebab Kid on Ponsonby Rd.

Locals swear by the hamburgers from *Al & Pete's* on Parnell Rd, opposite Domain Drive. *Bombay Junction*, the Indian takeaway next door, is also recommended.

NEWMARKET & EPSOM

Tribeca (Map 5; ☎ 379 6359, 8 George St) is between Parnell and Newmarket. It has a wide choice of entrees and mains, and the desserts are very good. There is outdoor dining under umbrellas on the lawn, or in the courtyard. Mains are mostly around $25.

Zarbo (Map 5; ☎ 520 2721, 24 Morrow St) is an upmarket deli with fresh salads, pasta, soups and so forth. *Kenzie* (Map 5), a licensed cafe, is a popular place for cake and coffee or light meals such as soup and pasta. For good coffee try *Colombus (7 Teed St)*, just off Broadway.

In and around Khyber Pass are several good, inexpensive places. *Poppadom Indian Restaurant (Map 5; ☎ 529 1897, 471 Khyber Pass)* is a long-standing favourite. For Chinese food there's *Sunny Town (Map 5; ☎ 520 7838)*, at No 410, with large/small-sized mains for around $22/15. For Thai try *Sri Siam (Map 5; ☎ 524 0903)*, at No 473, where most mains are under $16. *Ramses Restaurant & Bar (Map 5; ☎ 522 0619, 435 Kyber Pass)* is a long-running place. Mains include fish, chicken, steak and game.

Tucked away behind the Olympic Pool, *Rikka (Map 5; ☎ 522 5277, 73 Davis Crescent)* is a classy little place with good Japanese cuisine. Mains include free-range chicken, teriyaki, sashimi etc ($18 to $22). There is a good wine list and a range of sake (Japanese rice wine).

Safran (Map 5; ☎ 520 5664, 71 Davis Crescent), next door, has tapas, tortilla, tostadas, hummus, panfried mussels, steaks and pasta, as well as a bar. It's popular for brunch on Sunday.

A first class place in Epsom is *Splato (Map 1; ☎ 360 0898, 417 Maukau Rd)*. Its modern interior is one of Auckland's most striking, and the food (modern European) is excellent, although fairly expensive. It's open for lunch Tuesday to Friday, and for dinner Monday to Saturday.

MT EDEN (MAP 1)

At Mt Eden Village, on Mt Eden Rd, is an enclave of cafes and restaurants (licensed and BYO – although Mt Eden is a dry area). *Circus Circus (☎ 623 3833, 447 Mt Eden Rd)* is red and gold with posters and collectables redolent of the big top. There is a cafe area and a covered courtyard. It's open daily for breakfast from 7 am; at other times you can get light meals and snacks (cakes, panini and bagels).

Across the road, at No 464, is *Mt Eden Deli & Bakery*, with cases full of pies, cakes, rolls, quiches and more. A few doors down, at No 442, is *Tea Total*, which, as its name suggests, specialises in all manner of tea blends. It has a four-shelf 'sniffing wall' where you can inhale the exotic aromas of teas such as rooibus Madagascar, Waiheke blend or walnut. You can drink-in or buy packets to take out.

At No 425 is *Restaurant Berlin (☎ 630 6602)*, which specialises in authentic German cuisine – goulash, veal knuckles, strudel, torte etc. It's open Monday to Saturday evenings from 6 pm.

MISSION BAY & ST HELIERS (MAP 1)

Tamaki Drive has a string of good places. *Hammerheads (☎ 521 4400, 19 Tamaki Drive)*, on Okahu Bay, specialises in seafood. There is a large verandah with outdoor dining.

Mission Bay has numerous dining options. *Jewel of India* and *Scorpio*, the latter specialising in Italian cuisine, are at the city-end of St Heliers Bay. Further east are *Bar Comida*, *Cafe Riva*, *Capri Bar & Pizzeria*, *The Business*, *Mecca*, and *Positano* (all with Mediterranean-style cuisine) and the oh-so-sweet *Death by Chocolate*. If you're after takeaway fish and chips try *The Fish Pot Cafe*.

In St Heliers there are the award-winning *Saints Waterfront Brasserie* (☎ 575 9969, 425 Tamaki Drive); and *Kahve* (☎ 575 2929), on the corner of Tamaki Drive and St Heliers Bay Rd, which has a pleasant verandah for outdoor dining. Both are across the road from the beach.

DEVONPORT (MAP 6)

There are many cafes and restaurants in Devonport, most of them in Victoria Rd. The Devonport Wharf also has restaurants, as well as fast food and snack places.

Port-O-Call (☎ 445 9585) is in a great spot overlooking the harbour at the end of the wharf. There is a reasonably wide selection of food from which to choose, with mains from $20. It's open daily from 6.30 to 10.30 pm. *Torpedo Bay Tavern & Grill* (☎ 445 9770) is upstairs.

The Esplanade Hotel has a couple of dining rooms (*LIC* and *Pasta by the Sea*) as well as the *Grapevine Wine Bar*. Meals are moderately priced and are available daily from 10 am to 11 pm (weekends from 8.30 am).

Java House, tucked away down WJ Scott Mall, off Victoria Rd, has good coffee and a tasty selection of scones, muffins, cakes and light meals. It's open Sunday to Thursday from 8 am to 5 pm, later on Friday and Saturday evenings.

The Stone Oven Bakery (☎ 445 3185, 5 Clarence St) is the perfect place for breakfast. It's open daily from 6.30 am to 6 pm.

Manuka (☎ 445 7732, 49 Victoria St) is a popular place, with wood-fired pizza as well as pasta and other dishes. Pizzas cost $18.90 and pasta dishes start at $15. Local beer costs $5 and there is a selection of wines. It's open weekdays from noon to 2 pm and weekends from 9 am to 3 pm.

Bankers Arms is a non-smoking pub with seating outside or in. Mains start at $14.50. Monday is comedy night; book a table on ☎ 445 3010.

Monsoon (☎ 445 4263, 71 Victoria Rd) is a popular place serving good Thai and Malay

food, with mains starting at $14.50. It's open daily from 5 pm.

Portofino (☎ 445 3777, 26 Victoria Rd) has a good selection of Italian food, with mains starting at $17. It's open weekdays for dinner, and weekends from 11 am until late.

Cod Piece (☎ 446 0877, 26 Victoria Rd), near Portofino, is a reliable place for fish and chips and for hamburgers. You can order by phone; it's open 4 pm until late.

Ziganna Espresso Lounge is a good spot for coffee and light meals. Next door is *Bar 3*, a bistro-style place with a Hollywood movie theme that sometimes has live music.

Da Ciccio (☎ 445 8133, 99 Victoria Rd) has good pizza, pasta and seafood. Gourmet pizzas are $18, pasta $17 (main). It's open weekdays from 6 pm until late, weekends from noon.

Sigdi (☎ 445 1546, 161 Victoria Rd) is a BYO and takeaway place that specialises in North Indian food (mains from $13.50). It's open 5.30 to 10 pm.

Porterhouse Blue (☎ 445 0309, 57 Calliope Rd) has a very interesting menu, which includes venison, kangaroo and hare. Mains start at $25.50. If you are staying in the area, the restaurant will pick you up free of charge, or will collect you from the ferry if you are coming from the city. Generally, you should book two to three weeks in advance to ensure a table, although you may be lucky and be squeezed in sooner. The restaurant is open Monday to Saturday from 6.30 pm.

Watermark (☎ 446 0622, 33 King Edward Pde) offers a good buffet dinner ($25) from Wednesday to Sunday and brunch ($15) on Sunday from 9.30 to 11.30 am. Its set lunch starts at noon. Watermark is open daily for dinner (à la carte as well as buffet) from 6 pm until late.

Masonic Tavern (☎ 445 0484, 29 King Edward Pde) is the place to go for a cheap counter meal. There is a pool-playing area upstairs, and sometimes a band.

McHugh's of Cheltenham (☎ 445 0305, 46 Cheltenham Rd) has a great location overlooking the beach. The popular lunchtime (noon to 2 pm) buffet is $20.

PLACES TO EAT

Entertainment

Auckland has a good variety of places to go after the sun sets. Check the *NZ Herald*'s entertainment pages (Saturday's 'What's On' supplement and Thursday's '7 Days'). *What's Happening* is a free monthly magazine that lists all major events. It's available from visitor centres and other places. The weekly *Alive & Happening* from the Auckland Visitor Centre lists the latest in events, music, concerts, theatre, opera, dance and sports. Gig guides tend to come and go. The giveaway events calendar *The Fix* is available at record and music shops (try Real Groovy Records at 438 Queen St). It comes out each Thursday. *Re-Mix* and *Lava* also have gig guides. *Re-Mix* is free and you can pick it up at Real Groovy Records and from other record and music shops. *Lava* costs $2.50 and is available from bookshops such as Unity on High St. There is also a gig guide in *Backpackers News*, a giveaway you can get from any hostel, and in *Auckland City News*, which is also free (there is a stand for these near Victoria Yeeros in Victoria St West).

Sky City Casino, on the corner of Victoria and Hobson Sts, is one of the biggest entertainment venues in the city. The main attraction here is, of course, gambling, but it also has a 700-seat theatre, restaurants, bars, a hotel and observation decks. The Force Entertainment Centre, on Queen St, next to Aotea Square, is the most recent addition to the city's cinema culture. It has a giant Imax screen and a Planet Hollywood as well as numerous bars and restaurants. Under construction at the time of writing was the Princes Wharf development. This will be home to restaurants, bars and a boutique hotel.

PUBS & BARS

Auckland has plenty of convivial pubs and bars. Dress standards usually apply and the minimum legal drinking age is 18 (having recently been changed from 20).

City Centre (Map 3)

Down near the waterfront (Viaduct Basin) is the *Loaded Hog*, a pub brewery favoured by the mobile phone brigade and where the dress code is enforced. However, it has a good atmosphere and is always lively. New places at the recently opened Princes Wharf development include *Cafe Hoegaarden*, an authentic Belgium cafe with Hoegaarden on tap, the *Lenin Bar* (vodka and beer) and *Leftfield*, which has televised sport, and dance music on Friday and Saturday. Also busy during the America's Cup will be *Viaduct Central*, opposite the Princes Wharf.

Cal Neva, near the corner of Wolfe and Albert Sts, is an expansive bar with a good selection of the excellent Monteith's on tap (a South Island, West Coast beer). It's a popular spot and serves great food. *The Immigrant (104 Fanshawe St)* is a good traditional Irish bar with live northern-hemisphere sports telecasts and bands on Friday and Saturday.

Rat's Bar, in the Auckland Central Backpackers on Fort St, is a lively and popular backpacker hangout. It has low prices and is always active, even during the week. It has a 7th floor rooftop deck, plus an indoor cafe and a bar with weekly pool competitions. *Balzac (26 Wyndham St)* has DJs, and a backpacker special every Wednesday night ($2 per handle of beer). *Crow Bar*, a downstairs bar virtually next door, is a popular hangout with some class.

Soho Kitchen & Bar (2 Hobson St) is a popular and pleasant place for a drink, and the food is very good. *Margarita's (18 Elliot St)* is a popular bar with backpackers. It has cheap meal specials and entry is free on Monday when they also have a beer special. Above Margarita's is the classy *Chilli Lounge*, an open arena encased in rimu with big windows. The staff are friendly and the menu eclectic.

The *Rose & Crown (69 Customs St)* is an English-style pub with good counter lunches and live music from Wednesday to Saturday. The *Empire Tavern*, on the corner of Nelson and Victoria Sts, is popular with the after-work crowd. It has live music on Friday night.

The *Civic Tavern (1 Wellesley St West)*, near the corner of Queen St, has three bars on three floors, each representing a different part of the British Isles. Murphy's Irish Bar is on the ground floor, Younger Tartan Bar is downstairs, and upstairs is the London Bar, an English-style pub. Murphy's and the London both have live music (see later).

The *Queens Head Tavern (404 Queen St)* is an English-style, value-for-money pub with pool tables, poker machines and big-screen television. *Embargo (26 Lorne St)*, underneath the Central City Backpackers, is popular with travellers. It has pool tables, and live music on Thursday. It's also a good place for a Steinlager.

In nearby High St there's *Deschlers*, a trendy bar that has consistently good live jazz, and *Cause Celebre/The Box*, a popular late night venue – techno, house and live music (see later). High St crosses Victoria St East to become Lorne St. At No 28 is *Matisse*, an art bar that's a short walk from to the Auckland Art Gallery.

The Occidental – Belgium Beer Cafe in Vulcan Lane opened in 1999 to immediate acclaim. It has Stella Artois on tap. *Equinox*, next door, has a cigar bar and an upstairs lounge. The *Judder Bar (35 Vulcan Lane)* has DJs most nights (there is another Judder Bar at 198 Jervois Rd, Herne Bay, and two on the North Shore).

Tabac (6 Mills Lane), off Queen St, is a trendy hideaway that's worth seeking out. It has DJs and occasionally live jazz as well (see later in the chapter). *Bacchus*, at 5 O'Connell St, has dance music for the young, active crowd; the *Liquid Lounge*, upstairs, is more relaxed.

The *Muddy Farmer*, at The Heritage Auckland on the corner of Wyndham and Hobson Sts, is an Irish theme bar with Guinness on tap. *Brownies Bar (71 Victoria St West)* has Speights (pride of the south) on

tap. *The Dispensary* in Victoria St West, across from the Sky Tower, is open 24 hours.

Shakespeare Tavern (61 Albert St) boasts the title of 'NZ's first micro brewery'. It also serves inexpensive food that you can enjoy with its Willpower Stout and Sir Toby Belch's ginger ale.

Team Magic, at the Centra Hotel on Albert St, is a veritable shrine to the America's Cup, with plenty of memorabilia to gaze upon.

West of the City Centre (Map 2)

In Ponsonby, *Cavalier Tavern (68 College Hill)* is popular and good value, with regular live sports telecasts and Speights on tap. Other popular watering holes in Ponsonby include *Java Jive* and *Tuatara*, the *Garage Bar* (next to SPQR), *One Red Dog* (good pizzas), *GPK* and the *Safari Lounge* (all on Ponsonby Rd).

One of the newer places in Ponsonby Rd, and one of the coolest, is the *Hula Hut* cocktail bar at No 214. Rest your drink on a surfboard table while admiring the frangipani and butterfly ceiling decorations and the coconut-frond lampshades. Aloha.

Also pretty cool is *Lime*, at 167 Ponsonby Rd. It must also be one of the smallest bars in town. At No 126 is the cosy *Grand Central*; comedy night on Wednesday, a band on Thursday and DJs Friday.

East of the City Centre (Map 4)

In Parnell, *Iguaçu (269 Parnell Rd)* is a trendy bar/restaurant where it's a challenge to squeeze through the door on Friday night. The *Mink Cafe & Bar (99 Parnell Rd)* is a relatively new, trendy place with wood-fired pizzas.

South of the City Centre (Map 5)

In nearby Newmarket, popular places include the *Carlton Tavern*, on the corner of Broadway and Khyber Pass Rd, which is a renovated pub with a popular sports bar, live music on Friday night and live rugby telecasts on weekends, and *Claddagh (372 Broadway Rd)*, a traditional Irish bar with live music every night.

ENTERTAINMENT

Galbraith's Ale House, at 2 Mt Eden Rd, near Symonds St, is in a former public library. Some claim that it has the best ales in Auckland.

CLUBS (MAP 3)

Nightlife tends to be quiet during the week. On weekends the popular spots are full to overflowing and dress standards apply at many of the fancier bars. Among the most popular clubs is *Calibre* (☎ 303 1673, St Kevins Arcade, 179 K Rd); dance and house music from 11 pm to 8 am Thursday to Saturday.

The Khuja Lounge (☎ 377 3711) on the corner of Queen St and K Rd (above Westpac) is a popular venue with plenty of variety in musical style and a mix of DJ and live music. Pick up a copy of the monthly calendar that details what's on. It's open Tuesday to Saturday from 7 pm. *Roots*, at 322 K Rd, has a distinctly African theme, and provides live music, house and DJs for a young and active clientele. *The Club* (☎ 309 0215, 371 Queen St) has DJs on Friday and Saturday nights (10 pm start), as does *Cal Neva* (☎ 307 1500, 3 Albert St).

For more venues, see the section above on pubs and the later section on live music.

GAY & LESBIAN VENUES (MAP 3)

Most of the gay clubs and bars are along the western end of K Rd.

Legend (☎ 377 6062, 335 K Rd) is a dance bar that is open Monday from 5 pm to 2 am, Tuesday from 4 pm till 2 am, Thursday to Saturday from 4 pm to 4 am and Sunday from 2 pm to 2 am. *Sinners* (☎ 308 9985, 373 K Rd), another dance bar, is open Wednesday to Saturday from 11 pm till late (Friday and Saturday from 10 pm). On Friday night from 9.30 pm to 1.30 am it becomes the *K Bar* (the only bar in Auckland exclusively for women).

Urge (☎ 307 2155, 490 K Rd) is popular with the 30-plus crowd. It's open Monday, Wednesday, Thursday and Friday from 8 pm, and Sunday from 6 pm. *Kamo* (☎ 377 2313, 382-86 K Rd), a restaurant and bar, is open

during the week from 10 am to 11 pm and at weekends from 7.30 am.

A popular sauna and cruise club is *Club Westside* (☎ 377 7771, 45 Anzac Ave). It's open Sunday to Thursday from noon to 2 am and Friday and Saturday 24 hours.

LIVE ROCK, JAZZ & FOLK

For big international bands and major local ones, the main venues in Auckland are the *Powerstation* (Map 5; ☎ 377 3488, 33 Mt Eden Rd) and the *North Shore Events Centre* (Map 1; ☎ 443 8199), on Torana Rd, Glenfield. Big dance venues are at *Alexandra Park* (Map 1) and *Ellerslie Race Course* (Map 1).

The most popular small venue is currently *The Kings Arms Tavern* (Map 5; ☎ 373 3240, 59 France St, Newton), which has emerging bands, rock and alternative music on offer. You can hear live music Thursday to Sunday and on the second Wednesday of each month. A small cover charge usually applies on Sunday, Friday and Sunday.

The Temple (Map 3; ☎ 377 4866, 486 Queen St), a small cafe and bar with pool tables, has everything from solo acoustic to fully plugged bands, but is especially popular as a venue for local singer/songwriters performing original work. Monday is open mike night, Tuesday is 'soup of the day' with solo half-hour sets, and Sunday is basically the same but for bands. The rest of the week features a variety of bands. The Temple is open daily from 5 pm and there is no cover charge except on Sunday (a $5 entry includes a drink and a snack).

The *Classic Comedy & Bar* (Map 3; ☎ 373 4321, 321 Queen St) has occasional live music as well as comedy (see later).

The *Manifesto Espresso Wine Bar* (Map 3; ☎ 303 4405, 315 Queen St) mostly offers live jazz on Thursday and Sunday; you'll find that there's usually a cover charge. *Deschlers* (Map 3; ☎ 379 6811, 17 High St) is one of the most consistently good places in the city centre for live jazz, which you can hear on Monday, Wednesday and Saturday evenings.

Cause Celebre/The Box (Map 3; ☎ 303 1336, 33-35 High St) is a long-running, popular place with hip-hop on Thursday (The Box) and jazz and fusion bands on Friday and Saturday (Cause Celebre). There is usually a cover charge of about $5. *Rakinos Cafe* (Map 3; ☎ 358 3535, 1st floor, 35 High St) is another good jazz spot with live performances from Thursday to Saturday.

Papa Jack's Voodoo Lounge (Map 3; ☎ 358 4847, 9 Vulcan Lane) turns up the volume and attracts a mixed crowd with a bent for alternative music; live bands on Wednesday and Thursday. The cover charge varies according to who's playing. *De Bretts Bar* (Map 3), in High St, near the corner of Shortland St, has jazz on Monday and a varied program from Wednesday to Saturday. Around the corner the *Shortland Cafe & Bar* (Map 3; ☎ 367 1005, 23 Shortland St) has live Latin music Thursday to Saturday from 10 pm.

The Civic Tavern (Map 3; ☎ 373 3684), on the corner of Queen and Wellesley Sts, has two bars with regular live music: the London Bar – a long-standing jazz venue with live music on Friday and Saturday – and the Irish Bar, with live Irish music Thursday to Saturday. The *Rose & Crown* (Map 3; ☎ 373 2071, 69 Customs St East) pub has bands from Thursday to Saturday. A small cover charge applies.

Tucked away behind the Stamford Plaza is *Tabac* (Map 3; ☎ 366 6067, 5 Mills Lane), which has live jazz periodically; at the time of writing there was a DJ rather than live music, but there were plans to reintroduce live sessions, so it would be worth checking.

Soho Kitchen & Bar (Map 3; ☎ 377 6917, 2 Hobson St) is a popular bar with live jazz on Monday nights. The *Alto Bar* (Map 3), on level 3 of Sky City, has live music from Monday to Saturday; usually contemporary, but with occasional soul and jazz. The dress code here is smart casual, and enforced! *The Ministry* (Map 3; ☎ 373 3664, 17 Albert St) is a popular nightclub with a regular drum and base session on Thursday ($5 cover charge). *The Immigrant* (Map 3, ☎ 373 2169, 104 Fanshawe St) is a good

Irish pub. There are cover bands from Wednesday to Saturday, and traditional Irish music and dancing from about 3.30 pm on Sunday. *Cafe 223* (Map 5; ☎ 379 62243), on Symonds St, has reggae-style music, jazz and emerging talent. A blackboard outside details the coming week's events. It's open every night from 8 pm.

In Ponsonby, *Java Jive* (Map 2; ☎ 376 5870), on the corner of Pompallier Terrace and Ponsonby Rd, is a good, long-running live music venue. Music ranges from garage to jazz, and it's on every night of the week. Usually there's no cover charge. The *Safari Lounge* (Map 2; ☎ 378 7707, 116 Ponsonby Rd) is popular with the 18-plus crowd. It has DJs Wednesday to Saturday, and bands occasionally. The *Alhambra Restaurant & Bar* (Map 2; ☎ 376 2430, Three Lamps Plaza, 283 Ponsonby Rd) has a varied program of live music (it could be anything from blues or jazz to rock) from Thursday to Saturday. The *Gables Tavern* (Map 2, ☎ 376 4994), on the corner of Jervois Rd and Kelmarna Ave, Herne Bay, has live jazz Wednesday to Friday from about 7.30 pm, and various other types of music from time to time.

Up in K Rd, the *Dog's Bollix* (Map 3; ☎ 376 4600, 582 K Rd) is a lively Irish pub with live music (mostly traditional and modern Irish, with a bit of country and western) every night except Monday (quiz night). Friday and Saturday see the Dog's Bollix band playing traditional Irish, and on Sunday the Bollix Brothers perform Irish music and songs. In the arcade is the *Live Poets Cafe* (Map 3; ☎ 303 0555, 238 K Rd), a book-lined place with a piano and a live night on Friday featuring a varying program of Brazilian and Portuguese sound, and torch singing. *Beautiful Music* (Map 3; ☎ 379 0052, 300 K Rd), a CD listening lounge, is located on the first floor of a narrow little building that it shares with the gallery Artspace. It has a varying occasional program of DJ music and electronic artists.

For live Latin and Latin DJ try *Club Havana* (Map 3; ☎ 302 3354), on Beresford St, which runs parallel to K Rd. Live bands playing traditional Latin American music perform on Friday and Saturday from 9.30 pm, followed by DJs playing traditional, Latin house and European house until at least 8 am. Club Havana has Latin dance classes (beginner to advanced) on Monday, Tuesday, Wednesday, Thursday and Sunday evenings; you can also learn salsa and tango.

Opposite Club Havana is the *Supper Club (Map 3; ☎ 300 5040)*, situated at Auckland's most famous historic public toilet building. It has various artists on Wednesday, jazz and swing on Thursday and jazz on Sunday.

In Parnell, *Igauçu (Map 4; ☎ 358 4804, 269 Parnell Rd)* has consistently good live jazz on Sunday (usually three bands). *Starbucks Coffee (Map 4; ☎ 336 1599, 305 Parnell Rd)* recently introduced live jazz on Sunday (from 1 pm till 4 pm); get there early as tables fill up fast.

The *Gravity Bar (Map 3; ☎ 377 1224, 21 Stanley St)* has live music from Wednesday to Saturday, ranging from punk through to rock, hip hop and blues. Bands usually get going around 9 or 10 pm. Usually a cover charge applies on Saturday.

In Newmarket, *Claddagh (Map 5; ☎ 522 4410, 372 Broadway)* has live music every night, usually jam sessions during the week and traditional Irish on weekends.

In St Heliers, *The Cafe (Map 1; ☎ 575 8093, 417 Tamaki Drive)*, opposite the beach, has live jazz on Sunday starting at 6.30 pm.

In Devonport, *The Masonic Hotel (Map 6; ☎ 445 0485, 29 King Edward Parade)* has bands (usually alternative-style music) upstairs on Friday, and more mainstream sounds downstairs. Also in Devonport, the local folk music club meets at 8 pm on Monday at the bunker halfway up Mt Victoria. Club nights are held every other week. Entry is $4 for non-members.

CLASSICAL MUSIC

Most classical performances take place at either the Town Hall or the Aotea Centre (both Map 3). Historic Highwic (Map 5) at 40 Gillies Ave, Epsom, sometimes has classical performances (eg classical guitar) on Sunday afternoon. Other venues include the University of Auckland and St Matthew-in-the-City (Map 3) at 187 Federal St.

CINEMA

The newest theatre in town (opened in July 1999) is the big-screen *Imax Theatre (Map 3)*. The screen itself is 27m wide and 20m high and there is seating for 461 people. Up to six films are shown on rotation during 13 one-hour sessions screened daily from 10 am.

The mainstream cinemas in central Auckland include the new *Force Entertainment Centre (Map 3)*, a complex which houses the Imax theatre as well as a number of conventional cinemas and several restaurants and bars. Outside of the city centre *The Village (Map 5; ☎ 520 0806, 77 Broadway)* cinema complex and the *Rialto (Map 5; ☎ 529 2218)* are both in Newmarket; on the North Shore there is the *Devonport 3 Cinemas (Map 6; ☎ 446 0999, 48 Victoria Rd)*; and at Mission Bay is the *Berkley (Map 1; ☎ 528 5296)*.

The Academy (Map 3; ☎ 373 2761, 64 Lorne St), downstairs beside the main entrance to the Auckland Public Library, and the *Bridgeway Theatre (Map 3; ☎ 418 3308, 122 Queen St, Northcote Point)* on the North Shore, occasionally have art-house films.

Entry to cinemas is around $10.

THEATRE, OPERA & BALLET

The Auckland Theatre Company (ATC; Web site www.auckland-theatre.co.nz) is Auckland's only professional theatre company. Mainly subscriber-based, the ATC opened in 1993 with two performances. Today it runs several shows annually, featuring local and international contemporary theatre. It performs at three venues: the 186-seat *Herald Theatre (Map 3)* in the Aotea Centre, the 448-seat *Maidment Theatre (Map 3)* at Auckland University and the new 700-seat *Sky City Theatre (Map 3)*. Performances are advertised in the *NZ Herald* entertainment pages; tickets can be bought through Ticketet (☎ 307 5000).

The University of Auckland's Maidment Theatre organises a summer season of Shakespeare usually held in the grounds of the Old Arts Building on Princes St.

Big international shows are generally held at the Aotea Centre and are planned feature at the restored Civic Theatre.

There is an active amateur theatre scene: the *Dolphin Theatre (☎ 636 7322, Spring St, Onehunga)* and the *Howick Little Theatre Inc (Map 1; ☎ 534 1406, Lloyd Elsmore Park, Pakuranga Rd, Howick)* are two of the most well-known venues, plus *Lopdell House* in Titirangi. Unitech's *School of Performing and Screen Arts Theatre* at Mt Albert is another popular venue.

The Auckland Philharmonic Orchestra performs regularly and the Wellington-based NZ Symphony Orchestra (NZSO) performs at the Aotea Centre and the Town Hall when it tours this way.

Opera NZ puts on two major performances annually (at the Aotea Centre), although it is also involved with numerous, smaller events.

Local contemporary dance companies include The Auckland Dance Company, Black Grace (an all-male, Pacific Island dance company), The Human Garden, The Touch Company Trust (mixed ability dancers), Curves and the Graduate Company (both with Unitech performing arts graduates), and Quantum Flux. Keep an eye out for the Aotea Centre's dance series Made to Move, which features local talent.

The Wellington-based Royal NZ Ballet Company visits Auckland, as does the contemporary dance company of Wellington-based choreographer Michael Parmenter.

Performance Venues

Much money has been spent restoring the *Civic Theatre (Map 3)*, on the corner of Wellesley St West and Queen St. Built early in the the 20th century, the Civic has a spectacular eastern-style interior. Prior to its renovation it was a movie theatre; plans now are to use the it for long-running shows, such as big popular musicals like *Les Miserables* or *Phantom of the Opera*.

One of the city's key performance venues

TONY WHEELER

The *Aotea Centre (Map 3)* is the main venue for opera, ballet, orchestral performances and theatre. Aotea Square is a popular venue for community performances. The *Town Hall (Map 3)* is used more for classical musical performances. The *Silo Theatre (Map 3; ☎ 373 5151)*, at Lower Greys Ave, is a focus for new talent and fringe theatre; Web site www.silo.co.nz.

Other venues include the theatre at Sky City, the Silo theatre and the Maidment Theatre at the university. During the summer, outdoor opera and family concerts are held in the Auckland Domain. Two active North Shore venues are the *Bruce Mason Centre (☎ 488 2940, 1 The Promenade, Takapuna)* and the *Pumphouse (☎ 486 2386)* at Killarney Park, Takapuna.

COMEDY

The *Classic Comedy & Bar (Map 3; ☎ 373 4321, 321 Queen St)* is the main venue for comedy performance in Auckland; Web site www.comedy.co.nz. A bi-monthly calendar of events is available from the venue (you can pick one up at any time from just outside the front doors). Tuesday night is 'impro' night (Loose Tuesday; from 8pm) and the Late Show on Friday (from 11 pm) features stand-up comedy. It's open daily from 4 pm till late.

The *Gravity Bar (Map 3; ☎ 377 1224, 21 Stanley St)* often has comedy nights and is worth checking out.

ENTERTAINMENT

SPECTATOR SPORTS
Rugby & Rugby League
The Rugby Super 12 season kicks off in February and goes till the end of May (Auckland Blues is the local team). The All Black season starts in June and finishes around the end of August. The National Provincial Championships run from August to October. The Auckland Warrriors' (rugby league) season is starting a little earlier in 2000, in February (usually March); the last game is generally in August.

The Super 12 and All Black teams play either at *Eden Park (Map 1; ☎ 849 555, Reimers Ave, Kingsland)* or the *Ericsson Stadium (Map 1; ☎ 571 1699, Beasley Ave, Penrose)*. The Auckland Warriors play at the Ericsson Stadium. In February *NZ Rugby News*, a weekly publication, puts out a calendar for all rugby events (available from most newsagents). *League News* publishes a calendar of events every six weeks (also available from most newsagents). Tickets can be bought through Ticketet (☎ 307 5000).

Soccer
Matches are held at *North Harbour Stadium (Map 1; ☎ 414 0150)* in Albany. The *NZ Herald* sports pages carries details of matches and ticketing outlets.

Cricket
International games are held at Eden Park (for details see earlier). National matches are generally held here too, although very occasionally they are held at club grounds (eg Cornwall Park). Book for international games through Ticketet. The *Shell Itinerary*, free calendar of games, is available from petrol stations at the start of the season (October/November). Alternatively you can pick up a copy of NZ Cricket's calender at bookshops – it generally comes out around mid-October.

Kilikiti, cricket as it is played in the Pacific Islands, is played in Auckland from November to March. This is no restrained affair punctuated by the sound of leather on willow. There are no willow trees in the islands anyway – the bat (long and triangular) is made of a springy type of wood from the fau tree, and the ball is made of compressed rubber. The game, traditionally anyway, is mainly social. There are no set rules, no overs and no limits on the number of players per team – although numbers should be equal in any match (usually there are about 20 players per side). In the islands games can last up to two hours, but moves to modernise the sport in NZ have halved that.

Sports Waitakere's Pasifika Games (in November) features kilikiti and is a good opportunity to see the action. Entry to the games is free; contact Sports Waitakere (☎ 836 6645) for further information. The venue is usually Moire Park in the western suburbs. Kilikiti is also played during summer in suburban parks in Grey Lynn, Mt Roskill and Manukau.

Netball
The season starts in April and usually ends in October. International matches are generally held at the *ASB Stadium (Map 1; ☎ 521 0009)*, on the corner of Kepa and Kohimaramara Rds, Kohimaramara. Matches are publicised through the *NZ Herald's* sports pages and tickets can be bought through Ticketet.

Tennis
The *ASB Bank Tennis Centre (Map 3; ☎ 373 3623, 72 Stanley St)* is the venue for international matches. In January 2000 the centre is hosting international events for men and women.

Horse Racing & Trotting
The two main venues for racing are the *Ellerslie Race Course (Map 1; ☎ 524 4069, 90-100 Ascot Ave, Greenlane East)* and the *Avondale Racecourse (Map 1; ☎ 828 3309, 90 Ash St, Avondale)*. Races at Ellerslie are usually on Saturday and at Avondale on Wednesday. The *NZ Herald* sports pages on Wednesday and Saturday has details.

The annual Auckland Cup, which has four events, is held at Ellerslie. Contact the Auckland Racing Club (☎ 524 4069) for details. *Alexandra Park Raceway (Map 1;*

The rolling pastures of Waiheke Island with Great Barrier Island behind

Glenora Estate B&B, a mudbrick building built in Brittany style on Waiheke Island

CHRISTINE NIVEN

West Auckland is the region's primary wine-growing area.

CHRISTINE NIVEN

Memorabilia weaves its magic at the historic Puhoi pub.

☎ *630 6164)*, on Greenlane Rd, is the place for trotting. Night trotting is held on Friday and Saturday evenings from at 6.40 pm.

Boat Racing

Every summer Waitemata Harbour is full of sails, as all sorts of craft, from little P classes up, compete on the water. The yacht clubs along Tamaki Drive are always busy on weekends with kids and parents getting boats ready to take to the water. Unless you know someone competing, individual races may not mean a lot, but taking a picnic up to Bastion Point, above Tamaki Drive, or North Head, at Devonport, and watching the boats scooting around the courses makes for a pleasant summer afternoon.

Speedway

The speedway season starts in November and finishes mid-March. The main venues are the *Waikaraka Speedway (Map 1;* ☎ *636 5014)* in Penrose and *Western Springs (Map 1;* ☎ *849 2200)* near Auckland Zoo.

ENTERTAINMENT

Shopping

WHAT TO BUY

Just about anything that comes out of New Zealand is available in Auckland. Popular souvenirs include sheepskin products, paua shell items, bone carvings, greenstone, woodcarving and turning, knitwear, and leather goods. Also worth considering is wine (there are numerous vineyards in Auckland's west and south, as well as on Waiheke), books, ceramics and designer clothing.

WHERE TO SHOP

The harbour end of Queen St has the greatest concentration of souvenir and duty-free shops. Most are open daily. The Old Custom House (Map 3) on the corner of Customs St West and Albert St has upmarket brand-name clothing and other items.

Also in the city centre is Pauanesia (☎ 366 7282), at 35 High St, which has a range of homeware imbued with Pacific design. There are coconut-shell items, tapa cloth, paua, textiles with Pacific motifs and more. Another place for things with a Pacific influence is Plantation House (☎ 360 8229), at 47 Ponsonby Rd. Here you'll find tapa and textiles, glassware and ceramics, furniture and more. MasterWorks Gallery, at 77 Ponsonby Rd, also features contemporary crafts.

For designer homeware and collectables try Askew (Map 4), at 195 Parnell Rd and 28 Jervois Rd (Map 2), or The Vault (Map 3), at 13 High St, both of which carry local and international products. The Texas Art School's shop (Map 5), at 366 Broadway, Newmarket, has bright, innovative homeware and gifts by NZ's young and creative new designers.

Out at Kingsland, along the strip of New North Rd near the Kingsland train station, is an enclave of galleries and homeware designer outlets, as well as a greenstone factory and showroom called Regent Manufacturing, at 453 New North Rd. Here you can view and buy greenstone and bone jewellery.

The Great Kiwi Yarn (Map 3), at 107 Queen St, stocks a good selection of NZ-made knitwear, including items produced from possum fur, alpaca, merino and high-country wool.

For books on NZ and Auckland, including coffee table books, try Unity Books (Map 3; ☎ 0800 286 489); Parsons Bookshop (Map 3; ☎ 303 1557), on the corner of Lorne and Wellesley Sts, which specialises in art; and Whitcoulls (Map 3; ☎ 356 5400), at 210 Queen St. Dymocks (Map 3; ☎ 379 9919) and Atrium on Elliot (Map 3), at 21 Elliot St, are good bookstore chains.

For books that are out of print and generally hard to track down (eg many of those covering the history of Auckland) try Evergreen Books (Map 6; ☎ 445 2960), at 15 Victoria Rd, Devonport, or Hard to Find (But Worth the Effort) Secondhand Bookshop (☎ 634 4340), at 171-73 The Mall, Onehunga. There is also a branch of the excellent Hard to Find at 81a Victoria Rd Devonport (Map 6). For children's books, including those with a NZ theme, try Dorothy Butler Children's Bookshop (Map 2; ☎ 376 7283) on the corner of Jervois Rd and St Mary's Bay Rd in Ponsonby.

The Auckland Museum (Map 5) has a shop with interesting handicrafts and a good selection of books. The Auckland Art Gallery also has a small outlet selling art books and a select range of items.

There are many galleries and workshops in and around Auckland. The North Shore City Council and the Waitakere City Council both put out maps indicating which artist studios and workshops are open to the public (when and where). The maps are available from visitor centres and from the respective city councils.

For a listing of Auckland galleries and current exhibitions get a copy of *The Auckland Gallery Guide* (available from most galleries) or visit the Web site www .aucklandlive.co.nz/whats_on/eventsdiary/

gallery_guide/. Portfolio (Map 3; ☎ 279 0145), at 10 Lorne St in the city, specialises in works on paper; Compendium (Map 3), at 5 Lorne St, has sculpture, ceramics, glass, pottery, woodwork, clothes and shoes; Art by the Sea (Map 6; ☎ 445 6665), on the corner of King Edward Parade and Church St in Devonport, has a wide range of work including ceramics and prints; and the Watercolour Gallery (☎ 445 7845), at 29 Church St, Devonport, is well worth a visit.

The Ferner Gallery (Map 4), at 367 Parnell Rd, is a leading dealer in NZ historical and contemporary art. There are numerous little galleries around Lorne St, in the city centre, and Ponsonby Rd and Parnell are also good places for art and handicrafts.

For original and innovative jewellery from leading artists, a good place to go is Fingers, at 2 Kitchener St in the city centre. For glassware try the Gary Nash studio/shop at 20 MacKelvie St, Ponsonby. Also in Ponsonby is Pots of Ponsonby (Map 2), a long-running ceramics shop and exhibition space.

For NZ designer clothing try the boutiques in High St, Vulcan Lane and O'Connell St in the city centre – big names here include Karen Walker, Zambesi, Workshop, World and Kate Sylvester. Ponsonby Rd and Parnell are also good places for the label-conscious, and Minnie Cooper (Map 2), on Ponsonby Rd, makes quality handmade shoes.

K Rd is the place for vintage and ethnic clothing, and for garments from emerging young designers. In fact, K Rd has some of Auckland's more interesting shopping experiences. This is the place to come for hair extensions, henna hand-designs, collectables from Asia and the Pacific, and new and second-hand CDs and tapes. On the corner of East St and K Rd is Beautiful Music (Map 3), which has a CD listening lounge – espresso available. In St Kevins Arcade you'll find the colourful and fascinating Balloonski (Map 3), which specialises in juggling equipment.

St Lukes Shopping Centre (Map 1; ☎ 846 2069) is one of Auckland's best shopping complexes, with 120 speciality stores and a food court. It's open daily from 9 am to 5 pm;

bus Nos 22 and 24 from Victoria St in the city will take you there. Newmarket is another popular shopping area, with Two Double Seven (Map 5) – a supermarket, food court, bookshop, clothing outlet etc – and the newer Rialto complex (Map 5), plus many other shops small and large (clothing, shoes, electronics, homeware and so on). The shops are open Monday to Thursday from 9 am to 5.30 pm, Friday 9 am to 9 pm and Saturday 9.30 am to 4 pm. A few stores are open on Sunday. You can get to Newmarket on the Link bus.

Parnell, as mentioned, is full of boutiques: handicrafts, homeware, designer clothing, electronic goods, art and books. In the city, try the Atrium Shopping Centre (Map 3), on Elliot St (parallel to Queen St and near the Centra Hotel), which has stores with brand-name goods (Sportsgirl, Oshkosh etc). The Link bus goes up Parnell Rise and will take you past the village.

Victoria Park Market (Map 3; ☎ 309 6140), a 15 minute walk west of Queen St (or take bus No 005 from Customs St West), is open daily from 9 am to 7 pm. There's a huge variety of goods here, including clothes, pottery, leather work, handicrafts and so on.

For bargain clothing try the Dressmart Factory Outlet (Map 1; ☎ 622 2400) at 151 Arthur St, Onehunga (open daily from 10 am to 4 pm). More than 40 factory shops are located here and you may pick up a brand-name for a good price.

For local wines you can always visit the vineyards and buy the wine direct from the cellar door. Get hold of the pamphlet *Winemakers of Auckland* from the visitor centre for details on vineyard locations and opening hours.

Auckland has numerous handicraft and flea markets. The visitor centre has a full list of these, but those worth looking out for include:

K Rd Saturday Street Market (Map 3), Saturday from 10 am to 3 pm. Here you'll find clothing, collectables, tapa cloth and music.
Mission Bay Handicraft Market, Mission House (Map 1), the 1st and 3rd Sunday of the month (each Sunday in December) from 10 am to 4pm.

Avondale Sunday Market, Ash St entrance, Avondale Racecourse (Map 1), Sunday from 6 am to noon. This market offers a great multi-cultural experience and lots of superb food.

Otara Flea Market (Map 1), in the car park, Newbury St, Otara, Saturday from 6 am to noon. A prime place for a glimpse of Polynesian Auckland, and food that you won't get in city restaurants.

Devonport Handicraft Market, Community House, Clarence St, (Map 6), the 2nd Sunday of every month from 10 am to 3 pm. Visit this market for local arts and crafts.

Downtown Market, between the old Central Railway Station (Map 4) and the former Oriental Markets (enter from Beach Rd), Sunday from 9 am to 2 pm. Crafts, arts and food, plus second-hand goods.

Excursions

Hauraki Gulf Islands

The Hauraki Gulf off Auckland is dotted with islands (*motu*). Some are within minutes of the city and are popular as day trips. Waiheke, a favourite weekend escape, has become almost a dormitory suburb. It also has some fine beaches and hostels, so it's a popular backpacker destination. There is plenty of choice if you are seeking something more upmarket. Great Barrier Island, once a remote and little-visited island, is also becoming a popular destination and can be used as a stepping stone to Coromandel Peninsula. The islands are generally accessible by ferry or light aircraft.

There are 47 islands in the Hauraki Gulf Maritime Park, administered by the Department of Conservation (DOC). Some are good-sized islands, others are simply rocks jutting out of the sea. The islands are loosely put into two categories: recreation and conservation. The recreation islands are readily accessible to visitors and their harbours are dotted with yachts in summer. The conservation islands, on the other hand, have severely restricted access. Special permits are required to visit some and others cannot be visited at all, since these islands are refuges for the preservation of plants and animals, especially birds, often extremely rare or even endangered species. For information on Kawau Island and Goat Island, see the North of Auckland section in this chapter.

Information

The Hauraki Gulf Islands are administered by DOC, whose information centre in Auckland has the best information about natural features, walkways and camping. At the Auckland Visitor Centre you can learn about the more commercial aspects of the islands, such as hotels, ferry services etc. Trampers should get the 1:50,000 Topomaps for Wai-

HIGHLIGHTS

- Touring the wineries west of Auckland
- Discovering the Hauraki Gulf Islands, including the volcanic Rangitoto and the wild and remote Great Barrier Island
- Bushwalking in the picturesque Waitakere Ranges
- Taking a cruise through the Bay of Islands

heke and Great Barrier. A good Web site with interactive maps and information on accommodation, places to eat and activities is at www.islands.co.nz.

RANGITOTO & MOTUTAPU ISLANDS

About 600 years ago, **Rangitoto** (260m) erupted from the sea, and was probably active for several years before settling down; it's now believed to be extinct. Maori living on nearby Motutapu Island, to which Rangitoto is now joined by a causeway, certainly witnessed the eruptions; human footprints have been found there, embedded in the ash thrown out during the course of the mountain's creation. It is the largest and youngest of Auckland's volcanic cones. The distinctive bumpy profile (as viewed from Auckland) is the result of fire fountaining, which created these scoria cones and various others on the mountain. Hot lava oozing down the side of the mountain solidified into the dark basaltic rock, which is common all over the island, and hot lava flowing beneath the cooling crust created a series of caves near the centre of the island, which can be visited (bring a torch).

Rangitoto literally means 'blood red sky' although this is generally thought to allude not to the eruptions as such but to a battle

RANGITOTO & MOTUTAPU ISLANDS

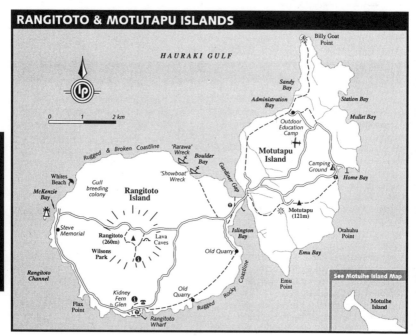

in which the commander of the Arawa canoe, Tamatekapua, was wounded. Rangitoto is an abbreviation of Te Rangi i totongia a Tamatekapua, a name meaning 'the day of Tamatekapua's bleeding'.

Pohutukawas were the first trees to establish themselves on the porous, basaltic ground; their deep roots can tap underground water reservoirs. This is the country's largest stand of pohutukawa and it provides moisture and shade for other forms of vegetation. Today more than 200 species of native tree grow on the island, despite its thin soil cover, and numerous types of orchid and fern have also become established. There isn't a great deal of birdlife, not surprising given the newness of the forests. But you may spot fantails, grey warblers, and silvereyes (all of which feed on insects). Tuis feed on the red pohutukawa flowers during summer. There are, however, many

sea birds, including black-backed gulls that nest in large numbers on the jagged scoria fields. Wallabies and possums let loose on neighbouring Motutapu in the 1880s quickly colonised Rangitoto, posing a serious risk to the pohutukawa forest. They have now been eradicated through a DOC program that began in 1990.

Before the arrival of Europeans, Maori used Rangitoto as a burial place, as a lookout, and possibly as a kaka (native parrot) reserve. There is evidence that small fishing villages may have been established on the coastline, but Rangitoto compared unfavourably with the more fertile islands nearby and was therefore never really settled. The government bought Rangitoto from the Maori in 1854 for £15, and it became a public domain in 1890. In 1892 a salt mine was set up, but later abandoned. Scoria was mined more successfully; convict labourers carved out the road to the summit in the 1920s and 1930s, and constructed stone walls near the landings. In the 19th century basalt from Rangitoto was used to build Kinder House (in Parnell), Mission House (in Mission Bay) and other structures that still stand today. Baches (holiday homes) sprang up after WWI, but from the late 1930s the government put a stop to further construction, and existing baches have been gradually removed. There are no permanent residents on the island today.

Rangitoto, 10km north-east of Auckland's city centre, is a good place for a picnic. It has many pleasant walks, a saltwater swimming pool, BBQs and a great view from the summit of the cone. There's an information board with maps of the walks and a shop that opens for the ferries. Before you go, get a copy of the DOC pamphlet *Rangitoto* ($1), which has a useful map and descriptions of several good walks.

The hike from the wharf to the summit takes about an hour. Up at the top, a loop walk goes around the crater's rim. The walk to the lava caves branches off the summit walk and takes 30 minutes (return).

There are other walks too, some easy enough for kids. Bring water – on sunny days the black basalt gets pretty hot – and sturdy footwear.

In contrast to Rangitoto, **Motutapu** (1508 hectares) is mainly covered in grassland, grazed by sheep and cattle. This is a very significant island from an archaeological point of view; the traces of some 500 years of continuous human habitation are etched into the landscape. Motutapu, which literally means 'sacred island of Taikehu', is thought to have been named by a Tainui *tohunga* (priest) after a place of significance in his homeland. The island was bought from the Maori in 1842 for 10 empty casks, four double-barrelled shotguns, 50 blankets, five hats, five pieces of gown material, five shawls and five pairs of black trousers. In 1869 it was bought by the Reid brothers and farmed by the family until WWII, when it was taken over by the army. An observation post, underground com-

Pohutukawa, or the NZ native Christmas tree

mand centre and various pillboxes were constructed, and the tunnels remain, providing an endless source of fascination to visitors. In 1992 DOC embarked on a 50-year conservation program, which has involved eliminating the introduced rock wallabies and possums. Extensive replanting with appropriate indigenous species is also part of the program.

There's an interesting three hour return walk between the wharf at Islington Bay and the wharf at Home Bay. Islington, the inlet between the islands, was once known as 'Drunken Bay' because sailing ships would stop here to sober up crews who had overindulged in Auckland.

There's a DOC *camping ground* at Home Bay on Motutapu Island. Facilities are basic, with only a water tap and a toilet provided. Bring your own cooking equipment, as open fires are not permitted; camping fees are $5 per night for adults and $2 a night for children. For more information, contact the island's senior ranger (☎ 372 7348) or DOC in Auckland.

Getting There & Away
The ferry trip to Rangitoto Island from the ferry building in Auckland takes about half an hour. Fullers (☎ 367 9120 for a faxed timetable, ☎ 367 9112 for advance reservations) has ferries leaving daily at 9.30 am, 11.45 am and an additional sailing at 2 pm during summer.

Ferries depart Rangitoto for the return trip at 12.30 and 3 pm with an extra boat leaving the island at 5 pm in summer. The return fare is $18 (children $9).

There are two tours to Rangitoto with Fullers. On the Volcanic Explorer tour you take a 4WD tractor-towed, canopied trailer to a 900m boardwalk leading to the summit. The trips depart daily from pier 3 at 9.30 and 11.45 am. There is a 2 pm sailing in summer. Bookings are essential. The cost (ferry and safari) is $35 per adult and $17.50 per child (five to 15 years) and $8.50 for children under five.

There are also guided walks on Rangitoto. For these you leave for the island on the 9.30 am ferry and return on the 3 pm ferry. The walks go via Kidney Fern Grove, Pioneer Track and the crater rim. At the time of writing they were running only on weekends, but check with Fullers. The tours cost $20 for adults and $14 for children plus the ferry fare. Fullers' two hour Coffee Cruise/Harbour Explorer tour also stops at Rangitoto. It departs daily from pier 3 at 9.30 and 11.45 am and 2 pm, with an extra departure at 4 pm in summer (adults/children $20/10).

BROWNS ISLAND (MOTUKOREA)
Browns Island erupted some 10,000 years ago, when the Waitemata Harbour was still a river valley. Its Maori name, Motukorea, means island of the oyster-catcher; these birds still frequent its shores. It's also an important breeding ground for the threatened NZ dotterel. The remains of gardens and *pa* (fortified village) sites have been found (at least 70 archaeological sites are recorded),

Browns Island, or Motukorea, one of the region's youngest volcanoes

and even in 1820, when the first Europeans visited the island, Maori were growing kumara and potato. The island was bought by William Brown and John Logan Campbell in 1840. For a short time they lived on the island in *raupo* (bullrush) huts, made for them by local Maori, and used the island as a trading base before moving to the fledgling Auckland settlement. The island passed into the ownership of two other families (the Alisons and the Featherstones) and for the first four decades of the 20th century was a popular picnicking spot for Aucklanders who made the journey with the Devonport Ferry Company (in which the Alison family had a major stake). The city was given to Auckland city in 1955 by Sir Ernest Davis, a wealthy brewer.

The island is uninhabited and the only access is by private boat or charter. You can also reach the island by kayak. See the Sea Kayaking section in the Things to See & Do chapter.

MOTUIHE ISLAND
Named for an ancestor of the Arawa tribe, Motuihe (178 hectares) contains much evidence of early occupation: pa, storage pits and gardens. The island was first sold to a European in 1839. John Logan Campbell and William Brown farmed the island soon after, and olive trees planted by Campbell still fruit. In 1873 it became a quarantine station; the cemetery is a memorial particularly

MOTUIHE ISLAND

Getting There & Away

Fullers runs ferries to Motuihe in summer. Call ☎ 367 9111 to get a faxed timetable.

TIRITIRI MATANGI ISLAND

Tiritiri Matangi was at one time occupied by Maori; there are remains of a pa site here. In 1841 it was bought by the Crown and eventually leased and farmed; its forests were mostly cleared. The historic and well-preserved 30m-high lighthouse was completed in 1865 and donated to Auckland city by the wealthy brewer Sir Ernest Davis. The island has been part of the maritime park since 1971. Since 1984 a not-so-small army of volunteers has planted many thousands of native trees. As the forest has regenerated, endangered native birds have been reintroduced to the island. They include red-crowned parakeets, brown

EXCURSIONS

to those who died during the 1918 influenza epidemic. During WWI it was used as a Prisoner of War camp, whose most famous escapees are the German Count Felix Von Luckner and his crew who made a successful bid for freedom in 1917. Between the wars the island served as a children's health camp, but it was closed to civilians during WWII when a naval training centre was established. The centre was finally abandoned in 1962 and the island is now part of the Hauraki Gulf Maritime Park. It is mainly farmland.

There are picnic grounds, barbecue sites, changing sheds and toilets on the northern end of the island where the old wharf is. Also in this area is a kiosk (open daily in summer and whenever there is a demand in winter), where you can get food, fishing supplies and information. The *camping ground* costs $5 for adults and $2 for children (contact ☎ 09-534 5419). If you plan to visit, buy the DOC pamphlet *Motuihe* ($1) from the DOC ferry-building shop. It has a map of the island, and a description of three walks.

TIRITIRI MATANGI ISLAND

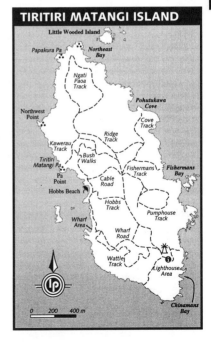

teals, little spotted kiwis, stichbirds and others.

You can do a guided tour with a DOC volunteer or employee. This is well worthwhile. The tour lasts an hour ($5 per adult, $4 per senior, $2.50 per child and $15 per family).

Getting There & Away

Fullers ferries go to Tiritiri Matangi on Thursday at 8.30 am, and at 9 am on weekends (leaving from pier 1 at the city centre ferry terminal). The return trip takes nine hours.

Reservations (☎ 367 9111) are essential. Tickets cost $30 for an adult return and $14.50 for a child (five to 15 years).

WAIHEKE ISLAND

Waiheke is the most visited of the gulf islands, and at 93 sq km is one of the largest. It's reputed to be sunnier and warmer than Auckland and has plenty of picturesque bays and beaches.

The island attracts all kinds of artistic folk, who exhibit their work in galleries and

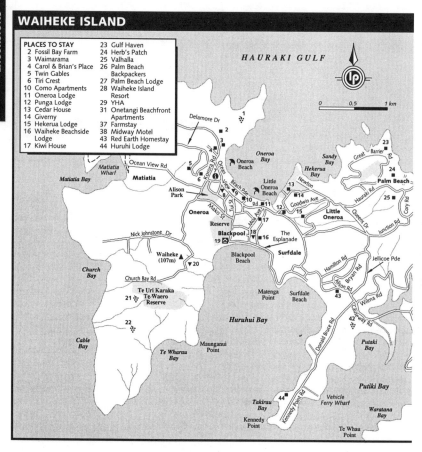

WAIHEKE ISLAND

PLACES TO STAY
2 Fossil Bay Farm
3 Waimarama
4 Carol & Brian's Place
5 Twin Gables
6 Tiri Crest
10 Como Apartments
11 Oneroa Lodge
12 Punga Lodge
13 Cedar House
14 Giverny
15 Hekerua Lodge
16 Waiheke Beachside Lodge
17 Kiwi House
23 Gulf Haven
24 Herb's Patch
25 Valhalla
26 Palm Beach Backpackers
27 Palm Beach Lodge
28 Waiheke Island Resort
29 YHA
31 Onetangi Beachfront Apartments
37 Farmstay
38 Midway Motel
43 Red Earth Homestay
44 Huruhi Lodge

craft shops on the island. There is also an increasing number of retirees and commuters. While it is slowly becoming an Auckland suburb, it is still a relaxed, rural retreat.

Waiheke was originally discovered and settled by the Maori. Legends relate that one of the pioneering canoes came to the island. Traces of an old fortified pa can still be seen on the headland overlooking Putiki Bay. Europeans arrived with the missionary Samuel Marsden in the early 1800s and the island was soon stripped of its kauri forest.

Orientation & Information

Waiheke's main settlement is Oneroa, at the western end of the island. From there the island is fairly built up through to Palm Beach and Onetangi in the middle region. But beyond this, the eastern end of the island is lightly inhabited. The coastline is a picturesque mixture of coves, inlets and private beaches.

The Waiheke Visitor Information Office (☎ 372 9999, fax 372 9919, waiheke@ iconz.co.nz) is at the Artworks complex, on

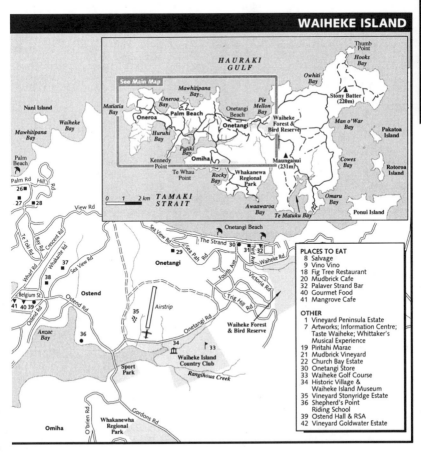

WAIHEKE ISLAND

PLACES TO EAT
8 Salvage
9 Vino Vino
18 Fig Tree Restaurant
20 Mudbrick Cafe
32 Palaver Strand Bar
40 Gourmet Food
41 Mangrove Cafe

OTHER
1 Vineyard Peninsula Estate
7 Artworks; Information Centre; Taste Waiheke; Whittaker's Musical Experience
19 Piritahi Marae
21 Mudbrick Vineyard
22 Church Bay Estate
30 Onetangi Store
33 Waiheke Golf Course
34 Historic Village & Waiheke Island Museum
35 Vineyard Stonyridge Estate
36 Shepherd's Point Riding School
39 Ostend Hall & RSA
42 Vineyard Goldwater Estate

EXCURSIONS

Ocean View Rd, in Oneroa, 1km from the ferry dock. It has maps and information, and makes bookings for tours and accommodation. It's open daily from 9 am to 5 pm (it closes earlier in winter).

The *Gulf News* ($1.50) is a weekly news magazine of island events. *Waiheke Island: A Tour* ($1.50), produced by the Waiheke Historical Society, is available at the information office.

Oneroa has a post office, banks and 24-hour ATMs. You can access the Internet at Waiheke Commercial Stationers (☎ 372 7174, 151 Ocean View Rd) during shop hours (weekdays from 8 am to 5.30 pm and Saturday to 4 pm). It costs $5 for 15 minutes and $20 an hour. The annual Waiheke Jazz Festival is held at Easter, and the Waiheke Arts & Crafts Fair in October.

Things to See & Do

The **Artworks** centre is home to a variety of art and craft galleries, and other businesses and community groups. Artworks is on the corner of Ocean View and Kororoa Rds, between Oneroa and Matiatia Wharf; it's open daily from 10 am to 4 pm. Whittaker's Musical Experience, in the Artworks Centre, is your chance to savour antique instruments; entry to the 1½ hour show (1 pm) is $7 ($5 children and seniors). It's open from 10 am to noon and from 2.30 to 4 pm.

At **Waiheke Potteries** (110 Ocean View Rd), at the Matiatia end of Oneroa's main shopping street, you can paint your own pots. Smaller pieces start at $10. Firing takes place between Wednesday and Saturday and your work can be sent to you (if you've already left the island). It costs $4 to send one piece back to Auckland and $10 to send a box on the ferry back to Auckland. It's open from 8 am to 6 pm daily.

On the road to Onetangi, between the airstrip and the golf club, is the small **Historic Village** and **Waiheke Island Museum**. The Historic Village (☎ 372 5168) suffered a blow when fire destroyed its 120-year-old woolshed in 1997. The museum survives, however, and is open daily in summer (1 to 4 pm) and on weekends and school holidays in winter. Rebuilding work was underway at the time of writing to replace the woolshed.

Waiheke has more than 30 **vineyards**, but you can only visit four of them (Goldwater Estate, Stoneyridge, Peninsula Estate and Mudbrick Vineyard) on a tour or by arrangement. Some will charge for tours and tastings. The information office has brochures.

Water Sports

Popular beaches with good swimming include Oneroa Beach and the adjacent Little Oneroa Beach. Palm Beach in a lovely little cove, and there is a long stretch of sand at Onetangi Bay. A number of the beaches have shady pohutukawa trees. There are nudist beaches at Palm Beach and on the west end of Onetangi Bay. Surf skis and boogie boards can be hired on Onetangi; there's snorkelling at Hekerua Bay.

Sea Kayaking

Waiheke's many bays and central position in the Hauraki Gulf make it ideal for sea kayaking. Operators include Ross Adventures (☎ 372 5550), which is based at Matiatia, and Kayak Waiheke (☎ 372 7262). Ross Adventures offers half-day (four hour) trips ($50 per person) to four-day camping excursions. There is also a night kayaking trip ($50 per person). Kayak Waiheke has daily guided tours (9 and 11 am, or by arrangement) and will pick up/drop off by taxi from Matiatia for free. It costs $50 for one person for one to three hours guided instruction/expedition (the price decreases according to the number of people on a trip). The kayak is available to you for the rest of the day at no extra charge provided conditions are favourable, but you are responsible for your own safety. Kayak Waiheke will organise personalised sightseeing and vineyard tours.

Walking

Waiheke has a system of walkways, outlined in the *Waiheke Islands Walkways* pamphlet, which is available on the island or at the DOC office in Auckland.

In Onetangi there's a forest and bird reserve with several good walks, one of them leading up to three large kauri trees. For coastal walks, a good, well-marked track leads right around the coast from Oneroa Bay to Palm Beach. It's about a two hour walk; at the Palm Beach end you can jump on a bus back to town. Another good coastal walk begins at the Matiatia ferry wharf.

The best walks are in the less-developed eastern part of the island. The **Stony Batter Walk**, leading through private farmland, derives its name from the boulder-strewn fields. From Man o' War Bay Rd, the track leads to the old gun emplacements with their connecting underground tunnels and sweeping views; from there you can continue north to Hooks Bay or south to Opopo Bay.

Other Activities

The Shepherd's Point Riding Centre (☎ 372 8104), at 91 Ostend Rd, between Ostend and the airstrip, has guided **horse rides** starting at $25 for an hour, $50 for a two hour beach ride, and $65 for a three hour beach and farm ride.

Scenic Flights (fixed-wing and helicopter), starting at $15 per person, are operated by Waiheke Airservices (☎ 372 5000, fax 372 5001, flingwing@hotmail.com).

Organised Tours

Fullers has a host of tours in conjunction with its ferry service. See the Getting There & Away section later. The Postie Run (☎ 372 9166) can take around seven people to the far end of the island ($15 per person). It leaves on Monday, Tuesday and Wednesday between 8.15 and 8.30 am from the Oneroa post office and returns between 1 and 2 pm. Waiheke Jaguar Tours (☎ 372 7312, 025 962 554) organises tours to the main sights in the west of the island, and will put together other tours for groups of at least 10 people. The bus will meet the ferry (it regularly meets Pacific Ferries from Auckland; see under Getting There & Away later). Ring to confirm which ferries the bus will be meeting.

Places to Stay & Eat

Waiheke has some 100 homestays, farmstays, B&Bs, beaches and flats for rent, costing anything from $20 to $200 a night. If you're on a really tight budget, there is a reasonable degree of choice, but if you can splash out, there are some real treats. Phone the information office (☎ 372 9999) in Oneroa and someone will help match you with the type of place you are looking for. Tourism Auckland also lists accommodation on Waiheke. The only camping ground on the island is at Rocky Bay, at the far end of the beach off Gordon's Rd in the Whakanewha Regional Park (and there are limited sites at Palm Beach Backpackers and Hekerua Lodge). Bookings for the camping ground must be made with Parksline (☎ 303 1530). Whakanewha costs $5 (children $2).

Church Bay & Around The Church Bay area, just south of Matiatia, is peaceful and lovely, with vineyards and small plantings of olives and lavender. There are a couple of places to stay.

Kowhai Close (☎ 372 6763, 92 Nick Johnston's Drive) has a self-contained one bedroom apartment and two rooms. The rooms share a bathroom; they cost $90 per couple, including breakfast. The apartment is fully self-contained and has a spa and good views. The owners will pick you up from the ferry. All linen is supplied.

Glenora Estate (☎ 372 5082, fax 372 5087, glenora.estate@xtra.co.nz, 160 Nick Johnstone Drive) is a stylish place – take a look at the Web site at www.waiheke.co.nz/glenora.htm. The farmhouse is fashioned after the style found in Brittany, northern France, and is set in lovely gardens. Accommodation in the farmhouse (breakfast included) centres on the Glenora suite ($270 for two) and the Crusoe Room ($230 for two). Both suites have sea views and are beautifully furnished, with private en suites. A separate barn caters to medium to long-term guests. It costs $350 a night for two (breakfast brought to your door included).

The *Mudbrick Vineyard & Restaurant (☎ 372 9050, fax 372 9051, Church Bay Rd)* is a top dining spot on Waiheke. From the patio you look across the rows of vines towards the harbour and Auckland city. It's open daily for lunch and dinner. The menu changes with the season, but is always good, with mains in the mid-to-high $20s. Naturally, there is an excellent wine list.

Oneroa Although it's the principal town of Waiheke, Oneroa is not very big. Straddling a ridge, it has sea views on both sides and contains most of the island's services and good restaurants.

To get away from it all, call in at the *Fossil Bay Organic Farm (☎ 372 7569, 58 Korora Rd)* near Oneroa. Singles cost $20, and doubles/twins cost $38. You can also camp here for $10. Self-contained units sleeping four/six are $60/80.

Waimarama Cottage (☎ 372 9206, fax 372 9209, 52 Korora Rd) is self-contained with a full kitchen, laundry, queen-sized bed and en suite. There is a deck from which you can take in the views towards Rakino Island. It's a quiet, private place next to the Peninsula Estate Vineyard (you can always pop across to buy a bottle of wine). It costs $250 for the first two nights (there is a two night minimum) and $100 a night thereafter. It's a great spot for honeymooners.

Carol & Brian's Place (☎ 372 8200, fax 372 8201, carolbpl@ihug.co.nz, 35 Kororoa Rd) is an impressive modern place with good views. A double room with en suite costs $80; children under five free.

Tiri Crest (☎ 372 5423, 528 4794, 025 223 5805, 16 Tiri Rd) has a neat, fully furnished house for rent, as well as a flat and a cute little cottage with polished floors. The house costs $140 a night; the cottage (one double bedroom) costs $110 and the flat $85. Weekly rates are available. You can enjoy views from the decks.

Twin Gables (☎ 372 9877, 17 Tiri Rd) is a modern place built to get the best of the lovely views. Doubles with a deck cost $90 and twin-share is $80, including breakfast.

Como Apartments (☎ 377 4970, 025 290 7970, 165 A & B Ocean View Rd) is very near Oneroa's restaurants and shops. Como A

is an older house on street level that has been renovated in apartment style with polished matai floors. It has the better views of the two apartments, as well as a deck. There are two bedrooms. The cost for two people is $180 a night (it can accommodate four people). Como B, which is below Como A, has one bedroom but no deck. It costs $120 a night for two people. The apartments are fully self-contained.

Oneroa Lodge (☎ 372 8897, fax 373 8244, 187 Ocean View·Rd) is a modern, Mediterranean-style lodge that catches the views from its cliff-top vantage point. Each of the three suites is individually designed, and has an en suite and private patio. Breakfast is included in the cost of $175 a single, $195 a twin/double.

Kiwi House (☎ 372 9123, 23 Kiwi St) is a pleasant modern place that sleeps 12 in double, twin and en suite rooms. Breakfast is included in the tariff of $25 per person. Kitchen and dining area facilities are shared. The Web site is at www.kiwi .co.nz/kiwihous.htm.

Waiheke Beachside Lodge (☎/fax 372 9884, 48 Kiwi St) is a modern, sunny place with views. It's close to the Fig Tree restaurant. There are two, self-contained one-bedroom apartments with en suites (one wheelchair accessible) for $110, and a bed and breakfast (en suite) room for $100.

Giverny (☎ 372 2200, fax 372 2204, givernyinn@ibm.net, 44 Queens Drive) has a self-contained cottage with polished floors, and a room in the new house next door. Both are set in beautiful gardens. A room in either the cottage or the house costs $180, including breakfast.

Cedar House (☎ 372 5407, 69 Queens Drive) is a self-contained one bedroom flat (king-size or twin beds) with great views over the gulf. It costs around $85 for two people.

Places to eat centre on Oneroa's main street. They include *Salvage (☎ 372 2273)*, a popular licensed venue where you can eat inside or out (open daily from 7 am to 11 pm). You can have a meal (steak, fish, pasta, burgers) or a coffee and a snack. *Vino Vino*

(☎ 372 9888) is at the end of View Mall. It's a popular licensed restaurant with good food. You get great views from the deck, but you should book if you want to ensure a place there. It's open daily from 11 am to late, and there is live music regularly. The little *Courtyard Cafe* tucked away one floor below is a quiet place for a cold drink or a coffee. The *deli* at the entrance to the mall serves good salads, sandwiches and soups. *Stjepan's* (☎ 373 8209) across the road has good pizzas and seafood ($18 to $19 for mains). It's open daily from morning till late. The *Dolphin Cafe (147 Ocean View Rd)* is one of the best places for good, inexpensive burgers and snacks.

The *Fig Tree Cafe & Restaurant (☎/fax 372 6363, 46 Moa Ave, Blackpool)* is near the waterfront, between Surfdale and Oneroa. This small, popular place has meat, seafood and vegetarian dishes from about $15. It's open from Wednesday to Sunday for lunch and dinner.

Bill of Blanchys (☎ 372 9068, 6 Miami Ave) at Surfdale, one beach along from Blackpool, serves duck, venison, eye fillet and chicken with delicious sauces. Mains cost around $25. In summer its open Wednesday to Sunday from 6 pm till late, and it's licensed. Blanchys will pick you up and drop you off anywhere on the island.

Little Oneroa Just east of Oneroa, Little Oneroa has a reasonable beach and one of the island's few areas of native bush. *Punga Lodge (☎/fax 372 6675, 223 Ocean View Rd)* is set in tranquil bush surroundings. B&B, en suite rooms and apartments are available and start at $95 per room.

Hekerua Lodge (☎ 372 2556, collrich@ clear.net.nz, 11 Hekerua Rd), also known as Waiheke Island Backpackers, is nestled in bush. Double/twin rooms with shared bathrooms cost $34 to $50, doubles with en suites $68, rooms that sleep up to 10 people cost $17 per person. There is a self-contained unit that sleeps six people for $130. Tent sites are available for $10 per person. There is a fully equipped kitchen, a BBQ and a swimming pool.

Hauraki House (☎ 372 7598, 50 Hauraki Rd) in Sandy Bay, is popular and has good views. The rooms cost $55/80 for a single/double, including breakfast. There are two bathrooms which are shared.

Herb's Patch (☎ 372 9937, 68 Hauraki Rd) has two rooms ($85), with a shared a bathroom. There are views and gardens.

Enclosure Bay *Gulf Haven (☎ 372 6629, fax 372 8558, 49 Great Barrier Rd)* has terrific views of the gulf; the lovely garden sweeps down towards the private foreshore where you can swim (the water's deep). There are two self-contained studio apartments (one queen, one twin/super-king) with en suites ($165), and two B&B rooms in the house (one double, one queen) for $90 to $100.

Palm Beach Palm Beach is in a beautiful little cove with a pleasant beach. On the hill above the beach are Valhalla and the Waiheke Island Resort.

Valhalla (☎ 372 8220, 72 Cory Rd) is a large, modern place with the sort of views you would expect from such a commanding position. There is a pool, a spa and four bedrooms with their own bathrooms.

The *Waiheke Island Resort (☎ 372 7897, 0800 924 4353, fax 373 8241, sales@ waihekeresort.co.nz)* is at the top of Palm Rd, which leads to the beach. The rooms vary in size and facilities but the basic cost is $199 per couple (this includes breakfast and transfers to the ferry). They have a Web site at waihekeresort.co.nz.

Palm Beach Lodge (☎ 372 7763, 23 Tiri View Rd), which is a few streets up from the beach, has three modern, self-contained apartments with decks (sea views) and BBQs. Each apartment has two double bedrooms and costs $240 a night.

Palm Beach Backpackers (☎ 372 8662, 54 Palm Rd), a sprawling place right across from the beach, has a school camp feel. A dorm bed in a three to eight bed room costs $20, doubles/twins are $45 to $54. All facilities are shared (there's a fully equipped kitchen). Tent sites cost $12 per person.

Ostend This village has shops and a couple of places to eat but it's a fair way from the beach. There is a colourful local market at the RSA (Returned Services Association) hall on Saturday (8 am to 3 pm in summer, closing earlier in winter).

On the main road, the *Midway Motel* (☎ *372 8023, fax 372 9779, 1 Whakarite Rd)* has studio units for $85, one-bedroom units for $95 and a spa bath unit for $120.

Tawaipareira Farmstays B&B (☎/fax 372 6676, 28 Seaview Rd) is an organic farm with plenty of activities to keep children busy. Singles/doubles/king (shared bathrooms) cost $45/75/85, including breakfast. Home-cooked organic meals are also available.

Surfdale & Kennedy Point *Red Earth Homestay (☎ 372 9975, 6 Kennedy Rd)*, off Mitchell Rd, is a cosy little backpacker homestay. Dorm beds cost and beds in a twin room costs $16, a single room costs $28. There is a fully equipped kitchen, a television, CD player, books and so on. French, German and Italian are spoken. The Surfdale-bound bus from Matiatia will take you to the start of Kennedy Rd from where it's a very short walk to the accommodation.

Huruhi Lodge (☎ 372 9761, fax 372 9706, 92 Donald Bruce Rd) is a very private water-front hideaway. The views are extensive and there's a private path to the water. The self-contained lodge is bright and welcoming and costs $65 to $110 a night.

There is accommodation at the *Kennedy Point Vineyard (☎ 372 5600, fax 372 9856, sunsethill@ihug.co.nz, 44 Donald Bruce Rd)*. Here you can relax among the grapevines and olive groves, while enjoying great views towards Rangitoto. A one bedroom en suite room with a lounge and kitchen costs $150 a night, a two bedroom with bathroom and lounge costs $150, and a three bedroom unit with two bathrooms and two lounges plus a kitchen and dining area costs $250 a night.

Onetangi Onetangi's long, sandy beach is popular in summer for swimming, surfing, windsurfing and other activities. Surf skis, surfboards and boogie boards can be hired at the store or on the beach in summer.

The popular *Waiheke Island YHA Hostel (☎ 372 8971, 419 Seaview Rd)* is on a hill overlooking the bay. The cost is $18 per person in a dorm (most dorms have two bunk beds), $40 to $45 for a double and $65 for an en suite room (one double bed and one bunk).

The *Onetangi Beachfront Apartments (☎ 372 7051, fax 372 5056, info@onetangi .co.nz, 27 The Strand)* has several options. Modern beachfront apartments are $185 for two people. Rooms in the motel complex range from about $95 to $150. They have a Web site at www.onetangi.co.nz.

Cowes Bay & Waikopu Bay The eastern end of Waiheke has a get-away-from-it-all feel. The main house at *Waikopu (☎ 372 7883, fax 372 9971, info@waikopou.co.nz, Cowes Bay Rd)* is a three bedroom mud-brick place, with a Japanese bathhouse, luxury kitchen and slate floors. It costs $250 for the first two people and $100 per person thereafter. There is also an annex that has two bedrooms (a double and a single) with en suite. Waikopu is set in extensive native bush and has its own beach. Kayaks and a fishing barge are available to guests.

Getting There & Away

Air Waiheke Airservices (☎ 372 5000) has a regular service to Waiheke (from $65 one way). You can arrange charter flights with Great Barrier Airlines (☎ 256 6500).

Boat Fullers Waiheke Island ferries depart from pier 2 at the city centre ferry terminal. There are up to 10 departures each way daily (☎ 367 9119 for a faxed timetable). The trip takes 35 minutes each way and costs $23 per adult return and $10.50 per child. Fullers' Waiheke Island Ferry & All Day Bus Pass costs $30 for adults and $13.50 for children. This is an all-day ticket that includes the return ferry and the freedom to use the island's own buses all day.

Fullers also offer the following tours: Vineyard Explorer, the Back & Beyond and

Karekare is just one of the west coast's fabulous surf beaches.

Unrivalled forest scenery at Karekare

Kerikeri is home to New Zealand's oldest stone building, built in the 1830s.

The Bay of Islands coastline is a maze of secluded bays and peninsulas.

EXCURSIONS

the Waiheke Island Explorer. Reservations are essential; for further information and for bookings phone ☎ 367 9111.

Pacific Ferries (☎ 303 1741) runs two services to Waiheke. The *Lady Wakefield*, a former Manly (Sydney, Australia) ferry, travels on weekends between Waiheke and the Auckland ferry terminal (pier 4; a kiosk at the entrance to the pier sells tickets). The trip takes 55 minutes one way. The return fare is $15 for adults, $3 for children. You may return from Waiheke on the 'fast ferry' with this ticket. There is a family pass (two adults, four children) for $33 return.

The 'fast ferries' also leave from pier 4. The return fare is $17 for adults, $9 for children. There is a family concession ($48 return; two adults and two children). The trip (one way) takes 25-30 minutes. All sailings are on weekends.

Subritzky Shipping (☎ 534 5663, fax 534 2933) has a vehicle ferry that leaves Half Moon Bay in south Auckland for Waiheke. There are at least five sailings each way on weekdays and four on weekends. The trip takes about an hour. There is also a Subritzky vehicle ferry to Waiheke from Wynyard Wharf in the city centre (Friday and Monday; one trip each way). It takes about 1½ hours and costs $100 return per car ($10 per adult one way; $5 per child one way).

Getting Around

Bus Two bus routes operate on the island, both connecting with the ferries. The Onetangi bus goes from Matiatia Wharf, through Oneroa, Surfdale and Ostend to Onetangi. The Palm Beach bus goes from Matiatia through Oneroa, Blackpool, Little Oneroa, Palm Beach and Ostend to Rocky Bay. Return bus fares (children are half-price) from Matiatia Wharf are: Oneroa ($1), Little Oneroa ($2), Surfdale ($2), Ostend ($2.50) Palm Beach, Rocky Bay, Onetangi ($3). An all-day bus pass costs $7.

Fullers' (☎ 367 9111) Waiheke Island Explorer and Vineyard Explorer tours include travel on the island's buses. You can get bus tickets from Fullers when buying your ferry tickets, or pay the driver on the bus.

Car, Scooter & Bicycle Waiheke Rental Cars (☎ 372 8635) has an office at Matiatia Wharf and at Artworks in Oneroa. Prices start at $45 for a car (plus 40 cents per kilometre). Motorbikes are cost from $35 and automatic nifty-fifty scooters from $30. You must be 21 years of age and be able to produce a current driver's licence (scooters only require a car licence, but be careful when riding on gravel). Waiheke Auto Rentals (☎ 373 8998) will deliver a car to you anywhere on the island. Its prices are the same as those mentioned earlier. Waiheke Shuttles (☎ 372 7756) charges per person per trip.

Attitude Rentals (☎ 372 7897) has motor-assisted mountain bikes for hire (minimum two hours) from $25 (two hours), $35 (four hours) and $45 (all day). You will need to pick up the bike from the Waiheke Island Resort at Palm Beach; you can get there by bus, or phone to arrange to be picked up. Insurance, helmets, and fuel are included in the cost.

Ordinary bicycles can be rented at various places. Wharf Rats (☎ 372 7937) has an office at Matiatia Wharf and rents out mountain bikes. Four hours costs $15, eight $25 and overnight $30. You must leave a $30 deposit. You can hire bikes from the information centre for similar prices. Pick up a copy of the *Bike Waiheke* pamphlet from the centre. The route takes you past most of the sites and usually takes four to six hours to complete although at least one speed freak has done it in just over two hours.

Taxi Taxi services are provided by Waiheke Taxis (☎ 372 8038), Dial-a-Cab (☎ 372 9666) and Waiheke Island Shuttle Service (☎ 372 7756).

PAKATOA ISLAND

Pakatoa is a small tourist resort 36km from Auckland and just off the east coast of Waiheke. The resort has a restaurant, one of the nation's 'choicest' bars, a cafe, pool and sporting facilities. There are views of the gulf and across to the Coromandel from the island's high point.

The *Pakatoa Island Resort Hotel* (☎ 372 9002, 0800 666 200, fax 372 9006) is the island's only accommodation. The resort mainly offers packages, such as a night for two people (all inclusive) for $296. A unit on its own costs between $110 and $200.

Pakatoa Ferries (☎ 379 0066) leave Auckland from pier 3 (Quay St) at 11.30 am on weekdays and at 9.30 am on weekends and public holidays. The trip to Pakatoa takes just over an hour and costs $45 per adult return ($25 one way) and $22.50 for children. The ferry returns from Pakatoa at 2.45 pm on weekdays and at 4.15 pm on weekends. The ferry also goes to Hanaford's Point Wharf in Coromandel (45 minutes from Pakatoa) and will stop off at Orapiu in Waiheke on request.

GREAT BARRIER ISLAND
• pop 1200   ☎ 09

Great Barrier, 88km from the mainland, is the largest island in the gulf. It is a rugged scenic island, resembling the Coromandel Peninsula, to which it was once joined. There's plenty of open space on this 110 sq km island. It has hot springs, historic kauri dams, a forest sanctuary and myriad tramping tracks. Because there are no possums on the island, the native bush is lush.

The island's main attractions are its beautiful beaches and its fine tramping. The west coast has safe sandy beaches; the east coast beaches are good for surfing. The best tramping trails are in the Great Barrier Forest between Whangaparapara and Port Fitzroy, where there has been much reforestation. Cycling, swimming, fishing, scuba diving, boating, sea kayaking and just relaxing are the other popular activities on the island.

Named by Cook, Great Barrier Island later became a whaling centre. The island implemented the world's first air mail postal service in 1897 (using pigeons) – the centenary was celebrated with the release of hundreds of birds. It has also been the site of some spectacular shipwrecks, including the SS *Wairarapa* in 1894 and the *Wiltshire* in 1922. There's a cemetery at Katherine Bay, where victims of the *Wairarapa* wreck were buried. There is a signposted NZ Walkways track from Whangapoua Beach (20 minutes

from Port Fitzroy by taxi) to the graves on the Tapuwai headland.

Great Barrier Island is decidedly isolated. Only two hours by ferry from Auckland, the Barrier (as it is called locally) is 20 years away. The island has no electricity supply, only private generators, most roads are unpaved and it has only a few shops.

Tryphena is the main settlement and arrival point for the ferries. It consists of a few dozen houses, some shops, a card phone (hidden away by the storage shed at the wharf), toilets, a school, a ferry wharf and a handful of accommodation places dotted around the harbour. From the wharf it is a couple of kilometres to the Mulberry Grove Store, and then another 1km over the headland to Pa Beach and the Stonewall Lodge.

The airport is at **Claris**, a small settlement with a shop (Kaitoke Store), the Great Barrier Island Information Centre, motels and a petrol station. **Whangaparapara** is an old timber town and the site of the island's 19th century whaling activities. **Port Fitzroy** is the other main town; it is also very small, but is the home of the DOC office.

From around mid-November to Easter the island is a busy holiday destination, especially during the Christmas holidays until the end of January, Easter and the Labour Day long weekend. At these times make sure you book transport, accommodation and activities in advance.

Information
The Great Barrier Island Information Centre (☎ 429 0033) is an offshoot of the Auckland City Council and is across from the airport in Claris. It's open weekdays from 8 am to 4 pm and weekends from 9 am to 4 pm. In Tryphena, the Fullers office (☎ 429 0004), next to the Stonewall Store, is a mine of information. The office maintains an extensive list of homestays and lodges. In summer it's open daily from 8.30 am to 5 pm and in winter from 9.30 am to 3.30 pm (Sunday 9 am to 4 pm).

The main DOC office (☎ 429 0044, fax 429 0071), in Port Fitzroy, is a 15 minute walk from the ferry landing. It has information

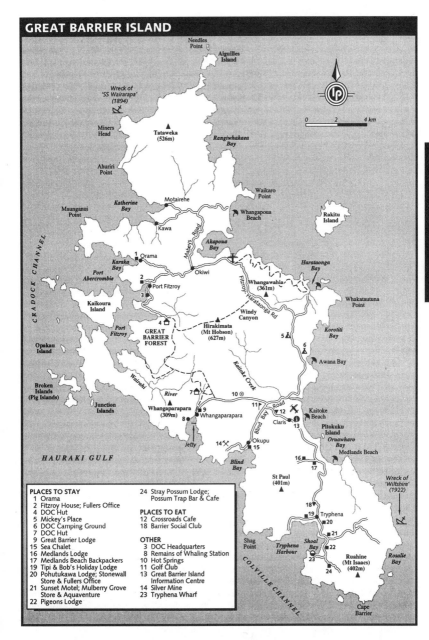

GREAT BARRIER ISLAND

Needles Point

Aiguilles Island

Wreck of 'SS Wairarapa' (1894)

Miners Head

Tataweka (526m)

Rangiwhakaea Bay

Ahuriri Point

Maunganui Point

Katherine Bay

Motairehe

Waikaro Point

Whangapoua Beach

Rakitu Island

Kawa

Akapoua Bay

Karaka Bay

1 Orama

Port Abercrombie

Okiwi

Harataonga Bay

2

Port Fitzroy

Whangawhia (361m)

3

Kaikoura Island

Whakatautuna Point

Port Fitzroy

Windy Canyon

4

GREAT BARRIER FOREST

Hirakimata (Mt Hobson) (627m)

Korotiti Bay

5

6

Opakau Island

Wairahi

Awana Bay

Broken Islands (Pig Islands)

Junction Islands

River

7

10

Whangaparapara (309m)

9

Whangaparapara

11

Road

Kaitoke Beach

8

12

Claris

13

Pitokuku Island

Oruawharo Bay

Jetty

14

Okupu

15

Medlands Beach

Blind Bay

16

17

Wreck of 'Wiltshire' (1922)

HAURAKI GULF

St Paul (401m)

18

19

Tryphena

Shag Point

20

21

Tryphena Harbour

22

Shoal Bay

23

Ruahine (Mt Isaacs) (402m)

Rosalie Bay

24

Cape Barrier

CRADOCK CHANNEL

COLVILLE CHANNEL

Fitzroy–Harataonga Rd

Kaitoke Creek

Blind Bay

Mabey's Road

0   2   4 km

PLACES TO STAY
1 Orama
2 Fitzroy House; Fullers Office
4 DOC Hut
5 Mickey's Place
6 DOC Camping Ground
7 DOC Hut
9 Great Barrier Lodge
15 Sea Chalet
16 Medlands Lodge
17 Medlands Beach Backpackers
19 Tipi & Bob's Holiday Lodge
20 Pohutukawa Lodge; Stonewall
    Store & Fullers Office
21 Sunset Motel; Mulberry Grove
    Store & Aquaventure
22 Pigeons Lodge

24 Stray Possum Lodge;
    Possum Trap Bar & Cafe

PLACES TO EAT
12 Crossroads Cafe
18 Barrier Social Club

OTHER
3 DOC Headquarters
8 Remains of Whaling Station
10 Hot Springs
11 Golf Club
13 Great Barrier Island
    Information Centre
14 Silver Mine
23 Tryphena Wharf

EXCURSIONS

and maps on the island, collects fees and sells hut tickets, and has a good camping ground. It's open weekdays from 8 am to 4.30 pm. Whangaparapara also has a small DOC office, which opens at irregular hours.

Most people on the island generate their own power by using solar, wind or diesel energy, but there are no street lights anywhere, so bring a torch (flashlight). The Barrier has an automatic telephone service and card-operated phones are dotted around the island. See the Places to Eat section for information on buying groceries.

Things to See & Do

Medlands Beach, with its wide sweep of white sand, is one of the best **beaches** on the island and is easily accessible from Tryphena. Whangapoua is a fine surfing beach, while Kaitoke, Awana Bay and Harataonga are also good. Whangapoua has an excellent right-hand break, while Awana has both left and right-hand breaks. Tryphena's bay, lined with pohutukawa, has sheltered beaches.

Many people come just for the **walks** – be aware that they are often not well signposted. The Great Barrier Forest walks are most easily reached from Whangaparapara or Port Fitzroy. You can take the ferry to either of these destinations and walk 45 minutes to one of the two huts that can be used as bases for exploring the forest.

The most spectacular short walk is from Windy Canyon to Hirakimata (Mt Hobson). **Windy Canyon**, only a 15 minute walk from the main road (Fitzroy to Harataonga), has spectacular rock outcrops and great views of the island. From Windy Canyon, an excellent trail continues for another 1½ hours through scrubby forest to **Hirakimata** (621m), the highest point on the island with views across to the Coromandel Peninsula and Auckland on a fine day. Near the top of the mountain are lush forests and a few mature kauri that survived the logging days. From Hirakimata it's two hours through forest to the hut closest to Port Fitzroy and then 45 minutes to Port Fitzroy itself.

Many other trails traverse the forest. From the road outside Whangaparapara you can walk to the **hot springs**, though the trail is usually very muddy and not well maintained. There is also a good, four hour walk west from Tryphena to Okupu Bay that eventually joins the Blind Bay Rd. There is a NZ Walkway track that goes along the coast from Okowi to Harataonga where there is an historic homestead (it's detailed in the NZ Walkways pamphlet available from DOC).

Mountain biking is popular on the island. There is diverse scenery, and biking is not too difficult here, even though the roads are unsealed. A popular ride is from Tryphena to Whangaparapara: cycle about an hour Medlands Beach, where you can stop for a swim, then an hour on to the hot springs, and from there it's a half-hour to Whangaparapara, where there is accommodation. You could catch the ferry out from Whangaparapara, or spend another day cycling through the forest up to Port Fitzroy, stopping on the way for a hike up to the kauri dams on a good, well-marked 4WD track. It's about a three hour ride, not counting stops; allow all day for the dams. (The easiest way to organise it would be with a Possum Pursuits Pass from the Stray Possum Lodge in Tryphena. See Getting Around later.)

Great Barrier provides some of the most varied **scuba diving** in NZ. There's pinnacle diving, shipwreck diving, lots of fish and over 33m (110ft) visibility at some times of the year (February to April is probably the best). There are no scuba operators on the island (although there are facilities for filling tanks). However, if you have a reasonable degree of experience and there are at least two of you, Fitzroy House (☎ 429 0091) will organise a trip. For information on arranging trips contact the information centre.

Sea Kayaking is a good way of experiencing Great Barrier from the water. Great Barrier Island Kayak Hire and Adventure Tours (☎ 429 0551) has a twilight mystery tour with a BBQ afterwards ($45); without the BBQ it's $25. You can also rent kayaks from this company (next to the Stonewall Store, Tryphena) for $10 an hour or $45 per day.

Aortae Sea Kayak Adventures (☎ 429 0664) hires out kayaks for $40 for half a day with snorkelling. You can also learn how to catch fish by towing lures. There is an evening twilight paddle to the Colville Channel. Some accommodation places also hire kayaks, for example Fitzroy House (☎ 429 0091).

Horse treks can be arranged through Adventure Horse Treks (☎ 429 0274), and Nagle Cove Horse Treks (☎ 429 0212). Prices start at about $25 for an hour.

Boat and fishing trips can be organised through Stanley Marine Charters (☎ 429 0570), Puriri Bay Fishing Charters (☎ 429 0485) and Tipi & Bob's (☎ 429 0550).

Fitzroy House (☎ 429 0091) will take you to the beginning of a track in a 4WD unimog and pick you up at the other end, usually at the beach, in a yacht and sail back. This costs about $50 per person.

Places to Stay

Most accommodation is in Tryphena, but places are scattered all over the island. Prices are steep in summer, but rates drop dramatically outside the peak period. Summer prices are quoted here.

Camping & Huts There are DOC camping grounds at Harataonga Bay, Medlands Beach, Akapoua Bay, Whangapoua, The Green (Whangaparapara), and Awana Bay, all with basic facilities including water and pit toilets ($6 per adult, $3 per child). Only Akapoua Bay has a BBQ; you are not allowed to light fires elsewhere. Camping is not allowed outside the camping grounds without a permit.

DOC also has two huts in the Great Barrier Forest near Port Fitzroy and Whangaparapara, each a 45 minute walk from the nearest wharf ($8 per adult, $4 per child). Each hut sleeps up to 24 in bunkrooms; facilities include cold water, pit toilets and a kitchen with a wood stove. Bring your own sleeping bag and cooking equipment. From November to January the huts are very busy; it's first come first served, so be early.

There are two camping grounds on private property: *Mickey's Place* (☎/fax 429

0170), at Awana ($4 per adult, $2 per child), and *The Great Barrier Island Campground (☎ 429 0184)*, at Puriri Bay, Tryphena ($8.50 per person). Facilities include toilets, BBQ sites and cold-water showers.

Hostels The *Stray Possum Lodge (☎ 429 0109, 0800 767 786)* in Tryphena is the best backpacker place on the island (and is YHA associated), providing good quality accommodation in a lovely bush setting. Dorms cost $17 to $20 and 13twins and doubles cost $50; there is also limited camping space for $12 per person.

Two great self-contained chalets, which sleep up to six people, are also available for $95 for the first two people and $15 for each additional person. The Stray Possum has a bus for transport around the island. For $45 you can use the pass as frequently as you wish and it includes the use of mountain bikes, boogie boards and snorkelling gear.

Pohutukawa Lodge (☎ 429 0211), in Tryphena, has some tight-fitting little rooms. The oddly shaped bunks are $17 per night; linen is an extra $5. A separate lodge has self-contained doubles costing $95.

Medlands Beach Backpackers (☎ 429 0320) is on Mason Rd, just inland from the main road at Medlands Beach. The hostel is fairly basic, but it's close to the superb beach. It costs $20 for a bed in a four bed dorm and $48 for a double. There is a one-off linen charge of $5.

Guesthouses & Motels *Pigeons Lodge (☎ 429 0437)* at Shoal Bay on the beachfront is in a bush setting. It charges $100 for an en suite room in the lodge and $120 for a double room with cooking facilities.

Tipi & Bob's Holiday Lodge (☎ 429 0550) has motel-style accommodation 50m from the sea, with a garden bar and restaurant. Good self-contained units, most with great sea views, start at $120. There is an older cottage sleeping up to eight that costs $250 a night.

Medlands Lodge (☎ 429 0352), on Mason Rd, Medlands Beach, is set on four hectares of park-like grounds at the foot of the hills inland from the beach. Excellent self-contained units sleeping four cost $120 for two (each additional adult is $15) and there's also a five bed bunkroom. You can cook or order meals.

At Whangaparapara, the *Great Barrier Lodge* (☎ 429 0488), on the water's edge, is a big place overlooking the inlet. It has a restaurant and bar; rooms cost from $40 to $110 for two in self-contained cabins.

Fitzroy House (☎ 429 0091) is an old homestead with fine views on the other side of the bay from the ferry wharf at Port Fitzroy. It has two self-contained cottages starting at $145, and is a good place for organising activities.

At Karaka Bay, in the next bay north of Port Fitzroy, *Orama* (☎ 429 0063) is a Christian Fellowship hostel that has self-contained flats for $100 in summer. Staff will pick you up from the Port Fitzroy ferry wharf. It has good facilities, including a swimming pool, but no alcohol is permitted.

Remoter possibilities abound. At Okupu Bay there is the *Sea Chalet* (☎ 429 0326), which is fully self-contained and right on the beach. There are two bedrooms, each with two single beds. It's available from August to Christmas and then from the end of January to Easter.

Baches Great Barrier Island has an array of holiday baches, all privately owned and maintained. The going rate is around $80 to $100 a double and many sleep four people or more. Fullers Auckland (☎ 372 9122) keeps a list (and will mark them on the map), so check with them before leaving the city. They will fax the list to you upon request.

Places to Eat

Restaurants are few, so all the places to stay provide meals and/or cooking facilities. In Tryphena *Tipi & Bob's* and the *Possum Trap Bar & Cafe* (in the Stray Possum), are the only fully fledged restaurants (each has a bar).

The *Barrier Social Club* (☎ 429 0421) in Tryphena has good value meals and cheap bar prices. It's open Saturday to Wednesday from 3 pm until whenever. A filling main meal costs about $14. Claris also has a social club and you can get a meal at the golf club.

Tryphena has two grocery stores, the Mulberry Grove Store and the Stonewall Store, but food is more expensive than on the mainland. Claris, Whangaparapara and Port Fitzroy have general stores. Wash down any meal with bush honey island mead, available from local stores.

Getting There & Away

Air Great Barrier Airlines (GBA; ☎ 275 9120, fax 275 6612), the main airline servicing the island, flies at least twice daily from the Air New Zealand domestic terminal at Auckland airport to Claris and Okiwi. The flight from Auckland takes half an hour and costs $89/169 one way/return. Special deals are often available in the off-season or there's a air-sea combination (see later for details). The airline operates a transfer bus ($10) from Claris to Tryphena and from Okiwi to Port Fitzroy. GBA also flies to Whitianga daily, and to Tauranga, Rotorua and Whangarei on demand.

Great Barrier Xpress (☎ 0800 222 123), run by Mountain Air, has three fights daily between Auckland and Great Barrier Island ($169 adult return, $99 child).

Boat Fullers has high-speed ferries departing from the Auckland ferry building (pier 2) on Friday and Sunday in winter, with extra sailings in summer (☎ 367 9117 for a faxed timetable). The trip takes two hours. On Friday the ferry leaves at 6.30 pm and goes directly to Port Fitzroy (arrived 8.45 pm). On Sunday the ferry leaves at 11 am and goes via Port Fitzroy (arriving 1.30 pm) to Tryphena (arriving 3.30 pm). The return trip is $89 for adults and $44 for children, with a $10/5 discount if you book and pay at least a day in advance. The option of going one way by ferry and the other by air is also available ($115 return for adults, $70 return for children at the time of writing, but check when booking).

Fullers also has a day trip package; you connect with a bus tour on arrival (adults/children \$67/33.50).

You can also get to Great Barrier Island with the car ferry service, Gulf Trans (☎ 0800 485 387) on *Sealink* or the *Tasman* (☎ 373 4036, 0800 485 387). *Sealink* departs Wynyard Wharf, Auckland city, for Tryphena daily in summer at 9 am, returning from Tryphena at 1 pm (there are fewer sailings and different sailing times in winter). The *Tasman* goes to Port Fitzroy from Auckland at 6 am on Tuesday and returns on Wednesday at 6 am. The cost for a vehicle plus driver (return) is \$399. Each additional passenger costs \$65 return and each child \$35.

There are several travel passes that allow you to take in Great Barrier and other destinations for very reasonable prices. These include the Explorer Pass, Possum Pursuits Pass, Barrier Island & Coromandel Pass, and the Barrier Island & Northland Pass. For information and bookings contact ☎ 0800 767 786.

Getting Around
From Tryphena in the south to Port Fitzroy in the north it is 47km by gravel road, or 40km via Whangaparapara using the walking tracks. The roads are graded but nevertheless rough.

Great Barrier Travel (☎ 429 0568) has a bus that meets the ferry and takes passengers into Tryphena (\$5). In theory it continues through Medlands Beach and Claris to Port Fitzroy, but unless enough passengers want to go you will have to get a charter.

Many of the places to stay will pick you up if notified in advance; the Stray Possum has a bus for its guests. In summer the best option for getting between Port Fitzroy and Tryphena is the daily Fullers boat.

Bob's Rentals (☎ 429 0988) has cars starting at \$55 a day. Down Under Rentals (☎ 429 0110) has 4WDs and cars from \$85 a day. Better Bargain Rentals (☎ 429 0092), in Tryphena, has cars from \$65 a day, vans from \$95 a day and 4WDs from \$85 a day. Great Barrier Lodge (☎ 429 0488), in

Whangaparapara, and Aotea Tours (☎ 429 0055) also have rental cars. These rental places also operate as taxi services.

Mountain bikes are readily available for hire for \$20 to \$25 per day. Most places to stay also rent out bikes and may give discounts.

OTHER GULF ISLANDS
Dotted around Rangitoto, Motutapu and Waiheke, and farther north, are many smaller islands.

Rotoroa is a Salvation Army alcohol rehabilitation clinic, just south of Pakatoa. **Ponui**, also known as Chamberlins Island, is a larger island just south of Rotoroa. It has been farmed by the Chamberlin family ever since they purchased it from the Maori in 1854. South again is **Pakihi**, or Sandspit Island, and the tiny Karamuramu Island.

Little Barrier Island, 25km north-east of Kawau Island, is one of NZ's prime nature reserves and the only area of NZ rainforest unaffected by humans, deer or possums. Several rare species of birds, reptiles and plants live in the varied habitats on the volcanic island.

Access to the island is highly restricted and a DOC permit, which is very difficult to obtain, is required before any landing can be made on this closely guarded sanctuary.

Motuora Island is halfway between Tiritiri Matangi and Kawau. There is a wharf and *camping ground* on the west coast of the island but there is no regular ferry service. Get a camping permit from the ranger (☎ 422 8882) on Kawau, or from the caretaker on Motuora.

The most remote islands of the Hauraki Gulf Maritime Park are the **Mokohinau Islands**, 25km north-west of Great Barrier. They are all protected nature reserves and visitors require landing permits.

North of Auckland

Beyond the suburbs of Devonport, Takapuna and the east coast bays is the Whangaparaoa Peninsula, Orewa, the hot pool

EXCURSIONS

complex of Waiwera and, inland, the quaint Bohemian settlement of Puhoi. Farther north is Warkworth, with its satellite station, and Sandspit, jumping off point for Kawau Island. You can do a circuit by car that takes you from Auckland city up the east coast on SH1 to Wellsford (96km) and back down along the west coast to Auckland on SH16 (109km), a good full-day trip with a few stops along the way. Tourism Auckland (☎ 366 6888) has a map (*Twin Coast Discovery Tour*) and details of what to see en route.

WHANGAPARAOA PENINSULA

Now virtually a suburb of Auckland, the Whangaparaoa Peninsula – just north of Auckland off SH1 – is good for water-based activities; windsurfers flock to Manly Beach, boaties leave from the Weiti River and gulf harbour and swimmers find great beaches around the tip of the peninsula at **Shakespear Regional Park**. Many native bush birds and waders can be seen, and the native forests of the park contain karaka, kowhai and old puriri. A number of walking tracks traverse the park. The park is just beyond the huge Gulf Harbour Marina development, which boasts a golf course and country club. Gulf Harbour Ferries (☎ 09-424 5561) stop here on their way to and from Tiritiri Matangi Island.

At Whangaparaoa there is a small **narrow gauge railway** where steam train rides are offered for $5/2.50/12 for adults/children/family. The train operates on weekends from 10 am to 5 pm. It's at 400 Whangaparaoa Rd, east of Silverdale (☎ 09-424 5018, fax 424 5065, whangaparaoa.rail@xtra.co.nz). You can get here from Auckland on Saturday on Bus No 899 from the Downtown Bus Centre and on Sunday on No 895; you'll need to change bus, to No 899, at Silverdale.

OREWA
- pop 6000   ☎ 09

Orewa is another Auckland satellite suburb with a large mall-style shopping centre. Its main attraction is the great beach, which runs next to the highway. The town also has a

statue of Sir Edmund Hillary, one of the first two people to stand on top of Mt Everest (the other was Tenzing Norgay). City buses from Auckland run to Orewa, so it is an easy first stop out of Auckland going north.

The Hibiscus Coast Information Centre (☎ 426 0076, fax 426 0086) is open daily from 9 am to 5 pm (closes 4.30 pm on weekends). It's on the highway south of town, next to KFC. Pick up a copy of *Let's go Walking on the Hibiscus Coast*, which outlines many good walks in the area. Orewa Cycle Works (☎ 426 6958, fax 426 6349) at 278 Main Rd has proved indispensable for cyclists heading up around Northland; staff hire out bikes ($12 per day), do repairs and sell parts. It's open weekdays from 8 am to 5.30 pm, Saturday from 9 am and Sunday from 10 am.

Places to Stay
There are two backpacker places in Orewa. *Pillows Travellers Lodge* (☎ 426 6338, 412 Hibiscus Coast Hwy) provides excellent accommodation for $15 in a dorm, $36 for twins and doubles and $49 for rooms with en suite. It is conveniently located near the centre of Orewa – opposite the beach and right on the highway – and boasts a spa.

The *Marco Polo Backpackers Inn* (☎ 426 8455, 2a Hammond Ave, Hatfields Beach) is just off the highway on the northern outskirts of Orewa. Take Bus No 884, 894 or 895 from Orewa. This hostel is nestled into hillside greenery; tent sites are $10 per person, dorm beds are $15 and singles/doubles are $28/38-40. Staff can arrange a variety of trips, including snorkelling trips to Goat Island ($50 for two people).

Orewa has a dozen motels and three camping grounds. *Puriri Park* (☎ 426 4648) on Puriri Ave is a well-equipped motor camp with a pool in a quiet setting. Campsites are $10 per adult (minimum $20; children half price), cabins are $59 for two, tourist flats are $76 for two.

Motels (all on Hibiscus Coast Hwy) include the following: *Orewa Motor Lodge* (☎ 426 4027, 0800 267 392, fax 426 4933, 290 Hibiscus Coast Hwy), across the road from the beach, has ground-floor units (studio, one and two bedroom) for $79 to $110 for two people. *Four Seasons Motel (☎ 426 5768, fax 426 9462, 383 Hibiscus Coast Hwy)*, has studio and one-bedroom units, costing $65 to $95 for two. *Best Western Golden Sands (☎ 426 5177, fax 426 4804, goldensands@xtra.co.nz, 381 Main Rd)* fronts onto the beach and charges $70 to $175 for two. *Edgewater (☎ 426 5260, fax 426 3378, 387-89 Main Rd)* has studios and units for $115/148 for off-beach/beachfront units and $75/90 for studio units (all prices for two people). Prices drop out of season at Edgewater, and there are always specials and discounts, so it's worth checking.

Homestays/B&Bs include *The Ambers (☎ 426 5354, fax 426 3287, gzwier@xtra .co.nz, 146 Pine Valley Rd)*, at Silverdale 4km south of Orewa. This is a lovely place full of romantic charm and set in spacious grounds. Rooms cost $110 to $120 a night, including breakfast for two. At Hatfields Beach, just north of Orewa, *Moontide Lodge (☎ 426 2374, 19 Ocean View Rd)* is right on the clifftop and has its own beach access. Its spacious rooms cost $150 to $180. German and French are spoken.

Places to Eat

Creole Bar & Brasserie (☎ 426 6250, 310 Main Rd) serves good seafood, with mains ranging from $16 to $19. There is usually some sort of live entertainment at weekends. It's open daily from 11 am to 1 am.

Thai Orewa (☎ 426 9711, 328 Main Rd) is a licensed Thai food eatery where rice and noodle dishes start around $12. It's open daily for lunch and dinner.

Behind these places, in Bakehouse Lane (above the Bin Inn Food Marker), is *The Eclipse Bar (☎ 426 2200)*. It has a dress code of no T-shirts, caps, jandals (flip-flops), leather jackets, vests. There's a party/dance on Friday and Saturday nights, and local bands.

Kebabs Cafe & Chinese Food (☎ 426 8422) on Tamariki Ave is a takeaway place with an electric Asian/Mid-East menu. Prices are reasonably low. It's open daily.

The *Walnut Cottage (☎ 426 6523, 498 Main Rd)* is off the main thoroughfare, beside Orewa's most historic house. It's open for lunch Thursday to Sunday from noon and for dinner Wednesday to Sunday from 6.30 pm.

Il Veneziano (☎ 426 5444), at the Red Beach Shopping Centre (about 2km south of Orewa), is one of the best places, with good Italian food and plenty of atmosphere. It's licensed.

Getting There & Away

Stagecoach buses (Nos 893, 894, 895 and 897) run between Auckland and Orewa/Waiwera via Takapuna, Albany and Silverdale. There are local Hibiscus Coast buses running between Orewa and Army Bay via Red Beach (Nos 991, 996, 997 and 998) approximately every hour.

WAIWERA

- **pop 264**   ☎ **09**

The coastal village of Waiwera, 48km north of Auckland (bus No 895 from the Downtown Bus Centre) is noted for its **thermal pools** (☎ 426 5369, fax 426 5850). This huge complex of hot pools, spa pools, waterslides (plus a luxury private spa and gym) is open daily from 9 am to 10 pm (until 10.30 pm on Friday and Saturday). Entry costs $14 for adults and $8 for children aged between five and 14, and there are family rates. The spa and gym cost extra. They have a Web site at www.waiwera.co.nz.

Horse riding is offering by Ti Tree (☎ 426 7003) for $20 an hour or $35 for two hours. Mountain bikes can be hired from Pedal Adventures (☎ 025 276 3835, 025 296 2610), Waiwera Holiday Park ($10 an hour, $35 a day; credit card imprint required as a bond). You can pedal to Puhoi and back, or else **kayak** to Warkworth and back on the Mahurangi River with Auckland Canoe Centre Adventures. The latter is an overnight trip (with a walking tour of Warkworth in the morning) and includes a swim at the Waiwera pools at the end ($239 per person). For details call ☎ 426 5369 or fax 426 5850; you can book at the Waiwera thermal pools. At least four paddlers are needed for a trip. The same people run trips up to Puhoi (8km one way; 2½ to three hours paddling) and Wenderholm to Puhoi (5km; two to 2½ hours paddling).

Just north of Waiwera is **Wenderholm Regional Park**, a coastal farmland park with a good beach, estuary and walks. Couldrey House (☎ 426 7778), the original homestead, is now a museum. It's open Saturday (Labour weekend to Easter) from 1 to 4 pm and Sunday year-round (adults/children $1.50/50c). Bus No 895 from the Downtown Bus Centre will take you close to the park.

Places to Stay & Eat

All the accommodation at Waiwera is within walking distance of the pools.

The *Waiwera Resort Hotel (☎ 426 4089, fax 426 6226, 15 Waiwera Rd)* has motel-style units for $75 a double. The restaurant opens at 6 pm, although bar meals are available during the day.

The *Waiwera Motel (☎/fax 426 5153, 25 Weranui Rd)* has five self-contained, ground-floor family and studio units with dinghies and kayaks for rent. Doubles cost $85 to $90 (each extra adult $15).

The *Coach Trail Lodge (☎ 426 4792, fax 426 9064, coachtl@hbc.kiwilink.co.nz, 1 Waiwera Rd)* has studio and family units and a licensed restaurant. Prices range from $95 to $150 for two people. Self-contained cottages are also available (☎ 426 4792, 14 The Strand) from $110 for two people.

The *Waiwera Thermal Resort Holiday Park (☎ 426 5270, fax 426 5250, 37 Waiwera Place)* has tent and campervan sites. It costs $13 per adult for a powered site and $9 per child, and $11 for a tent site.

Getting There & Away

The Stagecoach buses that pass through Orewa (see earlier) will also take you to Waiwera.

PUHOI

- **pop 2927**   ☎ **09**

North of Waiwera, 1km off SH1, Puhoi is a picturesque historic village that claims to be NZ's first Bohemian settlement. The small **Puhoi Bohemian Museum** is open on week-

ends from 1 to 4 pm (entry is free but a donation of $1 is appreciated). You can purchase the 56-page booklet *Puhoi Remembers* ($8) and a short history of the settlement *Bohemia to Puhoi* ($2). However, the main point of interest is the **historic pub**, crammed with old artefacts (open daily from 11 am to 10 pm).

At Puhoi you can hire canoes (☎ 422 0891). It costs $15 per hour for a paddle in a singe kayak down the river to Wenderholm Regional Park on the coast, or $25 in a Canadian canoe. You can also go on guided moonlight trips. The area is great for mountain biking. Puhoi Adventure Bike Tours (☎ 025 905 227 or 422 0625 after-hours) will take you mountain biking through the Puhoi Valley, along farm and forestry tracks, and for coastal rides through local regional parks. It costs $25 for two hours, $35 for half a day and $65 for a full day. Groups (of 40 or more people) can arrange to be entertained by the Puhoi Bohemian Dancers to the strains of the Puhoi Band. Lunch is included in the cost of $14 per person. Contact Jenny Schollum, c/- Post Office, Puhoi 1240 (☎ 422 0816).

Places to Stay & Eat

There is a *self-contained cottage (☎ 422 0704, fax 422 0708, 53 Puhoi Rd)* on the left as you approach Puhoi from SH1. There is no separate bedroom as such, and the bathroom is just outside, although there is a kitchen with a fridge. Breakfast is included in the price of $60 per night. '

Another option is *Our Farm Park (☎/fax 422 0626, ofp@friends.co.nz, RD3 Kaukapakapa)*, which is 4.5km west of Puhoi. This is an organic farm and your meals will include organic fruit and vegies as well as 'adrenalin-free' meat (assuming you are not vegetarian). There is one queen-sized bedroom and one twin with a child's bed. Bed and breakfast costs $110 for two people, and $85 for one. Children under five can stay for free, five to 12 years cost $10, and 13 to 17 are $20. Lunch and dinner are available for an extra cost. They have a Web site at www.friends.co.nz.

Puhoi Cottage, 500m past the Puhoi Store, has delicious Devonshire teas and home-cooked goodies. It's open every day except Wednesday from 9.30 am to 5 pm. Sitting outside in the garden on a sunny afternoon, listening to the birds, is tremendously relaxing.

Getting There & Away

Your own transport is best for getting to and from Puhoi. If you are relying on public transport the two services that pass this area from Auckland are the Northlander Express (☎ 307 5873) and Gubbs (☎ 0800 482 271). The Northlander Express can drop you off on SH1, from where you'll have to walk a few kilometres to Puhoi township. The other option is to hire a mountain bike at Waiwera (see earlier) and pedal there and back.

WARKWORTH

• **pop 2477**   ☎ 09

Just off the main highway, by the Mahurangi River, this pretty town was once connected to Auckland by steamships that docked at the town's old wharf. Now Warkworth is mainly a lunch stop on the drive north, but the surrounding area is a popular summer holiday destination.

The Warkworth Visitor Information Centre (☎ 425 9081, fax 425 9299), at 1 Baxter St near the river and bus station, has the complete run-down on the area. It's open weekdays from 8.45 am to 5.15 pm and on weekends from 9.30 am to 3 pm. Pick up a copy of the brochure *Warkworth, The Kowhai Town*, which has a heritage trail marked out that will take you past Warkworth's most historic sites. The trail takes one to 1½ hours to complete at an easy pace. Alternatively you can take the Kowhai Stage air-con shuttle van on a tour of Warkworth and its surrounds (☎/fax 425 7697).

On the outskirts of town, the **Parry Kauri Park** has short forest walks and a couple of monstrous mature kauri, including the 800-year-old McKinney kauri. Also at the park, the small **Warkworth Museum** (☎ 425 7093), open from 9 am to 4 pm in summer (until 3.30 pm in winter), has well-preserved pioneering exhibits (adults/children \$4/50c). Three kilometres north of Warkworth, at 42 Kaipara Flats Rd (400m west of SH1) is McKenzie Horse Riding (☎/fax 425 8517, rogerm@clear.net.nz), where you can do trail rides across farmland and forest.

Places to Stay & Eat

Warkworth's historic pub, the *Warkworth Inn* (☎ 425 7569), on Queen St, has typical old pub rooms with shared facilities for \$40/60 for a single/double.

Bridge House Lodge (☎ 425 8351, fax 425 7410), on Elizabeth St, is next to the river. It's a part-old, part-new establishment with some style. Rooms with attached bathrooms start at \$70.

Saltings B&B (☎ 425 9670, fax 425 9674), on Sandspit Rd, has been renovated to give it a French provincial flavour. There are four rooms, three with en suites, starting at \$80/95 for a single/double.

Sandpiper Lodge (☎ 422 7256, fax 422 7816, sandpiper.lodge@xtra.co.nz, Takatu Rd, Takatu Peninsula) is 15km east of Warkworth, overlooking the beach. There are en suite rooms from \$250 a double.

Bellgrove (☎/fax 425 9770, 346 Woodcocks Rd) is 4km west of Warkworth. The upstairs accommodation is \$50/80, and the bathroom is shared. Five kilometres west of Warkworth is a homestay called *Willow Lodge* (☎/fax 426 7676, 546 Woodcocks Rd), which has singles/doubles for \$60/80 (there are two en suites).

The licensed *Riverbank Cafe* (☎ 425 7383), on Wharf St, is open Wednesday to Saturday for lunch and dinner, and Sunday for lunch. It has a fine selection of wines. *Ducks Crossing* (☎ 425 9940), in Riverview Plaza, is open daily from 7.30 am to 5.30 pm. Both places have fine views over the river and old wharf.

Getting There & Away

Gubbs Motors (☎ 425 8348) has three buses a day during the week to Silverdale (which connect with Stagecoach buses to Auckland). The only way of getting to/from Warkworth by bus on weekends is on an

InterCity bus (☎ 357 8400). There is no bus from Warkworth to Sandspit for Kawau Island; the only option is a taxi ($14 one way).

AROUND WARKWORTH

The most unabashedly touristy attraction is 4km north of Warkworth on SH1. **Sheepworld** (☎ 09-425 7444, shirley@sheepworld .co.nz) demonstrates many aspects of NZ sheep farming and shearing, and offers things you can try yourself, such as carding, spinning and weaving. You can also feed the tame sheep and lambs. Recent additions include an adventure playground and a display of local arts and crafts. It's open daily from 9 am to 5 pm, with shows on Saturday and Sunday at 11 am and 1 pm, and an extra show in January at 3 pm (adults/children $10/5). They have a Web site at www .sheepworld.co.nz.

There is a *caravan park* and camping ground nearby (☎/fax 09-425 9962) with 22 powered sites ($25 per night for two people for a caravan site – including a private bathroom – and $10 per person for a tent site).

The **Dome Forest**, 10km north of Warkworth on SH1, is a regenerating forest that was logged about 90 years ago. A walking track to the Dome summit (336m), with its great views across the Mahurangi Peninsula, leads from the car park and takes about 1½ hours return. A three hour (return) walk leads beyond the summit to the **Waiwhiu Kauri Grove**, an unlogged stand of 20 mature kauri trees. The start of the walkway is some 6km north of Warkworth on SH1.

About 15km east of Warkworth, at 295 Point Wells Rd, Matakana, is the **Makulu Kraal Ostrich Farm** (☎ 09-422 9455). Tours (about an hour) run in summer at 11 am and 1 pm and during school and public holidays at some other times of the year (telephone for times). The cost is $10 per adult and $5 per child, and includes meat tasting. Accommodation is available on the farm.

On Sharp Rd (6km east of Warkworth, on the road to Leigh) is **Heron's Flight Vineyard** (☎ 09-422 7915). Tours, which include wine tasting in the vineyard cafe, run daily; the owners prefer at least five people, but will show you through if there is just one or

two of you. Tours cost $8 per person and you should book ahead.

Morris & James Pottery & Tileworks (☎ 09-422 7116) is at 48 Tongue Farm Rd, Matakana. This is the place where well-known Morris ceramics are made. You can tour the pottery on weekdays at 11.30 am, then relax in their excellent cafe with some Matakana-grown wine and good food.

Six kilometres south of Warkworth, the **Earth Satellite Station** has an information centre with hands-on exhibits explaining satellite communications; it was a Kiwi astrophysicist from Warkworth who, in 1970, picked the location of the disabled Apollo 13 in outer space, enabling NASA ground crew to bring it home. The station is open to the public from 9 am to 3 pm.

Four kilometres south of Warkworth on the corner of SH1 and Perry Rd is the **Honey Centre & Honey Cafe** (☎ 09-425 8003); open daily from 9 am to 5 pm October to May and from 10 am to 4 pm at other times. It's claimed to be the largest live bee display in the country. If you've never seen a worker bee doing the waggle dance, this is the place to come to view it. Honey-tasting is available, and the cafe serves a variety of snacks.

To the east of Warkworth, on the scenic Mahurangi Peninsula, is **Sandspit**, from where the ferry departs for Kawau Island. South of Sandspit are the beach suburbs of **Snells Beach**, with a trendy 'ye olde' English pub, shopping centre, motel and B&Bs, and **Algies Bay**. These shallow bays are pleasant enough, but 3km farther on **Martins Bay** is the pick of the beaches and has a motor camp.

KAWAU ISLAND
• pop 106   ☎ 09

Directly east of Warkworth, Kawau Island's main point of interest is **Mansion House** (☎ 422 8882), an impressive historic house built in 1846 by Sir George Grey, an early NZ governor. It was a hotel for many years before being restored and turned into a museum. It's open daily from 9.30 am to 3.30 pm (adults/children $4/2). It houses a collection of Victorian memorabilia including items once owned by Sir George Grey.

Copper was discovered on the island in 1844 and 10 years later some 300 people were living there. Floods and legal problems plagued the mining venture, which eventually ceased, although there were sporadic attempts to resurrect it in the 1850s.

Kawau has many beautiful walks, starting from Mansion House and leading to beaches, the old copper mine and a lookout. DOC publishes a pamphlet called *Kawau Island Historic Reserve* ($1), which has a map of Kawau with walking tracks. You can get it from the DOC office at the Auckland ferry building. Numerous wallabies, introduced from Australia, are housed in an enclosure on Pah Farm in Bon Accord Harbour.

Vivian Bay is the only sandy bay with accommodation on the island; attractions include a white, sandy beach, swimming, fishing, snorkelling and bush walks.

Places to Stay

There are a couple of places to stay at Vivian Bay, on the north side of the island, and a campsite and a couple of cottages at Bon Accord Harbour.

Heavenly Homestay (☎ 422 8887), at North Cove, is a new, self-contained place right on the beach. There is one double bedroom with an en suite, a kitchen and lounge. There is a generous deck. The cost is $100 for two people including breakfast. Other meals are available; dinner is $20.

St Clair Lodge (☎ 422 8850) is another upmarket B&B charging from $250 (all meals inclusive) for two people. The St Clair beachfront units cost $200 and there is a chalet for $180 (two people).

There is one self-contained DOC *cottage* for rent at Sandy Bay (contact Mansion House ☎ 422 8882). It sleeps five people and costs $60 per night.

At Swansea Bay there is a *cottage* with one double bedroom for rent for $120 per night (two people). All food is included. This place has its own jetty and a dinghy that you can use to row out to the Pah Farm bar and restaurant. Expect visits from Sally the friendly Labrador-cross. For bookings call ☎ 422 8816.

For a meal or a drink try the *Kawau Island Yacht Club (☎ 422 8845)*. It's open daily from 9 am to noon and again from 4 pm – check to see what time it's closing on any particular day. The *Pah Farm Restaurant & Lodge (☎ 422 8765, fax 422 8794)* is open

MARTIN HARRIS

Mansion House (1846), on Kawau Island

from about 9 am daily until late. Both places are in Bon Accord Harbour.

Pah Farm also has accommodation. A bunk in a four bunk room (there are 12 bunk rooms) costs $15 per night and a room in the house (four double bedrooms) costs $40, linen included. Bathroom facilities are shared and there is no kitchen. You may also camp here; 100 sites are available with a toilet, shower and basic kitchen with a fridge, freezer and stove. It costs $7.50 per adult per night ($5 per child).

Every year, in the last week of February, the four day Furuno fishing competition, one of the world's biggest, is held off Pah Farm's stretch of coast. The record for the biggest snapper ever caught by a competitor is 10.3kg. You must register in advance with the Furuno Fishing Club if you wish to enter. To replenish fish stocks the farm runs a snapper hatchery, which is open to visitors.

Getting There & Away

Two ferry companies operate trips to Kawau from Sandspit (one hour). The Kawau Kat (☎ 425 8006) has a Royal Mail run daily at 10.30 am, which stops at Mansion House and many coves, bays and inlets (adults/seniors/children $39/33/12; includes lunch).

Matata Cruises (☎ 0800 225 295) has a daily coffee cruise to Kawau for $25 return (children $10) at 10 am (returning around 2 pm). It also offers a combined three hour lunch-Mansion House cruise for $35 (children $22).

Fullers Auckland (☎ 367 9111) has cruises to Kawau from Auckland (from Labour weekend to Easter) at 10 am, returning at 4.30 pm. At the time of writing some uncertainty existed as to whether these would run in 2000, although charters are available. Check with Fullers.

WARKWORTH TO BREAM BAY

Less frequented than the main road to Whangarei is the scenic route from Warkworth to Leigh on the east coast, then north via Mangawhai and Waipu to Bream Bay. This route has a number of places where you can relax off the not-so-beaten track.

The first good beach, **Omaha**, is a short detour from the Leigh road and has a sweeping stretch of white sand, good surf and a lifesaving club. For a pleasant, sheltered beach try **Mathesons Bay**, just before you enter the small town of Leigh. **Leigh** sits above a picturesque harbour dotted with fishing boats. It has a motel, a sometimes lively pub popular with fishers, and a great fish and chip shop that cooks up the fresh, local catch. ***Leigh Sawmill Cafe*** *(☎ 422 6019)*, at 142 Pakiri Rd, is situated in a former sawmill, and has a good play area for children and lovely gardens. The coffee is great and the food is good. There is also live music regularly, and the occasional art exhibition.

Farther north, around the cape from Leigh, **Goat Island** is the site of the Cape Rodney-Okakari Point Marine Reserve, where the University of Auckland has a marine laboratory. The reserve is teeming with fish that can be hand fed, or viewed from a glass-bottomed boat (Habitat Explorer; ☎ 422 6334, fax 422 690). The trips run year-round, weather permitting. The most popular, the 45-minute round-the-island trip, costs $15 per adult and $10 per child.

Snorkelling and diving gear can be hired at Seafriends (☎ 422 6212, sea.friends@xtra.co.nz, 7 Goat Island Rd), 1km before the beach, for $23 per day for a snorkel, mask, flippers and wetsuit. Seafriends also has a good, inexpensive restaurant and a small aquarium. They have a Web site at www.seafriends.org.nz.

Continuing along the coast, a gravel road leads to **Pakiri**, a tiny rural settlement with a white-sand beach. A good way of seeing the unspoilt beach and the forests behind is on horseback. Pakiri Beach Horse Rides *(☎ 422 6275, 0800 274 334, pakirihorse@xtra .co.nz)* at Taurere Park, Rahuikiri Rd, has popular rides along the beach; these start at $30 for a one hour ride and range to $120 for a full day (including lunch). There are overnight safaris and moonlight rides as well. Staff can arrange farmstays (a self-contained beach house through to a *tipi* and a gypsy wagon).

From Pakiri, the gravel road via Tomarata eventually meets the sealed road to Mangawhai. You rejoin the coast at **Mangawhai Heads**, a growing summer resort town with a great surf beach and a lifesaving club. The **Mangawhai Cliffs Walkway** (1½ to two hours one way) starts at the beach and affords extensive views inland and out to the Hauraki Gulf Islands. Mangawhai has motels and caravan parks.

A particularly scenic part of the road goes over the headland to Langs Beach and then on to Waipu.

West of Auckland

No more than an hour's drive from the city, west Auckland has a dramatic, rugged coastline with black-sand beaches backed by regenerating bush. There are excellent surf beaches and some 143 bushwalks in the Waitakeres making this an important recreational zone for Auckland city.

This is also the place to go for vineyards and craft outlets. Enterprise Waitakere (☎ 837 1855, info@enterprisewaitakere.co .nz) puts out a map called *Art out West* (available from both the Auckland and the Arataki visitor centres), which provides information on galleries and studios throughout the region.

Lopdell House Gallery (☎ 817 8087, lopdell@lopdell.org.nz) is an exhibition space that showcases work from the region. It's on the corner of Titirangi and South Titirangi Rds, Titirangi, and is open daily. The **Titirangi Village Market** (☎ 817 3584) is held at the Titirangi Memorial Hall, South Titirangi Rd, on the last Sunday of each month from 10 am to 2 pm. There's food and live music, plus more than 100 stalls.

VINEYARDS

NZ wine has a worldwide reputation and there are a number of vineyards in the west Auckland area. The glossy map *Winemakers of Auckland* (available from the visitor centre) details the vineyards, their addresses and opening hours. Some, such as Delegat's

and Corbans, are within walking distance of Henderson, which can be reached by bus or Tranz Metro from Auckland. Other large and well-known vineyards, such as Matua Valley, House of Nobilo and Coopers Creek, are farther out near Kumeu. There are also a couple of vineyards as far afield as Matakana, near Warkworth.

Some of the wineries have excellent restaurants. For fine dining in a beautiful setting, the *Hunting Lodge* (☎ 411 8259) at Matua Valley is open from Friday to Sunday for lunch and dinner. Other restaurants are *de Vines* at Lincoln Vineyards, the *cafe* at Pleasant Valley Wines and *Allely House* at Selaks Vineyard.

Auckland Adventures (☎ 379 4545) does tours around any combination of four vineyards. A minimum of eight people is required, but if you're not already in a group you can arrange to join one. The trips start at 11 am and finish around 4 pm; you can be picked up/dropped off in the city. The cost for a group of eight to 15 people is $50 for the wine trail, $5 for the picnic (optional), and $5 for a vineyard tour (optional). The cost of the trip decreases for larger groups.

Waitakere Scenic Tours (☎/fax 817 4547, bhales@pl.net) runs vineyard tours in an aircon Mercedes Benz coach. Tours generally cost $95 per person including lunch, but groups can negotiate. You can be picked up/dropped off in Auckland city.

Bush & Beach (☎ 478 2882) also does tours (a minimum of five people) for $55, including pick up/drop off in Auckland city.

Robbies Double Decker Travel (☎ 413 8222) will organise bus trips round the vineyards for groups.

There are a couple of regular festivals out this way. Vintage Alfresco takes place in mid-March and involves the Coopers Creek (☎ 412 8560) and Matua Valley (☎ 411 8301) vineyards, which provide live music and food over a weekend. A $20 ticket buys you an entree-size meal and a glass of wine (plus there is a complementary glass) at either vineyard. A bus will be available to take people from Auckland to the vineyards and back again; there is one trip either way per day. Contact the vineyards directly for tickets and information.

Wine Waitakere takes place on Labour weekend (the Sunday and Monday) and involves three vineyards: Pleasant Valley, Lincoln Vineyards and Soljans Estate. Buses run between the vineyards from a car park in Henderson (corner of Alderman Drive and Edmonton Rd). At each of the vineyards there's live music and reasonably priced food – as well as wine of course. At the time of writing the cost of tickets had not been confirmed. Contact the vineyards directly for more information.

See also the boxed text 'For the Pleasure of the Palate' in the Places to Eat chapter.

WAITAKERE RANGES

These scenic ranges once supported important kauri forests, but these were logged extensively during the 19th century, though a few stands of kauri and other mature trees such as rimu survive. The **Centennial Memorial Park** now protects many native plants in the regenerating forest. Bordered to the west by the beaches on the Tasman Sea, the park's sometimes rugged terrain is the most significant forest area close to Auckland, and is popular for picnics and walks. Be aware that periodically people get lost in the Waitakeres; it's easier than you might think. Never wander off the tracks (which of course you shouldn't do anyway, in the interests of conservation) and never go walking alone. Always tell someone reliable where you are going and when to expect you back. Wear good, stout shoes (preferably boots) with plenty of ankle support, warm socks and a hat. Bring a daypack with plenty of water and food, and warm, waterproof clothing just in case you may need it.

The **Arataki Visitor Centre** (☎ 817 7134), on SH24, 6km north-west of Titirangi on **Scenic Drive** (which goes from Titirangi to Swanson), is a good starting point for exploring the ranges. It is open daily from 9 am to 5 pm. As well as providing a host of information on the area, this impressive

centre with its Maori carvings and spectacular views is an attraction in its own right. The **Arataki Nature Trail** opposite the centre indicates native species and contains mature kauri. It's an easy and educational walk designed to show you how forest regenerates and to explain the different types of vegetation.

The visitor centre has numerous pamphlets, including the excellent *Nga Tohu a Nga Tupuna* (indicating the carved ancestors of Te Kawerau a Maki) and maps for walking over 200km of trails in the ranges. Recommended is Jason's *Recreation and Track Guide* of Waitakeres ($8), which has detail on all walks in the ranges and as far north as Muriwai. You can also get information from the DOC information centre in Auckland. The AA puts out a guide called *New Zealand Leisure. Auckland: Waitakere Walks*, edited by Kathy Ombler, which maps and describes a variety of walks. Noted walks are the

DAVID WALL

Carved *pou* at the Arataki Visitor Centre

Karamatura Loop Walk (one hour return) near Huia, leading to the waterfalls and northern rata forest, and the **Cascade Kauri** area to the north, which has three good walks **Auckland City Walk**, the **Upper Kauri Track**, and **Pukematekeo Track**. Another popular walk is the **Kitekite Falls Track**, which starts at the end of Glen Esk Rd. It takes about 1½ hours return.

Not far from the visitors centre, farther along Scenic Drive on your, is **Rose Hellaby House**, a property bequeathed to the people

of Auckland in 1973. Part of the house is open to the public (weekend afternoons); the grounds are open daily and provide great views of the city and both harbours.

The **Waitakere Tramline Society** (☎ 832 330) is a small group of enthusiasts who have kept the Waitakere line operating for the public. Trips can only be made with bookings and they leave East Portal (turn down Christian Rd from Swanson and continue to the end; it's signposted) on weekends at 10 and 11.30 am and 1 and 2.30 pm.

Looking After the Land

Here are a few simple guidelines that you should observe if you plan to go tramping (hiking) in the bush.

Rubbish Carry out all your rubbish. If you've carried it in you can carry it out. Don't overlook those easily forgotten items such as aluminium foil, orange peel, cigarette butts and plastic wrappers. Empty packaging weighs very little anyway and should be stored in a dedicated rubbish bag. Make an effort to carry out rubbish that's left by others.

Never bury your rubbish: digging disturbs soil and ground cover. Buried rubbish will more than likely be dug up by animals.

Human Waste Disposal Where there is a toilet, please use it. Where there is none, bury your waste. Dig a small hole 15cm deep and at least 100m from any watercourse, tracks or huts. Consider carrying a lightweight trowel for this purpose. Cover the waste with soil and a rock. Use toilet paper sparingly and bury it with the waste.

Washing Don't use detergents or toothpaste in or near watercourses, even if they are biodegradable.

For personal washing, use biodegradable soap and a water container (or even a lightweight, portable basin) at least 50m away from the watercourse. Disperse the waste water widely to allow the soil to filter it fully before it finally makes it back to the watercourse.

Wash cooking utensils 50m from watercourses using a scourer or sand instead of detergent.

Cooking Portable fuel stoves are not as environmentally damaging as fires. If you do use a fire, keep it small and only used dead wood. Ensure it is out by dousing it with water and checking the ashes before you leave the campsite.

Conservation Always stick to the tracks to avoid damaging fragile plant life.

Cultural Considerations Some places may be of historical or cultural importance. Please treat these places with respect and consideration.

The train passes through two tunnels and the carriage lights are dimmed so passengers can see the glow-worms. The cost is $8 for adults and $4 for school-age children (this includes temporary membership of the society).

There are numerous tour operators who organise trips to the Waitakeres. They include Waitakere Scenic Tours (see Vineyards), which runs a coast and rainforest trip in a Mercedes unimog ($95 per person, including lunch). You can be picked up/dropped off in Auckland city. Off The Beaten Track (☎ 407 4086, fax 407 4186) tailors trips to your needs. Bush and coast walks are a specialty, but there are other possibilities. They will pick/drop off in Auckland city. Wilderness Walks Waitakere (☎/fax 838 9007, wildwalk@ihug.co.nz) does a two day walk (food, day packs and sleeping bags included) for $260 per person, and a one day walk for $100 per person (minimum of two people). You need boots with good ankle support for these walks. You can be picked up/dropped off in Auckland city. Bush & Beach (☎/fax 478 2882, bbl@bushandbeach.co.nz) takes half-day ($60 per person) and full-day ($99 per person) trips; no minimum numbers. For other companies, see Activities in the Things to See & Do chapter.

The Waitakere Park Lodge (☎ 814 9622, fax 814 9921, 573 Scenic Drive) is 5km from the Arataki Visitor Centre (towards Piha). There are 17 suites with en suites (plus conference and convention facilities), views across to the city and the harbour beyond, and native forest all around. Rooms in the lodge cost $92.50 per person (twin share); motel-style units with kitchen facilities cost $60 per person twin share. There are often weekend and other specials. Even if you don't stay here, you can avail yourself of the restaurant (mains are $20 to $25).

WHATIPU & KAREKARE

In the 19th century, steam trains hauled huge kauri logs along the surf-pounded coast to the wharf. The **Parahara Railway** was superseded in the early 20th century by another coastal railway that stretched to Piha,

although there is little evidence these days of either. The former mill manager's house now offers fairly basic accommodation.

Many ships have foundered on the treacherous sand bars near here. The most famous and tragic is the *Orpheus*, a 1700-ton, 21-gun steam corvette that went down in 1863, earning the dubious distinction of being NZ's worst maritime disaster.

Whatipu is an attractive spot on the northern side of Manukau Harbour at Manukau Heads. It is a 40km from Auckland via Titirangi and Huia, about a 50 minute drive from the city. The *Whatipu Lodge (☎ 811 8860)* is set in a quiet and isolated area, good for tramping and fishing. It has basic campsites at $12 per vehicle (up to four people), and hostel-style accommodation with single, twin and double rooms at $22 per adult ($10 per child). Take the bus to Huia and they'll pick you up. It's 10 minutes from the beach and there are plenty of walks, ranging from easy to challenging.

You can walk to Karekare from here (5km) or take the road (17km). Scenes from Jane Campion's film *The Piano* were filmed

Swimming Safe

The west coast beaches have powerful currents and heavy surf. Lifesaving clubs have been established to patrol the beaches to protect swimmers and surfers. You should always swim between the flags which are planted on the beach by lifeguards. Remember, that currents change and a place that's OK one day may not be the next. If you have been warned not to swim at a particular place, take heed. If in doubt, ask. The lifeguards will be happy to advise on conditions and explain which places are safe. You should never go out of your depth, and of course, children should be supervised at *all* times. Drownings along this coast are not uncommon.

here. The Karekare Surf Club patrols the beach on summer weekends. There is no accommodation.

PIHA & TE HENGA (BETHELLS BEACH)

Piha, with its iron-sand beach, has long been a favourite with Aucklanders as well as with artists and alternative types. The distinctive **Lion Rock** (101m), poised just off the beach, can be climbed although it's steep and best done before or after the heat of the day (30 to 40 minutes return; there are handrails). The **Tasman Lookout Track** takes you to a promontory at the southern end of the beach where you overlook **The Gap** and a blowhole that booms and froths in the heaving surf. **Whites Beach**, which is just over the promontory to the north of Piha, is accessible via a track at the northern end of Piha. The more remote **Anawhata** beach (no road access) is about 3km to the north of Piha.

Piha comes alive in summer with hundreds of beach-goers, holiday-makers and surfers. In summer, in addition to the beach life, there's tennis, lawn bowls, live bands at the surf club on weekends, and lots of partying. Surfing competitions are held in Piha and there are horse races on the beach towards the end of summer. There are many good bushwalks through the surrounding Waitakere Ranges and along the rocky coastline. It's a very enjoyable, picturesque spot, and a refreshing change from Auckland.

Some 8km north of Piha is Te Henga, or Bethells Beach, with its wind-swept sand dunes. Although much less visited than Piha, there is a surf club, and a walkway (part of the NZ Walkway system) that starts at the freshwater Lake Wainamu (the track is signposted near the bridge before the end of the road leading to Bethells Beach). The walk takes you along the coastline and through a farm valley before coming out at Constable Rd (three to four hours one way). Some 500m north along Constable Rd is the entrance to Goldie Bush and the Motutuara Scenic Reserve, which has kauri trees (some large). There is an easy route and a more difficult

The expansive surf beach at Piha

one here. It takes about three hours to do the loop back to where you started at Constable Rd. The walk is detailed in the free pamphlet *Auckland: NZ Walkways*, available from DOC or the Arataki Visitor Centre. The Te Henga section of the walk is closed between 1 August and 1 October (lambing season).

Places to Stay

There are numerous bed and breakfast places and interesting farmstay options in the Waitakere/West Auckland area. Tourism Auckland (☎ 366 6888) has details, but the specialist accommodation guides in the Facts for the Visitor chapter also list places to stay.

The *Piha Domain Motor Camp* (☎ 812 8815), right on the beach, has tent sites for $10 ($6 per child), caravans for $25/38/8 for a single/double/child.

Much more upmarket is *Grenvilles* (☎ 812 8870, 136 Garden Rd, Piha), which has one double/twin room with its own bathroom and wood burner, and one queen-size room with a shared bathroom. This attractive two storey cottage is made of adobe brick. Breakfast is included in the price of $95/140 to $160 for a single/double.

Bethell's Beach Cottages (☎ 810 9581, fax 810 8677, 267 Bethells Rd) has two, lovely self-contained cottages for $126 a

RONJ BIERI

EXCURSIONS

double (Turehu Cottage) and $195 (Te Koinga Cottage) a double. Meals are available for an extra cost.

MURIWAI BEACH

The road to Muriwai Beach is well signposted at Waimauku on SH16. Apart from the renowned **surf beach**, the main attraction here is the colony of **Australasian gannets**. The colony was once confined to a nearby rock stack but has now overflowed to the shore cliffs, even past the barriers erected to keep observers out. If you haven't seen these beautiful birds at close range before, take the opportunity to see them here. North of Muriwai is **Woodhill Forest**, a 12,500 hectare commercial plantation forest (40km north-west of Auckland) that has walking tracks and picnic sites. Entry is signposted from SH16 (there are two entries from here and one farther north at South Head Rd). No camping is permitted.

A good way to explore the beach and forest around Muriwai is on horseback with the Muriwai Beach Riding Centre (☎ 411 8480). A two hour ride (maximum of five people) costs $50 per person (includes a guide and hard hat).

Muriwai Four Wheel Drive Tours (☎ 411 8603) does trips across farmland, through Woodhill Forest and out onto Muriwai Beach. Tours are tailored to individual needs, but work out roughly at $30 per person for a two-person, two-hour tour, and $60 per person for a half-day tour.

4-Track Adventures (☎ 420 8104) takes guided tours over logging tracks in Woodhill Forest. There are one, two and three-hour tours starting at $85 per person. Helmets are provided. You need to be at least 14 years of age to drive the Honda 300ccs or the Polaris 250ccs. To get there turn off SH16 at the Carter Holt Harvey headquarters sign.

In most cases, the tour operators listed under the Waitakere Ranges will arrange trips to the gannet colony and Muriwai.

Places to Stay

At the small settlement of Muriwai, the *Muriwai Waterfront Camp (☎ 411 9262)* is adjacent to the beach; tent and powered sites are $10 per night.

The *Muriwai Beach Motel (☎ 411 8780, 411 9202, 280 Moturara Rd)* has single/double one-bedroom units for $85 (single rates are about $60 during the week).

HELENSVILLE
* pop 2080   ☎ 09

This town is less than an hour's drive from Auckland, 4km inland from the southern end of the Kaipara, NZ's biggest harbour.

MARTIN HARRIS

Australasian gannets have made a home of Muriwai's offshore rock stack.

Helensville itself is no great attraction, but you can make interesting **harbour cruises** on the MV *Kewpie Two* – advance bookings are essential (☎ 420 8466). There are three-hour trips on Saturday, Sunday and Monday at 1 pm (adults/children $12/6), as well as full-day trips and three-day trips. There are several interesting **gardens** to visit in the area and a pamphlet with details is available from the Helensville Garden Centre Care & Florist (☎ 420 8878), on 5 Commercial Rd; it's open daily. You need to arrange your visits in advance. The **Pioneer Museum** (☎ 420 7881) on Porter Crescent is open daily from 1 to 3.30 pm.

Four kilometres north-west of Helensville, at Parakai, **Aquatic Park** (☎ 420 8998) is a huge hot pool and swimming complex with indoor and outdoor mineral pools and various waterslides. The centre is open daily from 10 am to 10 pm (adults/children $10/6).

Tandem skydiving (☎ 420 8064, fax 420 8010, c.pine@xtra.co.nz) at Parakai Parachute Centre is also popular. Jumps take place daily in summer and, weather permitting, in winter. You can arrange in advance to be picked up from Auckland city on weekdays ($15). Jump prices are $195 and $225.

Places to Stay & Eat
Malolo House (☎/fax 420 7262, 110 Commercial Rd) has dorm beds (four beds to a dorm) for $17, twins for $44 and singles for $30. En suite rooms cost $80. There is a kitchen for guest use.

Whenuanui 'Rose Cottage' B&B Farmstay (☎ 0800 755 433, 2191 SH16, Helensville) has one queen-size room in a cottage with an en suite. It costs $95 for two with breakfast included. It's about 3.5km south of Helensville.

Getting There & Away
Whenuapai Bus Travel (☎ 416 9521) has buses that go from Lower Albert St in Auckland city to Helensville daily: Nos 066, 067 and 069 (the latter two are express buses). The one-way trip costs $7.20 for an adult; it takes 1½ hours in an ordinary bus and one hour 10 minutes in an express.

South of Auckland

At the foot of the market-garden region of the Bombay Hills the terrain flattens out into the Hauraki Plains. To the west are historic Waiuku and the Awhitu Peninsula, which juts into Manukau Harbour. To the east are Clevedon, the Hunua Ranges and the Seabird Coast – and the road to Coromandel Peninsula.

BOMBAY HILLS
At Bombay, some 45km south of Auckland city, is the Franklin Information Centre (☎ 09-236 0670, fax 236 0580), where you can pick up useful information on the Franklin District. It's open weekdays from 8.30 am to 5 pm and weekends 9 am to 3 pm. Get hold of the colour map *Country Trails of Franklin*, which details plenty of attractions in the region. Some 2km past the centre (on the north-bound lane, and next to Grandma's Kitchen) is the **Nyco Chocolate Factory** (☎/fax 09-236 0788) where, if you book in advance, you can tour the factory on weekdays ($1 per person including chocolate tasting).

At the foot of the Bombay Hills is Pokeno and the turn-off to Thames. Here, by the De Redcliffe Estate winery, is the luxurious *Hotel Du Vin (☎ 09-233 6314, fax 233 6215, reservations@duvin.co.nz, Lyons Rd, Mangatawhiri Valley)*. It's worth making the 45km trip from Auckland city to dine in the award-winning restaurant. There is also accommodation (starting at $343 for two) here, plus a heated pool, spas, a gym, croquet, petanque and various other facilities. Lyons Rd is off SH2, which is the road to Thames that branches off from the Southern Motorway.

THE SOUTH-WEST
Steam train enthusiasts can visit the **Glenbrook Vintage Railway** (☎ 09-236 3546 or the Waiuku Information Centre ☎ 09-235 8924) where they have 12km steam train rides (adults/children $9/4). Turn right off the Southern Motorway at Drury, just south of Papakura, and it's just before Waiuku

township. The train operates between late October and early June on Sunday and most public holidays, every hour on the hour between 11am and 4 pm.

Nearby, at 35 Farmpark Rd (off Glenbrook Station Rd), is the Glenbrook Farm Park (☎ 09-236 3628), which is open on Sunday and public holidays from October to June. This is a great place to bring kids; there are plenty of animals and birds, and there are pony rides for $1.50. Entry is $4.50 for adults and $2.50 for children. The restored sailing scow *Jane Gifford* takes 2½-hour trips on the high tide, which will give you a good view of the southern parts of the Manukau Harbour (adults/children $16/7). For bookings and sailing times contact the Waiuku Information Centre (☎ 09-235 8924).

Also based at Waiuku is Stressfree Adventures (☎ 09-235 9529), on Awhitu Rd, RD4 Waiuku, Auckland 1852, which specialises in taking beginners on kayaking, caving and abseiling excursions. Caving is done at Port Waikato, and a combined caving/abseiling experience starts at $90. Groups can arrange to be picked up from Auckland city.

At Waikaretu (near Tuakau), about 1½ hours from Auckland city (over 100km), is Nikau Cave, which is on a working farm (☎ 09-233 3199). There are two trips ($20): a relatively easy one that doesn't involve crawling, and another that takes you on a 1km journey past caverns filled with stalactites (1½ hours approximately); you'll probably also see glow-worms. Torches and helmets are provided.

THE SOUTH-EAST

The route south-east through the Auckland suburb of Howick takes you via the small coastal settlements of **Beachlands** and **Maraetai** through to **Clevedon** and from there to the **Hunua Ranges**, the **Seabird Coast** and **Miranda**.

There are several regional parks along this stretch of coast. Just before you get to Maraetai township, where there is a placid strip of shelly beach with a jetty and boat club, you'll find **Omana Regional Park**, which is situated

on a promontory overlooking Omana Beach. Once a pa site (home to the Ngai Tai tribe) and later a mission station and farm, it's now a popular place for picnickers and daytrippers from Auckland. There is an unstaffed information centre open daily from 8 am to 4.30 pm near the entrance.

Umupuia (Duder's) Regional Park (a farm park) to the south juts out into the gulf. There are walking tracks that take you to another old Ngai Tai pa site and, at low tide, along the coast to **Duder's Beach**. The land was bought from the Ngai Tai by Thomas Duder in 1866 and made a regional park in 1995.

Tapapakanga Regional Park, a farm park with great views across the Firth of Thames and a walking track, is just south of Orere Point. There is a basic *camping ground* here ($5 per adult, $2 per child); for information call Parksline on ☎ 303 1530.

To the south of these is **Waharau Regional Park** (there are two campsites, one with hot water; $5 per person, $8 for the hot-water site; closed mid-December to mid-February), which has an unstaffed information centre just inside the entrance, and **Whakatiwai**. There are several tracks into the Hunua Ranges from Waharau and one from Whakatiwai.

From Maraetai you can travel along the Pohutukawa-lined Maraetai coast road and North Rd to Clevedon, the base for Auckland's **Polo Club** (☎ 292 8556; games are held from December to April). There are now about eight **vineyards** in this area; for details get a copy of the brochure *Winemakers of Auckland* from visitor centres.

In Clevedon itself is **The Woolshed** (☎ 292 8615), on the corner of North Rd and Kawakawa Bay Rd, which showcases NZ knitwear, sheepskin and deerskin items, woodware, greenstone and paua jewellery. It's open daily from 10 am to 5 pm. Just 4.5km south of Clevedon, on Pioneer Rd, is **Montgomerie Farm** (☎ 292 8724), a working farm that's open daily to the public. There are shows (sheep shearing, lamb feeding, drafting, milking, working dogs and so on) at 11 am and 2.30 pm (adults/children $9/4). There's also horse riding

($20 for half an hour, $25 for an hour). You should book ahead for the horse riding, and for the shows if possible.

Only half a kilometre from Clevedon, at 123 Twilight Rd, is **Red Alert Paintball Games** (☎ 298 2265). You get 100 paintballs (food colouring and water in a gelatinous casing), a face protector and paintball gun ($30). You have to bring your own teams. Numbers of players vary from six to 35, and there are several game scenarios from which to choose: capturing the opponent's flag, capturing a central flag, saving the president, storming the fort and so on. Extra paintballs can be bought if needed ($10 for 50, $20 for 100). Wear old clothes.

From Clevedon it's about a 10 minute drive to Hunua Village, where there's an information centre that's open daily from 8 am to 4.30 pm (unstaffed on weekends). The Falls Rd entrance to the **Hunua Ranges Regional Park** is only a couple of kilometres from here; the Hunua Falls can be seen from the car park. There are *campsites* in the park ($5 per person), and numerous walking tracks ranging from easy to hard. Get a copy of the *Hunua Recreation and Track Guide* ($8) from the office, the nearby BP petrol station or from Auckland. Bigfoot Tours (☎ 273 3717) organises kayaking and hiking trips into the Hunuas for groups.

Following the coast road south of Maraetai, it's a 40 to 50 minute drive to the **Miranda Shorebird Centre** (☎ 09-232 2781), located on a 20km stretch of coast known as the Shorebird Coast. It's open daily 9 am to 5 pm. This vast mudflat on the Firth of Thames is teeming with aquatic worms and crustaceans that attract thousands of Arctic-nesting shorebirds over the Arctic winter.

The two main species are the bar-tailed godwit and the lesser knot, but it isn't unusual to see turnstones, curlew sandpipers, sharp-tailed sandpipers and the odd vagrant red-necked stint and terek sandpiper.

Miranda also attracts internal migrants after the godwits and knots have departed, including the pied oyster-catcher and the wrybill from the South Island, and banded dotterels and pied stilts from both main islands. For more information visit the Miranda Shorebird Centre, and pick up a copy of *Shore Bird Migration to and from Miranda* ($2).

The **Miranda Hot Springs** (☎ 867 3055) complex has open and covered hot pools, private spas, play areas and powered campsites. It's open from 9 am to 9 pm daily (adults/school children/preschoolers $7/4/2.50).

Places to Stay

The *Fairfield Country Homestay* (☎/fax 292 8852, Kawakawa Bay Rd, Clevedon), 7.3km north-east of Clevedon (en route to the coast) has a lovely queen-size en suite room for $80 single, $110 double. The home is set in two hectares of grounds and has sea views.

Clevedon Maritime Resort (☎ 292 8572, fax 292 8039, North Rd) has a self-contained guesthouse 2.5km north of Clevedon. This place has its own marina and spacious grounds. The cost is $100 for a single, $150 for a double.

The *Miranda Shorebird Centre* has clean and modern rooms. A bunk bed here is a reasonable at $15 for nonmembers ($10 for members), and a self-contained unit costs $45 for two. Kitchen facilities are available. Trust membership is $20 per year.

Not far south of the centre, next to the hot springs, is the tidy *Miranda Holiday Park* (☎ 07-867 3205) where tent and caravan sites are $12 per person, on-site vans $50 for two people and the leisure lodge is $100 for two for the first night and $80 thereafter.

North of the Auckland Region

WHANGAREI

• pop 69,700   ☎ 09

Whangarei is the major city of Northland and a haven for yachts. Travellers heading to or from the Bay of Islands will invariably pass this way. It is a pleasant, thriving city with an equable climate, though its main attractions are in the surrounding area. The

EXCURSIONS

beaches at Whangarei Heads, about 35km east of town, are incredibly scenic and have many tiny bays and inlets. The climate and soil combine to make Whangarei a gardener's paradise – many parks and gardens thrive in this city.

The helpful Whangarei Visitor Bureau (☎ 438 1079) is at Tarewa Park, 92 Otaika Rd on SH1 at the southern entrance to town. It's open daily in summer from 8.30 am to 6.30 pm; in winter it's open on weekdays from 8.30 am to 5 pm and weekends from 10 am to 4 pm. There's a cafe overlooking a 'kid-friendly' park, with weekend toy-train rides.

Getting There & Away

Air Both Air New Zealand and Ansett have flights between Auckland and Whangarei with onward connections. Great Barrier Airlines flies twice a week to/from the island.

Bus The InterCity bus depot (☎ 438 2653) is at 11 Rose St. InterCity has frequent buses between Auckland and Whangarei, continuing north to Paihia, Hokianga Harbour and Kaitaia, as well as to Dargaville.

Northliner has a daily Auckland-Whangarei-Bay of Islands service, with a route to Kerikeri via Paihia or directly to Russell on the Opua ferry. It operates from the Northliner terminal (☎ 438 3206, also at 11 Rose St.

BAY OF ISLANDS
☎ 09

Long famed for its stunning scenery, the Bay of Islands is one of the country's major attractions. The bay is punctuated by dozens of coves and its clear waters range in hue from turquoise to deep blue. Dotted with nearly 150 islands, the Bay of Islands is aptly named. The islands have escaped development as the townships are all on the mainland. Paihia is the centre of the Bay of Islands. Though only a small town, its population swells dramatically in summer. Waitangi Reserve is within walking distance. Only a short passenger ferry ride away, Russell has all the character that Paihia lacks.

Though also a popular tourist destination, historic Russell is a small, sleepy town with many fine old buildings and a delightful waterfront. To the north is Kerikeri – 'so nice they named it twice', claim the tourist brochures. Kerikeri is more like a real town and much less touristy.

The Bay of Islands has a mind-boggling array of activities and tours. Many are water-based to make the most of the natural surroundings. Backpacker discounts are available for many activities and tours, and the hostels arrange cheap deals. Fullers (☎ 402 7421) and Kings Tours & Cruises (☎ 402 8288) operate regular cruises that are popular. Best known is the Fullers Cream Trip, which takes about five hours. It leaves daily in summer and on Monday, Wednesday, Thursday and Saturday in winter.

A pleasant way to explore the Bay of Islands is on a sailing trip. Operators include:

A Place in the Sun	☎ 403 7615
Carino	☎ 402 8040
Great Escape Charters	☎ 402 7143
Gungha	☎ 025 760 670
Straycat	☎ 402 6130
Vigilant	☎ 403 7596

If you want to swim with the dolphins try Dolphin Discoveries (☎ 402 8234). You can go sea kayaking with Coastal Kayakers (☎ 402 8105). Scuba diver operators include Paihia Dive Hire (☎ 402 7551) on Williams Rd and Matauri Cat Charters (☎ 405 0525) near the Oceans Motel at Matauri Bay. Both take trips out to the *Rainbow Warrior*.

Other activities include fishing, scenic flights and horse riding. The tourist information centre at Paihia will provide details.

Paihia & Waitangi
• pop 1825

Paihia, the main town in the area, was settled by Europeans as a mission station in 1823, when the first raupo hut was built for the Reverend Henry Williams. Paihia still has a very pretty setting but the missionary zeal has been replaced with an equally fervent tourist industry. It's basically an accommodation, eating and tours centre.

Most of the information places are conveniently grouped together in the Maritime Building right by the wharf in Paihia. Here you'll find the Bay of Islands Visitor Information Centre (☎ 402 7345) on Marsden Rd, which can give information and advice and make bookings. It's open daily from 8 am to 8 pm in summer, 8 am to 5 pm in winter. Also here are Fullers', King's and other cruise and tour operators' offices, fishing boat bookings, the bus station and terminal for the ferry to Russell. The offices are open daily from 8 am to 5 pm.

Things to See & Do The **Treaty House** in Waitangi has special significance in NZ colonial history. Built in 1832 as the home of British resident James Busby, eight years later it was the setting for the signing of the Treaty of Waitangi. Beyond the great house a road climbs Mt Bledisloe, from where there are commanding views. Beginning from the visitor centre, a **walking track** through the **Waitangi National Reserve** passes through the mangrove forest around Huia Creek and on to the attractive **Haruru Falls**. At the foot of the falls there's good swimming, several motor camps, a licensed restaurant and a tavern. The reserve is open daily from 9 am to 5 pm.

A few kilometres from the falls is **Kelly Tarlton's Shipwreck Museum**. Beached beside the bridge over the Waitangi River is the barque *Tui*, an old sailing ship imaginatively fitted out as a museum of shipwrecks. It's open daily from 9 am to 5.30 pm; longer during holidays.

Just behind Paihia is the **Opua Forest**, a regenerating forest with a small stand of kauri and a number of walking tracks. DOC publishes pamphlets with details on all the Opua Forest Walks.

This region celebrates many special events. In January there is a Tall Ships Race at Russell. February has Waitangi Day on the 6th and a 10 day arts festival, with exhibits of touchable art, plays, music, comedy and dance.

Kelly Tarlton's Shipwreck Museum

There is the Country Music Festival in early May and the Jazz & Blues Festival in mid-August. September is foodies month, with Russell's Oyster Festival and the very popular Wine & Food Festival in Paihia, on the Waitangi foreshore.

In October, the Auckland-Bay of Islands Weekend Coastal Classic is held – NZ's largest yacht race.

Places to Stay *Camping & Cabins* There are many camping grounds around Paihia and Waitangi, most of them near Haruru Falls. Tent/powered sites cost around $10 per night. The camping grounds include: *Tradewinds Resort* (☎ 402 7525), in a beautiful setting beside the river and facing the falls; *Twin Pines Tourist Park* (☎ 402 7322), on Puketona Rd at the falls; *Falls Caravan Park* (☎ 402 7816), located beside Twin Pines; *Bay of Islands Holiday Park* (☎ 402 7646), 3km from the falls, 6.5km from Paihia on the Puketona Rd; and *Smith's Holiday Camp* (☎ 402 7678); a lovely waterside camp, 2.5km south of Paihia towards Opua.

The DOC office in Russell (☎ 403 7685) has details of accommodation in the Bay of Islands Maritime & Historic Park.

Hostels Paihia has a good selection of hostels; all make bookings for activities at discounted prices. Kings Rd is Paihia's hostel row and places here include: *Pipi Patch Lodge* (☎ 402 7111, 18 Kings Rd), where a dorm/single/double is $17/30/45; *Mousetrap*

EXCURSIONS

(☎ *402 8182, 11 Kings Rd*), where a dorm/twin/double is $15/32/38; and *Peppertree* (☎ *402 6122, 15 Kings Rd*), where these options cost $15/40/40.

Other hostels include: *Lodge Eleven* (☎ *402 7487*), on the corner of Kings and MacMurray Rds, which charges $16/35/44 for a dorm/single/double; *Pickled Parrot* (☎ *402 6222*), on Greys Lane, just off Kings Rd, which charges $16/25/38 (including breakfast); the *Centabay Lodge* (☎ *402 7466, 27 Selwyn Rd*), well positioned behind the shops, charges $15/37/45 for a dorm/double/double with en suite; *Tommy's* (☎ *402 8668*), on Davis Crescent, charges $14/36/36 for a dorm/twin/double; and *Mayfair Lodge* (☎ *402 7471, 7 Puketona Rd*), at the Waitangi end of Paihia, charges $16/36 for a dorm/double.

B&Bs & Guesthouses Several B&Bs are found in Paihia and the Bay of Islands. The information centre makes referrals and bookings.

Motels & Hotels In Paihia motels stand shoulder to shoulder along the waterfront. Doubles are usually around $120 during the peak summer months. Paihia also has quite luxurious tourist hotels. The *Quality Resort Waitangi* (☎ *402 7411*) is in a nice setting, north across the bridge. The *Paihia Holiday Motor Inn* (☎ *402 7911*), on Joyces Rd, has a pool and well-equipped rooms.

Russell
- pop 788

Russell is a short ferry ride across the bay from Paihia. It was originally a fortified Maori settlement that spread over the entire valley, then known as Kororareka. Russell today is a peaceful and pretty little place that justifiably features 'romantic' in its self-promotion. It's a marked contrast to the hustle of Paihia across the bay. There is no information office. Get a copy of *Russell: Kororareka* from the Bay of Islands Visitor Information Centre in Paihia. The excellent Bay of Islands Maritime & Historic Park Visitor Centre (☎ 403 7685) is in Russell.

The free *Russell Heritage Trails* pamphlet includes walking and driving tours.

Things to see in Russell include the **Russell Museum**, which is open daily from 10 am to 4 pm, **Pompallier House**, open daily 10 am to 4 pm, **Maiki (Flagstaff Hill)**, and **Long Beach**, which is 1km to the east of Russell.

You'll find there are numerous camping grounds, motels, hotels and B&Bs at Russell.

Kerikeri
- pop 4161

At the northern end of the bay, Kerikeri is a laid-back provincial town. It has plenty of accommodation and can be used as a base for exploring the Bay of Islands, but is primarily a service town for the surrounding agricultural district. The visitor centre at Rewa's Maori Village has pamphlets. Get information on walks in the area from DOC (☎ 407 8474) on Landing Rd.

Things to see in Russell include the **Stone Store & Kemp House, Rewa's Maori Village**, which is across the river from the stone store, and the **Waimate North Mission House**. There are also **arts & craft** shops and several interesting **walks**.

Getting There & Away
Air Air New Zealand has daily flights to Kerikeri from Auckland. Great Barrier Airlines has daily flights in summer from Auckland to Watea (Haruru Falls) airstrip then on to Great Barrier Island and Whitianga in the Coromandel.

Bus All buses serving Paihia arrive at and depart from the Maritime Building by the wharf. InterCity has buses daily from Auckland to the Bay of Islands via Whangarei and Opua. The trip takes about four hours to Paihia and goes to Kerikeri before continuing north to Kaitaia.

Northliner has an Auckland-Whangarei-Bay of Islands-Kaitaia bus service. It departs from the Downtown Airline Terminal in Auckland and stops in Paihia, Haruru Falls and Kerikeri. There's a connecting service to Russell and also a direct Whangarei-Russell service.

Pioneer Coachlines has a four hour trip from Paihia to Dargaville via the Waipoua Forest on weekdays (and a Sunday service in summer).

South of the Auckland Region

HAMILTON
- **pop 115,700**   ☎ 07

Hamilton is 129km south of Auckland and is the city that travellers generally pass through on their way to/from Rotorua. Built on the banks of the Waikato River, it is the Waikato region's major centre and in the past few decades has undergone spectacular growth. The Hamilton Visitor Centre (☎ 839 3580) is in the municipal building in Garden Place, between Victoria and Anglesea Sts. It's open weekdays from 9 am to 4.45 pm and weekends and public holidays from 10 am to 2 pm. It has information on Hamilton, Waitomo and the Waikato, and also sells bus and train tickets.

Things to see in Hamilton include the superb **Waikato Museum of Art & History**, on the corner of Victoria and Grantham Sts near the river, the **Mormon Temple**, 12km from the city centre, **Hamilton Zoo**, which is 8km from the city centre, and the huge **Hamilton Gardens**, on Cobham Drive on the east side of Cobham Bridge (they can be reached by walking south from the city along the river walkway).

There's plenty of accommodation in Hamilton. Ask at the visitor centre.

Getting There & Away
Air Air New Zealand has direct flights between Hamilton and Auckland and other major cities.

Bus All local and long-distance buses arrive at and depart from the Transport Centre on the corner of Anglesea and Ward Sts. Inter-City (☎ 834 3457) and Newmans (☎ 838 3114) are both represented. Frequent buses make the connection between Hamilton and Auckland and also leave for Rotorua and other southern destinations.

ROTORUA
- **pop 68,000**   ☎ 07

Rotorua is the most popular tourist area of the North Island. Nicknamed 'Sulphur City', it has the most energetic thermal activity in the country with bubbling mud pools, gurgling hot springs, gushing geysers and evil smells. Rotorua also has a large Maori population, descendants of the Arawa canoe. The cultural activities of Arawa are among the most interesting and accessible in the country.

The city itself is thriving, buoyed by the huge interest of tourists (earning another local nickname: 'Roto-Vegas'). It's located 280m above sea level on the shores of Lake Rotorua, which teems with trout. The name Rotorua means 'the second lake' (*roto* means lake; *rua* means two), as it was the second lake that the Arawa ancestor Ihenga discovered in the late 14th century. The area has numerous other lakes as well as interesting trout springs and wildlife parks.

Rotorua took off as a tourist destination in the early 1870s at the close of the land wars (see History in the Facts about Auckland chapter). The voices of government and army personnel joined with those of early travellers, broadcasting the scenic wonders of the place. People came to take the waters in the hope of cures for all sorts of diseases, and Rotorua's tourist industry was thus founded. The town's main attraction was the fabulous Pink and White Terraces, on the shores of the small, warm lake Rotomahana. The terraces, formed by water-borne deposits of silica from geothermal activity, were considered by many at the time as among the natural wonders of the world. They were destroyed in the 1886 Tarawera eruption.

Orientation & Information
The main shopping area is along Tutanekai St. Fenton St starts by the Government

CENTRAL ROTORUA

PLACES TO STAY
7 Dudley House B&B
8 Novotel Royal Lakeside Rotorua
14 Princes Gate Hotel
18 Hot Rock; Lava Bar
20 Kiwi Paka
21 Acacia Camping Ground
22 Cactus Jacks Downtown Backpackers
24 Rotorua Downtown Backpackers
27 Good Sports Hotel
30 Rotorua Central Backpackers
40 Rotorua YHA Hostel
41 Eaton Hall
42 Millennium
44 Lake Plaza Rotorua
49 Spa Lodge
53 Funky Green Voyager
54 Ann's Volcanic Rotorua
55 Morihana Guest House
58 Motel & Hotel Area
59 Baden Lodge

PLACES TO EAT
6 Pizza Hut
9 Lady Jane's
10 Lewisham's Austrian Restaurant; Zambique
11 The Thai Restaurant
12 Japanese Sushi Bar
13 Fat Dog Cafe Bar
17 Pig & Whistle Pub
34 Zanelli's
35 Rendevous Restaurant
45 Korea House Restaurant
46 Mr India
50 Sirocco; Finally Found It

OTHER
1 St Faith's Anglican Church
2 Tamatekapua Meeting House
3 Soundshell
4 Rotorua Lakefront Jetty & Lakefront Cruises
5 Hospital
15 Civic Theatre
16 Tourism Rotorua; Map & Track Shop; Bus Depot
19 Aquatic Centre
23 Carey's Sightseeing Tours
25 Laundrette; Nomad Cyber Cafe
26 Police Station
28 Rotorua Museum of Art & History
29 Orchid Gardens
31 Link Rent-a-Car
32 Air New Zealand; Thomas Cook
33 Post Office
36 Hoyts; Movieland 5
37 Ansett New Zealand
38 Rotorua Cycle Centre
39 Pins Cycles
43 Polynesian Spa
47 Blackmore's Galaxy Travel & American Express Agent
48 Automobile Association (AA)
51 Pac 'n Save Supermarket
52 Big Fresh Supermarket
56 Budget Rent-a-Car
57 Rent-a-Dent

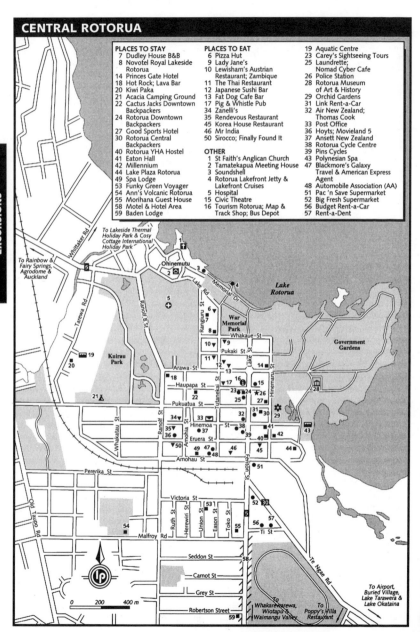

Gardens near the lake and runs all the way to Whakarewarewa ('Whaka') thermal area 2km away; it is lined with motels for much of its length.

Tourism Rotorua (☎ 348 5179, fax 348 6044, marketing@tourism.rdc.govt.nz), open daily from 8 am to 6 pm, is at 1167 Fenton St, on the corner of Haupapa St. It has much local information, makes bookings for everything around Rotorua and has a travel agency (www.rotoruanz.com). There is also a money changing bureau (open daily from 8.30 am to 5.30 pm), a cafe and other services for travellers, including showers, luggage storage, public telephones.

The Automobile Association (AA; ☎ 348 3069) is on Amohau St. The American Express agent is Blackmore's Galaxy Travel (☎ 347 9444) at 1315 Tutanekai St. Thomas Cook has a forex desk in the Air New Zealand office and there are plenty of banks that will change foreign currencies.

Thermal Air is a useful weekly tourist publication and the annual *Rotorua Visitors' Guide* is indispensable (both are free). Tourism Rotorua sells a good map, *Gateway to Geyserland* ($2) of the city and surrounding area.

Things to See & Do

Lake Rotorua This lake is the largest of 12 lakes in the Rotorua district. It was formed by an eruption and subsequent subsidence of the area. Two cruises on the lake depart from the Rotorua lakefront jetty at the end of Tutanekai St.

The *Lakeland Queen* paddle-steamer (☎ 348 6634) does one-hour breakfast ($24), luncheon ($26 for a buffet, $16 cruise only) and dinner cruises ($38.50 to $42.50) on the lake (luncheon cruises daily, breakfast and dinner cruises on demand); children are half-price. The *Scatcat* motorised catamaran (☎ 347 9852) does a one hour circuit of Mokoia Island (adults/children $25/free).

Ohinemutu This is a lakeside Maori village. Its name means 'the place of the young woman who was killed' – and was given by Ihenga in memory of his daughter.

The historic Maori **St Faith's Anglican Church**, by the lakefront, has a beautiful interior decorated with carvings, woven tukutuku panels, painted scrollwork and stained-glass windows. An image of Christ wearing a Maori cloak is etched on a window so that he appears to be walking on the waters of Lake Rotorua. Seen from this window, it's surprising how much Lake Rotorua does resemble the Sea of Galilee. The church is open daily from 8 am to 5 pm.

Opposite the church is the impressive **Tamatekapua Meeting House**, built in 1887. Named after the captain of the Arawa canoe, this is an important meeting house for all Arawa people. The Magic of the Maori Concert (see Maori Concerts & Hangi) is held here.

A good **craft market** is held every second weekend at the Soundshell.

Rotorua Museum of Art & History

This impressive museum (☎ 349 8334), better known as the Bath House, is in a Tudor-style building in Government Gardens. Built in 1908, it was once an elegant spa retreat. You can tour through some of the reconstructed spa rooms and marvel at the seemingly odd cures practised therein.

The museum has a very good exhibition of the *taonga* (treasures) of the local Arawa Maori, a rousing video (every 20 minutes) on the 1886 Mt Tarawera eruption and plenty of information on the region before and after the eruption that destroyed the Pink and White Terraces. The survivors' stories have been preserved, as has the strange tale of the ominous, ghostly war canoe that appeared before a boatload of astonished tourists hours before the eruption. The museum is open daily from 9.30 am to 6 pm in summer, until 5 pm in winter (adults/children $7.50/3). It also has a pleasant cafe serving good coffee.

Polynesian Spa

The popular Polynesian Spa (☎ 348 1328), off Hinemoa St in the Government Gardens, is open daily from 6.30 am to 11 pm (last ticket sale is 10.15 pm). A bath house was opened at these

EXCURSIONS

springs in 1886, and people have been swearing by the health-giving properties of the waters ever since.

Remember to take off anything silver that you're wearing; it'll instantly turn black on contact with the water. There is a safe deposit facility at the ticket office. The modern complex has several pools at the lake's edge. Entry to the main pools (temperatures from the high 30s°C to the low 40s°C; adults only) is $10, private pools are $10 per half hour (children $4), the luxury lakeside spa is $25 (adults only), and the family spa is $10 (children $4).

Orchid Gardens Located in Hinemaru St, the gardens contain an extensive hothouse of orchids that bloom year-round, as well as a micro-world display where you can get a microscopic view of living reptiles and insects. There is also a big water organ, really a huge fountain, with over 800 jets. It plays every hour on the hour from 9 am to 5 pm. The complex is open daily from 8.30 am to 5.30 pm (adults/children $10/4).

Te Whakarewarewa This is Rotorua's largest and best known thermal reserve, and a major Maori cultural area. It's pronounced Faka-raywa-raywa, but most people call it simply 'Whaka'. Mind you, Whakarewarewa is actually short for Te Whakarewarewatangaoteopetauaawahiao, which means 'the gathering together of the war forces of Wahiao'.

Whakarewarewa's most spectacular geyser is **Pohutu** ('big splash' or 'explosion'), which usually erupts at least once an hour. Pohutu spurts hot water about 20m into the air, for an average time of five to 10 minutes – though the longest eruption is reputed to have lasted for 15 hours!

Whaka, until recently a single thermal site, has been divided into two parts, with the division roughly where Pohutu spouts forth. One part contains the village, which you enter from Tryon St (adults $15, seniors and children aged seven to 14 $7.50, under fours free; open daily from 8.30 am to 5 pm). There are concerts in the meeting house at

MARTIN HARRIS

Detail from the gateway of the Maori Arts and Crafts Institute at Whakarewarewa

11.15 am and 2 pm, and regular guided tours (between 9 am and 4 pm) through the village and the thermal area (try the sweetcorn cooked in a hot pool – $2). The entry ticket includes the tours and the concerts.

The other part of Whaka contains the Maori Arts & Crafts Institute (☎ 348 9047), which has working craftspeople and an art gallery. It also has a replica Maori village, a kiwi house and a Maori concert performed daily at 12.15 pm. There are (free) guided tours daily at 3 pm. Entry is $16.50 for adults ($30 including the concert), $7.50 for children aged five to 15 ($13.50), and $4.50 for children under five ($8). It's open daily from 8 am to 6 pm in summer, 5 pm in winter (enter from Hemo Rd).

Whaka is 2km south of the city centre, straight down Fenton St. City buses will drop you near Tryon St, or the Sightseeing Shuttle bus will drop you at the Maori Arts & Crafts Institute.

Maori Concerts & Hangi Maori culture is a major attraction in Rotorua. Although it has been commercialised, it's worth investing in the experience. The two big activities are concerts and *hangi* (meals cooked in an earth oven) – often the two are combined.

Concerts are put on by local Maori. By the time the evening is over it's likely you'll have been dragged up on stage, experienced a Maori *hongi* (nose-to-nose contact), have joined hands for a group sing-in, and thought about freaking out your next-door neighbour with a *haka* (war dance) when you get home. Other features of a concert are *poi* dances, action songs and hand games.

For a concert only, one of the best performances is presented daily (8 pm) at Tamatekapua Meeting House in Ohinemutu, opposite St Faith's Church down by the lake (adults/children $15/5). You can show up at the door for the Magic of the Maori Concert or book directly (☎ 349 3949) or with Tourism Rotorua.

For a combined concert and hangi, Tamaki Tours (☎ 346 2823) does the excellent Twilight Cultural Tour to a marae and Maori village complex. They'll pick you up and along the way explain the traditional protocol involved in visiting a marae. A 'chief' is chosen from among the group to represent the visitors. The concert is followed by a hangi (adults/children $58/29).

Big hotels which also offer Maori concerts and hangi include:

Centra	☎ 348 1189
Lake Plaza	☎ 348 1174
Millennium	☎ 347 1234
Quality Hotel	☎ 348 0199
Novotel Royal Lakeside	☎ 346 3888
Sheraton Rotorua	☎ 349 5200

Zorbing Like bungy jumping, zorbing is another of those unusual Kiwi innovations. Rotorua is the only place where you can do it. The rules are simple: climb into an inflated double plastic sphere (the two spheres are held together with shock cords), strap in then roll downhill for about 150m, rotating within the sphere. Eventually you'll come to a stop. You can zorb dry for

$25 or try a wash cycle for $30 (wash and dry costs $45; a kid's zorb is $10). You can do zorbing at the Agrodome Leisure Park (☎ 332 2768), on Western Rd, Ngongotaha.

White-Water Rafting Several rafting companies make trips on the Rangitaiki River (Grade III to Grade IV). Day trips, with a barbecue lunch, cost around $89. The trips depart from the Rangitaiki River Bridge in Murupara; companies provide transport from Rotorua for an extra $5. Companies include:

River Rats	☎ 347 6049
Great Kiwi White Water Co	☎ 348 2144
Kaituna Cascades	☎ 357 5032
Raftabout	☎ 345 4652
Whitewater Excitement Co	☎ 345 7182
Wet & Wild Rafting	☎ 348 3191

Most popular are the shorter and more dramatic rafting trips on the Kaituna River over the Okere Falls – off SH33 about 16km north-east of Rotorua. You go over the 7m falls, then over another 3m drop, as well as various rapids, in about 40 minutes ($65). All Rotorua's rafting companies do a Kaituna trip.

Fishing You can hire guides to trout fish or go it alone, but a licence is essential and there are various regulations. Guided fishing trips cost about $65 per hour per boat, and you are almost guaranteed to catch a fish. Plan to spend about two to three hours on the trip. Ask at Tourism Rotorua or at the Rotorua lakefront for fishing operators.

You can wander down to the lakefront and fish if you have a licence and it's the season (October to June). Get your fishing licence directly from a fishing guide or from the Map & Track Shop (☎ 349 1845, 1225 Fenton St). Licences cost $13 per day, $25 per week or $65 for the season.

Organised Tours
Rotorua offers a mind-boggling array of tours – Tourism Rotorua can book any tours, as can hostels and hotels.

Carey's Sightseeing Tours (☎ 347 1197), 18 Haupapa St, has a large range. Carey's Capers visits most of Rotorua's favourite volcanic and thermal attractions, with a dip in an isolated hot-water stream along the way (tours are $99/50 for a full/half day).

Carey's 'world famous' Waimangu Round Trip, well-known in these parts since 1902, is one of the best. Focusing on the 1886 Mt Tarawera eruption, it includes the Waimangu Volcanic Valley, a cruise on Lake Rotomahana past the site of the Pink and White Terraces, a cruise on Lake Tarawera, a visit to the Buried Village and a dip in the Polynesian Spa (adults/children $140/80 for a full day). There's two shorter versions of the 'premier' Waimangu Round Trip: the 'de luxe' is $125/65, the 'budget' is $115/60.

Volcanic Wunderflites (☎ 345 6077) are particularly popular for flights over the awesome chasm of Mt Tarawera. Also available are trips in the Redcat biplane. Volcanic Air Safaris (☎ 348 9984) has fixed-wing and helicopter flights, the latter landing on the crater rim of Mt Tarawera ($240 per person). These companies are all based at Rotorua airport.

Places to Stay
Camping & Cabins The *Acacia Camping Ground* (☎ 348 1886, 129-37 Pukuatua St) is beside Kuirau Park. Tent/powered sites cost $10 each ($5 per child) and tourist flats cost between $40 and $55 for two (higher rates in the summer peak).

The *Cosy Cottage International Holiday Park* (☎ 348 3793, 67 Whittaker Rd) may be the only place in the world with heated tent sites – the ground warmth gradually warms your tent at night. It also has a mineral pool, a heated swimming pool, canoes, bicycles and fishing tackle for hire. Tent/powered sites are $10 per person ($5 per child), tourist cabins cost $40 to $46 a double and tourist flats start at $55.

The *Lakeside Thermal Holiday Park* (☎ 348 1693, 54 Whittaker Rd) has hot mineral pools and spas. Tent/powered sites are $10 per person, tourist cabins $40, tourist flats $55 and lakeside flats $65 (the latter three prices for two).

The *Rotorua Thermal Holiday Park* (☎ 346 3140), on the southern end of the Old Taupo Rd, is a large camping ground with hot mineral pools and a heated swimming pool. Tent/caravan sites are $9 per adult ($5 per child), cabins start at $45 for two people, and tourist flats are $65 for two. There is also a lodge with bunk beds for $18 per person, double rooms for $36 and en suite rooms for two are $45.

Hostels *Hot Rock* (☎ 347 9469, 1286 Arawa St) is the most popular backpacker hostel in town. It is a former motel, and a number of its spacious, thermally-heated rooms have en suites and kitchen facilities. There are also three hot pools (indoor and outdoor). Dorm beds start at $16, rooms for four are $18 per person, twin and double rooms around $44. Hot Rock shares its address with the popular Lava Bar, where you can play pool and listen to good sounds.

The *Funky Green Voyager* (☎ 346 1754, 4 Union St) is one of the smallest and nicest of Rotorua's hostels. In a tranquil residential neighbourhood, close to the city centre, the hostel is comfortable and casual with a spacious backyard and a pleasant sunny conservatory. Accommodation starts at $15 for a dorm bed, $36 for double or twin room.

The *Rotorua Downtown Backpackers* (☎/fax 346 2831), on the corner of Haupapa and Fenton Sts, is near Tourism Rotorua and the bus station. It has dorm beds from $15 to $16, singles for $30, doubles for $40 and twins for $34. There is a large kitchen area, guest bar and barbecue facilities.

Rotorua Central Backpackers (☎ 349 3285, 1076 Pukuatua St) has spacious rooms and a spa pool in a classic older building. The cost is $15 for a dorm bed, double and twin rooms are $36 (there is a bunk twin for $34). It's centrally located and quiet.

Rotorua YHA Hostel (☎ 347 6810), on the corner of Eruera and Hinemaru Sts, has twin and family rooms as well as a thermal spa pool. It charges $17 for dorm accommodation and $40 for a double room.

Rotorua is renowned for its geothermal landscape.

The old Bath House is now Rotorua's museum.

The Wharepuni, or meeting house, at Whakarewarewa, Rotorua

The gorgeous Champagne Pool at Rotorua's Waiotapu Thermal Reserve

The *Spa Lodge* (☎ 348 3486, 1221 Amohau St) is old and cramped, but the rooms are thermally heated. It charges $15 for a dorm bed, $25/30/30 for a single/double/twin.

As its name suggests, *Cactus Jacks Downtown Backpackers* (☎ 348 3121, 54 Haupapa St) is a building with a distinctly Mexican theme. It has rooms and cabins and there are spas for guests. It charges $15.50 for dorm accommodation and $30/39/35 for a single/double/twin.

The modern *Kiwi Paka* (☎ 347 0931, 60 Tarewa Rd) is 1.2km from the city centre (it runs a pick-up/drop off service for travellers). It charges $17 in four-bed shared rooms; doubles and twins in a chalet are $47 and in the lodge $40/38. A self-contained chalet sleeping four costs $84. You can camp for $8.50 per person. There is a thermal pool, a nice cafe and a bar (Under Canvas).

B&Bs & Guesthouses Toko St is quiet and well away from the tourist hustle of central Rotorua. At No 3 is the *Tresco International* (☎ 348 9611), where bed and breakfast costs $48/75 for a single/double. There are sinks in the rooms and it's a neat, tidy and comfortable place. The same can be said for the *Morihana Guest House* (☎ 348 8511) at No 20, which charges $40/75 for a single/double. Both places have hot mineral pools.

Central *Eaton Hall* (☎ 347 0366, 1255 Hinemaru St), opposite the Quality Resort, is a comfortable guesthouse with bed and breakfast for $45/75 a single/double. Book ahead in summer as this is a popular place.

The Tudor-style *Dudley House B&B* (☎ 347 9894, 6 Rangiuru St) is decorated in English country cottage style. It's comfortable, spotless and excellent value at $40/60 for a single/double.

Tourism Rotorua has a listing of nearly 50 homestays and farmstays, and can make bookings.

Motels & Hotels Rotorua has over 80 motels and Fenton St, as it heads south from town past the Big Fresh supermarket, has wall-to-wall motels as far as the eye can see.

In the off season they compete, with discounts displayed.

Ann's Volcanic Rotorua (☎ 347 1007, 107 Malfroy Rd) has one and two-bedroom units, each with its own spa, for $89/145 for a single/double and studio units for about $60.

Ashleigh Court Motel (☎/fax 348 7456, 337 Fenton St) has self-contained studio/one-bedroom units for $85/95 for two people. Each unit has a private spa.

Baden Lodge (☎/fax 349 0634, 301 Fenton St) has self-contained one-bedroom units with private spas starting at $120 a night for two people.

The *Birchwood Spa Motel* (☎ 347 1800, cnr Sala St and Trigg Ave) has studio/one/two-bedroom units with privates spas for $95/115/155 for two people.

Conveniently situated on the corner of Hinemaru and Pukuatua Sts, the *Good Sports Hotel* (☎ 348 1550) has typical pub rooms for $45/55 for a single/double. It has a large thermal pool and the Dobbo's Sports Bar, which has live bands on weekends.

The *Princes Gate Hotel* (☎ 348 1179, 1 Arawa St), on the corner of Hinemaru St, is a luxurious hotel with crystal chandeliers, canopies over the beds, an elegant restaurant and bar, a health facility and much more. It charges $123/146 for a single/double.

Top-End Lodges If expense is no obstacle, Rotorua has a few exclusive and secluded lodges: *Solitaire Lodge* (☎ 362 8208), Lake Tarawera; *Woodlands Country Lodge* (☎ 332 2242), Hamurana Rd, Ngongotaha; *Kawaha Point Lodge* (☎ 346 3602), 171 Kawaha Point Rd; *Okataina Lodge* (☎ 362 8230), Lake Okataina; *Waiteti Lakeside Lodge* (☎ 357 2311), 2 Arnold St, Ngongotaha.

Prices start at about $90 for a double room and range to over $500 (Kawaha Point Lodge).

Places to Eat

Lewisham's Austrian Restaurant, at 1099 Tutanekai St, specialises in traditional Austrian and Hungarian food. *Zanelli's*, at 1243a Amohia St, is a popular Italian dinner house that serves great gelati. *Sirocco*, at

EXCURSIONS

EXCURSIONS

1280 Eruera St, is a popular Mediterranean cafe/bar that is open daily for lunch and dinner. Meals are around $18. Next door, *Finally Found It* serves good, imaginative vegetarian cuisine (peanut pasta, vegetarian curry), as well as tasty seafood.

For genuine Pacific Rim cuisine, featuring innovative use of local ingredients, try the *Rendezvous Restaurant* at 1282 Hinemoa St; it is open from Tuesday to Saturday for dinner. Also highly recommended for its Kiwi fare is *Poppy's Villa*, at 4 Marguerita St (main courses are around $25). Both of these restaurants are in atmospheric old villas.

You can get good Thai food from the *Thai Restaurant*, at 1141 Tutanekai St. Main courses are around $18. *Mr India*, at 1161 Amohau St, is moderately priced and has all the authentic subcontinental favourites – vindaloo, korma, naan and vegetarian dishes.

The *Korea House Restaurant*, at 1074 Eruera St, is a pleasant, large and fancy place serving Korean food. If you're after Japanese your appetite will be satisfied at the *Japanese Sushi Bar*, at 1148 Tutanekai St. A sushi main course costs between $10 and $15. *Copper Criollo*, at No 1151 Arawa St, has Creole-style food, such as Cajun chicken and seafood gumbo. It also serves a $6.50 cooked breakfast.

The cosy *Fat Dog Cafe Bar*, at 1161 Arawa St, is popular for breakfast, and indeed at any time of the day for salads, soups, lights meals, cake and coffee. It's a good place to while away the evening with an espresso, and in winter it has a fire going.

Churchill's Bar, at 1302 Tutanekai St, is a good place for a pub meal. It's a comfortable English-style bar that serves lunch and finger food in big, satisfying portions; food is always available. The *Pig and Whistle*, a renovated police station on the corner of Haupapa and Tutanekai Sts, has soups and salads, burgers and generous-sized meals including fish of the day ($17), which comes with Pig Tail Fries. It has a number of brews on tap, including its own Swine Lager. On weekend nights you can guzzle a Swiney and listen to bands.

Getting There & Away

Air The Air New Zealand office (☎ 347 9564), on the corner of Fenton and Hinemoa Sts, is open on weekdays from 8.30 am to 5 pm. It also has a counter at the airport (☎ 345 6175). It offers daily direct flights to Auckland and other main centres.

Ansett New Zealand (☎ 347 0596) has an office at 1200 Hinemoa St and a ticket counter at the airport (☎ 345 5348). Ansett also offers daily direct flights to Auckland and other centres.

Bus All major bus companies stop at Tourism Rotorua (☎ 343 1740), on Fenton St, which handles bus bookings.

InterCity has daily buses to/from Auckland and numerous other places, as does Newmans bus company

Magic Bus and Kiwi Experience backpackers buses also stop in Rotorua.

Train The train station is on the corner of Railway and Lake Rds, about 1km northwest of the centre. The station opens only when trains are departing or arriving. Train tickets are available from Tourism Rotorua, not the station.

The *Geyserland* train operates daily between Auckland and Rotorua, stopping at Hamilton. It departs from Rotorua at 1.30 pm and arrives at Auckland at 5.45 pm. In the other direction, it leaves Auckland at 8 am and arrives at Rotorua at 12.15 pm.

Getting Around

To/From the Airport The airport is about 10km out of town, on the eastern side of the lake. Airport Shuttle (☎ 346 2386) and Super Shuttle (☎ 349 3444) offer a door-to-door service to/from the airport for $8 for the first person and $2 for each additional passenger. A taxi from the city centre is about $15.

Bus Magic of the Maori shuttle (☎ 021 674 354, freephone 0508 300 333) runs a constant loop each day, departing from Tourism Rotorua at 8.45 am (the last circuit leaves at 4.45 pm). It calls in at several hostels including Kiwi Paka YHA and Hot Rock, plus all the major attractions. It costs $4 for a one-way trip and $10 for an all-day pass. A timetable is available from Tourism Rotorua.

The Pink Bus (also The Thermal Connection; ☎ 348 2302, 0800 222 231) has a service to Waiotapu and Waimangu thermal areas (see Around Rotorua). It picks up passengers from Tourism Rotorua and some accommodation places at around 9 am (call The Pink Bus or Tourism Rotorua for precise times); buses return at 12.30 pm. The trip (including admission) to Waiotapu is $35 and to Waimangu $40.

Reesby Coachlines (☎ 347 0098) operates along several suburban bus routes on weekdays, with a limited service on Saturday. Route 3 runs to Whakarewarewa; route 2 to Rainbow Springs.

Car Rotorua has a host of car rental companies. The competition is fierce and they all seem to offer 'specials' in an effort to undercut the others.

Rent-a-Dent (☎ 349 1919), on Ti St, and Link Rent-a-Car (☎ 347 8063), at 108 Fenton St, are two economical companies. Ask about relocating cars to Auckland; you pay only for insurance and fuel.

Bicycle Rotorua is fairly spread out and public transport is not very good, so a bicycle is worthwhile. Bicycle hire places include Lady Jane's (☎ 347 9340), on the corner of Tutanekai and Whakaue Sts, the Rotorua Cycle Centre (☎ 348 6588), at 1120 Hinemoa St, and Pins (☎ 347 1151), at 161 Fenton St (the latter two are also good for repairs and parts). Expect to pay about $15 per hour for a mountain bike; around $45 for a full day.

AROUND ROTORUA
Hell's Gate

Hell's Gate (Tikitere) is a highly active thermal area, 16km east of Rotorua on the road to Whakatane (SH30). The reserve covers 10 hectares, with a 2.5km walking track to the various attractions, including the largest thermal waterfall in the southern hemisphere. It's open daily from 8.30 am to 5 pm (adults/children $10/5).

Waimangu Volcanic Valley

The Waimangu Volcanic Valley is another interesting thermal area, created during the eruption of Mt Tarawera in 1886. A walk through the valley (an easy downhill stroll) will take you past the Waimangu Cauldron (a pale blue lake steaming quietly at 53°C) and many other interesting thermal and volcanic features on the way down to Lake Rotomahana ('warm lake'). You can take a half-hour boat trip on the lake, passing steaming cliffs and the former site of the Pink and White Terraces, or get a minibus lift back to the start of the walk.

The Waimangu Volcanic Valley is open daily from 8.30 am to 5 pm. Entry costs $14.50/5 for adults/children for the valley walk only; $32.50/8 for the valley walk and boat trip. It's a 20-minute drive from Rotorua; 19km south on SH5 (the Taupo road), then about 5km on from the marked turn-off.

Waiotapu

Also south of Rotorua, Waiotapu ('sacred waters') is perhaps the best of the thermal areas to visit. It has many interesting features including the large, boiling Champagne Pool, various craters and blowholes, colourful mineral terraces and other rock formations. It is also home to the Lady Knox Geyser, which spouts punctually (with a little prompting) at 10.15 am, gushing for about an hour.

It opens daily from 8.30 am to 5 pm (last entry 4 pm), but is usually open later in summer (adults/children $12/4). The Waiotapu turn-off is signposted 30km south on SH5 (the road towards Taupo); it is 2km on from there.

Trout Springs

Several streams run down to Lake Rotorua, and the trout, lured by the free feeds from the tourists, swim up the streams to the springs.

The **Rainbow Springs Trout & Wildlife Sanctuary** is the best known of the trout springs. There are a number of springs (one with an underwater viewing facility), an aviary and a nocturnal kiwi house. The springs also have a wildlife area with wallabies, deer, birds, wild pigs and other native and introduced fauna, now all found in the wild in NZ.

Across the road, the Rainbow Farm Show is part of Rainbow Springs. It has shows at 10.30 and 11.45 am, 1 and 4 pm featuring sheep shearing and working sheep dogs.

Rainbow Springs is 4km north of central Rotorua, on the west side of Lake Rotorua – take SH5 towards Auckland or Hamilton, or catch the Magic of the Maori shuttle bus. It is open daily from 8 am to 5 pm (adults/children $16.50/7 – entry includes farm show and the springs).

Paradise Valley Springs is similar to Rainbow Springs, and is set in an attractive six hectare park with various animals. The springs, at the foot of Mt Ngongotaha, 13km from Rotorua on Paradise Valley Rd, is open daily from 8 am to 5 pm (adults/children $12/5).

Skyline Skyrides

Skyline Skyrides is on the west side of Lake Rotorua, near the Rainbow Springs. Here you can take a gondola ride up Mt Ngongotaha for a panoramic view of the lake area. Once there, fly the 900m back down the mountain on a luge (a sort of toboggan) or on a flying fox, then head back up again on a chairlift. The gondola costs $12 (children $5) for the return trip and the luge is $4.50 for one ride, less for multiple trips. The gondola operates daily from 9 am.

There is also a flight simulator, a shooting range and walking tracks.

Buried Village

The Buried Village is reached by a 15km scenic drive along Tarawera Rd, which passes the Blue and Green Lakes.

There's a museum just beyond the ticket counter that has many artefacts and provides interesting detail on the events before and after the devastating eruption. Of particular interest is the story of the *tohunga* Tuhoto Ariki who foretold of the destruction wreaked by the Tarawera eruption; his *whare* (house), in which he spent four days buried, has been excavated and is on display. In the park are the excavated remains of some of the buildings that were buried during the eruption. There's a peaceful bushwalk through the valley to the beautiful Te Wairoa Falls that drop 80m over rocky outcrops.

The village is open daily from 9 am to 5 pm in summer (until 4.30 pm in winter). Entry is $10.50/7.50 for adults/children; there are discounts for AA and YHA card holders.

Lake Tarawera

About 2km past the Buried Village is Tarawera Landing on the shore of Lake Tarawera. Tarawera means 'burnt spear', named by a visiting hunter who left his bird-spears in a hut and, on returning the following season, found both the spears and hut had been burnt.

Tarawera Launch Cruises (☎ 362 8595) has an 11 am cruise across Lake Tarawera towards Lake Rotomahana. The boat stays on the other side for about 45 minutes – long enough for people to walk across to Lake Rotomahana. The trip takes two hours and costs $25/12.50 for adults/children.

A 45-minute cruise on the lake leaves the landing at 1.30, 2.30 and 3.30 pm in summer ($17/9); 1.30 pm only during winter. Boats from Tarawera Landing can also provide transport to Mt Tarawera and to Hot Water Beach on Te Rata Bay.

Glossary

AA – New Zealand Automobile Association; the organisation that provides road information and roadside assistance
All Black – a member of NZ's revered national rugby union team (the name comes from 'All Backs', which the press called the NZ rugby team on an early visit to England)
Aotearoa – Maori name for NZ, literally 'land of the long white cloud'; jokingly translated as 'land of the wrong white crowd'
atua – spirit or god

bach – holiday home, usually a wooden cottage (pronounced 'batch'); in the South Island a bach is called a crib
Barrier, the – local name for Great Barrier Island in the Hauraki Gulf
baths – swimming pool, often referred to as municipal baths
Beehive – Parliament House in Wellington, so-called because of its distinctive shape
boozer – public bar; pub
bro – literally 'brother'; usually meaning mate, as in 'just off to see the bros'
bush – heavily forested area
Buzzy Bee – a child's toy as essential to NZ child development as dinosaur models; a wooden bee with spinning wings dragged along on a string to produce a whirring noise
BYO – bring your own (drinks and/or alcohol)

chilly bin – cooler; esky; large insulated box for keeping food and drink cold
choice – fantastic; great
ciggies – cigarettes
cuzzies – cousins; relatives

dairy – small corner store that sells just about everything, especially milk, bread, the newspaper and ice cream; convenience store
Dalmatian – a term applied to the predominantly Yugoslav gum diggers who fossicked for kauri gum (used as furniture polish) in the gum fields of Northland
deli – delicatessen

DOC – Department of Conservation (Te Papa Atawhai); the government department which administers national parks and all tracks and huts
duvet – doona; goose-feather quilt

farmstay – accommodation on a typical Kiwi farm where you are encouraged to join in the day-to-day activities
football – rugby, either union or league

Godzone – New Zealand (God's own country)
good as gold; good as – very good
greenstone – jade, pounamu

haka – the traditional challenge; war dance
handle – a dimpled glass beer mug with a handle
hangi – earth oven, where food in baskets is steamed over hot stones and embers in a covered hole; a traditional Maori feast
hapu – sub-tribe or smaller tribal grouping
hard case – an unusual or strong-willed character; humorous
Hawaiki – the unknown place in the Pacific from where the Maori tribes (the original seven waka) came
heitiki – carved, stylised human figure worn around the neck, often a carved representation of an ancestor; also called a *tiki*
hokey pokey – delicious variety of vanilla ice cream with butterscotch chips
hoki – a fish commonly sold in fish and chip shops
homestay – accommodation in a family house where you are treated (temporarily, thank God) as one of the family
hongi – Maori greeting; the pressing of noses and sharing of life breath
hui – gather; meeting; more casually, a party

Ika a Maui, Te – the North Island
Instant Kiwi – state-run lottery
Interislander – the Cook Strait ferry,

which crosses between the North Island and South Island

'Is it what!' – strong affirmation or agreement; 'Yes isn't it!'

iwi – a large tribal grouping with lineage to the original migration from Hawaiki; people; tribe

jandals – sandals; flip-flops; thongs; usually rubber footwear

jersey – jumper; sweater; usually woollen (also the shirt worn by rugby players, eg 'grab him by the jersey')

K Rd – Karangahape Rd

kai – food; any word with kai in it has some food connection

kainga – village; pre-European unfortified Maori village

ka pai – good; excellent

karakia – prayer

kaumatua – highly respected members of a tribe; the people you would ask for permission to enter a marae

kete – bag or basket woven from flax

kina – sea urchins; a Maori delicacy

kiwi – the flightless, nocturnal brown bird with a long beak which is the national symbol; the New Zealand dollar; a New Zealander; a member of the national rugby league team; an adjective to mean anything of or relating to NZ

kiwi bear – the introduced Australian ringtail possum; also called an opossum

kiwi fruit – small, succulent fruit with fuzzy brown skin and juicy green flesh; Chinese gooseberry

koe – you (singular)

koha – a donation

kohanga reo – schools where Maori language and culture are at the forefront of the education process; also called 'language nest' schools

koutou – you (plural)

kumara – Polynesian sweet potato; a Maori staple food

kune kune – a type of wild pig introduced by Chinese gold-diggers in the 19th century

Kupe – an early Polynesian navigator, from Hawaiki, credited with the discovery of the islands that are now NZ

league – rugby league football

mana – the spiritual quality of a person or object; authority of a chief or priest

manuhiri – visitor; guest

Maori – indigenous people of New Zealand

Maoritanga – Maori culture

marae – the complex of buildings associated with a particular Maori community; more formally, the sacred ground in front of the Maori meeting house (marae atea)

Maui – an important demi-God in Maori mythology

mere – flat, greenstone war club

MMP – Mixed Member Proportional; a cumbersome electoral system used in NZ and Germany; a limited form of proportional voting

moko – facial tattoo

motor camp – well-equipped camping grounds with tent sites, caravan and campervan sites, on-site caravans, cabins and tourist flats

motorway – freeway or expressway

nifty-fifty – 50cc motorcycle

NZ – the universal appellation for New Zealand; pronounced 'en zed'

pa – fortified Maori village, usually on a hill top

Pacific Rim – a term used to describe modern NZ cuisine; cuisine with an innovative use of local produce, especially seafood, with imported styles

Pakeha – white or European person; once derogatory, and still considered so by some, this term is now widely used for white New Zealanders

paua – abalone; tough shellfish pounded, minced, then made into patties (fritters), which are available in almost every NZ fish and chip shop; the multi-coloured shell of the abalone

poi – flax balls on lengths of string, used by women in poi dances

ponga – the silver tree fern; called a bungy

(pronounced 'bungee', with a soft 'g', in parts of the South Island)

pou – post

powhiri – traditional Maori welcome onto the marae

rap jump – face-down abseil

raupo – bullrush

Rheiny – affectionate term for Rheineck beer

scrap – a fight, not uncommon at the pub

section – small block of land

silver fern – the symbol worn by the All Blacks on their jerseys, representative of the underside of a ponga leaf

Steinie – affectionate term for Steinlager beer

Syndicate, the – the NZ defenders of the America's Cup in 2000

Tamaki makaurau – Maori name for Auckland

tane – man

tangata – the people

tangata whenua – people of the land; local Maori people

taniwha – fear-inspiring water spirit

taonga – something of great value; treasure

tapu – sacred; forbidden; taboo

tarseal – sealed road; bitumen

Te Kooti – a prominent 19th century Maori leader

Te Papa Atawhai – Maori name for DOC

tihi – summit; top; apex

tiki – short for *heitiki*

tohunga – priest; person of strong spiritual power; expert

tramp – walk; trek; hike; a more serious undertaking than an ordinary walk, requiring some experience and/or special equipment

tramper – one who tramps

tukutuku – wall panelling in some marae buildings and churches

umu – a Pacific Island version of a *hangi*, but cooked above ground

varsity – university

VIN – Visitor Information Network; the umbrella organisation of the visitor information centres and offices

wahine – woman

wai – water

waiata – song

Waitangi – short way of referring to the Treaty of Waitangi; a Northland town

waka – canoe

Watties – the NZ food and canning giant; NZ's answer to Heinz, until Heinz took over the company

whakapapa – genealogy

whare – house

whare runanga – meeting house

whare taonga – treasure house; museum

whare whakairo – carved house

whenua – the land

whitebait – small elongated translucent fish which is scooped up in nets and eaten whole (head, eyes and all!), often made into patties

wopwops – remote area; the middle of nowhere

LONELY PLANET

Phrasebooks

L onely Planet phrasebooks are packed with essential words and phrases to help travellers communicate with the locals. With colour tabs for quick reference, an extensive vocabulary and use of script, these handy pocket-sized language guides cover day-to-day travel situations.

- handy pocket-sized books
- easy to understand Pronunciation chapter
- clear & comprehensive Grammar chapter
- romanisation alongside script to allow ease of pronunciation
- script throughout so users can point to phrases for every situation
- full of cultural information and tips for the traveller

'...vital for a real DIY spirit and attitude in language learning'
– Backpacker

'the phrasebooks have good cultural backgrounders and offer solid advice for challenging situations in remote locations'
– San Francisco Examiner

Arabic (Egyptian) • Arabic (Moroccan) • Australian *(Australian English, Aboriginal and Torres Strait languages)* • Baltic States *(Estonian, Latvian, Lithuanian)* • Bengali • Brazilian • British • Burmese • Cantonese • Central Asia • Central Europe *(Czech, French, German, Hungarian, Italian, Slovak)* • Eastern Europe *(Bulgarian, Czech, Hungarian, Polish, Romanian, Slovak)* • Ethiopian (Amharic) • Fijian • French • German • Greek • Hebrew phrasebook • Hill Tribes • Hindi/Urdu • Indonesian • Italian • Japanese • Korean • Lao • Latin American Spanish • Malay • Mandarin • Mediterranean Europe *(Albanian, Croatian, Greek, Italian, Macedonian, Maltese, Serbian, Slovene)* • Mongolian • Nepali • Papua New Guinea • Pilipino (Tagalog) • Quechua • Russian • Scandinavian Europe *(Danish, Finnish, Icelandic, Norwegian, Swedish)* • South-East Asia *(Burmese, Indonesian, Khmer, Lao, Malay, Tagalog Pilipino, Thai, Vietnamese)* • South Pacific Languages • Spanish (Castilian) *(also includes Catalan, Galician and Basque)* • Sri Lanka • Swahili • Thai • Tibetan • Turkish • Ukrainian • USA *(US English, Vernacular, Native American languages, Hawaiian)* • Vietnamese • Western Europe *(Basque, Catalan, Dutch, French, German, Greek, Irish)*

Lonely Planet Journeys

J OURNEYS is a unique collection of travel writing – published by the company that understands travel better than anyone else. It is a series for anyone who has ever experienced – or dreamed of – the magical moment when they encountered a strange culture or saw a place for the first time. They are tales to read while you're planning a trip, while you're on the road or while you're in an armchair in front of a fire.

These outstanding titles explore our planet through the eyes of a diverse group of international writers. JOURNEYS books catch the spirit of a place, illuminate a culture, recount a crazy adventure or introduce a fascinating way of life. They always entertain, and always enrich the experience of travel.

ISLANDS IN THE CLOUDS
Travels in the Highlands of New Guinea
Isabella Tree

This is the fascinating account of a journey to the remote and beautiful Highlands of Papua New Guinea and Irian Jaya: one of the most extraordinary and dangerous regions on the planet. Tree travels with a PNG Highlander who introduces her to his intriguing and complex world, changing rapidly as it collides with twentieth-century technology. *Islands in the Clouds* is a thoughtful, moving book.

SEAN & DAVID'S LONG DRIVE
Sean Condon

Sean and David are young townies who have rarely strayed beyond city limits. One day, for no good reason, they set out to discover their homeland, and what follows is a wildly entertaining adventure that covers half of Australia.

'a hilariously detailed log of two burned out friends' – *Rolling Stone*

DRIVE THRU AMERICA
Sean Condon

If you've ever wanted to drive across the USA but couldn't find the time (or afford the gas), *Drive Thru America* is perfect for you. In his search for American myths and realities – along with comfort, cable TV and good, reasonably priced coffee – Sean Condon paints a hilarious road-portrait of the USA.

'entertaining and laugh-out-loud funny' – *Alex Wilber, Travel editor, Amazon.com*

BRIEF ENCOUNTERS
Stories of Love, Sex & Travel
edited by Michelle de Kretser

Love affairs on the road, passionate holiday flings, disastrous pick-ups, erotic encounters . . . In this seductive collection of stories, 22 authors from around the world write about travel romances. Combining fiction and reportage, *Brief Encounters* is must-have reading – for everyone who has dreamt of escape with that perfect stranger.

Includes stories by Pico Iyer, Mary Morris, Emily Perkins, Mona Simpson, Lisa St Aubin de Terán, Paul Theroux and Sara Wheeler.

Lonely Planet Travel Atlases

L onely Planet has long been famous for the number and quality of its guidebook maps. Now we've gone one step further and produced a handy companion series: Lonely Planet travel atlases – maps of a country produced in book form.

Unlike other maps, which look good but lead travellers astray, our travel atlases have been researched on the road by Lonely Planet's experienced team of writers. All details are carefully checked to ensure the atlas corresponds with the equivalent Lonely Planet guidebook.

- full-colour throughout
- maps researched and checked by Lonely Planet authors
- place names correspond with Lonely Planet guidebooks
- no confusing spelling differences
- legend and travelling information in English, French, German, Japanese and Spanish
- size: 230 x 160 mm

Available now: Chile & Easter Island • Egypt • India & Bangladesh • Israel & the Palestinian Territories • Jordan, Syria & Lebanon • Kenya • Laos • Portugal • South Africa, Lesotho & Swaziland • Thailand • Turkey • Vietnam • Zimbabwe, Botswana & Namibia

---

Lonely Planet TV Series & Videos

L onely Planet travel guides have been brought to life on television screens around the world. Like our guides, the programs are based on the joy of independent travel, and look honestly at some of the most exciting, picturesque and frustrating places in the world. Each show is presented by one of three travellers from Australia, England or the USA and combines an innovative mixture of video, Super-8 film, atmospheric soundscapes and original music.

Videos of each episode – containing additional footage not shown on television – are available from good book and video shops, but the availability of individual videos varies with regional screening schedules.

Video destinations include: Alaska • American Rockies • Australia – The South-East • Baja California & the Copper Canyon • Brazil • Central Asia • Chile & Easter Island • Corsica, Sicily & Sardinia – The Mediterranean Islands • East Africa (Tanzania & Zanzibar) • Ecuador & the Galapagos Islands • Greenland & Iceland • Indonesia • Israel & the Sinai Desert • Jamaica • Japan • La Ruta Maya • Morocco • New York • North India • Pacific Islands (Fiji, Solomon Islands & Vanuatu) • South India • South West China • Turkey • Vietnam • West Africa • Zimbabwe, Botswana & Namibia

The Lonely Planet TV series is produced by: Pilot Productions
The Old Studio
18 Middle Row
London W10 5AT, UK

LONELY PLANET

Lonely Planet On-line

W hether you've just begun planning your next trip, or you're chasing down specific info on currency regulations or visa requirements, check out Lonely Planet On-line for up-to-the minute travel information.

As well as mini guides to more than 250 destinations, you'll find maps, photos, travel news, health and visa updates, travel advisories, and discussion of the ecological and political issues you need to be aware of as you travel. You'll also find timely upgrades to popular guidebooks which you can print out and stick in the back of your book.

There's also an on-line travellers' forum where you can share your experience of life on the road, meet travel companions and ask other travellers for their recommendations and advice.

And of course we have a complete and up-to-date list of all Lonely Planet travel products including travel guides, diving and snorkeling guides, phrasebooks, atlases, travel literature and videos, and a simple on-line ordering facility if you can't find the book you want elsewhere.

Lonely Planet Diving & Snorkeling Guides

B eautifully illustrated with full-colour photos throughout, Lonely Planet s Pisces Books explore the world s best diving and snorkeling areas and prepare divers for what to expect when they get there, both topside and underwater.

Dive sites are described in detail with specifics on depths, visibility, level of difficulty, special conditions, underwater photography tips and common and unusual marine life present. You ll also find practical logistical information and coverage on topside activities and attractions, sections on diving health and safety, plus listings for diving services, live-aboards, dive resorts and tourist offices.

FREE Lonely Planet Newsletters

We love hearing from you and think you'd like to hear from us.

Planet Talk

Our FREE quarterly printed newsletter is full of tips from travellers and anecdotes from Lonely Planet guidebook authors. Every issue is packed with up-to-date travel news and advice, and includes:

- a postcard from Lonely Planet co-founder Tony Wheeler
- a swag of mail from travellers
- a look at life on the road through the eyes of a Lonely Planet author
- topical health advice
- prizes for the best travel yarn
- news about forthcoming Lonely Planet events
- a complete list of Lonely Planet books and other titles

To join our mailing list, residents of the UK, Europe and Africa can email us at go@lonelyplanet.co.uk; residents of North and South America can email us at info@lonelyplanet.com; the rest of the world can email us at talk2us@lonelyplanet.com.au, or contact any Lonely Planet office.

Comet

Our FREE monthly email newsletter brings you all the latest travel news, features, interviews, competitions, destination ideas, travellers' tips & tales, Q&As, raging debates and related links. Find out what's new on the Lonely Planet Web site and which books are about to hit the shelves.

Subscribe from your desktop: www.lonelyplanet.com/comet

LONELY PLANET

Guides by Region

Lonely Planet is known worldwide for publishing practical, reliable and no-nonsense travel information in our guides and on our Web site. The Lonely Planet list covers just about every accessible part of the world. Currently there are nine series: travel guides, shoestring guides, walking guides, city guides, phrasebooks, audio packs, travel atlases, diving and snorkeling guides and travel literature.

AFRICA Africa – the South • Africa on a shoestring • Arabic (Egyptian) phrasebook • Arabic (Moroccan) phrasebook • Cairo • Cape Town • Central Africa • East Africa • Egypt • Egypt travel atlas • Ethiopian (Amharic) phrasebook • The Gambia & Senegal • Healthy Travel Africa • Kenya • Kenya travel atlas • Malawi, Mozambique & Zambia • Morocco • North Africa • South Africa, Lesotho & Swaziland • South Africa, Lesotho & Swaziland travel atlas • Swahili phrasebook • Tanzania, Zanzibar & Pemba • Trekking in East Africa • Tunisia • West Africa • Zimbabwe, Botswana & Namibia • Zimbabwe, Botswana & Namibia travel atlas
Travel Literature: The Rainbird: A Central African Journey • Songs to an African Sunset: A Zimbabwean Story • Mali Blues: Traveling to an African Beat

AUSTRALIA & THE PACIFIC Australia • Australian phrasebook • Bushwalking in Australia • Bushwalking in Papua New Guinea • Fiji • Fijian phrasebook • Islands of Australia's Great Barrier Reef • Melbourne • Micronesia • New Caledonia • New South Wales & the ACT • New Zealand • Northern Territory • Outback Australia • Papua New Guinea • Papua New Guinea (Pidgin) phrasebook • Queensland • Rarotonga & the Cook Islands • Samoa • Solomon Islands • South Australia • South Pacific Languages phrasebook • Sydney • Tahiti & French Polynesia • Tasmania • Tonga • Tramping in New Zealand • Vanuatu • Victoria • Western Australia
Travel Literature: Islands in the Clouds • Kiwi Tracks • Sean & David's Long Drive

CENTRAL AMERICA & THE CARIBBEAN Bahamas and Turks & Caicos • Barcelona • Bermuda • Central America on a shoestring • Costa Rica • Cuba • Dominican Republic & Haiti • Eastern Caribbean • Guatemala, Belize & Yucatán: La Ruta Maya • Jamaica • Mexico • Mexico City • Panama
Travel Literature: Green Dreams: Travels in Central America

EUROPE Amsterdam • Andalucía • Austria • Baltic States phrasebook • Barcelona • Berlin • Britain • British phrasebook • Brussels, Bruges & Antwerp • Canary Islands • Central Europe • Central Europe phrasebook • Corsica • Croatia • Czech & Slovak Republics • Denmark • Dublin • Eastern Europe • Eastern Europe phrasebook • Edinburgh • Estonia, Latvia & Lithuania • Europe • Finland • France • French phrasebook • Germany • German phrasebook • Greece • Greek phrasebook • Hungary • Iceland, Greenland & the Faroe Islands • Ireland • Italian phrasebook • Italy • Lisbon • London • Mediterranean Europe • Mediterranean Europe phrasebook • Norway • Paris • Poland • Portugal • Portugal travel atlas • Prague • Provence & the Côte d'Azur • Romania & Moldova • Rome • Russia, Ukraine & Belarus • Russian phrasebook • Scandinavian & Baltic Europe • Scandinavian Europe phrasebook • Scotland • Slovenia • Spain • Spanish phrasebook • St Petersburg • Switzerland • Trekking in Spain • Ukrainian phrasebook • Vienna • Walking in Britain • Walking in Italy • Walking in Ireland • Walking in Switzerland • Western Europe • Western Europe phrasebook
Travel Literature: The Olive Grove: Travels in Greece

INDIAN SUBCONTINENT Bangladesh • Bengali phrasebook • Bhutan • Delhi • Goa • Hindi/Urdu phrasebook • India • India & Bangladesh travel atlas • Indian Himalaya • Karakoram Highway • Mumbai • Nepal • Nepali phrasebook • Pakistan • Rajasthan • South India • Sri Lanka • Sri Lanka phrasebook • Trekking in the Indian Himalaya • Trekking in the Karakoram & Hindukush • Trekking in the Nepal Himalaya
Travel Literature: In Rajasthan • Shopping for Buddhas

LONELY PLANET

Mail Order

Lonely Planet products are distributed worldwide. They are also available by mail order from Lonely Planet, so if you have difficulty finding a title please write to us. North and South American residents should write to 150 Linden St, Oakland, CA 94607, USA; European and African residents should write to 10a Spring Place, London NW5 3BH, UK; and residents of other countries to PO Box 617, Hawthorn, Victoria 3122, Australia.

ISLANDS OF THE INDIAN OCEAN Madagascar & Comoros • Maldives • Mauritius, Réunion & Seychelles

MIDDLE EAST & CENTRAL ASIA Arab Gulf States • Central Asia • Central Asia phrasebook • Hebrew phrasebook • Iran • Israel & the Palestinian Territories • Israel & the Palestinian Territories travel atlas • Istanbul • Jerusalem • Jordan & Syria • Jordan, Syria & Lebanon travel atlas • Lebanon • Middle East on a shoestring • Syria • Turkey • Turkish phrasebook • Turkey travel atlas • Yemen
Travel Literature: The Gates of Damascus • Kingdom of the Film Stars: Journey into Jordan

NORTH AMERICA Alaska • Backpacking in Alaska • Baja California • California & Nevada • Canada • Chicago • Florida • Hawaii • Honolulu • Los Angeles • Louisiana • Miami • New England USA • New Orleans • New York City • New York, New Jersey & Pennsylvania • Pacific Northwest USA • Puerto Rico • Rocky Mountain States • San Francisco • Seattle • Southwest USA • Texas • USA • USA phrasebook • Vancouver • Washington, DC & the Capital Region
Travel Literature: Drive Thru America

NORTH-EAST ASIA Beijing • Cantonese phrasebook • China • Hong Kong • Hong Kong, Macau & Guangzhou • Japan • Japanese phrasebook • Japanese audio pack • Korea • Korean phrasebook • Kyoto • Mandarin phrasebook • Mongolia • Mongolian phrasebook • North-East Asia on a shoestring • Seoul • South-West China • Taiwan • Tibet • Tibetan phrasebook • Tokyo
Travel Literature: Lost Japan

SOUTH AMERICA Argentina, Uruguay & Paraguay • Bolivia • Brazil • Brazilian phrasebook • Buenos Aires • Chile & Easter Island • Chile & Easter Island travel atlas • Colombia • Ecuador & the Galapagos Islands • Latin American Spanish phrasebook • Peru • Quechua phrasebook • Rio de Janeiro • South America on a shoestring • Trekking in the Patagonian Andes • Venezuela
Travel Literature: Full Circle: A South American Journey

SOUTH-EAST ASIA Bali & Lombok • Bangkok • Burmese phrasebook • Cambodia • Hanoi • Healthy Travel Asia & India • Hill Tribes phrasebook • Ho Chi Minh City • Indonesia • Indonesia's Eastern Islands • Indonesian phrasebook • Indonesian audio pack • Jakarta • Java • Laos • Lao phrasebook • Laos travel atlas • Malay phrasebook • Malaysia, Singapore & Brunei • Myanmar (Burma) • Philippines • Pilipino (Tagalog) phrasebook • Singapore • South-East Asia on a shoestring • South-East Asia phrasebook • Thailand • Thailand's Islands & Beaches • Thailand travel atlas • Thai phrasebook • Thai audio pack • Vietnam • Vietnamese phrasebook • Vietnam travel atlas

ALSO AVAILABLE: Antarctica • Brief Encounters: Stories of Love, Sex & Travel • Chasing Rickshaws • Lonely Planet Unpacked • Not the Only Planet: Travel Stories from Science Fiction • Sacred India • Travel with Children • Traveller's Tales

Index

Text

Bold indicates maps.

Boxed Text

MAP 2

PONSONBY & HERNE BAY

MAP 3

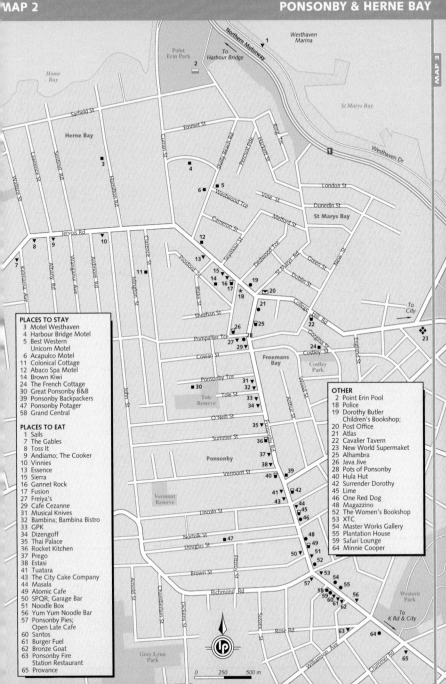

PLACES TO STAY
3 Motel Westhaven
4 Harbour Bridge Motel
5 Best Western
  Unicorn Motel
6 Acapulco Motel
11 Colonical Cottage
12 Abaco Spa Motel
14 Brown Kiwi
24 The French Cottage
30 Great Ponsonby B&B
39 Ponsonby Backpackers
47 Ponsonby Potager
58 Grand Central

PLACES TO EAT
1 Sails
7 The Gables
8 Toss It
9 Andiamo; The Cooker
10 Vinnies
12 Essence
15 Sierra
16 Gannet Rock
17 Fusion
27 Freiya's
29 Cafe Cezanne
31 Musical Knives
32 Bambina; Bambina Bistro
33 GPK
34 Dizengoff
35 Thai Palace
36 Rocket Kitchen
37 Prego
38 Estasi
41 Tuatara
43 The City Cake Company
44 Masala
49 Atomic Cafe
50 SPQR; Garage Bar
51 Noodle Box
54 Yum Yum Noodle Bar
57 Ponsonby Pies;
  Open Late Cafe
60 Santos
61 Burger Fuel
62 Bronze Goat
63 Ponsonby Fire
  Station Restaurant
65 Provance

OTHER
2 Point Erin Pool
18 Police
19 Dorothy Butler
  Children's Bookshop;
20 Post Office
21 Atlas
22 Cavalier Tavern
23 New World Supermaket
25 Alhambra
26 Java Jive
28 Pots of Ponsonby
40 Hula Hut
42 Surrender Dorothy
45 Lime
46 One Red Dog
48 Magazzino
52 The Women's Bookshop
53 XTC
54 Master Works Gallery
55 Plantation House
59 Safari Lounge
64 Minnie Cooper

MAP 3 - AUCKLAND CITY CENTRE

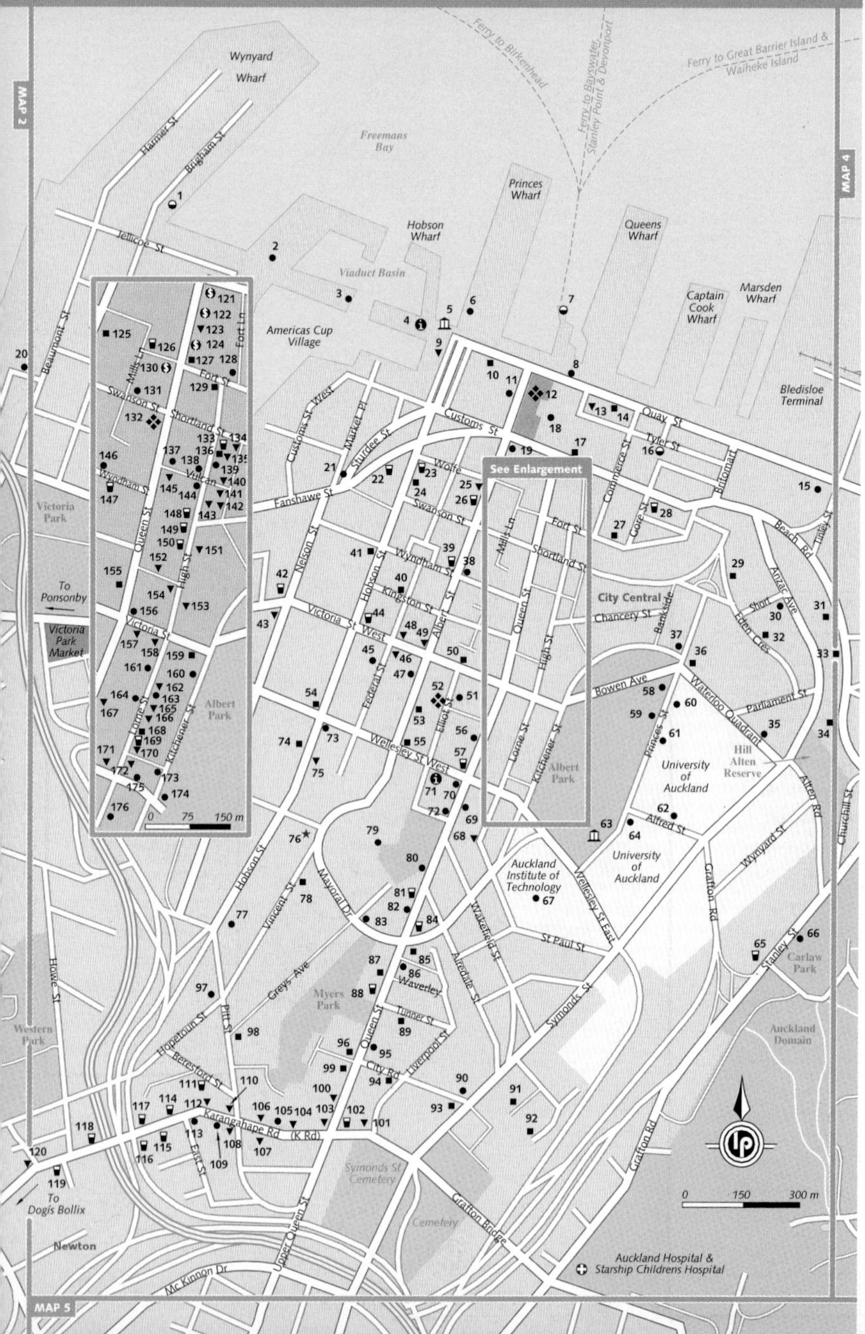

MAP 3 - AUCKLAND CITY CENTRE

PLACES TO STAY
10 Copthorne Harbour City
14 Quay Regency
17 Novotel
24 Nautilus Apartments
27 City Backpackers Hotel
29 Aspen Lodge B&B
31 Harbourview Station Hotel
32 Darlinghurst Quest Inn
33 Anzac Apartments Avenue
34 Bay City Backpackers
36 Hyatt Regency
40 Rydges Auckland
41 The Heritage Auckland;
   Muddy Farmer
50 New President Hotel
53 Centra; Team Magic
54 The Albion
55 City Central Hotel;
   Okonamai-yaki;
   Middle East Restaurant;
   Tony's Steak & Seafood
74 First Imperial Hotel &
   Apartments
78 Carlton Hotel
85 Kiwi Hilton Backpackers;
   Caravanserai;
   Merchant Mezze Bar
87 Quest Auckland
89 Auckland International YHA
91 Cintra Apartments
92 Best Western Whitaker Lodge
93 Sheraton
94 Auckland City YHA Hotel
96 Park Towers
98 YMCA
99 Kiwi International Hotel
125 Stamford Plaza
127 Downtown Queen St Backpackers
129 Auckland Central; Rat's Bar
   Backpackers; Discount Dialling
136 De Brett's International
   Backpackers; De Bretts Bar
155 Citylife Auckland;
159 Albert Park Backpackers;
   Cyber City
168 Central City Backpackers;
   Embargo

PLACES TO EAT
9 Kermadec; Viaduct Central;
   Santario; Loaded Hog
13 Daikoko Ramen
25 Food Alley
43 Toto
46 Sultan's Table
48 Brownies Bar; Mexican Cafe
   Cafe Midnight Express
49 Mai Thai
68 Pizza Pizza
75 Wun Loy
90 Five City Restaurant
100 Krisna Food for Life
101 Ken Yakitori Bar
103 KXQ
104 Wagamana; Verona
106 Rasoi; K Rd Kebab
110 Habanero
112 Mezzaluna
120 Armadillo
123 Mohammed's Curry Den;
   Queens Arcade
134 O'Connell St Bistro
135 Bacchus
140 Cafe Mecca
141 Cafe Melba; Judder Bar

142 Factory
143 Rosinis
145 Papa Jack's Voodoo Lounge;
   Sushi Factory; Vulcan Cafe
151 Ginger
152 Fireilos Cafe
153 Wofem Bros Bagelry; Cima;
   Paneton; Foodoo
154 Colombus; Jolt
157 Victoria Yeeros
158 Alba
162 Bokcholee Korean Restaurant
165 Chef 2 Asian Cafe
166 City Restaurant
167 Countrywide Bank Centre
   Foodhall
170 Tony's Steak & Seafood
   Restaurant
171 Noodle Fast Food;
   Sushi & Sake; Choice Plaza
172 Paramount Restaurant & Bar

OTHER
1 Subritzky Ferry Terminal
2 Syndicate Bases; Team NZ
3 Super Yacht Berths
4 NZ Visitors Centre
5 NZ National Maritime Museum;
   Pride of Auckland Ticket Office
6 Pacific Ferries Ticket Office
   Cafe Hoegarden; Lenin Bar;
   Leftfield
7 Ferries to Birkenhead,
   Bayswater, Stanley Bay,
   Devonport, Waiheke & Rangitoto
8 Ferry Building; Harbourside
   Fullers Ferry Office; Moneychanger;
   Kermadec; Viaduct Central;
   Loaded Hog; Cin Cin
11 Downtown Airline Terminal; Cal Neva
12 Downtown Shopping Centre
15 Extreme Air Bungy
16 Downtown Bus Centre
18 Chief Post Office Building
19 Old Custom House
20 The Yacht Club
21 Seamart
30 Club Westside
35 High Court
37 The Northern Club
38 Specialty Maps
45 Sky City; Skytower;
   Orbit Restaurant;
   Tamarind Restaurant;
   Fortuna Buffet; Bus Terminal
47 AA
51 Margarita's; Chilli Lounge
52 Atrium Shopping Centre;
   Dymocks
56 Hoyts Cinema; Live Wire
58 Old Synagogue
59 Princes St Merchants' Houses
60 Old Government House
61 Auckland University's Old
   Arts Building & Clock Tower
62 Remains of Albert Barracks Wall
63 Bruce Wilkinson Collection
64 Maidment Theatre
66 ASB Bank Tennis Centre
67 Auckland Institute of Technology
69 Force Entertainment Centre
70 Civic Theatre
71 Auckland Visitor Centre;
   Post Office & Post Restante
72 Force Entertainment Centre;
   Planet Hollywood; Imax Theatre

73 St Matthews-in-The-City
76 Police
77 Wah Lee
79 Aotea Centre; Herald Theatre
80 Town Hall
82 Classic Comedy Bar
83 Silo Theatre
86 Real Groovy Records
95 The Temple; Peter's Pies
97 Auckland Regional Authority
105 St Kevins Arcade; Alleluya;
   Mumbai; Balloonski;
   Calibre; Ambush
108 Brazil
109 Cyber Cafe
113 Beautiful Music; Artspace
121 Singapore Exchange
   Moneychanger
122 Travelex
124 Thomas Cook; Deka;
   Mega Mags
128 Clean Green Laundromat
130 American Express;
   Great Kiwi Yarn
131 Citinet
132 BNZ Facade & Shopping Centre
137 Occidental; Equinox; Khymer;
   Raw Power Cafe
138 The Vault
139 STA
144 Unity Books
146 Pride Centre
156 Whitcolls
160 Citinet Cyber Cafe
161 Net Central Cafe
163 Portfolio Gallery
164 Compendium
173 New Art Gallery
174 Auckland Art Gallery
175 Parson Book Shop
176 Auckland Public Library;
   Academy Cinema

PUBS, BARS & CLUBS
22 The Immigrant
23 Soho Kitchen & Bar
26 The Ministry
28 Rose & Crown
39 Shakespeare Tavern
42 Empire Tavern
44 The Dispensary
57 Civic Tavern; London Bar;
   Murphy's Irish Bar
65 Gravity Bar/Gasoline Alley
81 Manifesto Espresso Wine Bar
84 Queens Head Tavern
88 The Club
102 Khuja Lounge
107 Live Poets Cafe;
   Dead Poets Bookstore
111 Club Havanna;
   The Supper Club
114 Legend
115 Roots
116 Kamo
117 Sinners; K Bar
118 Monkey Bar;
   Caluzzi Bar & Cafe
119 Urge
126 Tabac
133 Shortland Cafe & Bar
147 Crow Bar; Balzac
148 Deschlers
149 Cause Celebre/The Box
150 Rakinos Cafe; Pauanesia
169 Matisse

MAP 4

PARNELL

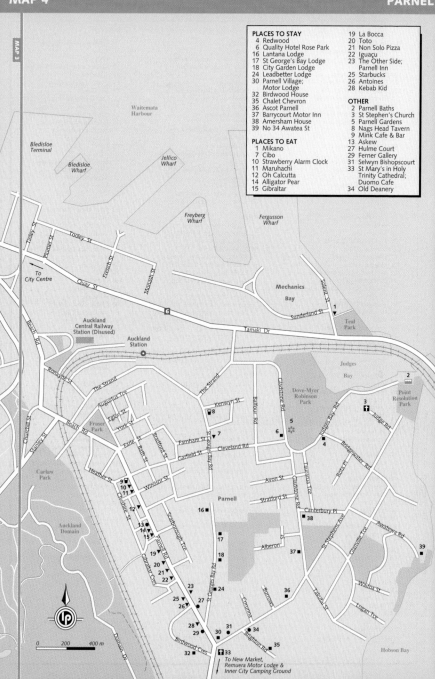

MAP 3

PLACES TO STAY
4 Redwood
6 Quality Hotel Rose Park
16 Lantana Lodge
17 St George's Bay Lodge
18 City Garden Lodge
24 Leadbetter Lodge
30 Parnell Village;
   Motor Lodge
32 Birdwood House
35 Chalet Chevron
36 Ascot Parnell
37 Barrycourt Motor Inn
38 Amersham House
39 No 34 Awatea St

PLACES TO EAT
1 Mikano
7 Cibo
10 Strawberry Alarm Clock
11 Maruhachi
12 Oh Calcutta
14 Alligator Pear
15 Gibraltar

19 La Bocca
20 Toto
21 Non Solo Pizza
22 Iguaçu
23 The Other Side;
   Parnell Inn
25 Starbucks
26 Antoines
28 Kebab Kid

OTHER
2 Parnell Baths
3 St Stephen's Church
5 Parnell Gardens
8 Nags Head Tavern
9 Mink Cafe & Bar
13 Askew
27 Hulme Court
29 Ferner Gallery
31 Selwyn Bishopscourt
33 St Mary's in Holy
   Trinity Cathedral;
   Duomo Cafe
34 Old Deanery

Waitemata
Harbour

Bledisloe
Terminal

Bledisloe
Wharf

Jellico
Wharf

Freyberg
Wharf

Fergusson
Wharf

To
City Centre

Quay St

Mechanics
Bay

Sunderland St

Teal
Park

Auckland
Central Railway
Station (Disused)

Auckland
Station

Tamaki Dr

Judges
Bay

Dove-Myer
Robinson
Park

Point
Resolution
Park

The Strand

The Strand

Kenwyn St

Balfour Rd

Gladstone Rd

Judge Rd

Augustus Tce

Taylor St

York St

Farnham St

Cleveland Rd

Fraser
Park

Beach Rd

Carlaw
Park

Auckland
Domain

Parnell

Avon St

Stratford St

Canterbury Pl

Alberon

Brighton Rd

To New Market,
Remuera Motor Lodge &
Inner City Camping Ground

Hobson Bay

0   200   400 m

MAP 5

NEWMARKET, GRAFTON & MT EDEN

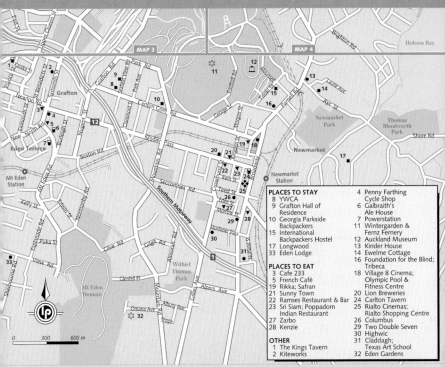

PLACES TO STAY
8 YWCA
9 Grafton Hall of Residence
10 Georgia Parkside Backpackers
15 International Backpackers Hostel
17 Longwood
33 Eden Lodge

PLACES TO EAT
3 Cafe 233
5 French Café
19 Rikka; Safran
21 Sunny Town
22 Ramses Restaurant & Bar
23 Sri Siam; Poppadom Indian Restaurant
27 Zarbo
28 Kenzie

OTHER
1 The Kings Tavern
2 Kiteworks
4 Penny Farthing Cycle Shop
6 Galbraith's Ale House
7 Powerstation
11 Wintergarden & Fernz Fernery
12 Auckland Museum
13 Kinder House
14 Ewelme Cottage
16 Foundation for the Blind; Tribeca
18 Village 8 Cinema; Olympic Pool & Fitness Centre
20 Lion Breweries
24 Carlton Tavern
25 Rialto Cinemas; Rialto Shopping Centre
26 Columbus
29 Two Double Seven
30 Highwic
31 Claddagh; Texas Art School
32 Eden Gardens

Auckland Museum

CHRISTINE NIVEN

MAP 6

DEVONPORT & CHELTENHAM

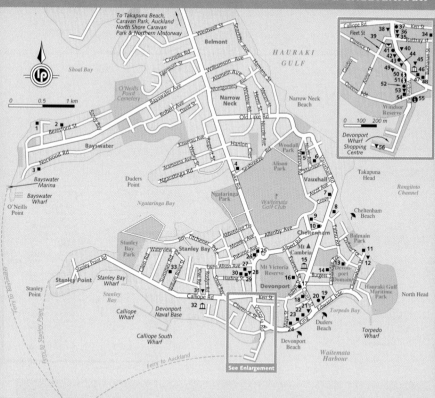

PLACES TO STAY

1 Bayswater Villa by the Sea
2 Bayview B&B
3 Bayswater Point Lodge
4 Duck's Crossing B&B
5 Ivanhoe
6 Wharemoana B&B
7 Cheltenham by the Sea
8 Devonport Villa Inn
9 Karin's Garden Villa
10 Villa Cambria
11 The Garden Room
13 The Secret Garden
14 Devonport Sea Cottage
16 Albertine
18 Khorasan B&B
22 Top of the Drive
23 Jeong-K Place by the Sea
24 Parituhu Beach Stay
25 Devonport Village Inn
26 Auntie Janet's Homestay

27 Amberley B&B
29 Aniwaniwa Cottage
30 Bakers' Place
33 Badger's of Devonport
34 Rainbow Villa
47 Peace & Plenty Inn
48 Hyland House
54 Esplanade Hotel

PLACES TO EAT

12 McHugh's of Cheltenham
19 Watermark
21 Masonic Hotel
28 Sigdi
31 Porterhouse Blue
35 Bar 3
36 Ziganna Espresso Lounge
38 Da Ciccio; High Flying Grapes
40 Portofino; Cod Piece; Paradox Books

42 Monsoon
44 Manuka Wood Fired Pizza Bar
45 Bankers Arms
49 The Stone Oven Bakery
53 Java House
56 Port-O-Call

OTHER

15 Devonport Museum
17 Watercolour Gallery
20 Art by the Sea
32 Royal NZ Navy Museum
37 Devonport Cinemas
39 Postshop
41 Hard to Find Bookshop
43 Gentronics
46 Jackson's Museum
50 Westpac Bank & 24-hour ATM
51 ASB Bank & 24-hour ATM
52 Evergreen Books
55 Information Centre; Library

MAP 7

To
Whangarei (56km) &
Bay of Islands

Bream Bay

Teranga
Island

Mokohinau
Island

Taipuha
Waipu
Braigh

Bream
Tail

Mangawhai
Head

Great Barrier
Island

Paparoa

Brenderwyn

Katherine
Bay

Port
Fitzroy

Maungaturoto

Little Barrier
Island

Kaiwaka

Cradock
Channel

Kaikoura
Island

Mt Hobson
(627m)

Te Hana

Pakiri

Cape Rodney

Broken
Islands

Leigh

Blind Bay

Tryphena

Wellsford

Matakana

Omaha Bay

Tauhoa

Warkworth

Tawharanui

Takatu Point

Tryphena
Harbour

Cape
Barrier

Kaipara
Flat

Sandspit

Kawau
Bay

HAURAKI

South Head

Glorit

Pohuehue

Mahurangi

Kawau
Island

GULF

Channel Island

Colville
Channel

Araparera

Puhoi

Motuora
Island

Cape Colville

Port
Jackson

Port
Charles

Waioneke

Shelley
Beach

Waiwera
Hatfield Beach

Whangaparoa
Bay

Coromandel
Forest
Park

Orewa

Red
Beach

Tiritiri
Matangi
Island

Colville Bay

Colville

Parakai

Silverdale

Shakespear
Park

America's Cup
Challenge and Defence
Courses

Rangitira
Beach

Helensville

Waitoki

Whangaparaoa

Long Bay

Dairy
Flat

Okura

Coromandel
Peninsula

Woodhill
Forest

Coatesville

Albany

Long Bay

Lake Pupuke

The Noises

Rakino
Island

Coromandel

Woodhill

Mt
Rangitoto
(260m)

Motutapu
Island

Waiheke
Island

Coromandel
Harbour

Waimauku

Kumeu

Takapuna

Devonport

Oneroa

Motuihe
Island

Pakatoa Island
Rotoroa Island

See Waitakere Ranges &
West Coast Beaches Map 8

Rangitoto
Island

Palm
Beach

Muriwai
Beach

Waitakere

Massey

Waitemata
Harbour

Auckland

Tamaki Strait

Te Henga
(Bethells Beach)

Henderson

Howick

See South-East of Auckland Map 9

Ahimia

Anawhata

Onehunga

Maraetai

Beachlands

Ponui
Island
Pakihi Island

Kereta

Piha

Waitakere Ranges
Regional Park

Waitarua

Titirangi

Mangere

Whitford

Orere

Orere
Point

Waikawau

Karekare

Laingholm

Papatoetoe

Takanini

Clevedon

Matingarahi

Tapu

Huia

Cornwallis

Manukau
Harbour

Manurewa

Matingarahi

Waiomu

Whatipu

Auckland
International
Airport

Cossey's
Reservoir

TASMAN
SEA

Grahams
Beach

Papakura

Mangatawhiri
Reservoir

FIRTH
OF
THAMES

Awhitu
Peninsula

Hunua

Kaiaua

Thames

Matakawau

Clarks
Beach

Drury

Hunua Ranges
Regional Park

Pollok

Ararimu

Paparimu

Miranda

Kopu

Waipipi

Patumahoe

Bombay

To
Thames (30km) &
Tairua (56km)

Pukekohe

Taurangaruru

Waiuku

Puni

Pokeno

Kopuku

Waitakaruru

Ngatea

Kerepeti

Otaua

Tuakau

Mercer

Aka Aka

Te Kohanga

Meremere

Okaeria

Kaihere

Onewhero

Pukekawa

Waerenga

Port
Waikato

Opuatia

Te Kauwhata

Maramarua
Forest

Nikau Cave

Lake
Whangape

Lake
Waikare

Taniwha

Glen Murray

Matahuru

To
Ragian
(30km)

To
Hamilton (50km) &
Rotorua (110km)

Waiterimu

0   10   20 km

ELEVATION

| 750 m |
| 600 m |
| 450 m |
| 300 m |
| 150 m |
| Sea Level |

MAP 8   WAITAKERE RANGES & WEST COAST BEACHES

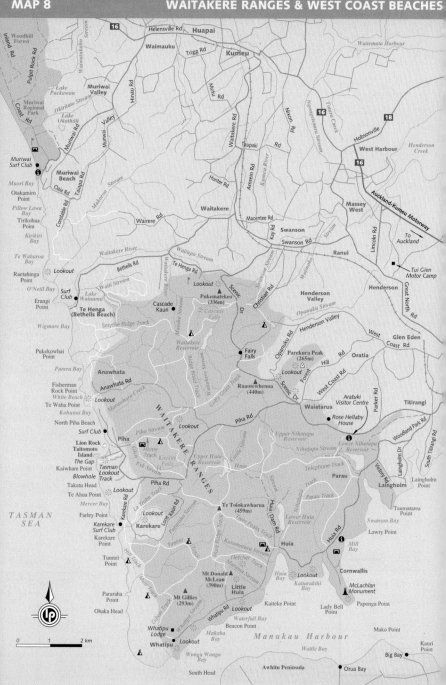

Woodhill Forest
Inland Rd
Pulpit Rock Rd
16
Helensville Rd
Huapai
Waimauku
Trigg Rd
Kumeu
Waitemata Harbour
16
Ngangararoa Stream
Tutira Creek
18
Hobsonville
West Harbour
Henderson Creek
16
Lake Packawau
Muriwai Valley
Okiritoto Stream
Hinau Rd
Motu Rd
Waitakere Rd
Nixon Rd
Lincoln Rd
To Auckland
Auckland-Kumeu Motorway
Muriwai Regional Park
Lake Okaihau
Muriwai Rd
Valley
Hunter Rd
Amrein Rd
Kumeu River
Massey West
Muriwai Surf Club
Muriwai Beach
Oaia Rd
Talapa Rd
Constable Rd
Maukoroa Stream
Tauraki Rd
Waitakere
Macentee Rd
Kay Rd
Swanson
Great North Rd
Maori Bay
Otakamiro Point
Wairere Rd
Swanson Rd
Swanson Stream
Ranui
Lincoln Rd
Tui Glen Motor Camp
Pillow Lava Bay
Tirikohua Point
Kirikiri Bay
Waitakere River
Waitipu Stream
Te Henga Rd
Chritian Rd
Henderson Valley
Waikumete Stream
Henderson
Great North Rd
Te Waharoa Bay
Lookout
Bethells Rd
Waiti Stream
Lookout
Pukematekeo (336m)
Scenic Dr
Cascade Falls
Opanuku Stream
Raetahinga Point
Surf Club
Lake Wainamu
Cascade Kauri
Mahoia Stream
Henderson Valley
West Coast Rd
Glen Eden
O'Neill Bay
Erangi Point
Te Henga (Bethells Beach)
Smythe Ridge Track
Waitakere Reservoir
Fairy Falls
Parekura Peak (265m)
Forest Hill
Oratia
Wigmore Bay
Pukekowhai Point
Anawhata
Ridge Road Track
Cutty Grass Track
Ruaotewhenua (440m)
Lookout
Scenic Dr
West Coast Rd
Parker Rd
Titirangi
Parera Bay
Anawhata Rd
Morsehorsa Creek
Waiatarua
Aratuki Visitor Centre
Rose Hellaby House
Fisherman Rock Point
White Beach
Lookout
Piha Rd
Rata Stream
Lookout
Upper Nihotupu Reservoir
Lower Nihotupu Reservoir
Woodland Park Rd
South Titirangi Rd
Te Waha Point
Kohunui Bay
North Piha Beach
Surf Club
Lookout
Piha Stream
Nihotupu Stream
Laingholm Dr
Lion Rock
Taitomoto Island
Piha
Home Track
Kitekite Falls
Upper Huia Reservoir
Kauke Stream
Telephone Track
Parau
Laingholm Point
The Gap
Kaiwhare Point
Blowhole
Tasman Lookout Track
Glen
Esk Stream
Piha Rd
Huia
Parau Track
Lower Huia Reservoir
Laingholm
Victory Rd
Huia Rd
Takatu Head
Te Ahua Point
Lookout
Karekare Rd
La Trobe Track
Te Toiokawharua (459m)
Hura Dam Rd
Twin Peaks Track
Whatipu Track
Taumatarea Point
TASMAN SEA
Mercer Bay
Farley Point
Lookout
Karekare
Karekare Surf Club
Long Kauri Rd
Parahaha Stream
Timber Track
Huia
Nihotupu Stream
Huia
Mill Bay
Lawry Point
Swanson Bay
Karekare Point
Huia Bay
Cornwallis
Tunnel Point
Hill Track
Huia Ridge Track
Kuramatunga Stream
Fletcher Track
Maraina Stream
Mt Donald McLean (390m)
Little Huia
Lookout
McLachlan Monument
Pararaha Point
Gibbon Track
Mt Gillies (293m)
Whatipu Rd
Lookout
Kaiteke Point
Kaitarakihi Bay
Lady Bell Point
Paponga Point
Ohaka Head
Waterfall Bay
Beacon Rd
Makaka Bay
Mako Point
Whatipu Lodge
Whatipu
Lookout
Wonga Wonga Bay
South Head
Manukau Harbour
Wattle Bay
Awhitu Peninsula
Orua Bay
Big Bay
Kauri Point

0   1   2 km
LP
N

MAP 9

SOUTH-EAST OF AUCKLAND

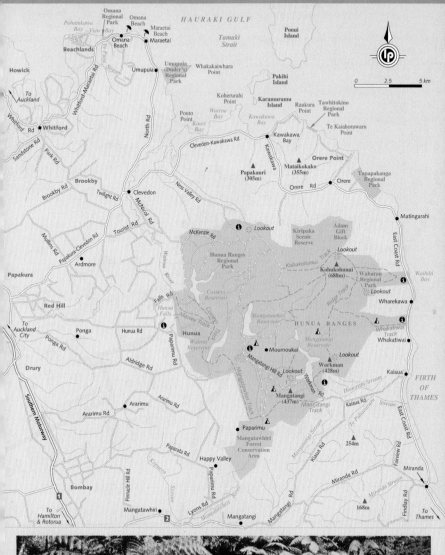

HAURAKI GULF

Pohutukawa Bay
Omana
Regional
Park
Omana
Beach
View
Omana
Beach
Beachlands

Maraetai
Beach
Maraetai

Tamaki
Strait

Ponui
Island

Howick

To
Auckland

Whitford-Maraetai Rd

North Rd

Umupuia

Umupuia
(Duder's)
Regional
Park

Whakakaiwhara
Point

Pakihi
Island

Whitford Rd
Whitford

Koherurahi
Point

Pouto
Point

Kauri
Bay

Wairoa
Bay

Karamuramu
Island

Kawakawa
Bay

Raukura
Point

Tawhitokino
Regional
Park

Te Kaiahorawaru
Point

Sandstone Rd
Park Rd

Brookby

Clevedon-Kawakawa Rd

Kawakawa

Kawakawa Bay

Orere Point

Matingarahi

Brookby Rd
Twilight Rd
Clevedon

Ness Valley Rd

Papakauri
(305m)

Mataikokako
(355m)

Orere

Orere Rd

Orere

Tapapakanga
Regional
Park

Mullins Rd
Papakura-Clevedon Rd

McNicol Rd

Tourist Rd

McKenzie Rd

Lookout

Hunua Ranges
Regional
Park

Kohukohunui

Kiripaka
Scenic
Reserve

Adam
Gift
Block

Lookout

Kohukohunui
(688m)

Waharau
Regional
Park

Lookout

East Coast Rd

Waihihi
Bay

Papakura

Ardmore

Wairoa River

Cosseys
Reservoir

Ridge Track

HUNUA RANGES

Wharekawa

Red Hill

Falls Rd

Hunua
Falls

Massey Track

Cosseys Creek

Mangatawhiri
Reservoir

Mangatangi
Reservoir

Whakatiwai
Track

Whakatiwai

To
Auckland City

Ponga

Ponga Rd

Hunua Rd

Paparimu Rd

Hunua

Wairoa
Reservoir

Moumoukai

Mangatangi Hill Rd

Lookout

Workman Rd

Lookout

Workman
(428m)

Kaiaua

FIRTH
OF
THAMES

Drury

Aldridge Rd

Ararimu

Ararimu Rd

Ararimu Rd

Mangatawhiri Track

Mangatangi
(437m)

Mangatangi Track

Honuroki Stream

Kaiaua Rd

East Coast Rd

Southern Motorway

Paparata Rd

Pinnacle Hill Rd

Paparimu Rd

Happy Valley

Paparimu

Mangatawhiri Forest
Conservation
Area

254m

Te Puhunurunu Stream

Miranda Rd

Miranda

Bombay

1

Kopuru Stream

Lyons Rd

Momongatanga River

Mangatawhiri

2

Mangatangi

Mangatangi Stream

Kaiaua Rd

168m

Pg Maupu Rd

Findlay Rd

Miranda Stream

To
Hamilton
& Rotorua

To
Thames

0   2.5   5 km

Ponga trees, characteristic of bush in the region

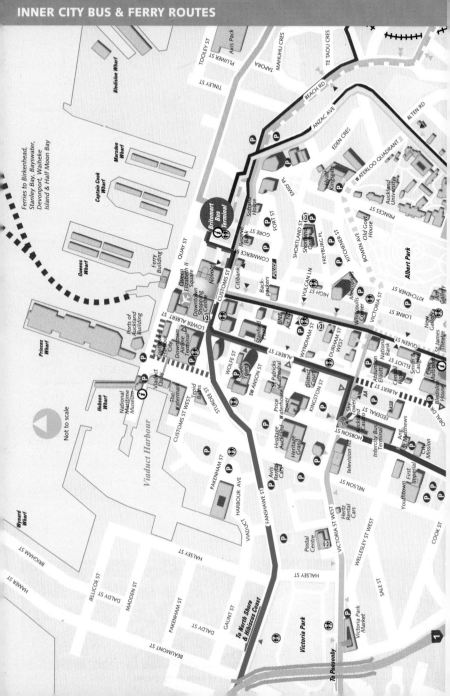

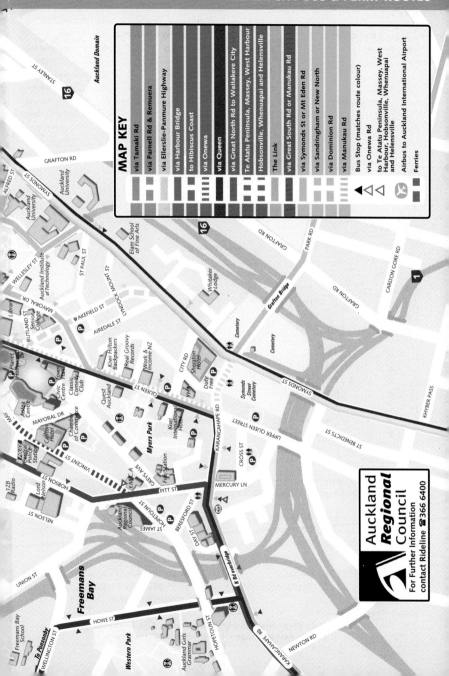

MAP KEY

- via Tamaki Rd
- via Parnell Rd & Remuera
- via Ellerslie-Panmure Highway
- via Harbour Bridge
- to Hibiscus Coast
- via Onewa
- via Queen
- via Great North Rd to Waitakere City
- Te Atatu Peninsula, Massey, West Harbour
- Hobsonville, Whenuapai and Helensville
- The Link
- via Great South Rd or Manukau Rd
- via Symonds St or Mt Eden Rd
- via Sandringham or New North
- via Dominion Rd
- via Manukau Rd
- Bus Stop (matches route colour)
- via Onewa Rd
- to Te Atatu Peninsula, Massey, West Harbour, Hobsonville, Whenuapai and Helensville
- Airbus to Auckland International Airport
- Ferries

Auckland **Regional** Council

For Further Information
contact Rideline ☎ 366 6400

MAP LEGEND

BOUNDARIES

— · — · — .... International
— · · — · · — .... State
— — — — .... Disputed

HYDROGRAPHY

.... Coastline
.... River
.... Creek
.... Lake
.... Intermittent Lake
.... Canal
.... Spring, Rapids
.... Waterfalls
.... Swamp

ROUTES & TRANSPORT

.... Freeway
.... Highway
.... Major Road
.... Minor Road
.... Unsealed Road
.... City Freeway
.... City Highway
.... City Road
.... City Street, Lane

.... Pedestrian Mall
.... Tunnel
.... Train Route & Station
.... Metro & Station
.... Tramway
.... Cable Car or Chairlift
.... Walking Track
.... Walking Tour
.... Ferry Route

AREA FEATURES

.... Building
.... Beach
+ + + × × × × .... Cemetery

.... Market
✿ .... Park, Gardens
.... Pedestrian Mall

MAP SYMBOLS

○ **CAPITAL** .... National Capital
◉ **CAPITAL** .... State Capital
● **CITY** .... City
● **Town** .... Town
● Village .... Village
○ .... Point of Interest

■ .... Place to Stay
⚠ .... Camping Ground
⛟ .... Caravan Park
⌂ .... Hut or Chalet

▼ .... Place to Eat
⚑ .... Pub or Bar

✈ .... Airport
☻ .... ATM, Bank
🚲 .... Bike Rental
🏛 .... Castle or Fort
✚ 🏠 .... Church
.... Cliff or Escarpment
☌ .... Embassy
✛ .... Hospital
☀ .... Lookout
⚱ .... Monument
☪ .... Mosque
▲ .... Mountain or Hill
🏛 .... Museum, Art Gallery
— .... One Way Street

ℙ .... Parking
★ .... Police Station
✉ .... Post Office
❖ .... Shopping Centre
○ .... Spring
🏛 .... Stately Home
▭ .... Swimming Pool
✡ .... Synagogue
☎ .... Telephone
▣ .... Tomb
ⓘ .... Tourist Information
◒ .... Transport
❀ .... Winery
🐖 .... Zoo

Note: not all symbols displayed above appear in this book

LONELY PLANET OFFICES

Australia
PO Box 617, Hawthorn, Victoria 3122
☎ 03 9819 1877 fax 03 9819 6459
email: talk2us@lonelyplanet.com.au

USA
150 Linden St, Oakland, CA 94607
☎ 510 893 8555 TOLL FREE: 800 275 8555
fax 510 893 8572
email: info@lonelyplanet.com

UK
10a Spring Place, London NW5 3BH
☎ 020 7428 4800 fax 020 7428 4828
email: go@lonelyplanet.co.uk

France
1 rue du Dahomey, 75011 Paris
☎ 01 55 25 33 00 fax 01 55 25 33 01
email: bip@lonelyplanet.fr

World Wide Web: www.lonelyplanet.com *or* AOL keyword: lp
Lonely Planet Images: lpi@lonelyplanet.com.au